A

Philip E. Lilienthal

BOOK

The Philip E. Lilienthal imprint
honors special books
in commemoration of a man whose work
at University of California Press from 1954 to 1979
was marked by dedication to young authors
and to high standards in the field of Asian Studies.
Friends, family, authors, and foundations have together
endowed the Lilienthal Fund, which enables UC Press
to publish under this imprint selected books
in a way that reflects the taste and judgment
of a great and beloved editor.

The publisher gratefully acknowledges the generous support of the Philip E. Lilienthal Asian Studies Endowment Fund of the University of California Press Foundation, which was established by a major gift from Sally Lilienthal.

VIETNAMESE COLONIAL REPUBLICAN

Peter Zinoman •

VIETNAMESE COLONIAL REPUBLICAN

The Political Vision of Vũ Trọng Phụng

University of California Press

Berkeley Los Angeles London

University of California Press, one of the most distinguished university presses in the United States, enriches lives around the world by advancing scholarship in the humanities, social sciences, and natural sciences. Its activities are supported by the UC Press Foundation and by philanthropic contributions from individuals and institutions. For more information, visit www.ucpress.edu.

University of California Press
Berkeley and Los Angeles, California

University of California Press, Ltd.
London, England

Portions of chapter 3 appear in "Hải Vân, *The Storm* and Vietnamese Communism in the Inter-war Imagination," in *Southeast Asia over Three Generations: Essays Presented to Benedict R. O'G. Anderson*, ed. James T. Siegel and Audrey R. Kahin (Ithaca, NY: Cornell Southeast Asia Program Publications, 2003): 125–43. This material is reprinted here with the permission of the publishers.

Library of Congress Cataloging-in-Publication Data

Zinoman, Peter, 1965–.
Vietnamese colonial republican : the political vision of Vu Trong Phung / Peter Zinoman.
pages cm
Includes bibliographical references and index.
Summary: "This volume is a comprehensive study of Vietnam's greatest and most controversial 20th century writer who died tragically in 1939 at the age of 28. Vu Trong Phung is known for a remarkable collection of politically provocative novels and sensational works of non-fiction reportage that were banned by the communist state from 1960 to 1986. Leading Vietnam scholar, Zinoman, resurrects the life and work of an important intellectual and author in order to reveal a neglected political project that is excluded from conventional accounts of modern Vietnamese political history. He sees Vu Trong Phung as a leading proponent of a localized republican tradition that opposed colonialism, communism, and unfettered capitalismand that led both to the banning of his work and to the durability of his popular appeal in Vietnam today"—Provided by publisher.
ISBN 978-0-520-27628-4 (cloth : alk. paper)
ISBN 978-0-520-95709-1 (e-book)
1. Vu, Trong Phung, 1912–1939—Political and social views. 2. Vu, Trong Phung, 1912–1939—Criticism and interpretation. 3. Vietnam—Intellectual life—20th century. I. Title.
PL4378.9.V86Z99 2014
895.9'2233—dc23 2013030955

23 22 21 20 19 18 17 16 15 14
10 9 8 7 6 5 4 3 2 1

For Alexander and Isaac

CONTENTS

ILLUSTRATIONS

ACKNOWLEDGMENTS

This book has been long in the works but I will keep my acknowledgments brief. Financial support for research and writing came from the University of California Committee on Research, the University of California Pacific Rim Program, the UC Berkeley History Department, the Hellman Family Faculty Fund, and the Fulbright Scholar Program. My research was assisted by the staffs at the National Library of Vietnam in Hà Nội, the General Science Library in Hồ Chí Minh City, the Bibliothèque Nationale de France in Paris, the Cornell University Library in Ithaca, New York, and the Doe Memorial Library at UC Berkeley.

This project began in Vietnam and my most important collaborators are located there. My greatest debt is to Lại Nguyên Ân, a scholar of immense talent and generosity, whose research and writing about Vũ Trọng Phụng deeply informs my own. I am grateful to Trần Hữu Tá and Nguyễn Đăng Mạnh, two eminent historians of Vietnamese literature who have helped me in many ways over the years. I was humbled by the kindness of the late Văn Tâm, perhaps the greatest scholar of Vũ Trọng Phụng, who welcomed me to his home on many occasions to share stories, ideas, and primary sources. I also thank Văn Tâm's widow, Cao Xuân Cam, who provided documents about the persecution of her husband in the 1950s. Đào Tuấn Ảnh, Bùi Tuấn, Phạm Xuân Nguyên, Lê Thế Quế, Nguyễn Việt Hà, Vương Trí Nhàn, and the late and sorely missed Hoàng Ngọc Hiến each discussed the project with me at some length. I also thank Vũ Trọng Phụng's son-in-law Nghiêm Xuân Sơn for helping to facilitate my access to his family archive.

Several friends and colleagues read all or part of the manuscript and deserve recognition. Christopher Goscha provided learned, detailed comments on every chapter as well as an inspiring model of scholarly excellence, integrity, and imagination. Alec Holcombe, Craig Reynolds, and Zachary Shore read drafts of multiple chapters and offered useful advice and encouragement. Sophie Quinn-Judge and Keith Taylor reviewed the manuscript for UC Press and made helpful suggestions for revision. I am fortunate to have received thoughtful feedback on the project from many of my Berkeley colleagues, including Andrew Barshay, Beth Berry, Karl Britto, John Connelly, Penny Edwards, John Efron, Basil Guy, Jeff Hadler, David Hollinger, Thomas Laqueur, Nancy Peluso, Mark Peterson, Yuri Slezkine, Tyler Stovall, James Vernon, and Wen-hsin Yeh. I also wish to acknowledge my dear departed colleague John Gjerde for his friendship and for helping me to get this project off the ground.

I have benefited from discussions with a global community of colleagues in Vietnamese studies and Southeast Asian studies. A partial list includes Susan Bayly, Mark Bradley, Ian Brown, Mary Callahan, David Chandler, Haydon Cherry, Eric Crystal, J. P. Daughton, Ginger Davis, David Del Testa, Michael Digregorio, David Elliot, Mai Elliot, Olga Dror, George Dutton, Christoph Giebel, Judith Henchy, Eric Jennings, Charles Keith, Ben Kiernan, Liam Kelly, Agathe Larcher-Goscha, Micheline Lessard, Greg Lockhart, Tamara Loos, Ken MacLean, Pam McElwee, Henk Maier, Shawn McHale, Edward Miller, Michael Montesano, Rudolph Mrazek, Lien-Hang Nguyen, Lorraine Patterson, Erica Peters, Philip Peycam, Phạm Quang Minh, Anthony Reid, Dana Sachs, John Schafer, John Sidel, Eric Tagliocozzo, Hue-Tam Ho Tai, Nora Taylor, Michelle Thompson, Nguyễn-Võ Thu-Hương, Trần Hạnh, Tường Vũ, and Alexander Woodside. I offer a special expression of gratitude to Shaun Malarney, who is both my oldest friend in the field and an important scholar of Vũ Trọng Phụng in his own right.

My graduate students at Berkeley have heard much about this project over the years and their engagement with my work has been a source of stimulation. I wish to mention Robert Acker, Sokhieng Au, Aparajita Basu, Mathew Berry, Trang Cao, Hà Thục Chi, Rebekah Collins, Va Cun, Adrianne Francisco, Cheong Soon Gan, Kimberly Hoàng, Alec Holcombe, Susan Kepner, Eric Jones, Siti Keo, Kevin Li, Ian Lowman, Natalie Miller, Alfred Montoya, Jason Morris-Jung, Lân Ngô, Khải Thư Nguyễn, Marguerite Nguyễn, Martina Nguyễn, Julie Phạm, Jason Picard, Jalel Sager, Gerard Sasges, Joe Scalice, Arjun Subramanyam, Adeline Trần, Ben Trần, Nữ-Anh Trần, Quang-Anh Richard Trần, Calvin Vũ, Linh Vũ, Leslie Woodhouse, and Wynn Wilcox.

Lưu Mỹ Trinh deserves special mention for proofreading the manuscript and producing the bibliography. I am grateful to Roberta Engleman for completing the index.

I also wish to thank my editors and other staff at UC Press, including Niels Hooper, Suzanne Knott, Kim Hogeland, Robert Demke, Wendy Dherin, and Pamela Polk.

For their love, support and patience during the lengthy process of producing this book, I thank members of my family including my mother-in-law Lê Thị Kim Chi, my late father-in-law Nguyễn Công Minh, my siblings Amanda and Jason, my parents Murray and Joy, and my sons Alexander and Isaac. Finally, it goes almost without saying that I thank Nguyễn Nguyệt Cầm for reading every word, checking every translation, challenging every dumb idea, and seeding every good one.

INTRODUCTION · A Political History of Vũ Trọng Phụng

Vietnamese readers need no introduction to Vũ Trọng Phụng but he has only recently come to the attention of outsiders.[1] For those unfamiliar with his remarkable life and body of work, it may be instructive to compare him to George Orwell. Both men were literary stars of the interwar era who died prematurely, Orwell (1903–50) at age forty-seven, Vũ Trọng Phụng (1912–39) at age twenty-eight. Both are known for stunning levels of productivity; Orwell's *Complete Works* comprises twenty volumes and nine-thousand pages, while Vũ Trọng Phụng, in a career spanning less than ten years, published eight novels, four books of narrative nonfiction, and hundreds of stories, plays, essays, editorials, and articles.[2] Both accomplished the uncommon feat of authoring canonical works in (the same) two literary genres: the novel and first-person reportage.[3] While both are regarded as masters of realism, they each earned acclaim for successful experiments with nonrealist fictional narratives: Orwell for the political fable *Animal Farm;* Vũ Trọng Phụng for the slapstick farce *Dumb Luck (Số đỏ)*. Moreover, despite very different backgrounds, the two men exhibited a similar prescience about the most pressing and divisive political issues of the day. In an influential study of the writer, the late Christopher Hitchens praised Orwell's opposition to colonialism, Stalinism, and fascism, during an era in which global public opinion about each of these coercive high modernist projects was disturbingly mixed.[4] As a native subject of French Indochina, Vũ Trọng Phụng naturally resisted colonialism, but he also opposed German fascism, Japanese militarism, and Soviet and Vietnamese communism. The two men also resented unrestrained capitalism, a sentiment that helps to explain Orwell's allegiance to socialism and Vũ Trọng Phụng's links to the noncommunist Vietnamese Left. However, while Orwell's well-known status as a "lower-upper-middle-class" Englishman during a period of British global hegemony provided him with a privileged vantage point from which to hone his craft and form his opinions, Vũ Trọng Phụng developed his similarly acute talents and views as a lower-class, untraveled, half-educated, opium-addicted, colonized subject from a remote outpost of France's second-rate empire. This contrast, together with the unyielding advance of English as a global language, helps to explain the gulf between Orwell's towering international reputation and Vũ Trọng Phụng's obscurity outside Vietnam.

In addition to his prodigious literary gifts and tragic early death, Vũ Trọng Phụng's high profile in Vietnamese cultural and political history rests on two controversies about his body of work. The first, which loomed large at the peak of his career in the late 1930s, concerns the explicit depiction of deviant and violent sexuality in his writing. "People say that Vũ Trọng Phụng is a pornographic *[khiêu dâm]* author," wrote his close friend Lan Khai in 1941. "They attack him, they boycott him, and they read him more than anyone else. The truth is that many of his characters are deeply perverted."[5] The conflicting positions in this controversy were neatly summed up by the critic Lê Thanh in 1937:

> Anyone interested in literature in our country must pay attention to new work by the realist writer Vũ Trọng Phụng. His novels such as *The Storm [Giông tố]*, *To Be a Whore [Làm đĩ]*, and *Dumb Luck*—and his reportage *Venereal Disease Clinic [Lục xì]*—have been understood in contradictory ways. Some believe that his valuable work may help to reform society. Others reject the notion that he possesses a lofty ideology or a firm aesthetic. They believe that he tries to boost sales through sexual titillation. These opposing views have generated intense curiosity—a curiosity that we feel as well.[6]

The crux of this particular dispute, in other words, was a disagreement over whether the lurid content of Vũ Trọng Phụng's writing reflected progressive ideals or crass commercial motives. Vũ Trọng Phụng's critics on this issue were older, culturally conservative intellectuals trained in the Confucian tradition as well as French-educated generational peers who boasted more elitist backgrounds and refined cultural tastes. His champions, on the other hand, were distinguished members of a loosely knit community of realist writers, liberal journalists, and unorthodox left-wing critics.

Also originating in the 1930s, but climaxing in response to the splintering of the Vietnamese communist intelligentsia after 1954, the second major controversy about Vũ Trọng Phụng concerns the content of his political vision.[7] It was fueled initially by the sensational depictions in his fiction of class struggle, colonial oppression, and the emergence of a local revolutionary movement. But it deepened during the late 1930s, when Vũ Trọng Phụng published two high-profile anticommunist essays, one harshly critical of the Moscow show trials, and another which denounced the shrill and divisive extremism of the local Vietnamese communist movement. With the rise of Stalinist and Maoist orthodoxy in the postcolonial Democratic Republic of Vietnam (DRV) during the 1950s, officials at the highest levels of Hồ Chí Minh's government denounced Vũ Trọng Phụng, now deceased for over a decade, as a dangerous political reactionary. His anticommunist writings from the late 1930s were recovered and denounced in public as "counterrevolutionary." His infamous depictions of sex and violence figured in this critique as well, as evidence of his decadent tastes and tawdry commercialism. Constrained by the narrow parameters of permissible political discourse during the era, liberal elements in the communist bureaucracy defended Vũ Trọng Phụng on the specious grounds that he had once been a clandestine Party sympathizer. In 1960, this deeply disingenuous debate was resolved in favor of Vũ Trọng Phụng's powerful opponents and his writing was pulled from the shelves and banned in communist Vietnam for over twenty-five years.[8] Just as his work remained inaccessible to the general public through the 1960s, 1970s, and early 1980s, it was chided in academic criticism as an example of "vulgar naturalism," a genre dismissed by communist critics as bourgeois and counterrevolutionary.[9] With the relaxation of censorship that accompanied the postwar Renovation reforms of the mid-1980s, a new generation of liberal cultural bureaucrats launched a successful campaign to rehabilitate Vũ Trọng Phụng.[10] By the start of the twenty-first century, multiple editions of his *Collected Works* had been issued by state publishing houses and his writing featured prominently in secondary-school and university curricula.[11] Research institutes organized conferences about the writer and city streets were named after him in Hà Nội and Hồ Chí Minh City.[12]

Those responsible for rehabilitating Vũ Trọng Phụng after the reforms of the 1980s came from a different generation than his failed defenders from the 1950s. But owing to the uninterrupted domination of the communist party over the state and the public sphere throughout this period, the arguments that they put forward to salvage his reputation were virtually the same. Without going so far as to suggest, in the absence of supporting evidence, that Vũ Trọng Phụng had been a secret Party sympathizer, they insisted that his work was intentionally crafted to undermine the bourgeois colonial order and to advance the revolution. This is how Vũ Trọng Phụng is taught in school today and, with a handful of exceptions, it remains the dominant public interpretation of his work.[13] Still, because of the length (and notoriety) of the earlier ban on his writing, a taint of political controversy clings to Vũ Trọng Phụng, and he remains a symbol of resistance, in some quarters, to the obscurantism and repressiveness of the existing social and political order.

This book explores three dimensions of Vũ Trọng Phụng as a historical figure: his life, his writing, and his reputation. The story of Vũ Trọng Phụng's life sheds light on broader trends within Vietnamese cultural history during the first half of the twentieth century, including the revolutionary impact of colonial language reform, the development of modern literature and journalism, and the substitution of a ruling-class educated in the Chinese classics by a French-schooled elite. Vũ Trọng Phụng's novels and reportage are read here both as manifestations of his social and political vision and as reflections of the spread of market relations, the growth of urban culture, and the fragmentation of Vietnamese politics along ideological lines. The turbulent history of Vũ Trọng Phụng's critical reception, both during his life and after his death, provides a revealing angle of vision into Vietnamese cultural politics and political culture during the late colonial and early postcolonial eras.

While each dimension of this study illuminates broader historical themes, Vũ Trọng Phụng's worthiness as a research subject derives as well from his popularity and influence inside Vietnam today. A darling of "progressive" critics and a member of the small pantheon of modern writers taught in public school, Vũ Trọng Phụng and his literary standing have endured, at a remarkably high level, since the 1930s—in spite of the official repression of his work for over a generation. With the exception of Hồ Chí Minh and the "national" poet Nguyễn Du, no Vietnamese writer has attracted as much critical attention.[14]

LATE COLONIAL REPUBLICANISM

In addition to providing the first serious introduction in a Western language to Vietnam's most illustrious modern author, this book argues that Vũ Trọng Phụng's body of writing expresses an inchoate but still coherent political vision that I term "late colonial republicanism." Although he never defined himself in these terms (he avoided political labels, preferring the literary moniker "realist"), this heuristic category captures Vũ Trọng Phụng's kinship with a moderately progressive political tradition with strong French roots that attracted many members of the Vietnamese intelligentsia in interwar Indochina and remains a modest presence in local intellectual life today. Despite the protean nature of "republicanism" as a concept, late colonial republicanism denotes a fairly stable cluster of political concerns and commitments and, as importantly, provides a useful alternative to the conventional communist/anticommunist frame of analysis for making sense of the writer and his work. In classifying Vũ Trọng Phụng in this manner, I hope to draw attention to an important ideological tendency within modern Vietnamese political life that has been neglected in the existing scholarship.

Rooted in the culture of French imperial rule, late colonial republicanism derived from an eighteenth-century political tradition that animated the Revolution of 1789 and persisted, in modified form, through the final decades of the Third Republic (1870–1940).[15] Its rhetorical bedrock was the triumvirate of Liberty, Equality, and Fraternity; its archenemies were the despotism of monarchy and the obscurantism of the Church; and its vocabulary was the revolutionary symbolism of 1789 and 1848. Republicanism supported the democratization of political life via the expansion of suffrage and the cultivation of a rational, civic-minded citizenry through mass education. It also promoted attachment to the nation as a substitute for the integrative force of the Church and the monarchy. Its foundational principles included a belief in the "transformative value of good laws and a quasi-mystical identification with 'the people.'"[16] Fluid and elastic, republicanism splintered during the tumult of the nineteenth century, and the politicians who established the Third Republic in the 1870s embodied multiple strains of the tradition.[17] They included the so-called left-wing radicals, described by one historian as "a cluster of advanced republicans who formed the extreme Left in the Chamber of Deputies."[18] Critics of "les puissances de l'argent" (the power of money), the left-wing radicals pursued progressive social reform through parliamentary action rather than revolution.[19] At the other end of the republican spectrum were the Forces of Order, who emphasized the protection of individual liberty through checks on state power, the regulation of capitalism, and the protection of property rights. In spite of different ideological emphases, most republican leaders opposed plutocracy, militarism, religious authority, and political despotism while sharing a common commitment to reason, education, the nation, and the rule of law.

The "late" French republicanism that Vũ Trọng Phụng encountered during the interwar era featured two additional elements that had moved to the forefront of the tradition during the nineteenth century in response to the rise of the Left. One was a growing faith in social science—a republicanism of Comte, Zola, and

Durkheim—which crystallized in the doctrine of Solidarism and led to support for a welfare state.[20] Championed by the largest political party of the Third Republic—the Republican Radical and Radical-Socialist Party (RAP)—Solidarism has been interpreted as a defensive response to the spread of scientific socialism.[21] A related feature of interwar republicanism was a virulent anticommunism that replaced the anticlerical obsession after the Third Republic enforced the separation of church and state in 1905.[22] Republican anticommunism attacked antidemocratic and totalitarian impulses in Leninism and Stalinism that mirrored the political culture of the church and the monarchy. It also criticized the corrupting influence of revolutionary violence and the absence of civil liberties in the Soviet Union. The replacement of anticlericalism with anticommunism as republicanism's preeminent bogeyman is illustrated in the speech delivered in 1927 by the Radical Prime Minister Albert Sarraut, "Le Communisme—voilà l'ennemi!," a direct play on Leon Gambetta's famous republican manifesto from 1871, "Le Clericalisme—voilà l'ennemi!"[23] It is instructive that Sarraut served as Governor General of Indochina during the course of Vũ Trọng Phụng's life and implemented the most explicitly republican reform agenda in the territory's history.[24]

Recent scholarship demonstrates the prominence of republicanism in the workings of the French Empire. Monographs by Alice Conklin and Gary Wilder affirm that republican ideals shaped France's colonial policy and practice in West Africa even while disagreeing about the character of the republican project.[25] The relatively thin scholarship on republicanism in Indochina dwells upon colonial Freemasonry and obscure local chapters of the civil rights organization the Ligue des droits de l'homme (League for the Rights of Man).[26] Focused on bounded institutions dominated by Frenchmen and the most privileged and aloof members of the Vietnamese elite (such as Phạm Quỳnh, Phạm Huy Lục, and Bùi Quang Chiêu), these studies do not account for the high profile of republican ideas in popular political discourse.[27] It is no coincidence that nearly all postcolonial Vietnamese states have billed themselves as republics (the Republic of Vietnam, the Democratic Republic of Vietnam, the Socialist Republic of Vietnam) and have featured familiar republican language in their founding documents.[28] To account for the persistence of this tradition in Vietnam, the spread of republican values and ideals during the colonial period needs to be explored.

In a study of "the roots of republican policy" in Indochina, Gilles de Gantès highlights the transformative impact on the local political culture of five outstanding republican Governor Generals: Jean-Marie de Lanessan (1891–94), Paul Beau (1902–08), Albert Sarraut (1911–14 and 1916–19), Alexandre Varenne (1925–27), and Jules Brévié (1936–39).[29] The latter three served during Vũ Trọng Phụng's lifetime and their reforms left a powerful imprint on his generation. Sarraut built the primary school system in which interwar Vietnamese youth learned French and gained a rudimentary exposure to republican civic values. By promoting the growth of a Vietnamese-language press, Sarraut's reforms provided an independent intellectual vocation for educated men (and some women) and incentivized a commitment to freedom of expression. Varenne reorganized local representative councils, opened civil service jobs to native applicants, and expanded state funding for public health and poverty relief. Brévié presided over the Popular Front's ambitious reformist agenda, the politics of which were fiercely debated in the writing of Vũ Trọng Phụng and his peers.

Just as the interwar republicanism that Vũ Trọng Phụng absorbed embodied a modified (and more moderate) variant of the political culture of 1789 and 1848, it also reflected the repression of progressive aspects of that culture in the colonial context. The French history curriculum in colonial schools downplayed the significance of "bloody civil wars, the French revolution or the taking of the Bastille."[30] The institutional racism of the colonial legal order violated equal protection under the law.[31] In defiance of the principle of popular sovereignty, elected representative bodies in Indochina remained relatively powerless and the colonial state enforced strict limits on suffrage, free expression, and associational life.[32] To a large extent, the "colonial" character of colonial republicanism derived from the failure of the colonial state to implement in practice the republican principles that it proclaimed in its public rhetoric. What local republicans in Africa and Asia shared was an insistence that republican ideals be thoroughly applied to the governance of their societies. In this way, colonial republicans resemble Gary Wilder's notion of "critical republicans" who "challenged France to extend republican institutions to all colonized peoples."[33] But unlike the francophone African intellectuals discussed by Wilder, Vũ Trọng Phụng and his colleagues opposed assimilation in any form, a position most clearly embodied in their rejection of the French language as a vehicle of expression.

Like many "modern" Vietnamese intellectual traditions such as nationalism and communism, late colonial republicanism represented a localized version of a generic global form.[34] The cumbersome dynamics of the transmission of ideas between very different cultures, during an era marked by slow travel and communications technologies, encouraged patterns of localization marked by anachronism, selectivity, and eclecticism. Vũ Trọng Phụng's republicanism was rooted in the interwar era, but its critique of market relations resembled the visceral anticapitalism of nineteenth-century romantic and naturalist French literature, which dominated the reading tastes of the late colonial Vietnamese elite. The dangers of religious obscurantism played a relatively modest role in Vietnamese republicanism owing to the weakness of local religious institutions, including the Buddhist church. On the other hand, local republicans inflated the significance of elements of the tradition that paralleled or reinforced aspects of classical Sino-Vietnamese political culture, such as a strong belief in the virtues of education.

Vũ Trọng Phụng is not generally interpreted in republican terms but there are good reasons to underline this connection. He enjoyed access to republican political culture through the colonial school system and the wide circulation in Indochina of metropolitan newspapers and books.[35] His heroes, Victor Hugo and Emile Zola, were giants of literary republicanism.[36] Most importantly, the fin de siècle republicanism dominant in the interwar era parallels, more closely than available alternatives, the combination of tendencies present in Vũ Trọng Phụng's writing: his passionate anticapitalism *and* anticommunism, his preoccupation with social science, his commitment to freedom of speech and the rule of law, his impatience with religious dogma, and his taste for literary realism. Even his "conservative" skepticism toward the emancipation of women resonated with the Third Republic's notoriously poor record on women's suffrage and gender equality.[37]

In contrast to the important studies of colonial-era Vietnamese intellectual history by David Marr, Alexander Woodside, Daniel Hémery, and Hue-Tam Ho Tai, each of which surveys a range of thinkers within a single analytic frame, this book explores late colonial republicanism through a close examination of one influential writer.[38] In this sense, it follows in the footsteps of Sophie Quinn-Judge's biography of Hồ Chí Minh and Christoph Giebel's study of Tôn Đức Thắng.[39] As with those single-person studies, what is sacrificed here in terms of sociological breadth is made up for with intellectual depth. Perhaps as a result, the picture presented of Vũ Trọng Phụng's social and political vision does not square neatly with any of the generic categories of commitment found in the existing scholarship, none of which captures the range and complexity of his ideas. Vũ Trọng Phụng was much more than a nationalist or an anticolonialist, and it would be difficult to pigeonhole him as a neotraditionalist or a modernist. His opposition to communism, unfettered capitalism, and premodern feudal authority further complicates efforts to characterize his agenda. Vũ Trọng Phụng's project also differs from southern Vietnamese "radicalism," the left-leaning "political mood" expertly dissected by Hue-Tam Ho Tai in her influential study of anticolonial political culture in the 1920s.[40] Despite the presence of significant overlapping republican concerns, Vũ Trọng Phụng's conservative views on gender relations, individualism, and the "modern woman" do not square with the conceptual coupling of personal emancipation and political freedom that Ho Tai identifies as the core feature of interwar Vietnamese radicalism. Hence, late colonial republicanism, as a related but distinct heuristic category, seems better able than radicalism to capture the precise contours of his project.

SOURCES, METHODS, AND CHAPTERS

In addition to addressing the most enduring controversy surrounding his work, my focus on Vũ Trọng Phụng's political vision rather than his broader biography reflects the unevenness of the relevant source material. The documentary record about the writer includes few conventional building blocks for biographical reconstruction such as letters, private notebooks, or material from family archives. Vũ Trọng Phụng's sole published interview, which I unearthed during the course of my research, skirts personal issues entirely.[41] Because he was too young to leave a memoir and too busy to keep a diary, it is difficult to access the intimate details of Vũ Trọng Phụng's personal life—including the circumstances surrounding his marriage in 1938 and the birth of his daughter the following year. Most of what can be established about his biography, therefore, must be gleaned from scattered reminiscences of friends and colleagues. Among the most useful examples are a series of brief recollections that appeared in the journal *Literary Circle (Tao Đàn)* several weeks after his death in 1939 and a short book-length tribute to the writer by his friend Lan Khai published in 1941.[42] On the other hand, a series of memoirs published in Hà Nội during the late 1950s suffers from patterned distortions stemming from constraints on free expression in the newly independent DRV. Other problems bedevil more recent memoirs such as the inevitable erosion of accuracy and specificity that comes with the passage of time. Hence, although my opening chapter describes Vũ Trọng Phụng's background, education, career, and the various urban and institutional settings in which he lived and worked, this book does not present anything like a full-fledged biography.

In contrast, a focus on the politics expressed in Vũ Trọng Phụng's work makes practical sense because of the voluminous quantity and deep political content of his literature and journalism (including novels, plays, short stories, documentary reportage, daily reporting, editorials, and published letters). During the course of my research, I discovered scores of long lost newspaper publications by Vũ Trọng Phụng that may now be added to his sizable collected oeuvre.[43] While his body of writing provides insight into a range of literary and historical issues, its most tangible value as an empirical source lies in the light that it sheds into the thinking of its author. This is especially the case for his reportage and newspaper writing that employed a first-person authorial voice to address the most pressing public issues of the day. The same holds true, to a large extent, for Vũ Trọng Phụng's novels, many of which place fictional characters amid politically significant current events such as the collapse of the local economy in 1930 or the mass amnesty of Indochinese political prisoners in 1936. On the other hand, the complexity and multivocality of Vũ Trọng Phụng's fiction necessitate a more cautious approach to the potential correspondence between textual content and authorial intent. In general, I try to forestall the dangers of interpretive overreach by focusing upon the most clearly expressed concerns and commitments in Vũ Trọng Phụng's most important works. To avoid reifying or exaggerating his fidelity to the message of any single text, I attend closely to changes over time in the author's treatment of key issues. My discussion of Vũ Trọng Phụng's fluctuating views on communism best exemplifies this approach. While assuming that the partisan agenda of a text is most easily discerned at the level of narrative content, I remain open to the possibility that intellectual and political commitments may also be conveyed through literary form. Hence, I occasionally supplement my treatment of the content of key works with rudimentary formal analysis.

The critical role of vernacular-language literature and journalism as colonial Indochina's most important public forum further validates an emphasis on the political content of Vũ Trọng Phụng's writing. French censorship repressed free speech in the colony's embryonic public sphere—an arena marked by token representative councils and toothless consultative committees—obscuring from the view of historians the variety of political projects championed by Vietnamese intellectuals and activists. These projects included local incarnations of Stalinism, Trotskyism, anarchism, moderate socialism, bourgeois constitutionalism, republican radicalism, neotraditional monarchism, fascism, anticolonial nationalism, and politicized religious sectarianism. Far from stamping out the diversity of local partisan agendas, however, French repression merely displaced the site of political expression to less tightly controlled discursive arenas such as fiction and newspaper writing.

But the richness and complexity of political commitment in late colonial Indochina have been underrated in the existing scholarship. Constrained by the ideological categories that structured interpretations of Vietnamese political history during the Cold War, standard accounts of late colonial politics depict a Manichean landscape split between pro-French collaborationist groups and an anticolonial movement dominated by the communist party.[44] Promoted by postcolonial Vietnamese communist historians and foreign scholars who rely uncritically on their work, this crudely binary depiction of local politics frequently ignores the presence or neglects to consider the significance, during the era, of alternative political agendas. As one of these alternatives, Vũ Trọng Phụng's late colonial republican vision deserves special attention both because of the widespread popularity of his work and because many interwar Vietnamese writers and journalists shared his concerns and commitments.[45] Recent research confirms the significance of late colonial republican themes in the discourse of southern "radicals" and members of the influential northern intellectual circle known as the Self-Strength Literary Group.[46] A similar sensibility may be observed in the writings of prominent intellectuals such as Phan Khôi, Lê Tràng Kiều, Ngô Tất Tố, and Lan Khai. Despite modest numbers relative to the population as a whole, these colonial republican intellectuals exerted a wide influence by expressing themselves in accessible forms such as serialized fiction, newspaper essays, and investigative reportage.

But, as the conflict between Vietnamese communist and anticommunist forces intensified during the global Cold War, the space for a moderate republican project contracted. It is no accident that Vũ Trọng Phụng was banned during the twenty-five years, between the late 1950s and the early 1980s, that marked the height of this period of polarization. On a happier note, the resurgent popularity of Vũ Trọng Phụng since the lifting of the ban in the mid-1980s and the mobilization of his work by progressive critics to expand the parameters of the country's cramped public sphere since the late 1990s highlights the surprising durability of a fragile but still palpable Vietnamese republican tradition.

The following chapters chart the rise of Vũ Trọng Phụng as a literary celebrity during the 1930s, the late colonial republican orientation of his most important writing, the harsh political campaign launched against him during the 1950s, and the repair of his reputation in the 1980s. Chapter 1 locates sources of his mature political commitments in some of the major "contact zones" and institutions of late colonial society: the city, the school, the department store, the white-collar office, and the colonial press. Chapter 2 examines Vũ Trọng Phụng's critical view of capitalism and his promotion of reformist measures to ameliorate its most pernicious effects. Chapter 3 explores a strain of anticommunism in his work that closely resembles a parallel strain in late Third Republic radical republicanism. Chapter 4 chronicles Vũ Trọng Phụng's social-scientific approach to the erosion of sexual morality and the growth of prostitution in Indochina. Chapter 5 explores the communist establishment's campaign against Vũ Trọng Phụng during the late 1950s, which culminated in the ban on his work. A brief conclusion explores the rehabilitation of the writer during the 1980s and examines the connection between the late colonial republican vision that animated his work and his enduring popularity during the contemporary era of late communism.

CHAPTER ONE • Sources of Vũ Trọng Phụng's Colonial Republicanism

Weeks after Vũ Trọng Phụng's death in October 1939, the bimonthly journal *Literary Circle* memorialized him in a special issue, the content of which provides a useful introduction to his celebrated reputation and controversial political vision.[1] Vũ Trọng Phụng's illustrious standing is reflected in the eminence of the eleven friends and colleagues who contributed to the issue. All but one were featured in the influential volume *Modern Writers (Nhà văn hiện đại)* published in 1942, Vũ Ngọc Phan's pioneering canon of contemporary Vietnamese authors.[2] The oldest was Ngô Tất Tố (1894–1954), almost twenty years Vũ Trọng Phụng's senior and renowned by the late 1930s for a series of realist narratives about the northern Vietnamese countryside. Three contributors were roughly a decade older than Vũ Trọng Phụng: Tam Lang (1901–86), whose *I Pulled a Rickshaw* (*Tôi kéo xe;* 1930) established Vietnamese reportage as a serious literary genre; Nguyễn Triệu Luật (1902–46), a writer of historical fiction; and the novelist Lan Khai (1906–45), who edited Vũ Trọng Phụng's work while serving as the editor-in-chief of *Megaphone (Loa)* in 1934 and *Literary Circle* in 1939. Like their deceased friend, most of the remaining contributors were in their middle to late twenties. They included the prolific Marxist critic Trương Tửu (1913–99), the talented essayist and short story writer Nguyễn Tuân (1910–87), the "social novelist" Nguyễn Vỹ (1912–71), and the leading "new poet" Lưu Trọng Lư (1912–91). Rounding out the group were the poet Tchya (1908–63), the humorist Đồ Phồn (1911–90), and the popular author-journalist Thanh Châu (1912–2007). Just as Vũ Trọng Phụng's prominence is reflected in the roster of luminaries who contributed to the memorial volume, it is also apparent in his funeral procession, which, according to Thanh Châu, included "all the literary stars of the capital."[3]

In addition to their youthfulness and stellar reputations, what united Vũ Trọng Phụng's eulogists is that they were regular contributors to the suite of periodicals published by the Tân Dân Publishing House, founded in Hà Nội in 1925 by the playwright and media magnate Vũ Đình Long.[4] Many appeared frequently in *Saturday Novel (Tiểu Thuyết Thứ Bảy)*, Tân Dân's flagship journal that featured short stories, essays, and serialized novels during its lengthy print run between 1934 and 1945.[5] Writers affiliated with Tân Dân shared modest backgrounds, limited educations, and, perhaps as a result, a preoccupation with lower-class characters and populist themes.[6] In short, the roster of contributors to the volume highlights Vũ Trọng Phụng's kinship with a well-regarded, loosely "progressive" subdivision of the literary community.

It would be a mistake, however, to assume that the vague social vision shared by Vũ Trọng Phụng's circle of friends and colleagues during the 1930s foreshadowed an allegiance to any of the partisan camps that came to dominate Vietnamese politics following World War II. Five of the eleven contributors to the special issue—Ngô Tất Tố, Nguyễn Tuân, Lưu Trọng Lư, Đồ Phồn, and Thanh Châu—joined the communist-led Việt Minh (founded in 1941) and worked for the Party's cultural bureaucracy during the following decades. Nguyễn Triệu Luật also joined the Việt Minh but he was killed under mysterious circumstances in 1946. At the other end of the political spectrum, Tam Lang, Nguyễn Vỹ, and Tchya opposed the communist movement and moved to the South in 1954. Lan Khai sympathized with the anticommunist Vietnamese Nationalist Party (VNQDĐ) and was likely assassinated by Việt Minh hit squads in 1945–46.[7] Finally, Trương Tửu joined the Việt Minh but he led an infamous protest against communist rule in 1956 and was excommunicated from public life in the DRV until his death in 1999.[8] The divergent trajectories of Vũ Trọng Phụng's closest associates attest to the complexity and fluid ambiguity of political allegiance during the late colonial era.

The most prominent theme expressed by contributors to the memorial volume was the immense sadness provoked by Vũ Trọng Phụng's premature death. "I grieve for you," wrote Nguyễn Vỹ, "I grieve for your friends. I grieve for the literature of our country *[nước nam]*, of which you are the most worthy representative."[9] According to Lưu Trọng Lư, the impact of Vũ Trọng Phụng's death touched not just fellow writers but "tens of thousands of anonymous and distant readers throughout the land."[10] Nguyễn Triệu Luật claimed that the news brought him to tears for the first time since the death of his father decades earlier.[11] Perhaps the most poignant account was Thanh Châu's description of the silent crowd of mourners attending the funeral. At the head of the procession, he observed the writer's widow dressed in white linen and cradling a baby girl in her arms.[12]

In addition to bemoaning his death, contributors decried the poverty and sickness that plagued Vũ Trọng Phụng throughout his life. Lưu Trọng Lư, Lan Khai, and Tam Lang each recalled his chronic tubercular cough and Nguyễn Tuân discussed his opium addiction, which deepened as he relied increasingly on the medicinal properties of the drug. Nguyễn Triệu Luật remembered his ghostly appearance six months earlier at the funeral of the poet Tản Đà, another beloved casualty of tuberculosis. While discussion of Vũ Trọng Phụng's illness tended to dwell on his final days, commentary on his economic difficulties focused on his childhood and teenage years. Ngô Tất Tố called Vũ Trọng Phụng's poverty a "family inheritance" since its origins lay in the death of his father when he was only seven months old.[13] Trương Tửu suggested that his antagonism toward the rich stemmed from financial hardship that forced him to leave school early to support his family. For some contributors, a history of economic deprivation provided the subtext for his legendary tightfistedness: his scrupulous approach to debt payment, his fondness for cheap pens and substandard paper, and his simple taste in food. For Nguyễn Tuân, poverty helped to explain his "humility, moderation, and prudence," while Lan Khai linked it to his legendary work ethic.[14] Others interpreted Vũ Trọng Phụng's hard life and tragic death as a cautionary tale about the wretched condition of all contemporary writers. "When I contemplate Vũ Trọng Phụng's death," wrote Tam Lang, "I can't help thinking of others who will soon follow. This makes me feel terrible for all poor writers."[15]

Finally, contributors discussed Vũ Trọng Phụng's remarkable body of work, focusing on its extraordinary literary quality and perplexing political content. Lưu Trọng Lư lamented that Vũ Trọng Phụng's death reduced the sum total of talent in the Vietnamese literary world by one half. For Nguyễn Vỹ, Vũ Trọng Phụng's work was a national treasure that brought "glory to Vietnamese literature."[16] Tam Lang acknowledged that his own celebrated achievements in the field of reportage paled beside Vũ Trọng Phụng's mastery of the genre. The closest analysis of his work was offered by Lưu Trọng Lư and Trương Tửu, each of whom employed a rudimentary Marxian analysis to liken Vũ Trọng Phụng to Balzac. Citing an argument about the revered French writer first put forward by Engels and embraced by communist critics throughout the interwar era, Lưu Trọng Lư argued that the virtues of Vũ Trọng Phụng's indictment of bourgeois society offset his failure to embrace a "constructive" revolutionary project:

> Vũ Trọng Phụng's power is the power of opposition to everything that is unjust, depraved, rotten, disgusting, and ugly about the bourgeoisie. All of his work mocks and derides that which is cruel and depraved in this class of men. In this way, Vũ Trọng Phụng is to Vũ Trọng Phụng's era what Balzac was to Balzac's era. They have their differences but both speak in a sour and dissatisfied voice. Both aim to destroy rather than rebuild, but such destruction is necessary if reconstruction is to proceed on a newer and more beautiful foundation.[17]

Trương Tửu provided a more elaborate analysis that characterized Vũ Trọng Phụng as a "vanguard servant of realism" and linked his "morally progressive work" to his lower-class background and poor material circumstances.[18] But he also criticized the limitations of his political vision. Departing from the laudatory tone of the memorial volume, Trương Tửu chided Vũ Trọng Phụng for locating the source of Indochina's "social corruption" in capitalist culture and not capitalism per se. In short, "he ignored the origins of this culture and the fact that customs and morals are only the reflection of a more concrete foundation."[19] As a result of this "mistaken sociological viewpoint," the criticism expressed in Vũ Trọng Phụng's novels dwelled upon cultural manifestations of capitalism such as dancing, fashion, bicycle riding, free love, and the cult of individual happiness. This led to an undeserved reputation for "conservatism." But Trương Tửu rejected this label. Like Balzac, Vũ Trọng Phụng diagnosed the ills of an emergent bourgeois society. While the shortcomings of his social analysis prevented Vũ Trọng Phụng from contributing to the liberation of his class, he followed Balzac in contributing greatly to the formation of a national literature. In conclusion, Trương Tửu speculated that "Vũ Trọng Phụng had moved recently toward socialism. What a shame that he died just as his pen and his soul were poised to raise his writing to a higher level."[20]

The characterization of Vũ Trọng Phụng's writing as critical of capitalist society but insufficiently Marxist or revolutionary highlights the idiosyncratic parameters of his broader political vision. This vision, which I call late colonial republicanism, featured core elements of the moderate republican agenda pursued by centrist and center-left parties in France during the Third Republic. In addition to opposing both communism and unfettered capitalism, it expressed strong support for democracy, education, scientific and social-scientific inquiry, social justice, and an open public sphere. The culturally unstable colonial context in which Vũ Trọng Phụng's commitment to this vision emerged encouraged, in addition, a special preoccupation with the erosion within Vietnamese society of traditional learning, morality, and gender norms. Such a project—marrying republican values and colonial preoccupations—appealed to a significant segment of the interwar Vietnamese intelligentsia, including most contributors to the memorial issue. While subsequent chapters explore the elaboration of these concerns in Vũ Trọng Phụng's work, this chapter locates their origins in some of the major "contact zones" and institutions of French Indochinese society: the city, the school, the department store, the white-collar office, and the newsroom.

URBAN TONKIN

Vũ Trọng Phụng was born on October 20, 1912, in Hà Nội, the capital of French Indochina and the headquarters of its northernmost Vietnamese territory, the protectorate of Tonkin.[21] Together with the central Vietnamese protectorate of Annam, Tonkin was incorporated into Indochina during the early 1880s and conjoined with the southern colony of Cochinchina and the protectorate of Cambodia, both of which had been seized by France in the 1860s.[22] The protectorate of Laos was added in 1893, becoming the fifth and final component of French Indochina. As a protectorate subject to "indirect rule," Tonkin remained under the titular authority of the Vietnamese Emperor and the administrative rule of a hybrid bureaucracy—part French colonial and part imperial Vietnamese—which insulated it, during the late nineteenth century, from many of the abrupt changes sweeping over the "directly ruled" "old colony" of Cochinchina. These included the replacement of Confucian scholar-bureaucrats with French officials and the development of a globally integrated market economy through the formation of a rice export industry in the Mekong Delta. In contrast, severe overpopulation in the Tonkin Delta and the preservation there of residual elements of the precolonial dynastic system discouraged economic development and administrative innovation.[23] While Governor General Paul Doumer transformed the protectorates at the turn of the century through the rationalization of the tax code and additional state spending on public works, modernization advanced slowly in Tonkin until the end of World War I.[24]

In spite of Tonkin's modest rate of development (especially in comparison with Cochinchina), the gradual commercialization of agriculture during the late nineteenth century and early twentieth forced farmers off their land and spurred migration to the cities. It was during this era that Vũ Trọng Phụng's parents migrated to Hà Nội from the lower Tonkin Delta, an old agricultural zone south of the capital marked by population densities that rivaled the most crowded regions of Bengal, Java, and southern China.[25] Vũ Trọng Phụng's mother, Phạm Thị Khách, came

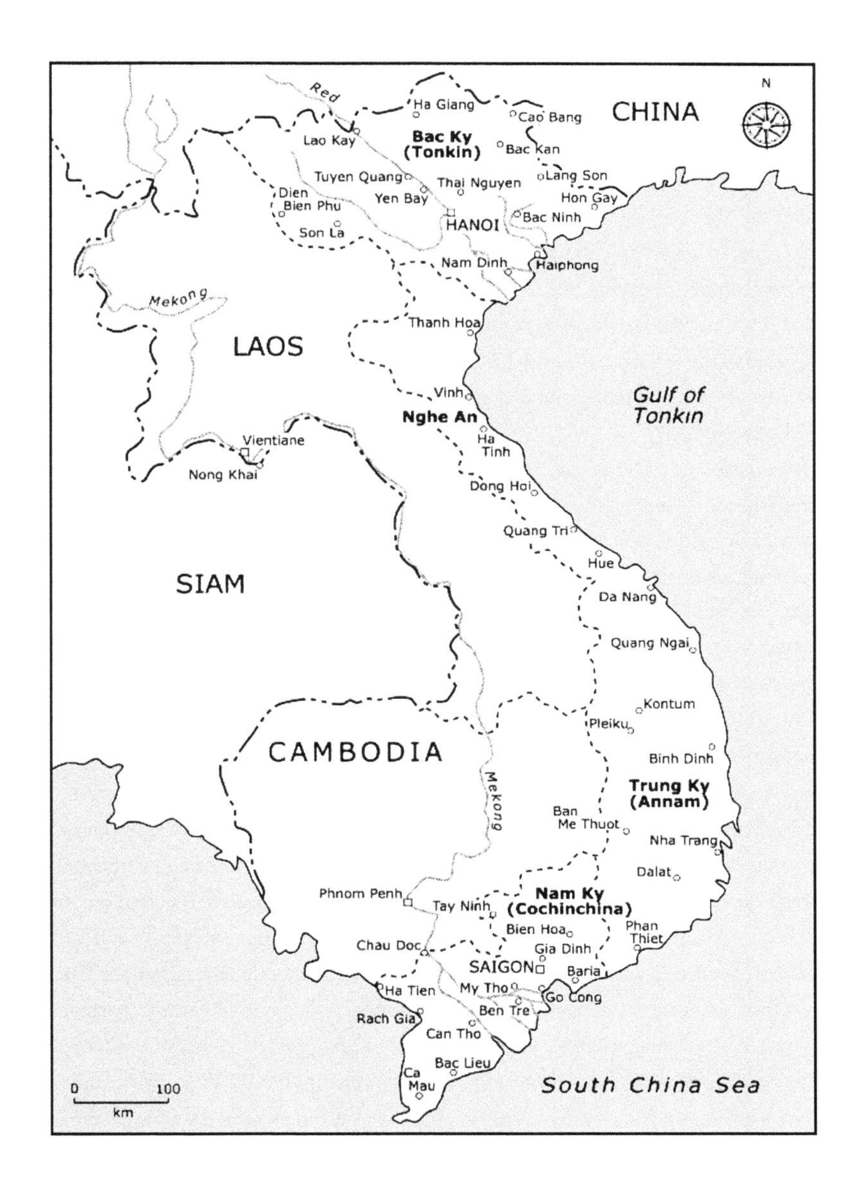

FIGURE 1.
Map of French Indochina

from Vẽ village in the Hoài Đức district of Hà Đông province.[26] In Hà Nội, she earned money as a seamstress, a career choice that may reflect her exposure to traditions of village textile production in her native Hà Đông.[27] Vũ Trọng Phụng's father, Vũ Văn Lân, was a landless farmer whose own father had once served as the mayor of Hảo village in the Mỹ Hào district of Hưng Yên Province.[28] After his family lost its land, Vũ Văn Lân found work in Hà Nội as an electrician at the Charles Boillot Garage. Many details of Vũ Trọng Phụng's background remain unknown but friends emphasize the poverty of his parents, a common predicament for recent migrants to the capital city. The death of his father during a cholera epidemic in the summer of 1913, when his mother was twenty-one, added further to his impoverished upbringing.[29]

Because of its political significance as the seat of French authority in Indochina, Hà Nội modernized more rapidly than the surrounding countryside. Attentive to the theatrics of colonial power, the French remodeled the royal citadel during the 1880s, removing walls, moats, and a vast examination compound and establishing a grid of roads that linked the workshops and warehouses of the "old quarter" to the original French concession along the banks of the Red River.[30] They also tore down the internal gates that had blocked circulation within the old quarter, transforming it into an integrated mixed-use neighborhood that was both residential and commercial. A separate French residential zone was developed as well through the drainage and filling-in of swamps and ponds south of Hoàn Kiếm Lake and the introduction of a modern sewage system.[31] By 1895, electricity and gas streetlights were in operation throughout the city along with a system for supplying fresh water and a network of electric streetcars. Urban development intensified at the turn of the century when the Doumer administration initiated an ambitious program of municipal public works. It included the construction of a central railway station, a palace for the Governor General, a monumental Opera House, an expanded central prison, and the massive Doumer Bridge. The population of the city increased in tandem with the expansion of its infrastructure, growing from roughly fifty thousand at the time of the French conquest in the 1880s, to eighty thousand around the turn of the century, to more than two hundred thousand by 1940.[32] In addition to drawing rural migrants from the chronically overcrowded Delta, Hà Nội maintained a steady expatriot population throughout the interwar era that included four to five thousand Chinese and an equal number of French residents, many of whom were naturalized citizens of France's West African and South Asian colonial possessions.[33]

While he lived in different parts of Hà Nội throughout the course of his life, Vũ Trọng Phụng mostly resided in the city's old quarter. Known as the "thirty-six streets" *(ba mươi sáu phố phường)*, this densely populated area featured a web of narrow lanes, each named after the particular item sold or produced there. Vũ Trọng Phụng lived for a time on Silver Street and Silk Street, where he shared small flats with his mother and maternal grandparents.[34] Virtually all of the newspaper offices and publishing houses where he worked were located in the old quarter as well. Its central architectural feature was the tube house, a vernacular rural housing type inserted into the urban environment and modified by the addition of a narrow shop façade facing the street.[35] Shaped by a precolonial tax calculated according to the width of each dwelling structure, the Vietnamese tube house evolved into an unusually narrow and deep urban shop-house.[36] By alternating rooms, open yards, and common spaces, they generated dense residential patterns and gave rise to a lively urban atmosphere. The latter was magnified in the late nineteenth century by the laying-down of pavement and sidewalks, which provided a public arena for the neighborhood's colorful street life.

The imprint of city life on Vũ Trọng Phụng's writing has been noted by many critics, including Đỗ Đức Hiểu, who once dubbed him "Vietnam's most urban author."[37] Given his long-term residence in the old quarter, it is no surprise that images of urban voyeurism and street scenes loom large in Vũ Trọng Phụng's writing and that well-known Hà Nội landmarks serve as crucial backdrops in both his fiction and nonfictional narratives. The façade of the Hà Nội Central Prison provides the setting for an important chapter in *The Dike Breaks (Vỡ đê)*, and several famous episodes in *Dumb Luck* occur at West Lake. Much of the action in *Household Servants (Cơm thầy cơm cô)* and *The Man Trap (Cạm bẫy người)* takes place on familiar streets in the old quarter, and *Venereal Disease Clinic* maps, street by street, the precise geography of commercial sex in the city.

Vũ Trọng Phụng's views on his native Hà Nội were intensely felt and generally negative. He portrayed it as an inorganic colonial metropolis plagued by social atomization, crass commercialism, racial segregation, class exploitation, political corruption, and moral perversity. In *The Storm* and *The Dike Breaks*, alternating chapters set in Hà Nội and the surrounding countryside function to highlight the growing distance between urban and rural society. At the same time, Vũ Trọng Phụng wrote eloquently, in *Household Servants* and elsewhere, about the magnetic pull that the "light of the capital" exerted over people from the countryside:

> Perhaps on nights when there are no moon and stars, the peasants of Nam Dinh, Thai Binh, Hai Duong, Bac Ninh, Son Tay, and Hoa Binh go out into their courtyards and see a shining halo each time they turn their heads and look

> far off into a corner of the sky. There, hovering over a thousand years of culture and glowing with easy riches, the peasants see a halo over Hanoi, and they are leaving their villages for it in droves. Soon they too will be able to lie in the corner of a courtyard beside a stinking drain amid the smell of chicken shit and human shit. Soon they too will lie curled up and starving as they look into the heavens on a night like tonight when bright moonbeams fill the sky.[38]

Vũ Trọng Phụng was also fascinated by the heterogeneity of life in the colonial city. Many of his works describe the mottled human diversity of public and quasi-public urban spaces: sidewalks, retail shops, opium dens, brothels, racetracks, tennis courts, restaurants, and hotels. A good example is his portrayal of an opium den in *The Storm,* which emphasizes the promiscuous communion of strangers and members of traditionally segregated social groups: "A roar of laughter arose from this mass of people bearing different complexions: locals, blacks, and white Europeans. . . . The beds were filled with opium smokers: five Vietnamese, eight Chinese including two women, a white French soldier, three black French soldiers, and an elderly French woman."[39] They included a "gambler, an unemployed and embittered school graduate, an elderly government clerk searching in vain for a second wife, an author of a recently banned book, an editor being sued for defamation, a reporter trying to craft a catchy headline, a jilted dancing girl, and a fading Cochinchinese opera star. Here we find a society of the aggrieved and the debauched taking collective action to dampen their sorrows. As in a loving family, feelings of misery and disgrace that are normally concealed are here brought into the open and loudly declaimed."[40]

Vũ Trọng Phụng's urban sensibility was rooted in the capital, but he experienced daily life in another colonial city when he worked for the *Hải Phòng Weekly (Hải Phòng Tuần Báo)* during roughly seven months in 1934–35—his only period of extended residence outside of Hà Nội. Opened to French commerce by a treaty of 1874, Hải Phòng became the second most populous urban center in Tonkin as well as its "leading industrial city" owing to its multiple economic roles as a railroad junction and a seaport.[41] It was also a hub for the transshipment and processing of Tonkin's abundant mineral wealth, especially its large coal deposits centered in Hòn Gai. When Vũ Trọng Phụng lived there during the mid-1930s, the city boasted a population of seventy thousand and provided a home for numerous medium-scale industrial enterprises, including an electric company, a shipyard, a glassworks, a brewery, a button manufacturer, a handful of rice mills and textile plants, and a massive cement factory that employed four thousand workers.[42] At the *Hải Phòng*

Weekly, Vũ Trọng Phụng wrote a series of articles entitled "Hải Phòng, 1934" that explored the impact of the global economic slump on the city and its residents.[43] He also oversaw (and perhaps authored) "Through the Streets" ("Qua các phố"), a weekly column about public spaces in the city that appeared under the pseudonymous byline "Le Flâneur."[44] Unlike his nineteenth-century Parisian counterpart who, according to Walter Benjamin, delighted in the frenetic spectacle of the French capital, the *flâneur* of the *Hải Phòng Weekly* drew attention to a range of problems plaguing Hải Phòng such as urban blight, social inequality, linguistic confusion, and the garish commercialization of the colonial cityscape.[45]

Just as republican political culture in nineteenth-century France thrived in urban areas, the growth of colonial cities in early-twentieth-century Indochina nurtured the emergence of related sensibilities among educated Vietnamese. Cities served as the nerve center for the colonial press, which, despite censorship and police harassment, offered a lively forum for "pen wars" *(bút chiến)* about current events and issues of public concern. They were also home to the upper tiers of the colonial legal system and institutions of higher education. As the natural habitat of the colonial bourgeoisie and a magnet for the rural poor, cities dramatized social inequality and inspired charitable initiatives and reformist projects.[46] They also provided the setting for civic rituals and limited representative institutions. During the interwar period, cities were the locus for a surprisingly robust form of electoral politics, as French and Vietnamese candidates vied for positions on the Colonial Council of Cochinchina and the Chamber of the People's Representatives of Tonkin and Annam.[47] While the colonial state limited their powers and restricted the franchise by which their members were selected, these primitive representative institutions evolved, during the 1930s, into contentious deliberative bodies that attracted widespread coverage in the local press. Cities were also the centers of a modest associational life spearheaded by local chambers of commerce, religious organizations, professional groupings, consumer cooperatives, welfare societies, labor unions, athletic clubs, and regional fellowship associations.[48] This nascent colonial civil society included progressive French law firms that championed the rights of native subjects in the courts and local chapters of fraternal organizations devoted to the promotion of republican values. Especially notable were the anticlerical Freemasons who admitted both French and Vietnamese members starting in 1925 and featured two all-Vietnamese lodges by the end of the 1930s.[49] Another proactive republican group was the Tonkin section of the League for the Rights of Man, founded in Hà Nội in 1903. According to Christopher Goscha, the mission of this local chapter of the League was "to promote republican ideals in the colonies, to check the abuses of colonialism, and not without serious contradictions, to make known such new ideas as 'individual rights and liberties,' 'citizenship,' and 'egalitarianism.'"[50]

Many scholars have rightly criticized the colonial state for restricting the development of civil society in Indochina by maintaining a racially discriminatory legal order and placing limits on freedom of association, expression, and political participation. While such restrictions prevented the realization in Indochina of a genuinely republican political order, they also inspired urban Vietnamese activists to articulate a reformist agenda in republican terms. Vũ Trọng Phụng provides a case in point. In an editorial published in 1937, he called directly for the introduction of a "democratic republic" in Indochina that guaranteed "a complete menu of freedoms" including "freedom to travel to France, freedom to go abroad, freedom of assembly, and freedom to do business."[51] While he rarely expressed his political aspirations in such a forthright manner, the failure of colonial civic institutions to live up to the republican ideals on which they were based runs like an unbroken thread throughout his writing. Many of his works addressed the corruption of the press by money and political influence. In a published interview with a member of the Chamber of the People's Representatives of Tonkin, he raised questions about the frivolous factional infighting that plagued the Chamber and lamented its limited capacity to express the popular will.[52] In a similar vein, *Dumb Luck* satirizes the hollowness of colonial civic rituals such as parades, sporting events, and political speeches, which were staged with increasingly regularity during the 1930s in his native Hà Nội.

ALBERT SARRAUT, FRANCO-VIETNAMESE SCHOOLS, AND *QUỐC NGỮ*

Another source of republican energy in the protectorate that coincided with Vũ Trọng Phụng's birth and childhood years was the appointment of the Radical Republican politician Albert Sarraut as the Governor General of Indochina, a position he held from 1911 to 1914 and again, during an unprecedented second term, from 1917 to 1919.[53] An exponent of a moderately liberal approach to colonial rule known as "association," Sarraut pursued a reformist agenda that set the terms for economic and political change in Indochina for over two decades. His vision for the colonial economy advocated state investment in infrastructure to stimulate economic development and, eventually, industrialization. Sarraut also favored the formation of a strategic alliance between the colonial state and enlightened sectors of the native elite. To forge (what he viewed as) this mutually beneficial partnership, he promoted the extension of education, medical services, and limited representative institutions to the native population.[54] Consistent with his republican values, he broke with his predecessors by suggesting that France should prepare the Vietnamese, gradually, for independence. While numerous obstacles prevented the realization of Sarraut's vision, his two terms in Indochina's highest office transformed the public expectations and standards of government against which colonial rule was measured.

Saurraut's republicanism is most dramatically manifest in his reform of the colonial school system. Education was a passion of the leaders of the Third Republic—known colloquially as *la république des professeurs*—who viewed it as a weapon to fight ignorance, illiteracy, and the power of the Church.[55] It could also promote republican virtues such as progress, rationality, science, and good citizenship. The school system Sarraut established suffered from serious shortcomings, but it was associated with republican ideals that touched the local population.[56] During his second term in Indochina, Sarraut introduced a comprehensive education law that codified public support for mass schooling and led to the closure of thousands of traditional schools teaching Chinese characters.[57] In their place, the colonial state established a centralized and standardized system of Franco-Vietnamese schools that provided instruction in French and Vietnamese. It comprised three years of elementary school in Vietnamese, three years of primary education in French, four years of primary superior education in French, and three years of French-language secondary education leading to an Indochinese baccalaureate.[58] Managed by a newly created office of public instruction based in Hà Nội, Franco-Vietnamese schools featured a distinctive curriculum tailored to the colonial environment. Between 1920 and 1938, the number of students enrolled in the Franco-Vietnamese system more than doubled from 125,688 to 287,037, with especially large increases in urban areas.[59] The absence of significant school fees—a republican innovation—enhanced access to the system for poor pupils like Vũ Trọng Phụng. Several years after Sarraut's reform, he enrolled in the Courbet School, also known as the Hàng Vôi School, located halfway between the French concession and his flat in the old quarter.[60] According to accounts by Nguyễn Triệu Luật and Nguyễn Văn Đạm, he also spent time at the Hàng Kèn School several blocks south of Hoàn Kiếm Lake.[61] Another friend and classmate from the era—the writer Vũ Bằng—claimed that Vũ Trọng Phụng completed six years of elementary and primary school before dropping out, at the age of fifteen, to find work to support his family.[62]

Colonial schooling influenced students of Vũ Trọng Phụng's generation in a variety of ways. Perhaps most importantly, it helped to wean them away from what colonial officials perceived as the pernicious influence of Chinese culture. During a millennium of formal Chinese rule in the Tonkin Delta between 111 B.C.E. and 939 C.E., a bilingual and bicultural Vietnamese elite emerged that viewed itself as part of a common East Asian cultural zone of "manifest civility."[63] While maintaining a series of independent dynastic states throughout most of the second millennium, the Vietnamese elite governed through tools of Chinese statecraft, including a Confucian educational and examination system that trained officials for posts in the state bureaucracy.[64] Even as they employed a nonsinitic spoken vernacular belonging to the Mon-Khmer language family, the local elite continued to use Chinese characters as the standard medium for academic instruction, civil service examinations, government documents, and high literary culture.[65] As a result, cultural developments in China remained easily accessible to educated Vietnamese up until the disruptions of the colonial era.

By the turn of the twentieth century, however, the growing circulation in Indochina of Chinese texts preaching revolutionary and nationalist ideas stimulated French efforts to destroy the ancient cultural and linguistic bonds that had long united the Vietnamese and Chinese elite. This effort was facilitated by the fortuitous availability of *quốc ngữ*, a little-used Romanized script for rendering spoken Vietnamese, first devised by missionaries and local Catholic priests in the mid-seventeenth century.[66] Following its successful introduction into colonial schools in Cochinchina during the 1860s, French officials came to see *quốc ngữ* as a useful instrument both for promoting mass literacy and for breaking the grip of Chinese culture over the local elite.[67] Consistent with this mission, Franco-Vietnamese schools emphasized the acquisition of literacy in French and *quốc ngữ* while neglecting instruction in Chinese characters. "In the elementary grades," explains Gail Kelly, "between nine and fifteen hours out of a twenty-seven hour school week were spent on languages, mostly on teaching Vietnamese. In the primary grades, between fifteen and eighteen hours each week was spent on language learning, mostly French."[68]

By promoting fluency in French and *quốc ngữ*, the Franco-Vietnamese school system transformed Vietnamese culture. Most importantly, it created the first generation of educated Vietnamese unable to read Chinese-language texts. This reduced Chinese influence in Indochina, but it also had the deracinating effect of severing Vietnamese from their own premodern textual tradition, virtually all of which had been written in characters.[69] Within a single generation, most educated Vietnamese lost the capacity to read anything that their ethnic forbearers had ever written with the exception of a tiny fraction of premodern works laboriously translated into *quốc ngữ*.[70] To the extent that nationalist ideology depends upon the establishment of continuities between a "modern people" and an "ancient" historical culture, the colonial school system's assault on Chinese-language literacy diminished the capacity of nationalists to shape a Vietnamese identity via the strategic mobilization of such continuities. In addition, the disproportionate growth of Franco-Vietnamese schools in the cities enhanced social distance between urban school graduates and rural communities, many of which continued, through force of habit, to provide local support for Chinese-language education. As an early product of this system, Vũ Trọng Phụng's intellectual development reflected its particular dynamics. He never learned Chinese and he wrote exclusively in the romanized script. He also acknowledged that the elimination of literacy in characters, fostered by Franco-Vietnamese schools, functioned to sever his generational fellows from their rural ancestry. In a generous review of Ngô Tất Tố's famous novel *Turn out the Lights (Tắt đèn)*, Vũ Trọng Phụng singled out the author's unusual fluency in Chinese as one of two "crucial conditions" that allowed him to paint a portrait of rural society that was both vivid and accurate (the second was an extended period of residence in the countryside). In contrast, he claimed that portrayals of the countryside in novels by Nhất Linh and Nguyễn Công Hoan seemed inauthentic because these writers did not know Chinese. "Without Chinese," he insisted, "it is impossible to understand what's going on in the rice fields, the communal houses, or the feudal law courts."[71] This sentiment may help to explain the relative neglect of rural life as a subject of Vũ Trọng Phụng's work.

The promotion of *quốc ngữ* by the Franco-Vietnamese school system also encouraged the growth of a Eurocentric cosmopolitanism among educated youth. Since the romanized script had rarely been used outside of segregated Catholic circles prior to the late nineteenth century, Franco-Vietnamese schools promoted literacy in a written language that did not possess a corresponding literature. As a result, intellectually inclined school graduates had little choice but to immerse themselves in the French literature and journalism that were becoming increasingly available in Indochina through the growth of libraries and bookstores and the circulation of metropolitan reading material. Vũ Trọng Phụng was a direct product of these changes. "No one in our group followed international developments as closely as Vũ Trọng Phụng," remarked Vũ Bằng, "or tried as hard to understand the obscure terms that we read in *Le Canard Enchaîné*."[72] An examination of foreign influence in Vũ Trọng Phụng's work reveals direct references to over sixty European writers, most of them French.[73] They include classical dramatists such as Corneille, Racine, and Moliere; romantics such as Hugo, Rousseau, Goethe, Lamartine, Musset, and

Chateaubriand; realists and naturalists such as Zola, Maupassant, Rolland, and Alphonse Daudet; and modernists such as Proust, Gide, and Malraux. Vũ Trọng Phụng read prodigious amounts of French pulp fiction as well as French journalism, criticism, and social science. Popular Freudian concepts influenced him greatly, as did the watered-down Marxism-Leninism that attracted numerous adherents throughout Indochina during the era.

In addition to shaping his reading habits, colonial schooling may have influenced Vũ Trọng Phụng in other ways. According to his close friend Lan Khai, Vũ Trọng Phụng's lifelong sympathy for underdogs derived from his failure to fit in socially at school.[74] Unable to afford the Western fashions favored by his wealthier classmates, he attended class dressed in a gown and turban—a traditional scholarly outfit that made him a target of ridicule among his more "up-to-date" peers. Fatherless, sickly, and poor, Vũ Trọng Phụng was ill equipped for the competitive school environment that emerged during the interwar years, in which male students vied for status and the attention of female classmates through displays of wealth and athletic prowess. "After all," Lan Khai continued, "this was an era in which tennis stars, wrestlers, and champion cyclists were applauded and adored by the general public."[75] The humiliations of student life deepened for Vũ Trọng Phụng when economic hardship forced him to leave school early to help support his family.[76] The sting of this episode endured throughout his career since many of his bitterest literary rivals—the members of the Self-Strength Literary Group (Tự Lực Văn Đoàn), for example—had earned postgraduate degrees or studied in France. When the Self-Strength newspaper *These Days (Ngày Nay)* dismissed Vũ Trọng Phụng as a "literary hack" whose "rudimentary education" *(sơ học)* rendered him unqualified to offer lessons about society and morality, his response betrayed more than a hint of class resentment.[77] "You accuse me of misinforming my readers because I possess only a rudimentary education," he responded. "So, does this mean that I'm not even allowed to argue? How should I respond to the charge that I am an uneducated hack? If your only point is to trumpet your superior education, I have nothing further to say."[78]

LIFE OF A CLERK

After leaving school around 1926 or 1927, Vũ Trọng Phụng worked for several dispiriting years in clerical jobs, including an unhappy tenure at Magasins Godard, Hà Nội's largest and most posh department store.[79] An ornate symbol of modern European consumer culture, Magasins Godard "followed the department store architecture made fashionable by the Parisian *Galeries Lafayette* and *La Samaritaine* with a domed ceiling, grand staircase and balconied upper floors."[80] It was located at one end of the Rue Paul Bert—"the *Champs-Élysées* of the colonial city"—alongside a series of up-market French shops, a tramway station, Le Palace Cinema, and the absurdly grand Municipal Opera House.[81] Reflecting the radical incongruity of life in the colonial city, this exclusive commercial boulevard was only several blocks from Vũ Trọng Phụng's cramped flat, situated on a run-down section of Silver Street, and described by Lê Tràng Kiều as a "dark corner" peopled by "rag-pickers, domestic servants, crippled beggars, and female street vendors with small children."[82] The contrast between Vũ Trọng Phụng's downtrodden neighborhood and his elegant office anticipated one of his central literary preoccupations and prefigured the recurring juxtaposition in his writing of scenes depicting the very rich and the very poor.

Vũ Trọng Phụng provided an instructive description of the atmosphere at Magasins Godard in a little-known work of reportage entitled "Life of a Clerk" ("Đời Cạo Giấy"), part of which was published in *New Youth (Tân Thiếu Niên)* in 1935. It examined the sensational double life of Đoàn Trần Nghiệp—also known as Ký Con—a neighbor of Vũ Trọng Phụng from Silver Street who joined the insurrectionary anticolonial Vietnamese Nationalist Party in his early twenties and rose to become a chillingly lethal leader of its security bureau. After achieving public notoriety during the late 1920s as a fugitive with a five-thousand-piastre bounty on his head, Đoàn Trần Nghiệp was arrested in February 1930, tried before an extraordinary Criminal Commission, and guillotined outside of the Hà Nội Central Prison.[83] At his interrogation, witnessed and reported on by the journalist Louis Roubaud, he admitted to having masterminded twenty assassinations of "enemies and traitors" plus a sequence of daring robberies and terrorist bombings.[84] Due to the sensitive subject matter of "Life of a Clerk," colonial security forces shut down *New Youth* and seized all issues in circulation.[85] Initial installments of Vũ Trọng Phụng's text indicate that he portrayed Đoàn Trần Nghiệp's mistreatment at Magasins Godard as a biographical prelude to his revolutionary career:

> When I first encountered Nghiệp as a clerk, his lowly position provoked widespread contempt. No one could have predicted that such a person would become the head of an assassination committee for the Vietnamese Nationalist Party. It was 1927; I was sixteen and Nghiệp was only a few years older. He worked in accounting and I worked as a security guard in the Godard showroom. Everyone in the office considered him slow and dimwitted. He was

> from a poor family and could not afford fancy clothes. Many Godard employees were the sons of village notables and they dressed well. Most worked as salesmen and earned ten dong per month, which they showed off back in their villages as proof that they worked for Westerners. This helped them to attract marriage partners. They disrespected Ký Con because their clothes were better than his. He was also bad at soccer. With skinny thighs like two reed sticks, he could not control the ball and he was easy to manhandle on the field. . . . One day, while passing by the accounting office, I saw Ký Con being called stupid by a Western bitch who happened to be his boss. While cursing him, she denounced the Annamese race as dirty, stupid as an ass, lazy, thieving, and so on. . . . The following month, I happened upon a pamphlet written by Ký Con called *The Parrot [Con Vẹt]*. It was as biting and satirical as any of our current humor magazines. It featured veiled criticisms of our office mates such as the heroic Mr. Francois whose greatest talent was to clutch the skirts of Western women, and an Annamese clerk who earned plaudits for going to the boss's house to bathe his wife's dogs. From that day onward, I no longer disrespected Ký Con. Eventually, I quit my job and he was promoted.[86]

Some claim that Vũ Trọng Phụng was fired from Magasins Godard for reading on the job, but the passage indicates that he left his position voluntarily. Although he doesn't explain the circumstances surrounding his departure, Nguyễn Văn Đạm recalled that Vũ Trọng Phụng resigned in protest after French managers accused his fellow Vietnamese employees of theft.[87] The surviving passage from "Life of a Clerk" suggests that the harsh appraisal of the urban middle classes found in Vũ Trọng Phụng's work grew out of his experience in the white-collar world. Indeed, the sniveling, status-conscious "horned senior clerk" in *Dumb Luck* dovetails perfectly with Vũ Trọng Phụng's description of Ký Con's tormenters in "Life of a Clerk."

Toward the end of the decade, Vũ Trọng Phụng worked as an "anonymous secretary" at the Imprimerie d'Extrême-Orient (IDEO), the largest French publishing house in Hà Nội.[88] The IDEO dominated the high end of the publishing market and handled the printing needs for many government offices. It also ran the largest bookstore in the capital.[89] According to Vũ Bằng, whose uncle also worked there, Vũ Trọng Phụng was a quiet employee who kept to himself and spent his free time reading and writing.[90] Another coworker at the IDEO, the future critic Thiều Quang, reported that Vũ Trọng Phụng was unhappy at the firm and complained about poor pay and toxic office politics marked by backstabbing, favoritism, and the vicious bullying of underlings by their superiors. This picture was affirmed by

Trương Tửu, who recalled Vũ Trọng Phụng's depiction of the work culture there as a vicious Darwinian struggle in which "the big fish devoured the small fish."[91]

Despite its evident drudgery, Vũ Trọng Phụng's position at the IDEO provided him with his first sustained exposure to the publishing world. Indeed, multiple accounts suggest that his first short stories appeared in print during the period that he was employed there. Tam Lang reports that, while working on the editorial board of the Hà Nội newspaper *Midday News (Ngọ Báo)* in 1930, he approved the publication of an unsolicited short story about a childless couple.[92] After it appeared, friends informed Tam Lang that the story might have been based on a real couple currently residing on Silver Street. Thereafter, he received several additional stories from the same writer, but they were rejected by his editor-in-chief, Bùi Xuân Học, due to their prurient subject matter. Several weeks later, Vũ Trọng Phụng visited Tam Lang at the paper and revealed his identity as the author of the recently submitted stories. He voiced frustration with his job at the IDEO and expressed a desire to become a journalist for *Midday News.* No positions were available, but Tam Lang hired him as a typist, his first full-time job in journalism.

In an idiosyncratic memoir published in 1957, Thiều Quang confirmed the broad outlines of Tam Lang's version of events, adding that Vũ Trọng Phụng may have lost his job at the IDEO because of his extracurricular literary activities.[93] According to his account, employees at the IDEO were scandalized when Vũ Trọng Phụng published a controversial story entitled "The Ploy" ("Thủ đoạn") in *Midday News.* It dramatized the homosexual exploitation of a Vietnamese office worker by his French supervisor and was considered shockingly graphic for its time.[94] After the story came out, Thiều Quang reported that "a fierce exchange broke out; many sought out the story but others didn't dare to read it."[95] In the midst of the outcry over "The Ploy," Vũ Trọng Phụng was charged with public indecency *(outrages aux bonnes moeurs)* and summoned to appear at court. He prepared a written defense that included a passionate appeal for free speech and realist literature (which he shared with Thiều Quang), but he was prevented from delivering it when his case was abruptly dismissed. Vũ Trọng Phụng was fired from the IDEO as a result of the controversy leading up his trial. If this account is accurate, it suggests that Vũ Trọng Phụng worked at the IDEO until early 1931 since "The Ploy" appeared in three installments during late January of that year.

While Vũ Trọng Phụng's employment history during the early 1930s is murky, he started to publish regularly during this period in the *Midday News.*[96] Between October 1930 and March 1932, roughly a dozen short stories appeared under his byline, some serialized in two or three installments.[97] Many explored pressing social issues in a realist or naturalist style. In "A Death" ("Một cái chết"), published on March 13–14, 1931, the son of a tax collector commits suicide after witnessing his father abusing a destitute beggar. Several stories such as "A Dishonest Person" ("Con người điêu trá") and "Love Trap" ("Bẫy tình") are misogynist in tone and belittle local incarnations of the "modern girl" and the cult of romantic love. Others, like "The Ploy" and "Miss Mai Loves Spring" ("Cô Mai thưởng xuân"), conjoin social critique with pejorative depictions of unrestrained sexual desire. During this period, Vũ Trọng Phụng also published in *Midday News* translations of Guy de Maupassant's short stories "Fou" and "Solitude" as well as excerpts from "Le roman," his famous treatise on literary realism.[98] Alongside this early engagement with French realism, Vũ Trọng Phụng exhibited a parallel interest in romanticism. In January 1932, he translated excerpts from Victor Hugo's romantic manifesto "Preface to Cromwell," which had appeared originally in 1827.[99] An interest in romanticism may also be discerned in his translation of essays by Alfred de Vigny and the "late-romantic" poet Jean Richepin, both of which dealt with the mistreatment of writers by politicians and moralists.[100] Although Vũ Trọng Phụng self-identified as a realist writer throughout his career, his engagement with well-known texts from both the realist and the romantic canon should come as no surprise since both traditions had entered Indochina at the same time and were similarly associated with colonial modernity.[101]

The *Midday News* was an exciting place to work in the early 1930s. It was founded in 1927 by the pioneering newspapermen Hoàng Tích Chu and Đỗ Văn, who modeled it after French broadsheets that they had encountered while studying journalism in Paris.[102] Hoàng Tích Chu introduced a simplified form of expository writing that eschewed the elaborate formal conventions of traditional Sino-Vietnamese prose. Đỗ Văn was responsible for the newspaper's high production quality and modern layout, which featured eye-catching headlines, parallel columns, thematic "sections," and a topical lead article on the front page. Both men embodied a new urban type—the hard-living newspaperman—who smoked opium, drank heavily, wore Western clothes, enjoyed dancing, and spoke easily in French. In an essay penned in 1935, Vũ Trọng Phụng recalled the glamorous aura that surrounded the *Midday News* at the start of the decade:

> The glorious days of the *Midday News* are over. I remember that when Hoàng Tích Chu was still there, readers anticipated the noontime release of each issue like lovers waiting for each other at a park. In those days, the *Midday News* sold well and was well respected, unlike daily papers today. Hoàng Tích Chu's

> contribution to the reform of our literature enhanced the reputation of the *Midday News*. Inspired by Hoàng Tích Chu, Ngọc Thỏ denounced bad things in his column "The Dark Side of Life," and Tam Lang's series "*Midday News* Stories" employed psychological analysis and a new literary style to explore the misery in people's hearts. In those days, people much preferred the *Midday News* to its old-fashioned rivals: Civilize *[Khai Hóa]*, *North Central [Trung Bắc]*, and *Profession [Thực Nghiệp]*.[103]

The popularity of the *Midday News* also derived from its stable of talented writers. "I first started to like reading newspapers," recalled the writer Vũ Bằng, "when Hoàng Tích Chu, Đỗ Văn, Phùng Bảo Thạch, Tạ Đình Bích, and Vũ Đình Chí wrote for the *Midday News*."[104] Vũ Đình Chí—aka Tam Lang—was an especially influential presence at the *Midday News* and his hugely successful nonfiction reportage narrative "I Pulled a Rickshaw" must have made a strong impression on Vũ Trọng Phụng.[105] Upon leaving the *Midday News* for Đỗ Văn's new weekly *New Day (Nhật Tân)* in 1933, Vũ Trọng Phụng began to follow in Tam Lang's footsteps.

COLONIAL JOURNALISM

Vũ Trọng Phụng's move to *New Day* in 1933 marked a turning point in his life in two respects. First, it signaled the beginning of his career as a full-time journalist after a transitional period during which his writing served merely to supplement the primary income that he earned as a clerk. Second, he published two pieces of long-format nonfiction reportage—*The Man Trap* and *The Industry of Marrying Westerners*—that attracted critical approval and popular acclaim. When Vũ Trọng Phụng left *New Day* in 1934, he was a twenty-two-year-old media celebrity.

Vũ Trọng Phụng's emergence as a journalistic luminary was made possible by the explosive growth of the Vietnamese-language press during the interwar era. Studies of the colonial press highlight the injustice of a plural legal regime that subjected Vietnamese journals to licensing rules and prepublication censorship while applying the Third Republic's famously liberal 1881 press law to periodicals in French. But this discriminatory dimension of French policy fails to convey the lively republican ethos conveyed by the colonial press.[106] Free from state control, French newspapers in Indochina were freewheeling and contentious, reflecting the diverse and conflicting interests of a fractious colon community of businessmen, bureaucrats, missionaries, lawyers, soldiers, and teachers. As early as the late nineteenth century, French newspapers attacked the colonial state for undermining the

Nhất Tân
Journal d'Opinion en langue annamite
15, rue des Cuirs, Hanoi

CARTE
de Service de Presse

Le Direct[illegible]r du NHAT TAN a l'honneur d[illegible] [illegible]diter, auprès des autorités civil[illegible] [illegible]nilitaires, de la Colonie, M. Vu Trong Phung Redacteur au Nhat Tan et les prie de bien vouloir, dans la mesure de leurs moyens, faciliter l'accomplissement de son devoir professionnel.

Le Titulaire. Le Directeur.

NHÂT-TAN

Vu pour légalisation des signatures de MM. [illegible] et Vu Trong Phung apposées ci-contre

Hanoï, le 28 Sept. 1933
l'Administrateur-Maire,
L. F. Eckert

VILLE DE HANOI
0.20
TIMBRE TAXE

FIGURE 2.
Vũ Trọng Phụng's Press Card for *Nhật Tân* (New day), issued on September 28, 1933 (collection of Nghiêm Xuân Sơn).

economic interests of the colon community. In the 1920s, state-subsidized newspapers such as Henry Chavigny's *L'Impartial* clashed openly with muckraking "scandal sheets" such as *Vérité, Saigon Rébublicain,* and *Indochine*—the latter founded in Sài Gòn in 1925 by the young republican novelist André Malraux.[107] The rise of literacy in French provided educated Vietnamese with access to this lively marketplace of ideas. Activists in Cochinchina participated in this discourse directly by exploiting legal loopholes that allowed native subjects to run French-language publications free from government censorship. During the mid-1920s, local participation in the French public sphere was embodied by Nguyễn An Ninh's impertinent political weekly *La Clôche Felée,* which billed itself as an "Organ of Propagation of French Ideas" and attacked French colonialism for violating republican principles.[108] The tradition inaugurated by *La Clôche Felée* peaked in the mid-1930s with the rise of a wide array of sectarian left-leaning journals such as the weekly *La Lutte,* which brought together a range of progressive writers in service to a common anticolonial and anticapitalist project.[109] A dynamic tradition of *quốc ngữ* journalism also developed in Cochinchina, spurred on between 1929 and 1935 by the popular weekly *Womens' New Literature (Phụ Nữ Tân Văn).*[110]

In Tonkin, the persistence of imperial Vietnamese law enhanced restrictions on free speech, but a vibrant print culture developed there as well. In 1917, Albert Sarraut authorized the establishment in Hà Nội of *Southern Wind (Nam Phong)*, a serious intellectual journal edited by the conservative nationalist Phạm Quỳnh.[111] While it supported the colonial project throughout its seventeen-year print run, *Southern Wind* addressed a wide range of current events, social problems, political questions, international issues, and cultural trends. It also intervened in public debates, including a famous controversy over the nationalist significance of the verse narrative *The Tale of Kiều*. Moreover, owing to the copresence of traditionalist and modernist impulses in Phạm Quỳnh's cultural nationalism, *Southern Wind* explored these issues in three languages: French, Chinese, and *quốc ngữ*. The legacy of *Southern Wind* provided a strong foundation for the development of a large, sophisticated *quốc ngữ* press in Tonkin. This growth accelerated during the mid-1930s when a leftward shift in French domestic politics (culminating in the formation of the Popular Front in 1934) eased censorship throughout the Empire. A result was the elimination of prepublication censorship for *quốc ngữ* journals in 1935 and the abandonment of discriminatory licensing rules in 1938.[112]

Owing to this relatively favorable legal environment, accelerated urbanization, the growth of French-educated youth, and the economic boom of the 1920s, the number of serialized publications tripled during the interwar years. According to one history of the colonial press, the number of periodicals published in Annam, Tonkin, and Cochinchina expanded from 96 in 1922 to 121 in 1925 and 153 in 1929.[113] In spite of the global economic slump, these numbers grew from 167 in 1931 to 267 in 1935, and growth enhanced diversity.[114] In addition to general interest daily and weekly newspapers, the press of the period included titles focused on niche issues such as women, youth, politics, business, international affairs, literature, fashion, sports, cinema, popular science, and humor. While the French-language press survived during this era, with the aid of state subsidies, its development stalled relative to the explosive growth of *quốc ngữ* journals (with their exponentially larger pool of potential consumers). At the start of the 1930s, the most popular daily broadsheets in *quốc ngữ* reached ten to fifteen thousand customers. Between 1936 and 1939, the nine most popular *quốc ngữ* journals were purchased by a total of eighty thousand readers.[115] Sales figures tell only part of the story, however, since single issues were typically read by more than one person. Vũ Trọng Phụng pointed this out in a review of the Tonkin press published in *Evolution (Tiến Hóa)* in 1935. "Currently, the newspaper *French Indochina (Đông Pháp)* prints ten thousand copies per day," he wrote, "but let's take a closer look. Everyone who buys one copy will typically share it with ten others. A subscriber will lend his paper to someone upstairs or out back and to neighbors on either side of his house or on the opposite side of the street. These borrowers, in turn, lend the papers to others. When the original buyer recovers his torn and wrinkled paper, he might send it to the countryside or up to the mountains. Hence, one buyer may represent one hundred readers. One hundred thousand readers per issue may be a more realistic estimate."[116]

This general context is critical for understanding Vũ Trọng Phụng's peripatetic employment history, which began amid this period of unprecedented media growth and diversification. Between the appearance of his first intermittent submissions to the *Midday News* in 1930 and the publication of his final handful of short stories in *Literary Circle* during 1939, Vũ Trọng Phụng's writing appeared in roughly two-dozen periodicals. While most were based in Hà Nội, papers in Huế, Hải Phòng, and Sài Gòn also featured his work. The uneven rhythm of his publication record reflects the brief life span of the periodicals for which he worked and the short terms of the staff positions that he held. Such factors explain the concentration of his work at the *Midday News* in 1931–32, *New Day* in 1933, *Megaphone* and *Hải Phòng Weekly* in 1934, *Hà Nội News (Hà Nội Báo)* in 1936, *The Future (Tương Lai)* and *Indochina Journal (Đông Dương Tạp Chí)* in 1937–38, *Thursday Novel (Tiểu Thuyết Thứ Năm)* and *The Mallard (Vịt Đực)* in 1938, and *Literary Circle* in 1939. These affiliations did not prevent him from placing his work in multiple venues at the same time. Starting in 1934, his work appeared simultaneously in numerous journals: four in 1934, six in 1935, four in 1936, five in 1937, five in 1938, and four in 1939. This record of simultaneous publication may also reflect the low commissions and ad hoc structure of payment characteristic of the colonial press—well described in memoirs by Nguyễn Vỹ, Nguyễn Công Hoan, and Phan Thị Mỹ Khanh.[117] What Theodore Zeldin observed about journalists in Third Republic France applied as well to their Vietnamese counterparts: "Journalists were ultimately wage earners with no security, at the mercy of arbitrary proprietors; many did not even have regular wages, but got paid by the line, and sometimes a small retainer."[118] The penurious state of the profession in Indochina determined the parameters of Vũ Trọng Phụng's social life. Journalists often lived together in newspaper offices, pooling their resources, eating communally, and socializing together. According to Nguyễn Vỹ, journalists during this era lived "free and undisciplined lives" and spent their leisure time patronizing the same cafes, salons, brothels, and opium dens. Nguyễn Vỹ placed Vũ Trọng Phụng in one such homosocial journalistic clique, grouping him along with Lan Khai, Đỗ Thúc Trâm, and Nguyễn Triệu Luật.[119]

Vũ Trọng Phụng expressed mixed emotions toward the journalistic profession to which he devoted his life. His novel *Dumb Luck* portrays journalists as pathetic and grasping and derides them for blurring the lines between news reporting and commerce. In a pair of essays published in 1935, Vũ Trọng Phụng scolded the Tonkin press for sensationalism and commercialism and for valuing timely scoops over accurate reporting.[120] Elsewhere he depicted journalists as unprincipled muckrakers or as "whores" who traded positive coverage for money and favors. Vũ Trọng Phụng's portrayal of newspapermen during the Popular Front era was more sympathetic. Fictional journalists employed by the magazine *Two Regions (Lưỡng Kỳ)* in *The Storm* and the newspaper *Labor (Lao Động)* in *The Dike Breaks* are described as activists who "criticize inhumanity and attack those who use their power and money to exploit the poor."[121] References to the Vietnamese press in *Venereal Disease Clinic* emphasize its oppositional posture toward the colonial state. The diverse portrayals of colonial newspapermen in Vũ Trọng Phụng's body of work mirror the range of images that circulated in postrevolutionary France. Depictions of French reporters as crusading social reformers date from the late eighteenth century owing to the high profile of journalists such as Marat and Mirabeau in the revolutionary leadership. "The Revolution established a tradition by which, in 1830 and 1848, journalists played leading roles in overthrowing governments," explains Zeldin. "The freedom of the press became a major political issue."[122] According to Philip Nord, positive portrayals of journalists surged during the Third Republic owing to the consolidation of a political establishment marked by an "alliance of press and republic."[123] At the same time, an aversion to the power of entrenched financial interests bred skepticism within republican discourse toward claims of journalistic objectivity and the corrupting influence of money on the press.

Vũ Trọng Phụng's similarly complex attitude toward colonial journalism may be seen in the brief autobiographical essay "A Dishonest Deed" ("Một hành vi bất lương") which he published in the Hải Phòng weekly *Life Stories (Chuyện đời)* on May 7, 1938.[124] It reveals the backstory behind the writing of *Venereal Disease Clinic*, a long piece of nonfiction reportage that he serialized in *The Future* during 1937. The essay opens with Vũ Trọng Phụng, brainstorming with colleagues, in search of a fresh writing project. "It was tough to find a topic," he complained, "because the good ones had all been done." The search was more difficult because the public had grown weary of reportage and skeptical of its claims to veracity. But then he hit upon an idea. "There was a lot of interest in prostitution at the time; everyone seemed to be writing about it. So I decided to investigate the municipal V.D. Clinic." Right away, the publisher of *The Future* began to advertise the imminent publication of the as yet unwritten series and requested permission from Mayor Virgitti for a site visit. When Virgitti failed to respond, Vũ Trọng Phụng approached Dr. Joyeux, the head of the clinic and the director of the Municipal Bureau of Public Health. Joyeux refused the request, but he forwarded to Vũ Trọng Phụng a collection of recent studies on prostitution in Indochina, including reports from the League of Nations. With a deadline looming, Vũ Trọng Phụng smoked a bowl of opium ("nothing strange here for a Vietnamese journalist") and crafted an opening vignette by knitting together material he had received from the French official with his own recollections of Hà Nội streetwalkers. Days later, a tour of the clinic was hastily arranged for the Popular Front Minister of Labor Justin Godard (who was visiting from Paris) and Vũ Trọng Phụng was allowed to tag along and to follow up with additional visits, which provided the basis for the early installments of *Venereal Disease Clinic*. Several weeks into the publication of the series, Mayor Virgitti abruptly terminated Vũ Trọng Phụng's access to the clinic, complaining that his coverage had been inaccurate and overly negative. During a meeting with Vũ Trọng Phụng to explain this reversal, the Mayor singled out sarcastic comments featured in the first installment of the series about a mnemonic poem taught to infected prostitutes to encourage good hygiene. While admitting to himself that he had, in fact, fabricated the offending passage during the period when he had been denied access to the clinic, Vũ Trọng Phụng (mis)informed the Mayor that he had made an error of mistaken identity and that the passage in question had been published by a rival at *Việt News (Việt Báo)*.[125] Chastened by this deliberate falsehood, the Mayor apologized profusely and reauthorized Vũ Trọng Phụng's access to the clinic. "This is the most dishonest deed that I have ever done in my career as a journalist," Vũ Trọng Phụng wrote in the last line of the essay. "But who knows what the future holds."

Despite the farcical and self-deprecating depiction of journalism in "A Dishonest Deed," a serious commitment to freedom of speech and freedom of the press is apparent, both in Vũ Trọng Phụng's written work and in his limited record of political activism. For reasons that will become clear, most of his writing on freedom of speech criticized efforts to censor pornography. For example, his historical essay "A Literary Case" ("Một cái án văn chương"), published in 1932, provides an approving summary of the French poet Jean Richepin's defense against obscenity charges launched in 1876 against his scatological poetry collection *Songs of the Down and Out (Chansons des gueux)*. After rehearsing Richepin's arguments in favor of a literature that exposes "the ugliness of social reality," the essay concludes: "Although he was jailed for a month and stripped of his civil rights, Richepin was never the object of public scorn. Among our writers, is there anyone who dares to follow in Richepin's footsteps? Go! Go! If you have talent and courage, go!"[126] Five years later, Vũ Trọng Phụng engaged in a public exchange with the critics Thái Phỉ and Nhất Chi Mai after they denounced several of his works for violating public decency. "A journalist must write the truth for everyone to see," he wrote in his defense. "If a story is true, it is our duty as journalists to amplify it irrespective of the pain or the benefit that it may bring."[127] In conclusion, he reiterated his belief in the social value of free expression. "People are often afraid of truths that are dirty or ugly," he wrote. "They often try to hide big, filthy wounds behind silk and velvet, but this will never cure the problem. Rather, wounds must be exposed and operated upon even if they smell bad and hurt our eyes. My work simply exposes the wounds of society in order that they might be cured."[128] In another public letter, Vũ Trọng Phụng linked his commitment to uncompromising truth-telling to the cause of social justice promoted by republican and left-leaning writers in Europe: "It is not petty-minded to tell the truth about this villainous society, to attack the luxury and lust of the rich, to lament the misery of the poor, the exploited, the persecuted, and the oppressed, to want justice, and to work to bring an end to the kind of filthy stories that I relate. If it is, then Zola, Hugo, Malraux, Dostoyevsky, and Gorky are also petty-minded."[129]

Vũ Trọng Phụng's commitment to the issue might be interpreted as a personal response to the legal persecution of his writing on multiple occasions during the early 1930s. In March 1932, newspapers in Hà Nội and Sài Gòn covered a suit brought against him and Nguyễn Văn Thìn, the editor-in-chief of a short-lived journal named *Sound of the Bell (Tiếng Chuông)*. The suit charged that a piece of writing by Vũ Trọng Phụng had slandered an unnamed notable and violated public decency, while also alleging that Nguyễn Văn Thìn was operating *Sound of the Bell* without a proper license. At a trial held on March 22, Vũ Trọng Phụng and Nguyễn Văn Thìn were each fined fifty francs and the latter was sentenced to six days in jail.[130] A complete run of *Sound of the Bell* has never been recovered, but Lại Nguyên Ân speculates that the offending item may have been a story entitled "Son or Father?" and attributed to the pseudonymous author "The Spittoon" ("Ống nhổ").[131] Together with the earlier attacks against "The Ploy" and "Life of a Clerk," this episode represents the third instance in which legal charges were raised against Vũ Trọng Phụng's journalistic activities.

In 1937, in his only documented foray into direct political activism, Vũ Trọng Phụng signed his name to a public petition that protested the arrest, on trumped-up charges, of the journalist Lê Bá Chấn.[132] Although he was arrested for allegedly kidnapping his fiancé, mainstream papers speculated that Lê Bá Chấn had been jailed for attempting to contact the Popular Front Minister Justin Godard during his recent visit to Hải Dương.[133] The twenty-odd signatories of the petition included many of Vũ Trọng Phụng's colleagues and employers such as Lê Tràng Kiều, Trương Tửu, Vũ Đình Long, Tam Lang, Ngô Tất Tố, Phùng Bảo Thạch, and Vũ Bằng as well as the future communist general Võ Nguyên Giáp, who worked, at the time, as a reporter for the left-wing journal *Rassemblement*. Lê Bá Chấn was eventually released but not before he staged a weeklong hunger strike, an episode that dominated front-page news throughout April 1937. "Not only does this case violate Lê Bá Chấn's personal freedom *[tự do],*" the petition read, "but it threatens the freedom of all journalists in our country."[134] As with his opposition to the censorship of pornography, Vũ Trọng Phụng's action in support of this case indicates that a republican commitment to the protection of the right to free speech and a free press loomed large within his political vision.

The final staff position that Vũ Trọng Phụng held before he died—as editor-in-chief of the *Indochina Journal* between August 1937 and January 1938—confirms the endurance toward the end of his life of the republican commitments that he expressed throughout his career. While featuring his name on the masthead on December 25, 1937, the *Indochina Journal* published a lengthy front-page manifesto that called for the formation in Indochina of a "social party with a national orientation." Its agenda included a demand for freedom to form political parties: "In civilized countries in Europe, a party is formed by the union of a big group of people who share the same ideas. This natural union is a sacred right of citizens who live in democratic countries. Our country is only a colony of France. Our people do not yet have the right to form a political party or to hold an open meeting." The essay asserted that the right to form parties was supported by the cause of "justice" and "human dignity." Consistent with its republican sensibility, it demanded that the state provide "mass education for all citizens of the country." It also drew attention to its republican vision by contrasting its rights-based agenda with the agenda of local conservative monarchists: "The principles of the Monarchy and the principles of the People are incompatible, especially when the People join together to demand multiple rights such as freedom of speech, freedom for organized labor, and the right to vote."[135]

LITERARY REPORTAGE

Vũ Trọng Phụng's republican sensibility may also be seen in his commitment to literary reportage, a cosmopolitan genre that thrived in many parts of the world during the interwar era. In 1942, Vũ Ngọc Phan defined reportage *(phóng sự)* as a literary form that fused objective observation of current events or milieus ("what the eye sees and the ear hears") with subjective commentary of a critical nature.[136] He also emphasized the genre's inherent antagonism toward the politically powerful and its utility as an instrument of social reform: "In our country, journalism is a new profession; hence, real reportage, worthy of the name, has only been around for ten years. The political situation in our country has been intolerant of reportage, stunting the growth of the genre. This is a shame because no genre is as concrete as reportage, promotes reform as well as reportage, or contributes as much as reportage does to the work of officials, lawyers, and sociologists."[137] Vũ Ngọc Phan implied that diverse national versions of the genre exhibited a similar crusading spirit: "In other countries, people believe that reportage has the capacity to modify the law, overturn unfair punishments, and reform society. Reportage there bears the responsibility of fixing what is flawed and eliminating what should be abolished. Writers of reportage are committed to the protection of rights and the defense of justice."[138]

Leading practitioners of literary reportage during Vũ Trọng Phụng's lifetime included the Americans John Reed, Upton Sinclair, Joseph North, and John Dos Passos; the Russians Ilya Ehrenburg and Sergei Tretyakov; the Englishman George Orwell; the Frenchman Albert Londres; and the Czech Egon Erwin Kisch. Although the narrative conventions of the genre varied little the world over, national traditions reflected a range of left-leaning political agendas. Soviet reportage, for example, followed an orthodox "line" established by cultural officials in Moscow. German reportage grew out of campaigns launched by the cultural wing of the German Communist Party to establish a system of "worker-correspondents whose task it was to report on conditions in the factories, in the lives of workers and in the bourgeois state."[139] Following guidelines devised by orthodox theorists such as the Hungarian critic Georg Lukács, communist reportage from different national traditions featured didactic commentary that guided readers toward "general" insights that they were expected to take away from "particular" scenes.[140] In contrast, interwar Chinese reportage expressed an array of progressive projects associated with Lu Xun's noncommunist League of Left-Wing Writers and an indigenous pre-twentieth-century documentary tradition.[141]

The most widely read reportage writers in interwar France married a left-leaning republican vision to a commitment to objective research that derived from the nineteenth-century *feuilleton* and Zola's naturalism. The most prominent French devotees of the form included the "staunch republican" Albert Londres as well as

Maryse Choisy, Roland Dorgeles, Louis Roubaud, and Andrée Viollis.[142] The latter three were moderate noncommunists with strong republican credentials, each of whom authored well-known exposés of French repression in interwar Indochina. Maryse Choisy's popular reportage-ethnographies of prostitutes, maids, monks, and female prisoners in interwar France expressed a similar social vision, although her thinking came to be dominated by psychoanalytic principles after she became a patient of Freud in the late 1920s.

Vũ Trọng Phụng was familiar with all of these figures. In 1934, he described Louis Roubaud as a "big shot journalist" and later appropriated him as a character in a short satirical play.[143] In a letter written in 1935, he acknowledged reading *Le Chemin de Buenos-Aires,* Albert Londres's popular account of the "white slave trade" in Argentina.[144] In 1937, he credited Andrée Viollis's book *Indochine SOS* with launching a powerful amnesty movement to free Indochinese political prisoners.[145] In the preface to *Household Servants,* he referred approvingly to the work of Maryse Choisy: "Not long ago, Maryse Choisy donned the garb of a maid, and wrote a long reportage, *Carnet d'une femme de chambre,* which was not without value for social scientists."[146] In 1937, he listed her as a major literary influence along with Jean Richepin, Victor Margueritte, Francis Carco, and Colette.[147]

In a letter written in 1935 that contrasted real reportage based on "what the eye sees and ear hears" to phony "armchair reportage" derived from hearsay and secondhand reports, Vũ Trọng Phụng alluded to a progressive social agenda inherent in his understanding of the genre that resembled its left-leaning republican incarnation in interwar France:

> What were the reasons that led me to reportage? When I was twenty-one, a thought sprang to mind: people do not want to see each other's pain or to revisit sad memories—in my case, memories from my childhood. I was fated from birth to become a writer, but the more I matured, the more I realized that many people are tormented by pain in their souls and their flesh. The gap between the rich and the poor grows wider each day. Rich girls curse when the silk hems of their skirts are soiled by contact with the patched skirts of poor peasant girls. Banquet tables are often hidden from view to conceal the tragedy of poverty and hunger. I learned recently that a match factory in Hà Nội plans to hire children who agree to chain themselves to machines because they lack food and clothes. As they are compelled to repeat the same gestures thousands of times per day, these children run the risk of turning into machines themselves. From North to South, innocent people languish in prison, "angels in hell" as Westerners say. Literature provides nothing but distraction if it only

> screams at the wind and yells at the clouds. For me, literature should serve as an instrument of struggle for writers who want to eliminate injustice from society or inspire sympathy for those whose dignity has been taken away or those who wish to help the weak, the damned, and the exploited or those who work all day to put food on the table but still must go to bed hungry. I am trying to explore the miseries of society. With luck, I may be able to find remedies that help to heal its wounds.[148]

The approach to reportage described by Vũ Trọng Phụng contrasts with the more rigid and didactic communist variant of the genre. Of special interest is his insistence that reportage should address hardships experienced by a broad category of exploited persons including children, prisoners, and the poor rather than focusing narrowly on the proletariat. This dovetails with the neglect of the industrial working class in Vũ Trọng Phụng's reportage and its preoccupation with the plight of "nonrevolutionary" social groups such as prostitutes, concubines, actors, servants, and con artists. In addition, Vũ Trọng Phụng's modest call for "remedies" points to a commitment to practical antidotes to social problems and a preference for piecemeal reform over revolutionary solutions.

The Man Trap, Vũ Trọng Phụng's first major piece of reportage, was serialized in *New Day* in thirteen installments between August and November 1933. It was initially published under his pen name—Thiên Hư—which referred to a fateful star in his personal horoscope chart.[149] Its subject was the community of clandestine con artists in Hà Nội who earned their living by manipulating popular games of chance played with cards and dice. The community was organized into a handful of overlapping syndicates, led by a criminal aristocracy of cardsharps and professional grifters. In addition to profiling the members of one syndicate and charting the course of their working lives over several months, *The Man Trap* revealed to its readers many of the cunning techniques that formed the industry's stock-in-trade.[150] These included various forms of sleight of hand, doctored equipment (such as loaded dice, arranged decks, and deceptive shirtsleeves), and the use of decoys and strategic distractions. Indeed, the popularity of the series likely derived from the insight it provided into a forbidden, subterranean world. While the politics of *The Man Trap* were more opaque than in any of Vũ Trọng Phụng's subsequent works of reportage, it alluded to broader themes concerning the harsh and deceptive character of capitalist modernity. The central subjects of *The Man Trap* were not members of the poor or exploited classes, but many had taken up con artistry after losing their jobs at the start of the Depression. Moreover, editorial asides in the

FIGURE 3.
Caricature of Vũ Trọng Phụng, *Loa* (Megaphone), January 24, 1934.

narrative return repeatedly to similarities between con artistry and "legitimate" professions in the capitalist economy. Like ordinary businessmen, con artists needed to hone their craft, make strategic investments, and work together with reliable partners to turn a profit. Success required ruthlessness, deceptiveness and a willingness to innovate. Another theme was the instrumental power of scientific rationalism, which Vũ Trọng Phụng associated with the intricate and well-tested techniques employed by con artists. Finally, *The Man Trap* promoted the paranoid idea that scams and con artists—like the forces of capitalist modernity—were omnipresent in colonial society, pulling invisible strings to determine outcomes that had previously been chalked up to the mysterious workings of fate.

The Man Trap earned rave reviews after it was republished as a short book in 1934.[151] "Readers first got to know Vũ Trọng Phụng through realist stories that he published in this newspaper," wrote Thái Phỉ in *Midday News* in February 1934.

> In these stories, this disciple of Gustave Flaubert described with great care the filth of society, in the manner of Guy de Maupassant. Vũ Trọng Phụng may be consumed with these two realist writers, but he has followed his own road. After tangling with a judge over a pornographic story in *Sound of the Bell*, he turned to criticism. But he grew dissatisfied with this approach and fell into reportage. With this genre, he is sure to reach his literary potential and to establish many benchmarks along the road. *The Man Trap* is valuable both as a piece of research and as a piece of literature.[152]

An admiring notice from *Literature Magazine (Văn)* read: "Our country has never before produced such refined reportage. Indeed this inside account of con artistry should be considered the first real reportage in our country *[nước Nam]*."[153] Positive notices also appeared in French-language journals including Nguyễn Văn Vĩnh's *L'Annam Nouveau*, which billed *The Man Trap* as "le reportage sensationnel."[154] In a private diary entry from 1934, the playwright Vi Huyền Đắc recalled expressing admiration for *The Man Trap* after being introduced to Vũ Trọng Phụng through their mutual friend, Thế Lữ. "Ah, Mr. Phụng, the author of *The Man Trap*," Vi Huyền Đắc stammered upon meeting the twenty-one-year-old writer. "I just finished reading our people's best work of reportage; it is written with great skill. Most works in our national literature are mediocre. Not so with *The Man Trap*. I read it from start to finish without stopping because the writing is so good. It is seductive, impossible to put down."[155]

During the following five years, Vũ Trọng Phụng published three additional book-length works of reportage, each of which is discussed at length in subsequent chapters. Also appearing in *New Day,* immediately after the conclusion of *The Man Trap* in December 1934, *The Industry of Marrying Westerners (Kỹ nghệ lấy Tây)* explored interracial conjugal unions in Tonkin, paying special attention to the lives of "professional" Vietnamese paramours of foreign legionnaires.[156] For *Household Servants,* serialized in *Hà Nội News* between March and May 1936, Vũ Trọng Phụng worked undercover as a domestic worker to produce a conjoined ethnography of local maids and their middle-class employers.[157] Published in *The Future* between January and April 1937, *Venereal Disease Clinic* detailed the segmented structure of Hà Nội's sex trade, the plight of female sex workers, and state efforts to regulate prostitution and prevent sexually transmitted disease. *The Industry of Marrying Westerners* was republished as a book in 1936, and *Household Servants* and *Venereal Disease Clinic* were packaged together in a single volume in 1937.[158] In addition, Vũ Trọng Phụng produced two partial, shorter works of serialized reportage—*Hải Phòng 1934* and a study of the theater in Hà Nội entitled *Clown Makeup (Vẽ nhọ bôi hề)*—both of which were left unfinished when the journals in which they appeared abruptly closed down.[159]

As with *The Man Trap,* Vũ Trọng Phụng's subsequent works of reportage earned high praise for their gripping prose and progressive social message. "*The Industry of Marrying Westerners* is a masterpiece that will deeply affect modern society," wrote Mai-Xuân-Nhân in 1936. "Everyone should read this magnificent and original book. The talented Vũ Trọng Phụng should be proud to have reached the same level as Louis Roubaud, Andrée Viollis, and Pierre Suze [sic]."[160] Vũ Ngọc Phan singled out the skillful and sympathetic portrayal of the underclass in *Household Servants.*[161] Reviews of *Venereal Disease Clinic* underlined Vũ Trọng Phụng's fearlessness as a researcher. "Vũ Trọng Phụng deserves praise," wrote Nguyễn Vỹ in 1938. "He has a talent for reportage and he has produced a very fine example of the genre. When confronted with a difficult issue such as prostitution, Mr. Phụng grows curious and embarks on intensive research. As a social writer, he does not flinch before the most disgusting scenes. . . . Few writers possess this special virtue."[162] Phùng Tất Đắc emphasized the value of Vũ Trọng Phụng's reportage as a historical document that will illuminate for "later generations" the "strange, unprecedented changes" occurring during the era.[163] Lãng Tử compared the political power of Vũ Trọng Phụng's writing to the finest French reportage: "In France, reportage is well respected and journalists such as Albert Londres, Roger Martin du Gard, and Pierre Mac Orlan have written powerful books with the potential to overthrow governments or bring about fundamental changes in society. Literature in our country remains poor and reportage is underdeveloped. But with

Vũ Trọng Phụng's *The Industry of Marrying Westerners,* we have reason for optimism. Long live reportage!"[164]

REALIST NOVELIST

The two years following Vũ Trọng Phụng's departure from *New Day* marked a temporary lull in his spectacular literary ascent. His most significant publication during 1934–35 was the naturalist play *No Echo* (*Không một tiếng vang*; discussed at length in chapter 2), but he is alleged to have written it in 1931.[165] He also completed his first novel, *Severed Love,* an overwrought love story with a strong but diffuse political subtext.[166] In addition, he published numerous minor pieces during this period, including short stories, one-act plays, news reporting, and editorials.[167] In 1934, he served on the editorial staff at *Megaphone* and *Hải Phòng Weekly,* for which he likely produced anonymous copy. The shuttering of *Women's Contemporary Forum (Phụ Nữ Thời Đàm), Hải Phòng Weekly,* and *New Youth* by censors and creditors forced him to abandon promising works of reportage: *Clown Makeup, Hải Phòng 1934,* and *Life of a Clerk.* It was also during this period that Vũ Trọng Phụng published his first story in Vũ Đình Long's *Saturday Novel,* a move that signaled the start of his association with the Tân Dân group.

However, 1936 marked a sudden and startling climax to his literary career. During the fifteen months between January 1936 and March 1937, Vũ Trọng Phụng released four major novels: *The Storm* (381 pages), *Dumb Luck* (228 pages), *The Dike Breaks* (266 pages), and *To Be a Whore* (290 pages).[168] All were serialized in weekly periodicals, the former two in *Hà Nội News;* the latter two in *Tuesday Novel (Tiểu Thuyết Thứ Ba)* and *Perfume River (Sông Hương).*[169] Remarkably, Vũ Trọng Phụng also completed over a dozen short stories in 1936–37, the lengthy reportage *Household Servants* (considered his finest by Vũ Ngọc Phan), and a translation of Victor Hugo's five-act play *Lucrecia Borgia.*[170] Is it any wonder that when he died three years later, rumors circulated that he had written himself to death? As notable as Vũ Trọng Phụng's productivity in 1936–37 was the critical acclaim that he inspired. "The literary style of *Dumb Luck* possesses a seductive power," wrote Hồ Xanh in *Industrial and Commercial News (Công Thương Báo)* in 1938. "I sincerely admire and respect it."[171] Writing in *Elite (Tinh Hoa)* in 1937, Nguyễn Lương Ngọc praised Vũ Trọng Phụng's eye for detail, full-bodied characters, and exciting storytelling.[172] "The author draws his characters with a fine pen," gushed Vũ Ngọc Phan in a review of *The Storm* penned in 1938. "But he is also capable of producing soft and sorrowful lines. . . . *The Storm* is one of our most valuable contemporary novels."[173] The critical reception of the novels was enhanced by expressions of approval for their reformist social message. "*To Be a Whore* offers a powerful indictment of our narrow-minded society," wrote Minh Tước in *Tomorrow (Mai)* in 1939. "Its audacious truthfulness will give moralists food for thought."[174]

In addition to their narrative ambition and acclaimed literary quality, the novels completed in 1936–37 are striking for their broad stylistic range. *The Storm* is a sprawling naturalist epic of rape, revenge, incest, corruption, class conflict, and communist espionage. *Dumb Luck* is an absurdist sex farce, satirizing the ignorance of the Vietnamese masses and the status anxiety of the urban elite. *The Dike Breaks* centers on a violent provincial labor struggle led by heroic political activists and reads like an earnest effort at socialist realism. And *To Be a Whore* stands as the first Vietnamese "psychological novel" structured explicitly by Freudian ideas. Indeed, the enduring confusion over Vũ Trọng Phụng's political and aesthetic orientation stems, more than anything else, from the extraordinary diversity of this novelistic quartet.

The novels of 1936–37 are also remarkable for their shocking portrayal of colonial Indochina as an immoral society plagued by sexual depravity, violence, corruption, and official abuse of power. Set in present-day Tonkin, all four novels depict sordid episodes of adultery as well as the deviant sexual habits of urban youth, modern women, and members of the nouveau riche. *Dumb Luck* and *The Storm* feature extended rape scenes and lurid accounts of nymphomania. Subplots involving incest and suicide figure prominently in *The Storm* and *To Be a Whore*. In an especially graphic episode in *The Dike Breaks,* colonial militiamen torture the novel's protagonist, subjecting him to a brutal beating, forced nudity, and anal penetration with hot candle wax. Both *The Storm* and *The Dike Breaks* include subplots about the corrupting influence of money on politics and government, and both novels feature characters who are political revolutionaries. Given this disreputable subject matter, it is no surprise that a sensational tone permeated public discourse about the novels. "Among all of our social writers, Vũ Trọng Phụng is the bravest," read a notice in *Tuesday Novel* announcing the publication of *The Storm*. "He alone utters aloud what nobody dares to say. He alone puts down on paper what nobody dares to write."[175] The critic Mộng Sơn was more emphatic: "Gentle wives and parents who worry about the happiness of your children! Young girls who are still innocent and pure! Don't read *To Be a Whore!*"[176]

By late 1937, at the age of twenty-five, Vũ Trọng Phụng's greatest works were behind him. Most of his output during the two years before his death in October 1939 comprised news reporting, short stories, and political commentary. His most intriguing political writing—including a series of essays and editorials attacking colonialism, capitalism, and communism—appeared between August 1937 and August 1938, when he served as chief editor at *Indochina Journal* and wrote a regular column for *Thursday Novel*. With his health deteriorating, he began to produce shorter, less taxing pieces, including poems and playful sketches for the humor magazine *The Mallard* as well as psychological short stories for the *Indochina Journal* and *Literary Circle*. Several of his stories lamented the modernization of gender norms and he referred to himself during an interview in 1937 as a "conservative on the question of women." Other pieces took issue with the arrogance of radical nationalism, a position that dovetailed with criticism he voiced of Japanese expansionism and militarism. His most substantial works during this period were two novels: *Winning the Lottery (Trúng số độc đắc)*, serialized in *Saturday Novel* starting in May 1939, and *The Prisoner Released (Người tù được tha)*, which was never published and remained incomplete at the time of his death. Depicting the grotesque transformation of a family after one of its wayward sons draws a winning lottery ticket, *Winning the Lottery* returned to the naturalist style and anticapitalist themes that marked Vũ Trọng Phụng's earliest published work. *The Prisoner Released*, on the other hand, resembled *The Dike Breaks* and *The Storm* in its romantic portrayal of the adventures of left-wing political activists. It has been widely cited as evidence for the leftward evolution of Vũ Trọng Phụng's political ideas at the end of his life. As chapter 3 will demonstrate, however, this thesis is not supported by Vũ Trọng Phụng's political writing of 1937 and 1938, which belittled orthodox communism in Indochina and the Soviet Union.

As a consequence of the fanfare that surrounded his novels, Vũ Trọng Phụng became a household name. His public profile was enhanced by the simultaneous appearance of his novels in multiple venues and by their speedy republication as stand-alone books with attendant publicity.[177] Notices and advertisements for his work appeared in scores of publications along with a wide range of criticism and commentary. *Megaphone* printed a full-page caricature of him dressed as a cardsharp, and *Thursday Novel* featured a photograph of him on its cover, in a space typically reserved for bathing beauties.[178] On July 2, 1937, *Youth Newspaper (Anh Niên)* advertised an upcoming response, by Vũ Trọng Phụng, to the question "What is Love?" but it never appeared.[179] In March 1938, newspapers posted congratulations on the occasion of Vũ Trọng Phụng's marriage to Vũ Mỵ Lương.[180] The strong praise and bitter condemnation that his work provoked from professional reviewers thrust Vũ Trọng Phụng further into the public eye, as did the rejoinders he published in response to his critics.

FIGURE 4.
Cover of *Tiểu Thuyết Thứ Năm* (Thursday novel), December 15, 1938.

CRITICAL DISCOURSE AND COLONIAL REPUBLICANISM

In addition to reflecting his growing celebrity, the large critical discourse about Vũ Trọng Phụng that appeared during his lifetime draws attention to the significance of republican sensibilities in his work. For example, many reviewers praised his commitment to research and careful observation, a compliment that underlined his republican preoccupation with social-scientific enquiry. Vũ Trọng Phụng's passion for social science was also noted by his detractors, many of whom chided his tendency to lard his narratives with pop psychology and faddish social theories borrowed from Freud and the German sexologist J. P. Liepmann. "Vũ Trọng Phụng should stick to the new and useful job of reporting," wrote Thạch Lam in 1938. "We hope that he will continue to write and that his pen will grow still sharper. But we also urge him to abandon useless theories in both his novels and reportage. There is nothing wrong with following theoretical principles as long as one first takes pains to depict psychology and behavior in a truthful manner."[181] Vũ Ngọc Phan raised a similar objection, advising Vũ Trọng Phụng to focus on "realistic description minus the theories and didacticism."[182] With reference to *The Storm*, he especially disliked the "author's preoccupation with the sexualism of Freud" and his fascination with "environmental determinism." For Vũ Ngọc Phan, the quality of Vũ Trọng Phụng's novel was compromised by his ambitious but clumsy appropriation of social science to explain the depraved behavior of the novel's major characters.

Vũ Trọng Phụng's republican sensibilities may also be seen in the hostility that his work inspired among orthodox communist critics. In 1939, the Marxist critic Uyển Diễm attacked *To Be a Whore* for promoting the "petty-bourgeois thesis" that the growth of prostitution in Indochina was caused by inadequate sex education rather than the growth of capitalism:

> The novel asks the question: Why does a girl from an "upstanding" family become a prostitute? It suggests that the answer lies in the lack of adequate sex education both at home and in school. But are we to believe that girls who receive a proper education will never become prostitutes? A thousand times no! Girls become prostitutes and boys become thieves because of the capitalist economic system! These rotten and disgusting things will continue to exist as long as the capitalist economy exists. In other words, we cannot eliminate the root of the problem unless we overthrow the capitalist economy and build socialism all over the world.[183]

While Vũ Trọng Phụng's interest in sex education as a possible solution to the problem of prostitution disappointed budding socialist-realist critics like Uyển

Diễm, it highlights the author's predilection for modest reformist measures (such as the quintessentially republican strategy of educational reform) as a preferred approach to solving pressing social problems.

Taking a tack similar to Uyển Diễm's, the Marxist critic Xuân Sa criticized Vũ Trọng Phụng's portrayal of class struggle and communist politics in *The Storm* for failing to conform to the recently prescribed dictates of socialist realism.[184] In a bitter response printed in *Sài Gòn Novel (Sài Gòn Tiểu Thuyết),* Vũ Trọng Phụng defended his portrayal of these topics as more "realistic" than the mechanical models proposed by Xuân Sa. In conclusion, he rejected Xuân Sa's narrow, prescriptive approach to literary criticism, which he dismissed as a "dictatorial posture toward literature."[185] Vũ Trọng Phụng's testy response to this form of criticism underscores his commitment to republican values of artistic freedom as well as his lack of patience with dogmatic efforts to enforce literary orthodoxy.

The most intense critical discussions of Vũ Trọng Phụng's novels, however, concerned pornography and realism—questions that touched upon standard republican concerns over censorship and free speech. "Recently, realist writers have adopted a new style for depicting the 'naked truth,'" wrote Phùng Tất Đắc in *Faithful Friend (Ích Hữu)* on October 27, 1936. "Realists expose what goes on in the dark and record the words and deeds of perverts. A debate has exploded in the North and the Center about pornography in literature. Some denounce pornography for stimulating uncontrollable lust. The realist group responds that it is better to expose the body of a scarred girl than to conceal it, although concealing it is certainly easier."[186] Phùng Tất Đắc expressed sympathy for the realists, but he admonished them to keep their work out of the hands of children. Nguyễn Vỹ raised the same issues in a consideration of Vũ Trọng Phụng's preoccupation with sex and the grotesque. "Vũ Trọng Phụng is an artist of ugliness. His pen is like a nasty child who enjoys scandalizing society, especially the bourgeoisie, through shock tactics and vulgarity. The author of *The Storm* and *The Industry of Marrying Westerners* is a cruel satirist who rejects refined and polite language. His pen dwells on the grotesque, disgusting and ugly qualities of the people that he hates."[187] Much of the remainder of the review addressed the novel's "strange obsession" *(ám ảnh kỳ quặc)* with sex, which, according to Nguyễn Vỹ, frightened away female readers. Vũ Ngọc Phan agreed that the novel's sexual content was its most notable feature:

> Moralists have argued that cinema is not a true art form because its main objective is to stimulate lust. For example, Georges Duhamel criticized cinema as a depraved form of entertainment consumed in a darkened room after

> dinner and before bedtime. People responded in a similar way when *The Storm* was serialized in the newspaper. "This novel is only good for provoking lust," they said. Since I am not a disciple of Duhamel, I replied: "But it is still better than other books." To which they responded: "Artists should have dignity and self-respect. A virtuous artist would not try to stimulate lust to achieve popular success." This response calls to mind Flaubert's anger when it was claimed that people rushed to buy *Madame Bovary* only after it was put on trial for public indecency.[188]

Perhaps the harshest charges of indecency came from religious officials such as Father J. M. Thích, the editor of Huế's largest Catholic Newspaper. He called on *Perfume River* to cease publication of *To Be a Whore* or risk triggering a boycott of the newspaper by Catholic readers.[189] Vũ Trọng Phụng chose not to respond in print, but he was defended by his close friend Phan Khôi, the editor-in-chief of *Perfume River*. In an essay published on August 22, 1936, Phan Khôi ridiculed the charges against *To Be a Whore*, pointing out that there was nothing in the novel that could not be found in the Bible. "After all," he added mischievously, "even Jesus Christ had grown close to a famous prostitute."[190] The following month, the conservative neotraditionalist critic Thái Phỉ charged local purveyors of pornography with hypocrisy and greed: "Pornographers sell their literature on the street. They take advantage of the fact that people who denounce pornography are secretly obsessed by it. Some claim that publishers put food on the table by selling filth like madams in a brothel."[191] He then denounced the effect on the public of pornography posing as realism: "Even radicals recognize the damage caused by pornography on an uneducated reading public that does not know right from wrong." Thái Phỉ blamed the proliferation of pornography on European influence, Western fashions, and romantic literature. He mentioned no particular offender by name, but he singled out the journal *Megaphone*, where Vũ Trọng Phụng had worked during 1934, as a squalid trailblazer in Vietnamese "pornographic literature."

In a letter published a month later in *Hà Nội News*, Vũ Trọng Phụng defended himself "as a realist, not a pornographer," by distinguishing between the portrayal of two types of lust.[192] The portrayal of "healthy lust," between husbands and wives, for instance, was pornographic and had no place in respectable literature. On the other hand, unhealthy lust that led to social evils such as rape, adultery, and incest must be exposed and analyzed in order to be combated effectively. Averring that his purpose was to inspire fury at social injustice (rather than fury at writers who expose injustice), he denounced Thái Phỉ, dismissing his arguments as "ignorant nonsense" and accusing him of being an old goat himself. Six months later, Vũ Trọng Phụng addressed the pornography controversy again in an "open letter" in *The Future*.[193] In response to fears raised about the impact of his work on impressionable girls, Vũ Trọng Phụng insisted that his purpose was to dissuade them from entering the sex trade. He then drew a contrast between his own graphic reportage that served the cause of social reform and sexually suggestive works that did little but inspire romantic longing such as Hoàng Ngọc Phách's novella *Pure Heart (Tố Tâm)* and the novels *Loneliness (Lạnh lùng)* and *Breaking Off (Đoạn tuyệt)* by the leader of the Self-Strength Literary Group, Nhất Linh. He also defended his use of profanity by comparing it to the explicit language featured in public advertisements for aphrodisiacs and venereal disease medicine. "Why attack me and not the kings of venereal disease medicine?" he demanded. "I also wrote *Venereal Disease Clinic* in a scientific spirit. Over a century ago, Victor Hugo demanded the right to call a pig a pig! I am not trying to pull a fast one by arguing in the manner of Zola, Flaubert, Baudelaire, Margueritte, and Richepin, figures once condemned for obscenity but now considered great writers. . . . Unlike stubborn and shy men like you, most people in the twentieth century respect science and truth even if it is ugly and hurtful. Ugliness is not pornography. Pornography is the seminaked, semicovered imagery in the bourgeois film *Music Hall* or the magazines *Beauty* and *Sex Appeal*. It is a modern dancer in a see-through dress, or the kind of 'noble' love story that inflicts real harm on both children and adults."

Three days later, (the pseudonymous) Nhất Chi Mai of the Self-Strength Literary Group attacked Vũ Trọng Phụng directly in an essay published in *These Days* entitled "Pornographic or Not?"[194] He opened by insulting Vũ Trọng Phụng as a "half-baked writer" with "a rudimentary education." Rejecting the defense of explicit prose based on the social utility of realism, he called attention to a notoriously lurid scene in *The Storm*, depicting the pregnant protagonist Thị Mịch assuming an awkward coital position to facilitate penetration from behind: "If that's not pornography, what is it?" Turning from the issue of pornography, Nhất Chi Mai targeted the unrelenting pessimism of Vũ Trọng Phụng's realist ideology:

> Vũ Trọng Phụng's work leaves me annoyed, irritated, even furious—not at the wounds of society that it purports to describe, but at the writer's dark, hateful, and petty ideology. Writers have a duty to reveal human misery and ugliness, but they also need a noble purpose, an altruistic sensibility, a belief in progress, or a shred of optimism that humans can escape the darkness and grow better and happier. But Vũ Trọng Phụng's work is bereft of hope. The unhappy

world that he depicts is a hell peopled by foulmouthed murderers and prostitutes. This is a mirror reflecting little more than the ideology of a writer who views the world through dark glasses and a darker mind.

In a letter published in *The Future* eleven days later, on March 25, 1937, Vũ Trọng Phụng responded at length to Nhất Chi Mai, his third intervention in the controversy within six months.[195] Accusing the Self-Strength Literary Group of pursuing a vendetta against rivals at Tân Dân, he announced that he would answer Nhất Chi Mai's charges "line by line, word by word." He dismissed Nhất Chi Mai's claim that he was uneducated as an ad hominem attack. He criticized him for cherry-picking one unrepresentative salacious passage out of a three-hundred-page novel. He denied that his graphic prose was crafted for commercial reasons, while reiterating the virtues of straightforward description over poetic euphemism. Moving from defense to offense, he suggested that prurient motives lay behind campaigns for the liberation of women and modern fashion promoted by the Self-Strength Literary Group. In response to the charge that the preoccupation with sexual immorality in his novels was a reflection of his own sick mind, he noted that the recent growth of the sex trade and moral perversity had been widely documented by authoritative European sources: "Don't you know about Margueritte's exposé of prostitution in the book *Prostituées?* Don't you know of the sexual depravity of the old and new regimes in France as portrayed in the journal *Craponillot?* Don't you know about the disastrous pederasty movement followed by millions of Germans and spearheaded in France by Gide, Rostand, and Verlaine? What I describe is not merely a world of my own making." In conclusion, he rejected the sunny optimism of the cult of youthfulness, happiness, and leisure promoted by the Self-Strength Literary Group, which he contrasted with his own hard-nosed vision of social reform.

CONCLUSION

The critical discourse surrounding the four novels published in 1936–37 affirms the presence of republican concerns in Vũ Trọng Phụng's broader view of the world. While his clumsy engagement with sexology and Freudian theory irritated his critics, it highlights his commitment to social science as an instrument for crafting social policy and writing realist literature. His spat with leftist critics reveals an aversion toward the subordination of literary expression to political orthodoxy, a position with affinities to interwar republican anticommunism. A republican sensibility is also evident in his rejection of obscurantist attacks by conservative Catholics and

Confucian moralists against the forthright depiction of sexuality in his work. His opposition to censorship and defense of the right to free speech may be seen in a similar light. Finally, the French figures that he invoked while defending his work—the writers Hugo, Zola, Flaubert, Baudelaire, Margueritte, Richepin, and Gide and the journalists Viollis, Roubaud, Dorgeles, and Londres—were all associated, in one form or another, with a broader republican vision. Vũ Trọng Phụng's commitment to a local variant of this vision, nurtured within the institutions and general political environment of French Indochina, forms the subject of the following three chapters.

CHAPTER TWO • Capitalism and Social Reform

Vũ Trọng Phụng was an emotional critic of colonial capitalism, blaming it for the spread of greed and immorality and the rise of a repugnant nouveau riche and a wretched subaltern class. Although he occasionally employed a rudimentary Marxian vocabulary, Vũ Trọng Phụng's critique of the socioeconomic order differed from the anticapitalism of local communists.[1] He paid little attention to the plight of the industrial working class or the poor peasantry, focusing instead upon the petty bourgeois and the lumpen proletariat. He ignored the underlying structural dynamics of the market economy while fixating on its damaging impact on traditional culture and morality. Most importantly, in spite of the scorn he expressed for the local political economy, he neither predicted nor advocated revolutionary change. Instead, he favored modest reforms, crafted with the help of social-scientific research, to ameliorate colonial capitalism's most pernicious effects.

Vũ Trọng Phụng's moderate anticapitalism stemmed from two sources. The first was his direct experience of the economic tumult of the interwar era, a period marked by extreme instability, the rise of colonial conglomerates, and increased class stratification, especially in the cities. The second was a broadly republican tradition of hostility toward concentrated wealth, social inequality, and the arbitrary exercise of state power that he encountered in realist—and more specifically naturalist—French literature and in the thinking of liberal colonial officials. The influence of this republican discourse helps to explain the empiricism and reformism that shaped his approach to the problems generated by colonial capitalism.

This chapter explores the evolution of Vũ Trọng Phụng's views about capitalism and social reform as expressed in his fiction and reportage. His dismay at the ruthlessness of market relations is apparent in his first major published work, the five-act play *No Echo,* which portrays a lopsided conflict between a venal, sexually depraved landlord and a poor tenant family in Hà Nội. Written in 1931, the play reflects the devastating impact of the Depression in Indochinese cities as well as the influence on Vũ Trọng Phụng's thinking of French naturalism, a late nineteenth-century literary credo with strong republican and anticapitalist overtones. The negative social consequences of capitalism are explored most directly in Vũ Trọng Phụng's popular works of reportage such as *The Industry of Marrying Westerners* and *Household Servants.* The former explores the commodification of love and marriage in colonial society, while the latter exposes the exploitation of domestic servants by members of a vulgar urban middle class. In contrast to *No Echo,* which merely describes capitalism's destructive force, these works depict popular resistance to capitalism and consider a range of reformist measures to deal with its negative consequences. They also confirm a strong connection in Vũ Trọng Phụng's thinking between the forces of colonial capitalism and the growth of sexual perversity, a theme explored extensively in his book-length reportage *Venereal Disease Clinic.* Drawing on an extensive body of social-scientific research, this book denounced the growing scourge of commercial sex in Indochina and advanced a case against state regulation of prostitution that drew heavily upon an influential French reformist movement known as "republican abolitionism."

COLONIAL CAPITALISM

Vũ Trọng Phụng's critique of capitalism was shaped by distinctive features of the interwar Indochinese economy.[2] The most important was a pattern of acute volatility produced by the integration of Indochina into the world economy as a colonial dependency of France. Beginning during his childhood in the 1910s and intensifying over the course of his career through the late 1920s and 1930s, this instability contrasted with the territory's more predictable economic trajectory during the early decades of colonial rule, marked by a modest expansion of commercial rice production in the Mekong Delta and anemic growth everywhere else.[3] The increasing vulnerability of the economy to external shocks was dramatized by World War I, during which ninety thousand Vietnamese laborers were recruited to work in France.[4] The war also disrupted maritime trade routes and export markets, while encouraging the development of rubber cultivation and coal mining in response to growing industrial demand in France and East Asia.[5] Rapid economic flux continued into the interwar period. A brief postwar downturn tied to a recession in France in 1921–22 was followed by a sensational boom during 1924–28, the dramatic bust of the Depression in the 1930s, and a gradual recovery later in the decade.

A prime cause of this volatility was the subordination of the Indochinese economy to the French economy as an exporter of raw materials and a market for consumer goods. Due to the influence of French business interests over colonial economic policy, tariffs and public spending in Indochina encouraged speculation in high-profit export commodities and discouraged investment in local manufacturing that threatened to compete with French industry.[6] Indochina's economy was also buffeted by global shifts in industrial production, trade, and fiscal policies, over which local actors had no control. The fluctuating fortunes of Indochina's important rubber industry illustrate the point.[7] Following its introduction into Indochina in the late nineteenth century, rubber production soared during the 1910s, fueled by military spending in Europe and the automobile industry in the United States.[8] Expansion ceased in 1921 when a crisis of global oversupply driven by high production in British Malaya and the Dutch East Indies caused the price of rubber to plummet.[9] The market recovered in spectacular fashion the following year due to a British scheme (the Stephenson Plan) to raise the price of rubber through restrictive quotas on exports from Malaya and Ceylon.[10] "The resulting sharp rebound in the world price triggered a huge expansion of rubber plantations in Indochina and contributed to record profit levels. Between 1925 and 1929, the land under rubber cultivation expanded from 15,000 hectares to 90,225 hectares with capital investment of 700 million francs."[11] Rubber plantations were concentrated in Cochinchina, but their fortunes impacted Tonkin and Annam, which provided 80 percent of their labor.[12] The rubber boom paralleled a more general spasm of investment and speculation throughout Indochina during the late 1920s that involved coffee, sugar, mining, finance, and urban real estate and benefited from the relative strength of the local currency—the piastre—and the weakness of the franc.

But a massive bust, caused by the global economic slump, cut short the dynamic boom of the late 1920s.[13] A sharp drop in the price of rice, Indochina's most important commercial crop, during the fourth quarter of 1930 devastated the southern economy.[14] Rice exports plunged from a record high of 1,797,000 tons in 1928 to 959,000 tons in 1931. At the same time, capital investment throughout Indochina fell dramatically from 750 million francs during the height of the boom in 1928 to a paltry 34.7 million francs in 1935.[15] Company dissolutions and capital reductions hurt the economy further; failures of local firms cost the economy 239.3 million francs during the low point of the slump in 1933.[16] Economic contraction led to painful belt-tightening by the colonial state.[17] Both the general budget and the five local budgets (for Tonkin, Annam, Cochinchina, Cambodia, and Laos) were cut in half between 1931 and 1935, throwing out of work tens of thousands of public and private employees.[18]

A second important feature of the colonial economy was the concentration of wealth in foreign-owned conglomerates, including the powerful Bank of Indochina. The interwar era witnessed a shift in the local political economy as the traditional dominance of Chinese consortiums that controlled lucrative public monopolies (in opium, alcohol, salt, transportation, and postal services) gave way to the rising power of a handful of French conglomerates that enjoyed preferential treatment from the colonial state.[19] Focused on growing interests in plantation agriculture, mining, light manufacturing, finance, and real estate, they included the Fontaine group, the Denis frères group, the Bernard group, the Homberg group, the Hermenier group, and the Mazet group.[20] The largest beneficiary of this realignment, however, was the Bank of Indochina, whose supremacy derived from its unrivaled capital reserves and its multiple roles as a retail bank, as a commercial bank, and as Indochina's sole bank of issue.[21] As bankruptcies piled up during the Depression, the Bank acquired hundreds of failing enterprises and emerged as "the effective caretaker of the Indochinese economy."[22] "By the mid 1930s, representatives of the Bank had come to occupy literally hundreds of positions on the board or as president or CEO at the majority of the colony's major enterprises. . . . By 1939, most colonial conglomerates and the monopolies that formed the basis of their activities had become assets in the investment portfolio of the Bank of Indochina."[23] The hegemony of the Bank provoked a backlash from the colon business community, which drew upon a familiar right-wing discourse to rail against "the plutocracy, the Jews and the subservience of the government to the capitalists."[24] These grievances dovetailed with a growing left-wing discourse about the unchecked power of trusts, monopolists, and financiers that intensified in France and throughout the Empire with the rise of the Popular Front.

Given the volatile and monopolistic character of the local economy, it is no coincidence that Vũ Trọng Phụng dwelled upon the problems of economic insecurity and concentrated wealth in both his journalistic writing and his fiction. All of his reportage takes place against the backdrop of the Depression and the wild plot twists and abrupt reversals of fortune in novels such as *Dumb Luck* and *Winning the Lottery* (note the titles!) mirror the instability that dominated the economy during his lifetime. His two most famous villains are crooked business magnates with diversified holdings and shady connections to the colonial state. *Dumb Luck*'s Victor Ban runs two parallel commercial empires—a chain of brothels and a chain of medical clinics—while the aspiring politician and sexual predator Nghị Hách from *The Storm* owns mines, plantations, and a government-authorized monopoly on fish sauce. The falling price of export commodities, the rise in bankruptcies, and growing unemployment at every social level provide important context to the general atmosphere of economic desperation dramatized in Vũ Trọng Phụng's writing.

NO ECHO AND REPUBLICAN NATURALISM

The earliest example of Vũ Trọng Phụng's critical treatment of economic insecurity and concentrated wealth may be found in the play *No Echo,* which he completed in May 1931, the precise moment that the full brunt of the Depression began to be felt in Indochina.[25] The play dramatizes a classic conflict over payment of rent between a venal, francophone landlord and a petty-bourgeois family that has fallen on hard times. The family comprises a husband and wife employed at menial jobs—he is an office boy, she is a street peddler—and the husband's father, who is blind and seriously ill. The play takes place one year after the old man's house burned down, destroying his fortune and killing his wife. Following an opening scene during which the landlord threatens the penniless family with eviction, two catastrophes occur offstage that set the plot in motion: police officers confiscate the wife's merchandise because she lacks a vending permit and the husband is threatened with dismissal unless he pays a bribe to a corrupt supervisor. Taking a knife from the kitchen, the husband announces that he will steal money to pay the rent, bribe his boss, and buy medicine for his father. His wife tries to dissuade him from this reckless course of action by appealing to his conscience as a Buddhist. But the husband rejects her entreaties, expressing the core anticapitalist theme of the play: "These days, the only God, the only Buddha, is money. Only money is sacred. It controls our lives. We must worship it if we want to live. Morality, law, God, and Buddha—none of these can withstand the power of money! It is the only thing that everybody worships!"[26] The husband also denounces the law as an instrument of class oppression. In response to an additional appeal from his wife about the immorality of breaking the law and the dangers of ignoring his conscience, the husband responds: "We have come to this point of desperation and all you can think about is the law and my own conscience!? The law deserves scorn not respect because it punishes those who undertake reckless acts but it pays no attention to the forces that drive them to behave this way. And why should I worry about my conscience when I live in a conscience-less society?"[27] The collusion between the moneyed elite and the forces of law and order is dramatized further in the play by a pair of uniformed officers who briefly appear and do the landlord's bidding and by the wife's mistreatment at the hands of the policemen who confiscate her wares.

After the husband is jailed for robbing his workplace, the landlord, reeking of liquor, visits the remaining members of the family and offers them a deal. He agrees to allow the wife and her father-in-law to reside temporarily in a small factory that he owns and to work there to pay off their debts. But he also insists that the wife accompany him, at once, to secure a work permit, even though it is the middle of the night. Alerted by his leering tone, the old man volunteers to beg for money on the street and urges his daughter-in-law to reject the landlord's proposal. She refuses and leaves together with the landlord. Later that night, the old man overhears the whimpering moans of his daughter-in-law after she has been raped by the landlord. As the final curtain falls, the daughter-in-law returns home to find that the old man has hung himself.

No Echo's portrayal of the landlord as an agent of unrepentant evil clearly reflects Vũ Trọng Phụng's youthful animosity toward colonial capitalism. As a factory owner as well as an urban landlord, the character embodies the diversified economic interests of Indochina's new business class. It is also significant that the landlord holds a day job as an interpreter for a French enterprise in Hà Nội.[28] This important detail, implying a connection between Vietnamese and French business interests, underlines the colonial character of the capitalist forces wreaking havoc within the play. Vũ Trọng Phụng's pathetic portrayal of the victimization of the family, including the arrest of the husband, the rape of the wife, and the suicide of the father, dramatically underlines the unforgiving nature of the market economy. The triumph of the landlord and the ruin of the family illustrate the play's central theme about the immoral and destructive power of money in colonial society.

While *No Echo* clearly reflects the devastation to Indochina caused by the Depression, it was also shaped by Vũ Trọng Phụng's engagement with late-nineteenth-century literary naturalism, a subset of the French realist tradition closely associated with Émile Zola. Vũ Trọng Phụng cited Zola approvingly in his writing, referring to him as a "great writer" *(văn hào)* in a letter published in 1937.[29] He also exhibited significant interest in Zola's most successful disciple, Guy de Maupassant.[30] The influence of naturalism on *No Echo* is signaled explicitly by an epigram from Zola that Vũ Trọng Phụng cited at the opening of the play script: "To install real human drama in place of absurd untruths."[31] Taken from Zola's essay collection *Naturalism in the Theatre: Theories and Examples*, published in 1881, the epigram suggests that the formal conventions of classical and romantic drama produce only "absurd untruths" and are inferior to the techniques of naturalism as a mode of representing reality on stage.[32] In *Naturalism in the Theatre* and elsewhere, Zola described these techniques as empirical methods borrowed from the natural sciences.[33] To facilitate the application of these methods, he urged writers to set their stories in observable contemporary settings (rather than in the inaccessible past preferred by classicists and romantics) and to investigate, at first hand, the topics of their works. He also insisted that the behavior of literary characters should be shaped by a combination of heredity and the environment, two deterministic forces that loomed large in scientific and social-scientific thinking during the late nineteenth century. In the same scientific spirit, he depicted the ideal creative process as a kind of "literary experiment" that involved introducing a catalytic shock to a group of characters whose behavioral tendencies had been established by environment and heredity.[34] The working out of the plot, therefore, represented an effort to "prove" the relative deterministic significance of various factors in human affairs.

Naturalist narratives exhibited additional generic features that derived from Zola's prescriptive blueprint. An emphasis on human impotence in the face of deterministic forces made naturalist narratives unusually sad and bereft of hope. Naturalism's commitment to the re-creation of the visible world encouraged a fixation on the accurate representation of settings, costumes, and speech, while discouraging speculative psychological analysis. Finally, although Zola insisted that the exploration of sexuality was incidental to his project, naturalist works treated sexual matters explicitly, and hence they were often denounced by conservative critics as sensational and pornographic.[35]

No Echo resembles naturalist drama in its realistic portrayal of a slice of contemporary life. It does not rely on traditional Vietnamese theatrical conventions such as stylized speech, stock characters, or abstract costumes and scenery. The main characters are ordinary members of the lower middle class, and all the events take place in a dingy rented house. The action of the play is propelled forward by the prosaic dialogue of the characters during the course of their normal interactions with one another. A naturalist sensibility may also be located in the gloominess of the play and in its lurid plot twists involving the rape, suicide, and imprisonment of its three main characters. Consistent with naturalism's penchant for the unflinching representation of the "real," the audience witnesses the suicide of the old man and the discovery of his corpse by his daughter-in-law. In addition, *No Echo* manifests a localized version of naturalism's preoccupation with the power of deterministic forces in human affairs. The critical role of poverty in driving the husband into a life of crime stands out as a classic naturalist theme. The most important deterministic force in the play, however, is a patriarchal Confucian worldview that plays a decisive role in catastrophic decisions made by each of the main characters as the narrative moves toward its tragic conclusion. The father commits suicide after learning that the virtue of his daughter-in-law has been violated. The son's reckless decision to rob his office is triggered by anxiety that his wife may turn to prostitution to solve the family's financial crisis, thereby sullying his honor. And the wife agrees to work for the landlord because she fears that her reputation for filial piety will be damaged by the sight of her aged father-in-law begging on the street.

Vietnamese critics of the day recognized *No Echo*'s naturalist pedigree. In a review of a production of the play staged in Hà Nội in 1937, Khái Hưng of the Self-Strength Literary Group likened *No Echo* to Henry Becque's drama *The Vultures (Les Corbeaux)*.[36] Written in 1882 at an early peak of Zola's influence in France, this quintessential example of late-nineteenth-century naturalism concerns the harassment, by creditors and other financial "vultures," of a bourgeois family recently impoverished by the death of the father.[37] As in *No Echo*, the family confronts its predicament by sacrificing the virtue of one of its daughters.[38] The tragic ending of *The Vultures* shares with the hopeless conclusion of *No Echo* a fatalistic refusal to entertain utopian fantasies about effective resistance to the ravages of the market. "I was going to compare Vũ Trọng Phụng to Henry Becque," Khái Hưng wrote, "but I was afraid that this might anger him. Becque's *The Vultures* also describes a family in steep decline; it is exploited mercilessly after the father passes away. But in the French play, there are no long-winded speeches that curse life and denounce the legal system in the manner of the Annamese play. Plus, Vũ Trọng Phụng's play is much more dark, messy, and tragic."[39]

Vũ Trọng Phụng's enthusiasm for naturalism extended to its explicitly republican political project. In an important essay entitled "The Influence of the Republic in Literature," Zola argued for a direct correspondence between literary naturalism and a moderate political republicanism.[40] Identifying both naturalism and the Republic with the causes of social justice and liberty, he suggested that the scientific quality of mind nurtured by naturalism encouraged support for republicanism by undermining the irrational authority of religion and monarchy. Zola also distinguished the moderate, gradual reformism promoted by "naturalistic republicanism" from messianic and revolutionary impulses present in left-wing utopianism. "The naturalistic republican takes into consideration the surroundings and the circumstances," he reasoned. "He does not work on a nation as in clay because he knows it has its own life and reason for existing, the mechanism of which must be studied before trying to manipulate it."[41]

In February 1877, Zola drew a finer distinction between the pragmatic progressivism of "naturalist politics" and the "idealist" politics of the radical Left: "I call idealist that politics which talks in bombastic slogans, which speculates about men as if they were pure abstractions, which dreams utopias without studying the real world. I call naturalist that politics which takes its cue from experience, which is based on facts, which treats a nation according to its needs."[42] Further emphasizing the connection between empiricism and an inclusive democratic republic, responsive to the will of the people, Zola wrote: "The naturalistic republican does not build until he has studied and sounded the ground. He is a man of facts and he will make a republic not a protestant temple, not a Gothic Church, not a prison opening upon a place of execution but a large and beautiful mansion, where all the classes may be accommodated, full of air and sunlight and so appropriate to the tastes and wants of its inhabitants."[43]

While Vũ Trọng Phụng's political thinking evolved throughout the 1930s, he exhibited a consistent predilection for aspects of Zola's naturalist republicanism. His commitment to both realism and nonfiction reportage dovetailed with naturalism's affinities for research and empirical observation. His integration of specific reform proposals into his work is consistent with Zola's belief in the symbiotic relationship between empirical research and the art of republican governance. His misgivings about communist political culture parallel Zola's skepticism toward the utopian fantasies of the radical Left. Most importantly, Vũ Trọng Phụng shared with Zola a deep antipathy toward what William Gallois refers to as "the impoverishment of the world by capitalist values."[44] Just as Zola's twenty-volume novel cycle has been seen as an effort to "detail the whole of capitalism through a series of descriptions of its parts," Vũ Trọng Phụng's body of work returned obsessively to the negative economic and cultural impact of colonial capitalism.

THE INDUSTRY OF MARRYING WESTERNERS AND THE COMMODIFICATION OF LOVE

While *No Echo* dramatized the destructive impact of colonial capitalism on the urban petty bourgeoisie, *The Industry of Marrying Westerners* lamented the saturation of Vietnamese culture and society by capitalist values. Serialized in 1934, it investigated semiconjugal unions between Vietnamese women and foreign legionnaires stationed in Bắc Ninh province, thirty kilometers north of Hà Nội.[45] Few of the unions were sanctioned by the state but the couples lived together and accepted in principle (if not practice) the conventions of modern marriage: sexual monogamy, communal

5 Décembre 1934 — Nhật Tân

KỸ NGHỆ LẤY TÂY

Phóng sự dài — Vũ Trọng Phụng

I — Đâu chả phải, phải tai !

Nhà bà bán hàng nước đã bắt đầu run. Trước một cơn thịnh nộ vô lý của một kẻ có sức lực hơn mình, tôi vội phải đứng ngay lên và lùi mấy bước lại đằng sau, hòng giữ thế thủ. Giữ thế thủ một cách kể cũng... hèn, vì cái thế mình đứng là mình không dám lộ ra tí nào cả, vẫn phải giữ cho như là mình chỉ khuất phục, vì sợ nó có thể khiêu khích kẻ địch khởi thế công. Những lời dọa nạt vẫn không hỏi hắt vào mặt tôi như cơn mưa nặng hạt :

— Phải, một trăm thằng thì lấy cớ là đến du lịch cả một trăm.

Nhưng bọn chúng ta không ai còn lạ gì ! Cái đất Thị Cầu này vẫn là chỗ để cho bọn trẻ tuổi vô nghệ nghiệp đến để ăn trộm ái tình, hoặc giở những thủ đoạn hèn mạt khác ! Bọn khốn nạn người bản xứ ấy thường cũng có cái bộ dạng khả nghi y như anh !

. . . .

Tôi đợi hắn trông trọc nhìn tôi cho chán chê đi, rồi mới đáp :

— Anh đừng vội nhầm. Tôi chẳng phải là hạng người để anh phải gặp thì mới xong đâu.

. . . .

Sau cùng, hắn lâu nhâu :

— Tôi cũng mong như thế lắm. Mà nếu, thí dụ chẳng may tôi sẽ bắt gặp anh làm chuyện gì bất lịch sự, thì bất cứ là thiệt hại cho tôi hay cho anh em bạn hữu của tôi quanh đây, tôi cũng xin sẽ sẵn lòng hầu hạ anh ngay !

— Xin vâng !

Thế xong hắn mới chịu quay đi, lộp cộp in xuống mặt đường lầy bùn dấu giầy đầy những đanh khuy to tướng.

Buổi sáng, tiếng chuông đương khua động cả kinh thành.

Bốn chục chiếc xe hơi từ thềm nhà thờ nối nhau một hàng dài vắt ra phố Lagisquet, như một con rắn nằm vươn mình : một đám cưới tây. Mặt trời tươi tỉnh rọi ánh sáng để tô điểm thêm cho những bộ áo của ngày đại lễ. Hàng đám một, người ta đón chào vồn vã nhau, ồ ạt kéo nhau vào nhà thờ. Tại một góc thềm nọ, hai nhà, một gia đình Pháp với một gia đình Pháp Việt, tưng bừng chào hỏi nhau. Gia đình Pháp chỉ có hai vợ chồng : người vợ còn đẹp nhưng ông chồng tóc đã bạc phơ. Còn cái gia đình Pháp Việt thì có bốn người : vợ ta, chồng tây, hai con, trai và gái, là lai. Hai vợ chồng kia đã bắt tay bà « đầm ta » một cách kính trọng không ngờ. Bà này cũng cười nói oang oang, bắt chuyện một cách rất tự nhiên, mà bệ vệ, mà xang trọng ! Khi hai vợ chồng kia cáo biệt vào nhà thờ trước rồi, bà « đầm ta » này quay lại ra lệnh cho con gái, cô đầm lai. Cô này cúi đầu chịu lệnh. Bà mẹ lại nói gì với cậu con trai, nhưng cậu này đáp lại một cách không bằng lòng. Lập tức bà làm cho biết phép bà, nghĩa là lên giọng gắt gỏng, mặc lòng là gắt khe khẽ. Thế rồi người con gật đầu sợ hãi, trong khi ông chồng lắc đầu và so vai.

. . . .

Lại một cảnh khác...

Một cái nhà tây nhỏ, vùng châu thành Hanoi. Ngoài sân. Dân quê qua đường thường phải ngạc

Giáng điệu tuy khả ố, song mặt trông cũng dễ coi.

— Tên là gì ?

— Nguyễn Thị L...

— Bao nhiêu tuổi ?

— Hăm nhăm.

— Làm nghề gì ?

— Trước lấy một ông tây đoan, sau lấy một ông,..

— Im ! Nghề gì chứ ai hỏi chồng !

— Sau lấy một ông *cạp lên* !

— Không có nghề gì ? Phải không ? Vô nghệ nghiệp. . *Sans prof...*

— Việc gì mà vô nghệ nghiệp ?

— Thế làm nghề gì ?

— Làm nghề gì ? Làm... làm nghề lấy tây !

Cả tòa chợt cười ồ. Viên mõ tòa đứng lên *suỵt suỵt* hoài mà tự cuối tòa vẫn có tiếng cười khúc khích. Đáp một câu hỏi của quan chưởng lý, viên thông ngôn bực mình cứ việc :

— *Elle déclare exercer le métier d'épouser les Français !*

Quan chánh án cau mặt rồi nhìn quan chưởng lý. Trước còn ra vẻ muốn gắt, sau quan chưởng lý chỉ... mỉm cười.

. . . .

Sao thị dám khai sưng sưng như thế ? Hay là có nghề lấy tây thật ? Mà sao quan chưởng lý lại chỉ mỉm cười ? Chỉ lấy cái cười mà tha thứ, ngài đã hiểu rõ những nguyên nhân nào mà có thể khiến sự phối hợp của hai giống lại đến nỗi thành ra sự buôn bán chăng ?

Cho nên, một buổi sáng mưa phùn gió bấc, tôi đã đáp chuyến xe hỏa thứ nhất đi Thị - Cầu.

là phải lắm. Vợ mới tháng trư[ớc] bị bắt gặp đi chơi với trai.

— Thảo nào !

Nói xong tôi cũng cười. Khôn[g] phải cười vì cái khoái trá th[...] mà là vì mình đoán đã khôn[g] sai. Bà hàng tiếp :

— Hôm ấy chẳng may nó l[...] là *săng ti nền* nên không làm gì được. Sau về nhà, căn vặn v[...] thì vợ bảo đó là một người em trai sang chơi. Phúc làm sao chồng chỉ cho có mấy cái tát!

Bị mấy cái tát mà lại còn là có phúc! Độc giả có hiểu tại sao không chứ người nói câu ấy không hóa dại một tí nào. Mà nếu mình lại đi tưởng rằng bà ấy nói thế để pha trò thì lại không là tri kỷ với nhau !

— Thế ông ở đâu đến đây làm gì ?

— Tôi là một người viết báo, sang đây thăm thú rồi. . . làm việc.

— Thế à!

Bà hàng nước gật gù và cười một cách tinh quái làm sao ! Thôi chết tôi rồi ! Còn trách gì anh lính lê dương kia! Bà ta cũng nghi tôi nốt ! Vội vàng phải nói cho gãy nghĩa :

— Không, bà chớ vội ngờ. Tôi không có nhân tình nhân ngãi với ai ở đây đâu. Tôi sang đây để làm việc thật.

Rồi tôi bầy tỏ bao nhiêu việc cần làm cho bà hàng nghe. Trời vẫn rả rích mưa to nhưng tôi không cho thế là mất thời giờ. Nhờ cuộc trò chuyện, tôi mới biết Thị Cầu, ấy là nói đại khái.

Tuy chỉ

FIGURE 5.
Original Serialization of *Kỹ Nghệ Lấy Tây* (The industry of marrying Westerners), *Nhật Tân* (New day), December 5, 1934.

eating, joint finances, and shared child rearing. Vũ Trọng Phụng interviewed a dozen Vietnamese women and foreign men involved in these stable, short-term relationships. One chapter featured a long conversation with a Eurasian woman named Suzanne, the offspring of an interracial union.[46] As with all of Vũ Trọng Phụng's nonfiction reportage, the text was written in the first person and included ironic editorial commentary, digressions on the journalistic process, and verbatim interview transcripts. The interviews focused on the life histories of the women and the culturally hybrid character of their family life.

The central theme of the text, however, is the domination of capitalist values over a sphere of social life—marriage—that, according to traditional morality and modern custom, ought to be regulated by emotions or ethical sentiments. In traditional Vietnam, marriage was organized around Confucian norms of duty, virtue, and filial piety. During the interwar era, an ideal of romantic love, imported from France, dominated modernist notions about marriage.[47] But in *The Industry of Marrying Westerners*, the regulatory impact upon marriage of romance and filial duty pales beside the culture of the market. This idea is introduced at the outset of the narrative in a humorous episode that inspired Vũ Trọng Phụng to research the topic:

> One morning in court, an Annamite *dame* said something that made everyone forget where they were. The courtroom erupted in laughter like the audience at a comedy.
>
> After the interpreter had called her name, a woman approached the witness stand, swiveling her hips back and forth and clicking her heels. She was easy on the eyes but her manner was inappropriate, impolite and rude.
>
> "What's your name?"
>
> "Nguyen Thi Ba," she replied.
>
> "Age?"
>
> "Twenty-five."
>
> "Occupation?"
>
> "First I married a deputy officer. Then, I married Mr . . . ."
>
> "Be quiet! I asked about your profession not your husband."
>
> "Later, I married a captain," she continued.
>
> The interpreter quickly finished it for her:
>
> "You don't have a job; is that correct?" the interpreter asked. "You are unemployed." He turned to the judge: "*Sans profession.*"
>
> "What do you mean unemployed?" the woman replied to the interpreter.
>
> "What is your occupation, then?" the interpreter asked again.
>
> "What is my job? My occupation is . . . marrying Europeans!"

The courtroom roared with laughter. The judge stood up and motioned for quiet but laughter still echoed from the back of the room. The interpreter turned to the prosecutor:

"Elle a déclare exercer le métier d'épouser les Européens!"

[She states that her profession is marrying Europeans!]

The prosecutor looked at the judge; the judge looked back at the prosecutor. They both cracked a knowing smile.

Her statement was funny and audacious. Why would she dare to reveal this in public? Could it be that marrying Europeans was, indeed, a profession?[48]

Some version of Nguyễn Thị Ba's forthright admission that she married European men to earn a living is repeated by all of the women that Vũ Trọng Phụng interviewed.[49] Moreover, *The Industry of Marrying Westerners* employs the language of business, in tongue-in-cheek fashion, to underscore the dominance of capitalist values within cross-cultural marriage. Vũ Trọng Phụng discussed the relative availability of legionnaires and young women in terms of "the laws of supply and demand" *(luật cung, luật cầu)*.[50] He described Madame Kiểm Lâm's "marital" history—starting with a civilian administrator and ending with "a soldier in the colonial regiment"—as a "career path" that was "bumpy, muddy and tortuous." Reflecting on the downward trajectory of her conjugal career, he remarked: "It was like earning a bachelor's degree first followed by a high school diploma and then an elementary school certificate after that. This analogy applies to the career path of women who marry Europeans because each marriage possesses a specific value that contributes to her occupational advancement (just like a certificate or a diploma)."[51] Later, Vũ Trọng Phụng questioned Suzanne about the taste of European men for "big, fat, well-endowed women": "Is it because European men prefer durable goods that last a long time?"[52] Upon catching a glimpse of the bed of Madame Bú-Dách, he remarked: "The bed of a *dame* is like the baton of a policeman, the hammer of a carpenter or the neck of a congressman. Within the industry of marrying westerners, it is a crucial piece of equipment."[53]

Given the application of economic language to relationships typically defined by traditional notions of duty or modern sentimental love, it is not surprising that local critics read *The Industry of Marrying Westerners* as a critique of the hegemony of market values within colonial society. "After reading this important work," wrote Lãng Tử in 1938, "I realize that marrying a Westerner is not merely a profession. It is, rather, an industry embedded in a market and driven by the power of consumption and the fluctuation of prices."[54] Another review claimed that *The Industry of*

Marrying Westerners revealed how "the inequitable economic system has spoiled our customs and made our traditions uncouth; the inhuman power of money has driven our people into a deep hole full of mud."[55]

In addition to noting the anticapitalist sentiment expressed in the text, critics interpreted the insincere interracial relationships described by Vũ Trọng Phụng as a veiled critique of a colonial political strategy to rationalize French rule by redefining it as a symbiotic partnership between Europeans and Asians. This legitimizing rhetoric was promoted by the Radical politician Albert Sarraut during his tenure as Governor General following World War I.[56] Despite its meager results, Sarraut's agenda was championed by moderate Vietnamese nationalists throughout the 1920s under the slogan: "Franco-Vietnamese collaboration and harmony" *(Pháp-Việt đề huề)*. In a review of *The Industry of Marrying Westerners* published in *Enduring Peace (Tràng An)* in 1936, Mai-Xuân-Nhân suggested that the text was crafted to undermine this collaborationist discourse: "Vũ Trọng Phụng understands his sacred duty as a writer during this transitional era in a land where the East and the West are endeavoring to come together, cooperate, and coexist in an intimate and conflict-free manner. By focusing on women who must sell their bodies to put food in their mouths, Vũ Trọng Phụng exposes the painful and shameful sacrifices demanded by the cause of 'East-West Cooperation' *[Đông Tây hợp tác]* and 'Euro-Asian harmony *[Á Âu đề huề]*.'"[57] The presence of this message also impressed the critic Lãng Tử: "Vũ Trọng Phụng studies the East-meets-West encounter between French soldiers and Vietnamese women and exposes the true character of their reluctant unions. . . . He depicts the characters as subjects of a painful East-West experiment." Citing Kipling to reflect on the larger meaning of the unions depicted in the text, Lãng Tử continued:

> We should look deeper into the East-West family, but we should not waste time looking for happiness since it does not exist here. Rather, what we find are people lowering themselves to the level of animals. We find pain and sorrowful tragedies occurring as regular as a daily meal. We find chronic misunderstandings and we find numerous cases where the subjects of this experiment are destroyed. This proves, once again, that East is East and West is West and never the twain shall meet. The wisdom of Rudyard Kipling's comment is immortal. The bringing-together of these distant worlds leads to nothing but irreparable harm.[58]

French readers also recognized in *The Industry of Marrying Westerners* a metaphor for the disharmony of colonial rule. In the final chapter of the text, Vũ Trọng Phụng reported that an anonymous Frenchman had sent him a letter threatening to sue the newspaper: "The letter writer stated that I should not claim that Europeans and Orientals will never live together in harmony and that I should not sow doubts in the minds of my readers. He insisted that I had no right to destroy the many wonderful Franco-Annamese unions by insinuating that for Westerners, marrying a local wife is like buying a piece of merchandise."[59]

Vũ Trọng Phụng's portrayal of the infiltration of the market into the marital sphere resembles, in a general way, the dominance of capitalist values over Vietnamese society depicted in *No Echo*. But while the play adopts a grim point of view toward this development, the tone of *The Industry of Marrying Westerners* is arch and ironic. This playful attitude coincides with a shift in Vũ Trọng Phụng's depiction of subaltern resistance to the dangers posed by predatory market forces. Unlike the defenseless family in *No Echo*, the women in *The Industry of Marrying Westerners* appropriate the logic of the market to advance their own interests. "I am poor so I am not afraid that people will laugh at me," explained Madame Kiểm Lâm, dismissing those who criticized her mercenary approach to love and marriage. "My goal is to get rich so I can get even with those who despise me."[60] While this may not constitute resistance to the culture of the market, it suggests a refusal by socially marginal Vietnamese women to remain passive victims of the colonial socioeconomic order. *The Industry of Marrying Westerners* documented numerous tactics that the women employed to retain the upper hand in their relationships. In one, women cheated on their Western "husbands" with local lovers to provoke a "divorce," so as to marry a different European man with more money or better prospects. This tactic was first described by the Russian legionnaire Dimitrov, who regaled Vũ Trọng Phụng with stories of betrayal and abandonment initiated by each of his nine Vietnamese "wives": "All of my wives cheated on me," he explained, "and each of them did it in different ways."[61] Another "dame" allowed Vũ Trọng Phụng to read the correspondence that she maintained simultaneously with three "husbands," each of whom had been posted out of Indochina. The letters juxtaposed declarations of love and fidelity with pleas for money. "Why do you bother keeping copies of the letters that you send, like some kind of merchant," Vũ Trọng Phụng asked. "Why?" the woman responded. "If I don't keep good records, I might mix-up my stories. What will I do when they stop sending money?"[62] Madame Sergeant Tứ *(bà Đội Tứ)* explained to Vũ Trọng Phụng the strategic value of feigning jealousy: "Men like it when you act jealous because it makes them think that you really love them. Understand? In fact, we are only acting. Who has the energy to be jealous?"[63] According to Vũ Trọng Phụng, the success of such strategies derived from the different motivations that the two parties brought to these relationships. "The women appear to be driven solely by money," he concluded after listening to these stories, "while the men think only of physical pleasure. This gives rise to a wall between them, blocking honest communication, destroying true affection and sowing mutual mistrust."[64]

HOUSEHOLD SERVANTS AND EVERYDAY RESISTANCE

Consistent with the anticapitalist themes that he had been exploring since the start of the decade, Vũ Trọng Phụng's reportage published in 1936, *Household Servants,* juxtaposed the wretchedness of the poor and the cruelty of the rich.[65] It explored these themes in a series of vignettes about the lives of domestic workers collected over a two-week period "in boarding houses, on sidewalks, outside of movie theatres and around public water taps."[66] In a chapter entitled "Tragicomedy," Vũ Trọng Phụng interviewed five servants at a run-down boarding house about their entry into the profession.[67] "Before I started to do this work, a dike broke and swept away my house, livestock and belongings," explained a bald-headed man. "My wife went to work as a wet nurse and never returned. I searched for her but to no avail. After locating her, I found work pulling a rickshaw but then I was thrown in prison." A teenager suffering from a severe tubercular cough explained that he became a servant after being expelled from home following the death of his father. Another small boy claimed that his impoverished mother sold him to a rich household to make ends meet. Perhaps the saddest account came from a dim-witted eight-year-old boy who was unable to name his mother, father, or native village. "Are you very poor?" the narrator asked. "I don't really know," replied the boy. In contrast to the tales of woe related by his interview subjects, employers of household servants are depicted as cold, selfish, cruel, and decadent. One servant describes members of a wealthy family so estranged from one another that adult children refuse to share food with their elderly parents.[68] Another worked for a rich master who severely mistreated his father but lavished affection on his Japanese dogs. The servant's main tasks involved feeding fresh beef to the dogs, bathing them daily, and "wiping their asses with toilet paper."[69]

Another chapter entitled "Value Makes the Person" dwelled on the dehumanization of household servants as commodified labor.[70] The chapter describes an outdoor labor market where domestic workers are examined by potential employers "like wares in a bazaar." After observing several "mistresses" comparing the going rates for children and elderly women, the narrator witnesses the workings of a niche market for wet nurses. "An older woman looked over the wet nurse from head to toe, nodded and said, 'She looks pretty clean. Let's see what her milk is like.' The other woman responded quickly, 'She's from the country, the wife of deputy village chief. She's never set foot in a field.' The wet nurse opened her blouse to reveal her soft white breasts. She squeezed some milk into the palm of her hand. 'That'll do,' the old woman said quickly."

Subaltern resistance in *Household Servants* appears in the insolent running commentary of poor, uneducated servants about the cruelty and greed of their wealthy employers. Indeed, Vũ Trọng Phụng noted the inevitability of such class hostility: "Just as the God of all creation is unable to prevent specialists in herbal medicine from tooting their horns, or victims of syphilis from moaning in agony or bell-hops from despising hotel guests or monks from fantasizing about dog meat, it is impossible to stop household servants from denouncing their masters."[71] An elaborate example is provided by a young maid named Ms. Đũi, who opens her heart to the narrator just like in a "romantic novel" except that they are "standing on the sidewalk beside a pile of garbage."[72] "What was your first master like?" he asks. "She made my life miserable," Ms. Đũi responds. "I thought I was going to die."[73] She then related how her employer worked her to the bone, abused her verbally, and colluded with a South Asian merchant to rape her although she was just thirteen at the time. "After that I went to work for a really rich family," she continued, "thinking that they would be more humane. But God damn it! The richer they are the stingier, meaner and more brutal."[74] The mistress of the house watches Đũi's every move, accuses her of stealing, and subjects her to a constant barrage of insults and beatings. But Đũi does not passively accept this mistreatment. In a ruthless act of vengeance, she arranges secret romantic liaisons for her employer's sexually curious thirteen-year-old daughter. She then seduces and blackmails her twelve-year-old son.

In addition to recording such everyday forms of resistance, *The Industry of Marrying Westerners* and *Household Servants* exhibit a reformist impulse that was to persist in Vũ Trọng Phụng's work for the remainder of his career. In the former text, it appears in the chapter devoted to Suzanne, the daughter of Madame Ách and one of her legionnaire husbands. Although it barely figured in the revolutionary nationalist agenda, the legal and social status of mixed-race children attracted sustained attention from officials, lawyers, philanthropists, and intellectuals throughout the interwar era. Reformist efforts were driven by anxiety over the legal categorization *métis non reconnus*, illegitimate mixed-race children, unrecognized and abandoned by their fathers.[75] Originally classified as "native subjects" but marked as partially European by their upbringing and physical appearance, *métis non reconnus* provoked a range of concerns. Their hybrid identity and low social standing blurred the distinction between colonizer and colonized and threatened to undermine French prestige. French officials also worried that this deracinated community might congeal into a political force. To contain the threat, philanthropists founded orphanages to support and socialize abandoned *métis*, while advocates pursued legal reforms on their behalf. Reformist efforts peaked several years before the publication of *The Industry of Marrying Westerners* with the passage of a watershed decree in 1928 granting abandoned *métis* French citizenship once their "racial identity" had been confirmed.[76]

Public concern with the problem of *métis* children may explain Vũ Trọng Phụng's eagerness to interview Suzanne about her life and hopes for the future.[77] Finding himself alone with her during an evening stroll, he exclaimed: "This was a perfect opportunity to learn what was on the mind of a young and pretty Franco-Annamite girl."[78] He then quotes extensively from his interview with her: "What a curse to have been born a Eurasian," she complains. "The Europeans don't fully respect us. The Annamites don't really love us. In respectable Western society, a drop of Annamese blood is a disgrace, and to the noble Annamese society, a drop of French blood is far from an honor. Oh God! I don't have a country!" In response to her description of the difficulty of finding a suitable French or Vietnamese husband, Vũ Trọng Phụng suggests that she marry someone of mixed-race like herself: "I have thought about it," she replies. "A Eurasian would also have French nationality and he couldn't really despise me. If he is rich, then I'll dress like a Westerner. If he is not, for example, if he is a soldier, then I'll dress like an Annamite woman. I used to study at a school for unwanted Eurasians but I missed my mother. If I didn't worry so much about my mother, I would have gone to France a long time ago." Suzanne's loyalty to her mother impressed Vũ Trọng Phụng because it departed from stereotypes of social-climbing mixed-race women who downplayed their "native" background to enter French society. Praising Suzanne's selfless decision, Vũ Trọng Phụng wrote: "Her filial piety towards her mother had made her into a heroine."[79]

Although the predicament of mixed-race children was not the only topic of *The Industry of Marrying Westerners*, Vũ Trọng Phụng identified it as a core concern of his investigation. "I want to know if the relationships between Annamese women and European men are stormy or peaceful," he explained when questioned about his motives by Madame Bú-Dích.[80] "But I am also interested in the offspring of these unions. This is a growing population and I am sure they will pose problems for our lawmakers in the future." Later, he observed mixed-race children being mistreated by their parents and expressed sympathy for them: "These innocent children suffer bitter punishments at the hands of their parents who view them with suspicion and regret. They deserve to be loved but Madame Corporal doesn't seem to give a damn about them. She is just like the government!"[81] In a footnote, Vũ Trọng Phụng provided context for this comment by explaining that "the government has stopped helping unwanted Eurasian children since the onset of the Depression." These references to shifts in government policy over "the *métis* problem" confirm that Vũ Trọng Phụng was aware that his research might shape public opinion and policy regarding a social issue of modest importance. Instead of advancing a specific proposal to address the issue, however, Vũ Trọng Phụng's intervention presented original research on the topic and amplified the sympathetic voice of a member of the community in question. This judicious, empirically minded approach recalls the republican naturalist impulses that he first exhibited in *No Echo*.

Like *The Industry of Marrying Westerners, Household Servants* does not advance a coherent strategy to overcome capitalism's destructive force, but it does acknowledge that a partial solution to the exploitation of domestic workers may lie in the organization of trade unions. Observing a mob of unemployed servants waiting in vain to be hired at the outdoor labor market, Vũ Trọng Phụng wrote: "I couldn't help thinking of the unemployed workers at the Port who plotted to meet at a predetermined place and succeeded in staging a large demonstration. It is too bad that there is not yet an analogous organization for these servants. This throng of low-class people splits up and disperses everywhere in the city so that sophisticated people think that it is a civilized place. Even social scientists think that there is no adversity there."[82] While Vũ Trọng Phụng did not pursue this point further, his reference to the positive social potential of trade unions parallels his stated belief in the capacity of the institutions of a civil society, such as the press, to ameliorate social injustice.

CAPITALISM AND SEXUAL PERVERSITY

As both *The Industry of Marrying Westerners* and *Household Servants* indicate, Vũ Trọng Phụng's critique of capitalism posited a relationship between the forces of economic exploitation and the growth of immorality, perversity, and sexualized violence. This connection is also illustrated in works like *No Echo* that depict rich and powerful characters as sexual predators. Vũ Trọng Phụng's earliest exploration of this theme may be found in "The Ploy," a sensational short story that triggered legal charges of public indecency against the author when it appeared in the *Midday News* in January 1931.[83] The story dramatizes the sexual victimization of a recently married Vietnamese white-collar worker—referred to as "Clerk H"—by a wickedly perverse French businessman who employs him.[84] In an opening scene set in a cramped apartment building, Clerk H and his wife—referred to as "L"—are introduced through the perspective of a prying female neighbor who eavesdrops on their domestic quarrels. She obsesses over L's former occupation as a prostitute and fantasizes about the "stacks of coins and piles of paper money" that she imagines clutter Clerk H's desk. The scene establishes a "noirish" atmosphere of urban voyeurism, avarice, and illicit sexuality.

The most menacing and corrupting agent in the story is the French businessman. Unmarried and childless after twenty years of working overseas, he copes with his homesickness by smoking opium and sleeping with random Vietnamese women procured for him by his employees. A description of his bedroom, decorated with tiger skins, pornographic paintings, and a statue of a nude woman on a pedestal, underscores his depraved state of mind. In the story's central episode, which utilizes the same voyeuristic perspective as the opening scene, two Vietnamese employees peer through the keyhole of this garish bedroom and witness the businessman chastising Clerk H for failing to find him a woman for the evening. Clerk H protests that the woman he had recruited backed out in order to care for a sick child. Enraged, the businessman calls him a liar and demands that he "play the part." Shifting abruptly to the reactions of the two voyeurs at the keyhole, the narrator describes their shocked expressions as they hear "the unfastening of a belt buckle and the sound of clothing being stripped off and thrown to the ground."[85]

The following scene describes Clerk H walking home, furious and humiliated. In an interior monologue, he curses his wife—who had "defiled her body with many men in the past"—for refusing to consent to have sex with his boss (this conflict is now revealed as the subject of the domestic quarrel overheard at the beginning of the story). He determines to give her a sound beating, but upon arriving home, he discovers her dead body and a suicide note. The note reveals that it was her husband's request that she sleep with his boss that prompted her to take her own life. It also suggests that while she had once believed that Clerk H had intended to rescue her from a life of prostitution, she now understood their marriage to be a "ploy" devised by her husband to improve his standing with his boss. The story concludes with the final lines of L's note, which express the hope that her suicide will purify her defiled body.

At first glance, the most remarkable aspect of "The Ploy" is its unprecedented account of the (homo)sexual violation of a Vietnamese clerk by his French employer. This episode was shocking to the notions of aesthetic refinement that prevailed at the time and, very likely, pregnant with anticolonial undertones. Since the story appeared during the heightened political repression that followed the eruption of left-wing strikes and peasant insurrections at the start of the Depression, it is tempting to interpret this scene of sexual violence as a kind of generic critique of French brutality and Vietnamese victimization during a period marked by extreme state violence against civilians. Indeed, Thiều Quang's memoir hints at the possibility that "The Ploy" may have been singled out for legal persecution because of the sensational political symbolism implicit in its depiction of cross-cultural rape.[86]

On the other hand, the homosexual dimension of the rape scene may also be read as a protest against French depictions of Vietnamese men as effeminate, licentious, and responsible for the spread of homosexual practices among the French in Indochina.[87] A famous exponent of this view was the French naval doctor Jacobus X, who characterized "the Tonkinese race" as "lascivious, lubricious, pederastic and sodomitical" and insisted that "the Europeans did not import the vice of Sodom into Cochin-China. . . . It was the vanquished people who corrupted the European."[88] In contrast, the emasculation of the Vietnamese male protagonist in "The Ploy" is depicted as a direct consequence of the exercise of a malicious and perverse form of French power and not as a reflection of the natural weakness or effeminacy of Vietnamese men. As a result, the story may have been read as a counterdiscursive tactic to turn the tables on an insidious colonial stereotype.

In the context of Vũ Trọng Phụng's overall body of work, "The Ploy" anticipated a number of additional themes that he would return to repeatedly in his writing on sex and colonial modernity. One was a particular focus on the moral corruption of the Vietnamese urban middle classes. While the psychosexual degeneration of the peasant girl Thị Mịch in the novel *The Storm* stands as an obvious exception to this trend, most of his serious writing about the dilemmas of modern Vietnamese sexual culture (including virtually all of his short stories about the topic) focused on the experiences of clerks, civil servants, students, teachers, and journalists.

Another theme of "The Ploy" that emerged as a core concern in Vũ Trọng Phụng's subsequent writing was the connection between city life and moral depravity. Early scenes in the story suggest that a new style of urban living characterized by crowded apartment complexes and cramped flats separated by paper-thin walls incited envy, covetousness, and voyeurism. City streets are portrayed in even more malevolent terms. Walking home after midnight, Clerk H passes a series of urban landmarks on the deserted streets at the outskirts of Hà Nội's old commercial quarter—"the Central Prison, the Lock Hospital for Prostitutes, the infirmary, and the morgue"—that together conjure an image of the city as a site of crime, sexual vice, disease, and death.[89] His solitary journey through this bleak cityscape is only interrupted by the appearance of a seedy rickshaw-man who advertises "a new batch of lost calves" *(bò lạc)* from Bắc Ninh province.[90]

Moreover, certain formal features of "The Ploy" allow it to be read as an indictment of the saturation of Vietnamese society by sexual perversity, despite the fact that the story's concise narrative focuses narrowly on a handful of specific characters. Perhaps the best example is Vũ Trọng Phụng's refusal to particularize any of the characters in the story by providing them with personal names. Indeed, the use of a single initial to refer to the clerk and his wife calls attention to the relatively abstract way that they are characterized and, hence, the ease with which their individual predicaments may be transposed to the social body as a whole. In addition, the repeated employment of a voyeuristic point of view underlines the generic interchangeability of anonymous and inquisitive contemporary readers with the eavesdropping, keyhole-peeping minor characters in the story. An effect of these overlapping, self-reflexive manifestations of voyeurism is to heighten an impression of the general spread of illicit, immodest, deviant, and commercialized sexuality throughout society and to implicate readers as active participants in this general crisis of moral degeneracy.

Another important theme of the story is the damaging impact on relations between Vietnamese men and Vietnamese women of the intrusive presence of a large community of sexually active French men. While studies of the sexual politics of imperialism tend to focus narrowly on the objectification and mistreatment of colonized men and women by the discourses and policies of the colonial state, the link between the European presence and changing relations between native men and native women has received far less attention.[91] In contrast, this connection emerges as arguably the central theme of "The Ploy." The sexual abuse of Clerk H may appear to be the tragic climax of the story, but its deeper significance within the overall structure of the narrative lies in its devastating impact on the marriage of Clerk H and his wife and, even more disastrously, in its role as the indirect catalyst for her suicide.[92] Three years after the publication of "The Ploy," Vũ Trọng Phụng would revisit the connection between the sexual practices of Frenchmen in colonial Vietnam and local relations between the sexes in *The Industry of Marrying Westerners.*

It is perhaps also significant that the wife's decision to commit suicide is triggered—as described in her note—by a sudden realization that her husband had never intended to rescue her from a life of prostitution, as she had once believed. This episode exposes the hollowness of one component of a broader romantic illusion about the social reform of sex work that Vũ Trọng Phụng associated with literary rivals in the Self-Strength Literary Group and denounced in his later writing. As he explained in subsequent works, the solution to the growth of the commercial sex industry was not to be found in fantasies promoted by literary "romantics" regarding the rescue of good-hearted prostitutes by enlightened reformers. Rather, it lay in the painstaking development and implementation of practical social policies connected to sex education and public health.

The connection between economic power and sexual perversity dramatized in "The Ploy" is also explored in Vũ Trọng Phụng's novel *The Storm,* published in 1936, in which the evils of capitalism are embodied in the business tycoon Nghị Hách—perhaps the most villainous figure in modern Vietnamese literature. Nghị Hách's expansive economic interests resemble the diversified business portfolio of the landlord in *No Echo,* but the scale of his wealth is exponentially greater. He possesses "five hundred hectares of farmland, a coal mine in Quảng Yên province, thirty French villas in Hà Nội, and another forty houses in Hải Phòng."[93] Many of his most profitable enterprises derive from government concessions, including a two-hundred-hectare tea plantation and a provincial monopoly for the production and sale of fish sauce.[94] In a minor subplot of the novel, Nghị Hách uses his money and influence to manipulate the provision of government-issued grain for famine relief in order to win election to the Consultative Council of Tonkin.

In addition to depicting Nghị Hách's corrupt business practices, *The Storm* portrays him as a deviant sexual predator. He sets the plot in motion by brutally raping the naïve peasant girl Thị Mịch. Nghị Hách rapes Thị Mịch despite the fact that his opulent household includes a private harem made up of a dozen concubines and secondary wives. In one especially lurid episode, he attempts to force himself upon Thị Mịch a second time despite the fact that she is pregnant and repulsed by his crude advances. Ignoring her resistance, "he hugs her close, kissing and groping every part of her body with both hands."[95] Toward the end of the novel, Vũ Trọng Phụng depicts Nghị Hách engaging in sexual foreplay with two of his concubines simultaneously while drinking champagne, smoking opium, and watching a pornographic film. A flashback further illustrates Nghị Hách's sexual aggression by showing him seducing the wife of his best friend. Finally, the resolution of a complex case of mistaken identity at the close of the narrative reveals that Thị Mịch is, in fact, the fiancé of Nghị Hách's biological son—a shocking revelation since he has already raped her and taken her as secondary wife.

As with the French businessman in "The Ploy," it is tempting to view Nghị Hách's predatory sexual aggression as a metaphor that intensifies his standing as an agent of economic exploitation. Such an interpretation calls attention to the uses of pornographic representation as political critique, a tradition with roots in popular republican discourse from the French revolutionary era.[96] Vũ Trọng Phụng insisted, however, that his characterization of Nghị Hách simply reflected the well-documented sexual decadence of the Vietnamese nouveau riche. "In writing *The Storm*, my only purpose was to present a snapshot of contemporary society," he explained in an interview published in 1937. "And when you look closely at this society, it is hard to be optimistic. Society today is decaying; we have never seen anything like it before in our history. It is rotten and stinking. We live in an era during which those with money and power live only for sensual pleasure. Certainly you have heard stories about members of the nouveau riche who, despite having half-a-dozen wives, still commit obscenities just like my character Nghị Hách."[97]

The erosion of sexual morality by the forces of colonial capitalism may also be seen in Vũ Trọng Phụng's treatment of commercial advertising. "This is the era of advertising," he once told his close friend Nguyễn Triệu Luật, "anyone who ignores this is destined to fail even if they have talent."[98] The stimulation of lust by modern advertising stands as a major theme of Vũ Trọng Phụng's novel *Dumb Luck*, much of which takes place at a boutique that specializes in lingerie and suggestive female fashions. Upon his first visit there, the uneducated vagabond Red-Haired Xuân encounters a group of workmen installing eye-catching but hard-to-read lettering on the storefront façade.

> Xuân inched towards the five wooden letters on the pavement. Try as he might, he was unable to make out the specific letter that each was supposed to symbolize. There was a round one with a hole in the middle and a strange square one with two round holes in the middle. Even more bizarre were three triangle-shaped ones with holes in the middle! Ever since he was six, Red-Haired Xuân's coarse mind knew that a triangular shape with a hole in the middle could only signify one thing—one very dirty thing. He smiled to himself.[99]

This ironically humorous passage illustrates the notion, recurrent throughout *Dumb Luck*, that the stimulation of lust is an inevitable consequence of the abrupt encounter between modern commercial culture and traditional Vietnamese society.[100]

Dumb Luck's gently mocking tone toward the stimulation of Red-Haired Xuân's libido by the forces of colonial capitalism contrasts with the disgust and outrage that Vũ Trọng Phụng usually expressed about the issue. In the novel *The Dike Breaks,* for example, the ex–political prisoner Minh is revolted by the lascivious behavior of Vietnamese youth that he observes at an open-air festival. "Why such lewdness?" he asks his friend Quang. "Why such decadence and loose morals? What I've seen today is a premonition of our ruin. How can these merry and stuck-up young men and women behave in such a carefree way with one another—hanging around together and dancing all night? This kind of behavior is destroying the country."[101] In the interview from 1937 with Lê Thanh, Vũ Trọng Phụng explained that his work dwelled on the obscene consequences of capitalism in order to instill a sense of revulsion in his readers and to jolt them out of their own perverse fascination with sex. "People often feel disgusted when they read my novels," he acknowledged. "They feel disgusted because my work reveals to them a filthy truth. This disgust can turn into bitterness. I hope that the feelings of disgust and bitterness provoked by my writing may be strong enough to make my readers forget their own feelings of sexual arousal."[102]

VENEREAL DISEASE CLINIC AND THE REFORM OF COMMERCIAL SEX

Both the link between capitalism and moral decay and the republican orientation of Vũ Trọng Phụng's reformist vision are on display in *Venereal Disease Clinic,* a wide-ranging study of venereal disease and state regulation of prostitution in Hà Nội, first published in 1937.[103] As with the rise of an "industry of marrying Westerners" on the outskirts of his native Hà Nội, the explosive growth of commercial sex and venereal disease symbolized for Vũ Trọng Phụng the corrosive impact of colonial capitalism on Vietnamese culture. But whereas local left-wing discourse about prostitution tended to dismiss the potential significance of reformist measures short of social revolution, Vũ Trọng Phụng adopted a pragmatic republican approach. Not only did *Venereal Disease Clinic* exhibit his now familiar empirical orientation toward the issue, but it attacked the French system of regulated prostitution for violating ideals such as liberty, equality, freedom from arbitrary arrest, and equal protection under the law. Indeed, the "abolitionist" solution championed by Vũ Trọng Phụng in the final chapter of *Venereal Disease Clinic* was a stock element in the political agenda of activist French republican groups and individuals, both at home and throughout the Empire, during the interwar years.

Pitched as "a work of scientific research," *Venereal Disease Clinic* opened by citing a recent statement by Mayor Virgitti that Hà Nội contained no fewer than five thousand prostitutes.[104] Given an overall population of 180,000, Vũ Trọng Phụng calculated that "one out of thirty-five people earn a living by spreading venereal disease." The problem was more severe because the Mayor did not account for hundreds of unregistered "singing girls and taxi dancers" who sold sexual services on Khâm Thiên Street, just outside the city limits. *Venereal Disease Clinic* provided equally alarming figures about the growth of sexually transmitted disease. It referred to a medical report from 1914 that placed the infection rate for colonial troops at 74 percent as well as more recent evidence that an astonishing 92 percent of all unregistered prostitutes suffered from venereal disease.[105] It also cited data collected from medical surveys showing that sexually transmitted diseases were responsible for 70 percent of all cases of blindness and 25 percent of the infant deaths reported in the city.[106]

An early chapter traced the history of the system of state regulation of prostitution in Hà Nội from its founding by French naval officers immediately after the conquest of Tonkin in the mid-1880s.[107] Based on the "French model" established in Paris at the start of the nineteenth century, this coercive regulatory system required prostitutes to register with the police, carry identity cards, undergo medical checkups, work within licensed brothels, and—in the event of infection—submit to incarceration and medical treatment in state-run lock hospitals.[108] It also introduced a powerful vice squad charged with policing the bodies of prostitutes who acquiesced to registration and hunting down those who did not. Vũ Trọng Phụng discussed the legislative decrees that structured the system and traced changes in the regulatory regime over time. He also argued that the state's commitment to regulation in Indochina stemmed from concerns over the health and sexual needs of colonial troops.

The centerpiece of *Venereal Disease Clinic* was an eyewitness account of the Hà Nội lock hospital, which Vũ Trọng Phụng was able to visit thanks to a stopover in Indochina by the French Minister of Labor. He described its state-of-the-art facilities and its modern regime of sex education and gynecological treatment. Interviews with doctors, nurses, and sex workers revealed a range of views about its internal workings. *Venereal Disease Clinic* also reported on a visit to the corrupt and undermanned vice squad. Other chapters cataloged (literally) the segmented, hierarchical structure of prostitution in Hà Nội and recounted the life histories of individual sex workers. The vast quantity and range of data on display—based on scientific studies, historical documents, and firsthand reporting—underline Vũ Trọng Phụng's remarkable commitment to empirical research.

An empirical orientation is further evident in Vũ Trọng Phụng's exhaustive effort to explain the growth of prostitution. In contrast to local Marxists and traditionalists who relied on well-worn theories (economistic for the former, moralistic for the latter), Vũ Trọng Phụng recorded almost two-dozen discrete explanations that he encountered during the course of his research.[109] Mayor Virgitti highlighted the loose character of Vietnamese women, who, he claimed, "enjoy working as prostitutes." Traditionalists linked the growth of prostitution to the erosion of morality that followed the decline of Confucianism, Buddhism, and Taoism. An experienced French nurse emphasized the dire financial situation of unemployed rural girls and their families. Adopting a broader comparative perspective, the Director of the Municipal Hygiene Service (Bernard Joyeux) noted that prostitution and venereal disease always spread in zones marked by intense intercultural contact such as port cities and Europe during World War I. Others focused on the indulgent preoccupations of modern youth: the seduction of new professions, the attraction of easy riches, and the frisson of the Western city, combined with a lack of adequate parental supervision. Another argument dwelled on the recruitment of naïve country girls by predatory urban pimps. Vũ Trọng Phụng rehearsed the Augustinian thesis that prostitution will always exist because it serves an essential social function. He also explored antifeminist explanations in which "the movement for women's rights and freedom of marriage" foster promiscuity in impressionable young girls. Most colonial officials (Le Roy Des Barres, Coppin, Joyeux, and Virgitti) condemned the impact of Westernization and the growth of materialism in the local population. Dr. Coppin charged that "the wild spread of greed corrupts men and leads women into debauchery." Vũ Trọng Phụng agreed, noting that "romantic girls" were especially vulnerable, as were Eurasians, whose moral fiber had been weakened due to deracination and discrimination. Joyeux contended that the growth of taxi dancers and bar girls reflected the eagerness with which Vietnamese borrow from foreign cultures. "There is nothing western that they do not find worth researching, copying, recording or absorbing," he remarked with an air of condescension. Vietnamese intellectuals, on the other hand, pinned blame on the moral laxity of French culture. "Contact with Europe has damaged our civilization," a Vietnamese student told Coppin. "French moral laxity promotes divorce and adultery and incites a taste for luxury and perversity." Coppin agreed that relaxed attitudes toward sex and eroticism in France (as opposed to Britain) encouraged promiscuity in subject populations. He also suggested that the risqué tenor of French popular culture ("as embodied by Rabelais") struck a receptive chord because it dovetailed with the bawdy informality of Vietnamese folkways. Although he clearly favored economic theories to explain the growth of the sex trade, the range of hypotheses and arguments that Vũ Trọng Phụng recorded and considered testifies to the wide-ranging empiricism of his approach. Rather than privileging a particular mode of analysis, he appears genuinely open to insights into the problem provided by economic, sociological, philosophical, historical, and journalistic research.

As with Vũ Trọng Phụng's painstakingly empirical approach to the causes of prostitution, his favored solution to the shortcomings of the regulationist system points to the broadly republican character of his political vision. Since the turn of the century, officials in Indochina had been debating a range of reformist strategies that mirrored metropolitan proposals to combat the social consequences of prostitution in France.[110] Led by military doctors, "regulationists" argued that the existing system of surveillance needed to be strengthened and updated. They proposed expanding the size and power of the vice squad, increasing the capacity of the lock hospital to accommodate more inmates, and establishing replicas of these coercive institutions in suburbs and provincial towns. A hyperregulationist subset of this conservative group supported the concentration of licensed brothels in red-light districts to increase the ease of surveillance. "Abolitionists," in contrast, favored the elimination of lock hospitals, vice squads, and licensed brothels. In their place, they advocated sex education for commercial sex workers and heightened legal prosecution of pimps and procurers. With the closing of the lock hospitals, abolitionists proposed to treat infected prostitutes in ordinary medical hospitals alongside the rest of the population. Between the poles of regulationism and abolitionism lay a widely endorsed compromise position known as "evolutionism" or "opportunism" that accepted the continuation of regulation in Indochina under the supervision of medical officials rather than the police. While sympathetic to the arguments advanced by the abolitionists, the colonial-minded advocates of this middle position insisted that Indochina's backward state of development prevented the implementation there of the abolitionist program.[111]

The abolitionist movement in France attracted support from republicans, feminists, and religious moralists, but it was dominated in the colonies by socially progressive technocrats who supported it on republican grounds exclusively.[112] Crystallized in the "liberal abolitionism" promoted in France by the crusading journalist Yves Guyot during the 1870s and 1880s, this potent strand of abolitionism took issue with the incarceration of infected prostitutes because it took away their civil rights even though the transmission of venereal disease was not technically a crime. It also denounced the system's unequal treatment of men and women since men who spread venereal disease received no sanction. Inspired by the principles of the Declaration of the Rights of Man, "liberal abolitionism" associated the vice squad with police brutality, arbitrary rule, and illiberal state repression.[113] The presence of this strain of abolitionism in Indochina may be seen in a special issue of the Hà Nội-based *Bulletin de la Société Médico-Chirurgicale de L'Indochine*, which Vũ Trọng Phụng consulted extensively while researching *Venereal Disease Clinic*. The issue reprinted a series of studies of prostitution and venereal disease in Indochina carried out between 1912 and 1930 along with transcripts of meetings, held over a twenty-year period, in which colonial health officials deliberated about the topic. In 1912, an official named Gauducheau used classic republican reasoning to challenge the efficacy and fairness of the regulationist approach. "Before we endorse measures of coercive hygiene such as forced visits and internments," he argued, "we must first prove with certitude that such measures are not just useful but indispensible for the protection of public health. . . . We must avoid committing abuses of power in the name of hygiene and be careful to respect individual liberty including the liberty of the prostitutes."[114] In a study from 1915, Dr. Abadie-Bayro referred defensively to republican abolitionists as "sociologists who place individual liberty above all other issues, reject all special measures against prostitutes, and view measures of mandatory hygiene as an abuse of power."[115] Another conservative, M. Guillemet, concurred with Abadie-Bayro, criticizing abolitionist doctors who viewed "all acts of sexual life, including prostitution, as an exercise of the rights that each person possesses, to use or abuse as he or she sees fit."[116] In response, the abolitionist Gauducheau launched a stirring critique of the despotic and illiberal character of the current regime:

> I consider regulation to be one of the most disgraceful and useless abuses of our time. When an unfortunate girl falls into prostitution, the administrative authorities seize her immediately and begin to impose on her a tax which simply must be seen as immoral. Next comes the forced examination. We have all seen in the course of our careers these young prostitutes, subjected for the first time to this infamous ordeal, struggling with all of their might not to be nakedly exposed in the light of day in the examination room. Next is the lock hospital where she must pay for treatment and board. After having paid for the costs of her own imprisonment, she must recoup the money, and because she has lost her clients, the brothel supervisor reduces her ration of rice. Hunger follows misery and dishonor. Then, there is the secret exactions of the vice police—they not only look after the preservation of public morals but the brothel receipts as well. . . . We should allow, therefore, prostitution to be freely exercised under a common law legislation that requires decency, discretion, and propriety on the street. We should not forget that these women have declared their misconduct in public. We should respect their liberty if we

> do not want catastrophic results. Under the influence of a regime of liberty, there will be produced a gradual amelioration of the material and sanitary conditions of prostitutes.[117]

Summing up the position of the abolitionists in a study completed in 1930, Dr. Joyeux noted that they found it "unacceptable to weaken individual liberty in the name of venereal disease."[118]

Vũ Trọng Phụng cited this republican discourse repeatedly during the course of *Venereal Disease Clinic* and endorsed the abolitionist position. "Shut down the lock-hospital," he wrote, and "close the brothels."[119] He was especially critical of the vice squad's reputation for corruption, arbitrary arrest, and abuse of power: "Abolish the vice-squad; it is an embarrassment for a civilized nation."[120] On the other hand, he praised abolition as "fair" and "humanitarian" because it was "founded on the equality of men and women."[121] In the final chapter of the text, he approvingly cited the view of Victor Basch, the president of the quintessentially republican League for the Rights of Man, that the regulationist system was "unjust" and "autocratic" and that "laws restricting prostitution run counter to the guiding principles of the equality of all before the law."[122] He then called for the immediate application in Indochina of an abolitionist scheme known as the Sellier Law that had been proposed by the new Popular Front government the previous year.[123] In place of the institutions of regulation slated for elimination by the law, Vũ Trọng Phụng put his faith in the power of education, advocating a massive public health campaign including films, propaganda, and sex education in school.

While denouncing regulation and defending abolition, Vũ Trọng Phụng devoted most of the final chapter of *Venereal Disease Clinic* to attacking evolutionism, the popular "compromise" position in the debate over the management of prostitution in Indochina. Although its champions in the colonial bureaucracy framed evolutionism as a concessionary move to the middle ground, it mandated little concrete change to the existing system of regulation. Rather, it put forward a different justification for the persistence of regulation, citing the backwardness of "Annamese" society as an insurmountable obstacle to the implementation of an effective abolitionist program. On evolutionism, Vũ Trọng Phụng quoted Professor Labrouquere of the University of Hà Nội Law School: "The application of an abolitionist regime in Indochina will founder due to many obstacles: flawed records regarding family background, births, deaths and marriage, weak primary education, poor public health systems and the general ignorance of the population. We must strive to devise reforms to address the problem of venereal disease that accord with the level of the people."[124] In response, Vũ Trọng Phụng suggested that the triumph of abolition in "nearly all civilized countries in Europe and America" and its endorsement by the League of Nations indicated that French policy in Indochina (and in France for that matter) was out of step with an emerging universal norm.[125] As with the unequal treatment of women by the institutions of regulation (an aspect of the system firmly rejected by the abolitionists), the cultural (and racial) chauvinism of the local evolutionist position violated republican ideals of universalism. Rejecting the condescending notion that the "Annamese lack capacity," Vũ Trọng Phụng called on the native elite to demand abolition immediately: "Journalists and people's representatives—if you want to liberate our country's women from the slavery of prostitution—demand the Sellier Law with the same zealousness that you demand Freedom."[126] In addition to expressing support for abolition as a moderate reformist solution to a pressing social crisis, Vũ Trọng Phụng's appeal endorsed an approach grounded in an open, democratic process that involved journalists and elected representatives working together for the public interest. These elements of his argument reinforce the impression that, as with his opposition to the dominance of commercial values in Vietnamese society more generally, Vũ Trọng Phụng's opposition to state regulation of commercial sex was grounded in a republican sensibility.

CHAPTER THREE • The Question of Communism

Vũ Trọng Phụng's attitude toward communism has attracted enormous attention since the late 1930s, but it remains controversial and poorly understood. In light of his anticapitalist views explored in the previous chapter, many of his contemporaries assumed that he was sympathetic toward communism.[1] Others, more familiar with his entire body of work, denied that it expressed a coherent ideological viewpoint or provided support for an organized political movement.[2] With the rise to power of the Indochinese Communist Party (ICP) after World War II, supporters of Vũ Trọng Phụng within the cultural bureaucracy of the DRV defended his work from the threat of state censorship by exaggerating his communist sympathies.[3] To buttress the case, they pointed to his positive portrayal of the Comintern agent Hải Vân and the ex–political prisoner Teacher Minh in the novels *The Storm* and *The Dike Breaks*, both published in 1936. This plausible defense strategy collapsed in the late 1950s, however, when several anticommunist essays from the late 1930s surfaced in Hà Nội, bearing his byline. The circulation of these essays contributed to the ban on his work in communist Vietnam that was enforced for roughly twenty-five years starting in 1960. As part of a campaign to rehabilitate Vũ Trọng Phụng in the late 1980s, sympathetic critics amplified his critique of colonial capitalism, while downplaying the significance of his anticommunist writing. With several important exceptions, most contemporary treatments of the writer adopt this approach to his political orientation or skirt the issue entirely.

A close look at Vũ Trọng Phụng's treatment of communism over the course of his career reveals a more complex story. Given his youth and the erratic fluctuations of the "party line" (in both the Soviet Union and Indochina) during the 1930s, it should come as no surprise that Vũ Trọng Phụng's views on communism evolved over time. After ignoring the movement during the first half of the decade (perhaps due to state censorship), he expressed leftist sympathies following the rise to power in France in 1936 of the communist-socialist-radical alliance known as the Popular Front. But this burst of enthusiasm dissipated by early 1937 owing to the failings of the new government, revelations about the Stalinist purges and the Moscow show trials, and the sectarianism and unprincipled political machinations of local communists. His last explicit engagement with communism, a stinging satire published in August 1938, was harshly disapproving of the movement. Hence, although Vũ Trọng Phụng's political sympathies waxed and waned during the 1930s, the general arc of his thinking moved toward an increasingly critical appraisal of the communist project.

Just as the fluidity of Vũ Trọng Phụng's views complicates efforts to affix a concrete label to his ideological orientation, the criticism of communism that he expressed late in his career does not square with conventional interpretations of the dynamics of Vietnamese anticommunism. In standard accounts, anticommunism in Indochina was pioneered after the Russian Revolution by a hidebound Catholic Church and promoted by the colonial state, the French business community, and the local bourgeoisie. According to this interpretation, the anticommunism advanced by these conservative forces was "reactive, lacking in positive content, and generally premised on the indefinite maintenance of the colonial status quo."[4] In contrast, Vũ Trọng Phụng's anticommunism appears to have been animated by two sentiments that barely figured in the thinking of the most reactionary elements of the Church, the colonial state, or the local bourgeoisie. The first was a strong nationalism, inspired by colonial rule, which prompted hostility to the divisiveness of communist sectarianism and resentment at the control of the ICP by foreign patrons. The colonial roots of Vietnamese nationalism may have encouraged as well skepticism about the shallow and derivative nature of local communist activism. The second sentiment shaping Vũ Trọng Phụng's attitude toward communism was a strain of late colonial republicanism that encouraged his opposition to Stalinist despotism. As Peter Lamour has argued, the fin de siècle republicanism that reigned at the twilight of the Third Republic indulged in an "orgy of anticommunism."[5] Foreshadowing post–World War II "liberal" anticommunism, this political posture in France is often traced to the antitotalitarian writing of Raymond Aron and Soviet refugees in Paris during late 1930s.[6] Vũ Trọng Phụng encountered this emergent tradition through reporting on global communist politics in the French press as well as coverage of apostates from communism based in Paris like André Gide, Boris Souvaraine, and Victor Serge. His direct experience with the mercurial Vietnamese Left buttressed the critical appraisals of communist totalitarianism that he encountered in the French press. Together with his nationalist concerns about the divisiveness and derivativeness of Vietnamese communism, this tradition deepened his fears about the despotism, lack of freedom, and persistent mendacity of communist rule. It may also be responsible for Vũ Trọng Phụng's preoccupation with the insincerity of communist behavior.[7] The significance of this republican-inflected nationalist anticommunism is enhanced because it enjoyed support from many intellectuals during the interwar era and because it has never been acknowledged in the existing scholarship.

THE CONTEXT OF EARLY VIETNAMESE ANTICOMMUNISM

Prior to 1936, Vũ Trọng Phụng referred to communism in print on only two occasions. An aside about the gambling boss Mr. B in the reportage *The Man Trap,* published in 1933, alluded to Stalin's penchant for self-aggrandizement. "Outdoing Stalin in every respect," Vũ Trọng Phụng wrote, "Mr. B referred to his own house on Fish Street as 'The Capital for Gamblers' well before Stalin boasted of 'Moscow, Capital of the World.'"[8] In *The Industry of Marrying Westerners,* published the following year, Vũ Trọng Phụng touched upon recent Russian history in his interview with Dimitov, a former officer in the White army now serving in Tonkin with the French Foreign Legion: "In front of me, next to the opium lamp, lay a courageous man, formerly a 'hero' of the Kerensky government, who had bravely resisted the communists."[9] Pursued by the secret police, Dimitov fled to France where he hoped to find a home under a "regime that respects the freedom of the individual." Instead, he found work in a hotel kitchen. But the disappearance from Paris in January 1930 of the White Russian general Alexandre Kouteipoff—allegedly seized by Bolshevik agents on his way to church—made him fear for his safety and he joined the Foreign Legion. These brief references to the megalomania of Stalin and the aggressive tactics of his secret police imply that Vũ Trọng Phụng shared some of the harsh perceptions of Soviet communism that were widespread during the era both in Indochina and throughout the French Empire.

Reflecting an anachronistic tendency in colonial political culture, anticommunism came to Indochina prior to communism, provoked by the anxieties of French officials and the colon business community. These concerns stemmed from the October Revolution and the birth and bolshevization of the French Communist Party (PCF) during the 1920s.[10] The efforts of the Third International to "quicken the forces of world revolution" fueled additional fears of a global red menace. "After 1920 the Comintern's agents were everywhere," wrote Michael B. Miller, describing the paranoid mindset of the time, "in North Africa, in Persia, in Afghanistan, in India, in Singapore, in the East Indies, in Indochina, in China. They fomented insurrection, disseminated propaganda, built communist parties, joined nationalist movements, and recruited local revolutionaries who slipped into Russia, trained in revolutionary doctrine and methods, and then infiltrated back to their homelands."[11] Colonial officials were especially susceptible to these fears. According to Martin Thomas: "Those charged with formulating new colonial policies to assure the empire's survival were increasingly animated by an anticommunism that meshed recent colonial experience with domestic ideological ferment in 1920s France."[12] For officials in Indochina, sources of anxiety included the rise of radical nationalism during the early 1900s but not significant communist activity until the mid-1920s. In October 1922, intelligence services could identify only twelve suspected communists throughout the colonial territory, all of them Frenchmen.[13] Three years later, the public profile of the movement was so low that Nguyễn An Ninh claimed: "it would be almost impossible to find a Vietnamese who would be capable of giving a clear definition of communism or Bolshevism."[14]

Since communism was barely present in Indochina, local impressions of it prior to about 1925 were dominated by the views of French officials. An important figure in this respect was Governor General Albert Sarraut.[15] While serving his first term in office, Sarraut aggressively pursued "revolutionary" and "anarchist" networks linked to the scholar-patriot Phan Bội Châu. But his second term was dominated by the communist threat.[16] During this period, he helped found the Sûreté Générale (the General Security Police), which would evolve into the colonial state's most vigilant anticommunist institution. As Minister of Colonies between 1920 and 1924, Sarraut kept a close eye on the first sustained flurry of Vietnamese communist activism, carried out by students in France and exiles in southern China. He also followed Hồ Chí Minh's remarkable rise as a communist militant in Paris and as a Comintern agent in the Soviet Union, China, and Southeast Asia. Sarraut aired his concerns on these matters in the best-selling book *Grandeur et servitude coloniales* and in the influential public address that he delivered in Algeria in April 1927: "Le communisme, voilà l'ennemi."[17]

One of Sarraut's most successful initiatives to neutralize Vietnamese political radicalism was the journal *Southern Wind*, founded in Hà Nội in 1917 and edited by the brilliant neotraditional nationalist Phạm Quỳnh.[18] Unrivaled in influence until its closure in 1934, *Southern Wind* promoted a gradualist reform agenda incompatible with the demands for immediate independence favored by more radical nationalists. Founded three months before the October Revolution, *Southern Wind* provided the first Vietnamese-language account of the event. It quickly adopted a critical stance, chiding the violence and disorder of the Bolshevik seizure of power and the "high-handedness" *(hách-dịch)* of the revolutionary leadership.[19] It continued to follow Soviet developments with a critical eye for the next seventeen years as well as the growth of communism in Asia, Europe, and the colonial world.[20] In addition to reflecting the elitism and conservatism inherent in Phạm Quỳnh's neotraditionalist agenda, the anticommunism of *Southern Wind* drew on diverse foreign sources. For example, it published Trotskyite criticisms of Stalin's failed "Popular Front" strategy in China in 1926–27 as well as an anti-Bolshevik diatribe by the Fabian socialist H. G. Wells.[21]

Following the tone set by Sarraut, officials in Indochina were quick to interpret reformist sentiment as communist subversion. The scandal-plagued Governor of Cochinchina Maurice Cognacq (1921–26), for example, routinely dismissed critics of his corrupt administration as "Bolsheviks" and "revolutionaries."[22] He used the same tactic to reject reforms proposed by progressive activists such as Nguyễn An Ninh. According to one account of an infamous meeting between the two men: "Ninh talked about the necessity of freedom of the press and free exchange of ideas to a successful meeting of the French and Vietnamese worlds, but Cognacq cut him off: 'In this country, we don't need any intellectuals! The country is too simple. If you want to intellectualize, go to Moscow.'"[23] Anticommunist smear campaigns were deployed to similar ends in the conservative French-language press. *L'Opinion* accused the moderate politician Bùi Quang Chiêu of "Bolshevik calculations" after he publicly requested a constitution for Cochinchina.[24] When André Malraux and Paul Monin founded the liberal muckraking journal *Indochine* in Sài Gòn in the mid-1920s, the procolonial newspaper *L'Impartial* denounced them for "following the directives of the Moscow communists to the letter."[25] Monin and Malraux may have added to public wariness toward the Left by rejecting the affiliation and treating the growth of communism in Asia as a "problem" that could be solved through clean colonial governance.[26] This torrent of charges and countercharges cast communism in a sinister light and contributed to a climate of foreboding surrounding the topic.

Reactionary sentiments were further reinforced by the shrill anticommunism of the Vietnamese Catholic Church. "If you want to know the outcome of Communism simply look at China," explained the Catholic writer J. M. Thích in *The*

Question of Communism (Vấn đề cộng sản), published in 1927. "Over the past fifteen years Communism has been responsible for overturning the monarchy, establishing democracy, fomenting civil war, and pushing the populace ever deeper into the mud. Liang Qichao and Kang Youwei are the Engels and Marx of China. Sun Yatsen is the Lenin."[27] Drawing on an established set of arguments worked out by the global Church, the anticommunism of Vietnamese Catholics emphasized the godlessness of Marxism-Leninism and the persecution of religion in the Soviet Union.

While most published material about communism between 1925 and 1930 remained sharply critical, procommunist writing circulated underground and appeared on occasion in left-leaning French-language publications.[28] The first positive discussions of communism in the legal press appeared in Sài Gòn journals such as André Malraux's *Indochine* and Nguyễn An Ninh's *La Cloche Fêlée*. The inaugural issue of *Indochine* featured news about Soviet politics lifted from the French wire service ARIP. On November 26, 1925, *La Cloche Fêlée* printed an editorial that explained differences in the colonial policies of the French communist and socialist parties.[29] Four months later, it started serializing *The Communist Manifesto*.[30] Around this time, activists from the protocommunist Revolutionary Youth League disseminated underground writings featuring the avidly Stalinist discourse that Hồ Chí Minh promoted in his Canton training courses.[31]

The spread of procommunist propaganda peaked with the foundation of the ICP in 1930 and the outbreak of mass protests among peasants and workers at the start of the Depression. Although the precise role of the ICP in fomenting this unrest remains in dispute, there is no question that Party members helped craft the language and political symbolism featured in the protests. Demonstrators staged marches on May Day, unfurled red banners, and chanted communist slogans.[32] Peasant insurgents in Nghệ An and Hà Tĩnh replaced local officials with governing councils known as Soviets. Many parts of Indochina were awash in illegal communist propaganda during this period, and the colonial state countered with anticommunist propaganda of its own. Governor General Pierre Pasquier supported new publications in troubled areas and enlisted progovernment newspapers to denounce the communist scourge.[33] They depicted communists as atheistic, uneducated extremists who preach the destruction of family and community and take orders directly from Moscow.[34] One inflammatory leaflet featured a "communist spider spreading its legs over Indochina." According to David Marr: "Many Vietnamese city folk were shocked at stories of roving peasant gangs arbitrarily confiscating private property and meting out summary punishments. Colonial apologists naturally used these stories to attempt to discredit Vietnamese radicals in general and the Communist Party in particular."[35]

An unintended consequence of the rash deployment of both communist and anticommunist discourse during this period was a growing skepticism about the sincerity and authenticity of expressions of partisan political commitment. Colonial officials perceived the airing of local grievances as veiled instruments of subversion by foreign communist agents. Savvy readers viewed the state's anticommunist campaigns as pretexts for attacking political enemies. Conservative newspapers fed these suspicions by inflating the radicalism of moderate critics of the status quo. The Constitutionalists, for example, were denounced as "the enemies of order . . . who cunningly wish to set up soviets in Indochina and whose praises are sung by the 'proletarian Revolution.'"[36] In their defense, the Constitutionalists bemoaned the use of anticommunism to ignore genuine grievances underlying political unrest.[37]

Because Vũ Trọng Phụng wrote so little about communism prior to 1936, it is difficult to know which aspects of this mottled discourse he consumed and favored. He was doubtless familiar with the anticommunist invective disseminated by the Catholic Church and the colon community, and he certainly consumed the reactionary propaganda that saturated government discourse following the unrest of 1930–31. Indeed, his references to the global ambitions of Stalin and to the aggressive tactics of the Soviet secret police are broadly consistent with this trend. Less clear is the level of access he enjoyed to proleftist writing that circulated during the era.[38] Vũ Trọng Phụng read radical French-language journals based in Sài Gòn, but the availability of southern publications in Tonkin was uneven. It is also unclear the extent to which he read propaganda circulated underground by activists who had returned from training in China and the Soviet Union. Moreover, Vũ Trọng Phụng's extensive writing on communism during the late 1930s does not provide clear insight into his earlier thinking because his shifting opinions toward the end of the decade provide an inconstant index of his previous views.

LEFTWARD TURN: INDOCHINA AND THE POPULAR FRONT

The political content of Vũ Trọng Phụng's work changed abruptly in 1936 when vivid portrayals of class struggle, collective action, and heroic left-wing activists began to appear in his writing. The most famous example occurs in *The Storm*—serialized in *Hà Nội News* between January and September 1936—which centers upon a conflict between the villainous business tycoon Nghị Hách and a heroic communist agent. As the final installment of *The Storm* went to press, Vũ Trọng Phụng started publishing a second explicitly political novel—*The Dike Breaks*—that featured sympathetic communist characters as well as the first portrayal in Vietnamese fiction of a "mass" protest. The positive treatment of left-wing themes and characters in these novels dovetailed with a shift in the local political climate triggered by the rise of the Popular Front in France.[39] Founded with Comintern support in 1934 as both an anti-Fascist mass movement and a political coalition of the Communist Party (FCP), the Socialist Party (SFIO), and the Radical Party (RAD), the Popular Front won legislative elections in May 1936 and formed a government headed by the SFIO leader Léon Blum. The Blum ministry pursued a progressive domestic agenda, the centerpiece of which was a new labor law mandating higher wages, a right to strike, paid vacations, and a forty-hour workweek. Although the Empire was not a priority for the new government, its electoral platform signaled support for a reform of colonial policy. Political opposition and cracks within the alliance undermined most of the Popular Front's program, and the Blum administration was replaced after twelve months in power by a conservative government led by the Radical politician Camille Chautemps. The Popular Front survived as a weakened political coalition for an additional year before it dissolved for good in the autumn of 1938.

Despite its internal fragility, short life span, and vague colonial agenda, the Popular Front transformed the political atmosphere throughout the French Empire.[40] Its platform generated enthusiasm by calling for a general amnesty for political prisoners and the "formation of a parliamentary Committee of Enquiry into the political, economic and cultural situation in France's territories overseas." Upon taking power, Blum appointed the longtime critic of colonial policy Marius Moutet to head the Ministry of Colonies and ordered a purge of conservative colonial governors.[41] Support for the new government within the Empire increased further after it proposed an extension of voting rights to twenty-five thousand Algerian Muslims and a treaty granting limited self-rule to Syrian nationalists. The impact of the Popular Front in Indochina followed this general pattern. "Many people hope that the Popular Front ministry will liberalize colonial policy," wrote Hoài Thanh in *Enduring Peace* on May 22, 1936. "They believe that the government will care for the poor, pass laws protecting workers, and provide the colonies with civil rights that pose no threat to France such as freedom of speech and freedom of association."[42] These early hopes appeared justified when the Ministry of Colonies replaced the unpopular Governor General René Robin with the liberal Jules Brévié and ordered the amnesty of thousands of political prisoners. Brévié introduced a new labor code in December 1936 along with liberal decrees on naturalization and political organization.[43] In response to the appointment of the parliamentary committee, activists in Cochinchina formed grassroots "action committees" as a first step toward the foundation of an "Indochinese Congress." The purpose of the

Congress was to assemble a record of public opinion about colonial rule that could be presented to the Committee of Enquiry during its upcoming visit. At the same time, Indochinese workers staged a series of strikes that were widely covered in a newly energized press.[44]

In addition to upending the political climate, the rise of the Popular Front hastened a change within a slowly evolving public discourse about the nature of communism. Starting around 1933, the vilification of communism in the colonial press as a sinister foreign movement prone to violence and subversion started giving way to more evenhanded portrayals. This change was first felt in Sài Gòn as left-wing activists associated with the La Lutte group took advantage of the liberal legal framework for French-language publishing in Cochinchina to launch newspapers and compete in local elections for seats on the Municipal Council.[45] Political discourse remained muted in the protectorates of Annam and Tonkin, where imperial Vietnamese law held sway, but a growing interest in left-wing politics found expression there as well. On January 10, 1934, the Hà Nội weekly *New Day* reprinted a French article on life in the Soviet Union that reported dispassionately on the living conditions there for workers, soldiers, intellectuals, and peasants.[46] At the same time, local journalists started expressing left-wing sentiments through discussions of *bình dân*, a neologism denoting both the "common people" and the ideology of "populism." This discourse was especially important in Annam and Tonkin as a surrogate for open exchanges about socialism and communism. An essay published in 1934 by the editors of *Fraternity* defined populism *(chủ nghĩa bình dân)* as an effort by Western-educated intellectuals to encourage empathy for workers and the poor. "We have recently observed the appearance of populism throughout Vietnamese society," the editors wrote. "Many people promote populism in literature and in newspapers in order to oppose the dominance within society of the aristocracy and the middle class."[47] An article entitled "Populist Culture" *(Văn hóa Bình dân)* by Hoàng Tân Dân published in *Literature Weekly* encouraged enlightened intellectuals *(dân trí thức tỉnh ngộ)* to resist the ruling class by founding schools to teach the poor about "populist culture" *(văn hóa bình dân)*. Its Marxist-inflected curriculum included "the history of the evolution of nations, sociology, socialism, and political economics."[48] While interest in *bình dân* drew on a leftist French discourse connected to the rise of the Popular Front, it also owed something to a neonaturalist literary movement known as Le Roman Populiste.[49] Founded in the late 1920s, this initiative promoted a non-Marxist literature about the lower classes grounded in observation, sincerity, and sympathy. In 1931, leaders of the movement endowed a national literary award. The critic Thiếu Sơn linked this development to the recent Vietnamese preoccupation with *bình dân* in an essay entitled "Populist Literature" *(Bình dân Văn học)*, published by 1935. The essay traced a genealogy of the recent discourse on *bình dân* to "writings by French authors with a socialist orientation" including Rousseau, Sue, Hugo, and Balzac and finally to the "prix du roman populiste."[50]

With the rise of the Popular Front, the colonial state eased censorship throughout Indochina, and interest in the Left that had been expressed obliquely through the discourse on *bình dân* found expression in extensive news coverage of global communist politics and local radical activism.[51] Animated by an educational mission in addition to journalistic imperatives, colonial newspapers ran stories on the history of socialism and communism and doctrinal differences between European parties of the Left. The mounting hostility between the forces of fascism and communism in Spain and East Asia loomed large in the local press through regular translations of items from the global wire services. The signing of the Franco-Soviet Treaty of Mutual Assistance in May 1935 stimulated coverage of the shifting contours of Stalin's foreign policy. The maneuverings of the PCF and the SFIO before, during, and after the election of 1936 attracted sustained attention as well. Interest in local leftist activism also increased as newspapers covered the dramatic growth of the labor movement and the reemergence of ICP networks overseas and in prison. The La Lutte group in Sài Gòn and the Le Travail group in Hà Nội provided a boost to this burgeoning discourse since they both spearheaded leftist initiatives and publicized them in their influential in-house newspapers. The mass amnesty of political prisoners in 1936–37 resulted in the release of thousands of Party members and fellow travelers whose histories of activism and resistance were chronicled subsequently in press reports and published memoirs.[52]

COMMUNISM IN *THE STORM*

Coinciding precisely with the rise of the Popular Front and the surge of local political journalism that arose in its wake, the serialization of *The Storm* commenced five months before the election in 1936 and concluded four months after the Blum government assumed power. The novel opens with the brutal rape of the peasant girl Thị Mịch by the rich and powerful business tycoon Nghị Hách. In the first of many coincidences, it is revealed that Thị Mịch's fiancé, Long, is employed at a "reformist" school run by Nghị Hách's son Tú Anh. The first two-thirds of the narrative follows the efforts of these four characters—Thị Mịch (the rape victim), Long (her fiancé), Nghị Hách (the tycoon and rapist), and Tú Anh (Nghị Hách's son and Long's boss)—to deal with the consequences of the rape. Nghị Hách uses his power and influence to thwart legal proceedings launched against him by Thị Mịch's family. Thị Mịch attempts suicide, discovers that she is pregnant by the rape, breaks off her engagement with Long, and suffers a mental breakdown that results in the perversion of her heretofore innocent personality. Long undergoes a parallel psychological meltdown and tries to recuperate by sleeping with Thị Mịch and Nghị Hách's frivolous "modern" daughter Tuyết. Meanwhile, Tú Anh upbraids his father and persuades him to atone for the rape by taking Thị Mịch as a second wife.

In the midst of this overwrought melodrama, a mysterious figure named Hải Vân materializes and initiates secret meetings with several characters, paying special attention to Nghị Hách. After a brief period of confusion over Hải Vân's true identity, Nghị Hách recognizes him as an old friend whom he once framed for a crime that he didn't commit. Nghị Hách compounded this act of betrayal by sleeping with Hải Vân's wife, who died, subsequently, in childbirth. The remainder of the narrative dramatizes a revenge plot launched by Hải Vân against Nghị Hách. It involves Hải Vân laying the groundwork to blackmail Nghị Hách by exposing his wife's infidelity along with a pair of shocking revelations about his family: Tú Anh is actually Hải Vân's son, and Long is, in fact, the son of Nghị Hách. The discovery of Long's true paternity is devastating to Nghị Hách as it brings to light several instances of unnatural sexual relations within his family: Nghị Hách's rape of Thị Mịch is revealed as a father's sexual violation of his son's fiancé; the sexual intercourse that transpires between Long and Thị Mịch (after she has married Nghị Hách) is exposed as a case of a son sleeping with his father's wife; and Long's seduction of Tuyết is recast as an incestuous liaison between siblings. Near the end of the narrative, Hải Vân reveals to Tú Anh—newly acknowledged as his son—that he is in fact a communist agent who has engineered the blackmail of Nghị Hách as a means to raise money on behalf of the Party. The novel concludes with Hải Vân bidding adieu to Tú Anh as he sets sail for further adventures in the middle of a violent storm off the coast of Móng Cáy.

At the time of its publication, the most striking feature of *The Storm* was its portrayal of the communist Hải Vân. While ill-defined political activists had appeared previously as characters in Vietnamese literature, Vũ Trọng Phụng's depiction of Hải Vân as a high-ranking Communist Party member was unprecedented.[53] *The Storm* stops short of identifying the Party by name, but Hải Vân's account of training in Moscow at the "Stalin School for Far Eastern Revolutionaries" points clearly to an affiliation with the Indochinese Communist Party.[54] Hải Vân's powerful position is underlined by the gravity and international scope of his political work. Not only does he represent the Party at "a Far Eastern Conference for delegates from the Philippines, Australia, Java, and Taiwan," but he works to "bring together the old Nationalist Party and the new Internationalist Party."[55] In a controversial detail excised from later editions of the novel, Hải Vân alludes to his high rank by admitting that he had once been assigned to "replace Nguyễn Ái Quốc (aka Hồ Chí Minh) as an instructor at Moscow's Collège d'Asia."[56]

As noteworthy as Hải Vân's high profile in *The Storm* is the novel's remarkably flattering depiction of him. Brave, wise, and charismatic, Hải Vân presents a perfect contrast to the thuggish Nghị Hách. His magnetic presence is enhanced by the delay of his appearance until over halfway through the narrative and because readers are privy to the thoughts of every major character in the novel except for him. He also possesses an extraordinary repertoire of talents and skills. He is a gifted linguist, an expert hypnotist, a capable ocean navigator, and a master of disguise. He possesses extensive knowledge of Western medicine and Eastern feng shui. He is a lethal marksman and a skilled martial artist. Hải Vân owes his facility in these areas to the training he received at the Stalin School. "Students there are trained in swordsmanship, shooting, horseback riding diving, swimming, driving cars, flying planes, Western and Japanese martial arts, and political subversion," he explain to Tú Anh. "They also learn rhetorical techniques to win over the masses, the arts of disguise and intimidation, and how to run a security organization and an intelligence service."[57] During the course of the novel, Hải Vân deploys this remarkable skill set to blackmail an enormous sum of money from Nghị Hách to be used for the revolutionary cause.

Some scholars interpret the idealization of Hải Vân as marking the start of a sustained leftward shift in Vũ Trọng Phụng's political orientation. On the other hand, Hải Vân's narrative function as a deus ex machina that abruptly materializes and resolves the plot of *The Storm* may reflect the fleeting and superficial nature of Vũ Trọng Phụng's fascination with the Left in the immediate wake of the Popular Front victory. The latter interpretation gains support from Hải Vân's uneven integration into the structure of the novel and from the way that his belated appearance shifts its focus from the rape of Thị Mịch to Hải Vân's politically motivated plot against Nghị Hách.[58] This narrative U-turn is extraordinary, owing to the absence of even the slightest foreshadowing, during the first half of the novel, that Hải Vân exists and will soon upend the lives of the story's main characters. Equally surprising is the vanishing act of Thị Mịch, who does not appear in the novel's final eight chapters despite the fact that the first half of the narrative conveys an impression that her story forms the centerpiece of the plot.[59]

When seen in light of the novel's fractured structure, the timing of the publication of *The Storm*'s serialized chapters suggests that Vũ Trọng Phụng may have modified the subject of the novel in midstream in response to the electoral victory of the Popular Front. Chapters 1 through 10, which foreground Thị Mịch and provide no inkling that Hải Vân's arrival is imminent, came out between January 2, 1936, and March 18, 1936—months before the rise to power of the Popular Front. *Hà Nội News* ceased publication of the novel for seven weeks following the appearance of chapter 10 (for reasons that remain obscure), but it started up again with chapter 11 three days after the Popular Front's stunning electoral victory on May 3. Chapters 11 through 20, which continue the narrative flow established in chapters 1 through 10, came out in May and June—a two-month transition period during which the new administration in Paris was being assembled. The Vietnamese intelligentsia was preoccupied by rumors during this period that the new government planned to reform colonial policy.

Given this atmosphere of hopeful anticipation, it is perhaps no coincidence that the official formation of the Popular Front government in July 1936 coincided precisely with the publication of chapter 20, in which Hải Vân makes his first appearance and launches the narrative in a new, politically proactive direction. The remaining ten chapters, in which Hải Vân's story comes to the fore while Thị Mịch's fades away, were published from August to late September, amid the euphoria that marked the first months of the Blum administration. The timing of the serialization of *The Storm* raises the possibility that the unexpected victory of the Popular Front may have prompted Vũ Trọng Phụng to insert Hải Vân into a half-finished narrative that had not been assembled initially with his eventual intervention in mind. This justifies a view of Hải Vân as a remarkably literal offspring of the Popular Front victory. Indeed, it is difficult to imagine the appearance of Hải Vân without the relaxation of censorship triggered by the rise of the new government or the onset of a widespread belief that a global confluence of leftist forces was poised to deliver Indochina from its colonial predicament.

While Hải Vân may not reflect a durable or deeply considered ideological conversion on the part of Vũ Trọng Phụng, the portrayal of the character does illuminate important aspects of his understanding of communism. First, it indicates that he was relatively well informed about recent changes in the policy of the Comintern and the ICP. This comes across in Hải Vân's description of the Party's political strategy:

> At the recent Comintern congress in Moscow, Stalin ordered the Indochinese party to put itself under the authority of the French Party so that the Vietnamese people will follow the French proletariat. We predict that the

> Socialists will secure a majority in the 1936 elections and that the party of the Third International will support the new government. Hence, our people should prepare to do whatever is necessary to reform society through legal means. In three more years, our people will have freedom of speech, freedom of assembly, and freedom of movement. You will see organizations of workers and peasants in all three territories of Indochina publicly unfurling banners, demonstrating, and making speeches. As long as they do not attempt to provoke risings against the social order, political activists will no longer be arrested and jailed.[60]

Hải Vân's comments reflect recent changes in the local communist party line in response to directives issued at the Seventh Comintern Congress in July 1935 that provided a formal endorsement of the Popular Front strategy.[61] Triggered by the mounting threat to the Soviet Union posed by Nazi Germany, the Comintern ordered communist parties the world over to join with social-democratic forces in an alliance against Fascism. It also urged them to replace their commitment to class struggle with a moderate anti-Fascist agenda that emphasized the defense of democracy and civil liberties. Parties operating in colonial countries were encouraged to soften their opposition to imperialism in order to focus on the Fascist threat and to refashion their underground networks into legal organizations devoted to mutual aid, sports, and cultural activity. To implement the new policy, the Comintern reorganized its global chain of command, placing communists in the colonies under the authority of more easily controlled metropolitan parties. Allied with the Popular Front, the PCF advised communist parties in French colonies to tone down the intensity of their attacks against imperialism. Hải Vân's assurance that "organizations of workers and peasants" would "reform society through legal means" confirms Vũ Trọng Phụng's awareness of these new developments.

The portrayal of Hải Vân also reveals Vũ Trọng Phụng's appreciation of Vietnamese communism's antagonism toward Vietnamese nationalism. This view was also shaped by the new Comintern line which attacked nationalism as a right-wing political creed that had contributed to the growth of Fascism and militarism. Consistent with this position, Hải Vân condemned nationalism in an exchange with Tú Anh about his political beliefs.

> "Are you a nationalist or internationalist," Hải Vân asked Tú Anh.
>
> "Nationalist, Sir," replied Tú Anh.
>
> Hải Vân frowned.
>
> "How stupid of you!"[62]

Connected to his enmity toward nationalism, Hải Vân rejected extreme anticolonialism as a reactionary form of racism. Instead of dismissing all Frenchmen as imperialist oppressors, he urged Tú Anh to embrace French progressives as potential allies in the anti-Fascist struggle. But because nationalism in the colonies was linked less to the political Right than to a broadly popular anticolonialism, the new Comintern line placed the ICP in the uncomfortable position of having to condemn radical anticolonialists as racists. Hải Vân's awkward fidelity to this new antiracist and antinationalist agenda may be seen in the following passage:

> We should not consider France as our enemy and allow the Japanese militarists to secretly advance their ambitions of establishing a united Asian empire under the slogan "Asia for the Asians." The old regime that oppressed our people originated with the big capitalists—the kings of oil, the kings of mining, the kings of banking, the kings of the automobile industry—but they do not represent all of France. We can perhaps place our hopes in the ideas of popular France expressed by Rousseau, Danton, Robespierre, Blum, and Moutet. This kind of Frenchman can relieve our misery once they gain power even though they have not yet done so. We should not consider France to be our exclusive enemy. On the contrary, real enemies may be found within our own race—those like Nghị Hách who live off the labor of others and oppress the working class. Your ideology of nationalism is narrow and unachievable. To make distinctions based on race is ignorant. You must abandon this ideology and be willing to befriend poor and miserable Frenchmen. The nouveau riche of Annam is your true enemy.[63]

Later in the conversation, Hải Vân exhibits a more tolerant attitude toward Tú Anh's political ideals, admitting that nationalist sentiments were preferable to materialism and bourgeois romanticism. "Don't be like the hundreds of thousands of people who possess hearts and brains but selfishly cling to life and do everything possible to avoid death," he advised him. "If you end up living like those bourgeois dogs and pigs—motivated only by money, love, and fame—that would be a tragedy for our race."[64]

Hải Vân's hostility toward nationalism is of historical interest because most studies of late-colonial Vietnamese political culture tend to downplay the antagonism between nationalism and communism. Indeed, these two ideological currents are often portrayed as naturally supportive of each other.[65] The origins of this interpretation lay in the efforts of DRV scholars and propagandists during the course of the postcolonial civil war to portray the Communist Party as the exclusive standard-bearer of the nationalist movement.[66] Hải Vân's intense antinationalism undermines this view and suggests that the conflation of the Vietnamese nationalist and communist projects dates from a later period.

Finally, the portrayal of Hải Vân reveals a jaded acknowledgment of the Machiavellian nature of communist politics. Driven by his secret plan to blackmail Nghị Hách, Hải Vân's behavior is marked by dissimulation and pretense. His sanctification of ends is apparent in his use of an especially sordid form of blackmail (connected to the sexual peccadilloes of Nghị Hách and his family) as a fund-raising instrument. It may also be discerned in his willingness to engage in conventionally amoral forms of behavior in order to keep his plot on track. He plies Vạn Tóc Mai with opium in order to enlist him in the plot against his father. He does not act to prevent Long from committing incest with Tuyết, although he is the only character in the novel who knows that they are brother and sister. He arranges for Nghị Hách's wife to be caught committing adultery in front of her husband and two sons. But the most shocking example of Hải Vân's amoral instrumentalism occurs when he attempts to cement his renewed friendship with Nghị Hách by joining him at a drunken party in his mansion. The scene opens as follows:

> When Hải Vân entered the room, Nghị Hách was lying with two young girls. They were extremely beautiful and their clothes were so thin and flimsy that they seemed almost nude. The sweet smell of opium wafted through the air. There was almost no furniture in the room, just several plush carpets surrounded by hand-embroidered pillows. Animal skins and stuffed tiger heads lay on each side of the opium tray. A set of champagne bottles sat upon a small table. Next to the wall was a small movie screen that faced a film projector. Miss Kiểm sat on a pillow beside the projector.[67]

Hải Vân is taken to bathe by one of the girls and returns dressed suggestively in a silk kimono. He drinks a toast with Nghị Hách; the lights go dim and, as the scene comes to a close, a pornographic film entitled *Les 32 caresses* is projected onto the screen.[68] The abrupt ending of the scene implies that Hải Vân sticks around to watch the blue movie, smoke opium, and perhaps take part in an orgy. In this case, Hải Vân's cavalier violation of communist ethical norms in pursuit of larger political goals stands as striking testimony to his Machiavellian nature.

Vũ Trọng Phụng reconfirmed key elements of the view of communism expressed in *The Storm* in a public exchange about the novel with the leftist critic Xuân Sa. Writing in the Sài Gòn journal *Woman (Nữ Lưu)* on May 28, 1937, Xuân Sa commended *The Storm* as the first genuine treatment of class struggle in the history of Vietnamese literature and praised Vũ Trọng Phụng as a "populist writer" *(văn sĩ bình dân)* who had "exposed the terrible impact on society of the landlord class represented by the character Nghị Hách."[69] Xuân Sa also lauded the novel's portrayal of Hải Vân as "an enlightened agent of the proletarian class who favors an expansive internationalism over a narrow nationalism."

Following these positive opening remarks, Xuân Sa chided Vũ Trọng Phụng for the passage (cited above) in which Hải Vân refers to the "tragedy of our race." To Xuân Sa, Hải Vân's reference to "our race" *(giống nòi)* implied a nationalist orientation incompatible with the character's internationalism. "This is the sort of language that we would expect from one of those great nationalists from twenty years ago such as Ngô Đức Kế or Phan Bội Châu," he argued. "It is too bad that Vũ Trọng Phụng portrays an internationalist like Hải Vân speaking the language of race. Internationalists do not distinguish between races; this is how old-fashioned nationalists think. To avoid this contradiction, Vũ Trọng Phụng should have replaced the word 'race' with the word 'class' *[giai cấp]*." "*The Storm* would have been a more valuable book," he concluded, "if it had more clearly expressed a 'class spirit.'"

Vũ Trọng Phụng responded to Xuân Sa in a letter published three weeks later in *Saturday Novel*.[70] Appealing to the standards of "realism," he defended himself by pointing out that Vietnamese internationalists frequently employed nationalist language and symbolism in their political appeals. Pressing the point, he noted that the nom de guerre of Indochina's greatest internationalist—Nguyễn Ái Quốc—means "Nguyễn who loves his country." "If internationalists ignored their race," he argued, "why would the leader of the Indochinese Communist Party take the name Nguyễn Ái Quốc?" Reiterating his commitment to realism, Vũ Trọng Phụng argued that he had no choice but to depict this contradiction. "My realistic pen is absolute," he wrote. "I only describe people as they actually are, not—as Mr. Xuân Sa seems to prefer—as they ought to be."

In an additional line of defense, Vũ Trọng Phụng drew attention to communism's Machiavellian tendencies. In response to Xuân Sa's charge that Hải Vân's language contradicted his ideology, Vũ Trọng Phụng insisted that the character had used a discourse of race as a ploy to appeal to Tú Anh's nationalist sympathies:

> It would be foolish and inappropriate to change the word "race" in that passage to "class." The main reason is that Tú Anh is a nationalist from a wealthy class background. Since he is not a worker, he might even be considered an enemy of the common people. Hence it would be unreasonable to expect a savvy

> revolutionary like Hải Vân to talk about class with him. When revolutionaries try to propagandize among the wealthy, they often appeal to "race" to make a real impact. It would be stupid to speak like a communist to a rich person. Moreover, all revolutionaries—whether nationalist or internationalist—feel entitled to behave in whatever way they please as long as it benefits the revolution.

Vũ Trọng Phụng's assertion that Hải Vân's amoral instrumentalism reflects the behavior of all revolutionaries—"whether nationalist or internationalist"—dovetails with a broader skepticism toward partisan political discourse that ran like an unbroken thread through his writing during the second half of the 1930s. Indeed, *The Storm* features several additional depictions of the duplicitous manipulation of political expression. In an important subplot of the novel, Nghị Hách retaliates against the villagers bringing rape charges against him by denouncing the accusations as part of a communist plot. "Landowners today are under siege from the communist movement," he explains to the local magistrate investigating the case. "Workers at my coal mines in Quảng Yên are threatening to strike and even the peasants employed on my plantations are starting to cause trouble."[71] Linking this general growth of communist sentiment to hidden motives behind the rape accusation, he insists: "The people of this village are accusing me falsely. They are following the rebels . . . who put outrageous words into their mouths. They have unjustly accused me of murder, rape, labor exploitation, and every imaginable crime. Their motive is simple: to sow seeds of hatred against the rich."[72] Later that evening, Nghị Hách instructs his henchman to plant phony communist leaflets and red banners in the village of his accusers. "Make sure to drop some behind the magistrate's office," he tells him, "and scatter a few around the assembly hall."[73] The discovery of the leaflets triggers an aggressive search of the village by the district chief and the local gendarme:

> The search terrorized the village, making the atmosphere unbearable. Everyone in the village—young and old—was gripped by fear when they saw both the chairman and vice chairman of the Council of Elders and the mayor and deputy mayor of the village trembling like leaves before the upturned mustache of the militia commander and the shiny bayonets of the four militiamen. The commander held aloft the red banners and the leaflets written in purple lettering and chastised the village officials who cowered before him. A militiaman shouted at a crowd of trembling onlookers and they scattered in confusion like flies swarming from the buttocks of a cow that has just lashed itself with its tail.[74]

This act of intimidation has the desired effect: "That afternoon, the village elders met to discuss the rape case. They worried aloud about the consequences of the incriminating leaflets that had been boldly and anonymously distributed in their midst."[75] With the tables turned against them, the villagers drop the suit.

Another episode from *The Storm* conveys a similar but more complex picture of the duplicitous subtext behind communist, anticommunist, and reformist discourse in the colony. Coveting an elected position as chairman of the Tonkin Economic Council, Nghị Hách enlists the help of an experienced French fixer who has lived in Indochina for thirty years. The Frenchman advises Nghị Hách to bribe newspaper editors to slander his opponent as a "traitorous capitalist." "And will they praise me in turn?" asks Nghị Hách.

> The Frenchman laughed. "Don't be naïve. The newspapers that I plan to bribe will not praise you either. Instead, they will attack you even more fiercely. I will help you to draft an ambitious agenda of social reform that will include enhanced rights for workers and peasants. As a result, French newspapers will accuse you of being a revolutionary . . . a communist. Vietnamese newspapers will then report that you have been attacked by the right-wing French press and your election will be ensured. It will be as easy as falling off a log."[76]

In the victory speech that he delivers after winning the election, Nghị Hách alludes slyly to his reputation as a left-wing radical within the right-wing press:

> "I am full of empathy for my fellow countrymen and I feel compelled to give up some of my property to help them. That is why I decided to organize two campaigns of poor relief. However, a newspaper with a significant interest in acquiring a monopoly over the production of fish sauce has subjected me to withering attack. It accuses me of fleecing the people, of being a communist agent, and of taking bribes from Russia." Nghị Hách laughed. "But I have decided to ignore this so-called public opinion since my conscience is clear. I was born a commoner and I will remain loyal to the masses until the day that I die."[77]

To repeat, critical discourse about *The Storm* in the DRV has focused overwhelmingly on what the novel indicates about Vũ Trọng Phụng's attitude toward communism. For some critics, the amoral behavior of Hải Vân was crafted to slander the leadership of the ICP. Others identify a largely procommunist sentiment in the narrative juxtaposition of the heroism of Hải Vân with the villainy of Nghị Hách.

Ignored by critics, however, is a deeper antipolitical subtext embedded in the novel that raises questions about the sincerity and authenticity of all local forms of partisan commitment. In other words, the novel's attitude toward the main political projects of the day may be less significant than its critique of the general corruption of Vietnamese political culture under colonial conditions. The presence of this theme in *The Storm* foreshadows the negative turn in Vũ Trọng Phụng's thinking about communism that would emerge in full force the following year. Prior to this ideological about-face, Vũ Trọng Phụng published *The Dike Breaks,* his second major political novel.

COMMUNISM IN *THE DIKE BREAKS*

Serialized in *The Future* between September 1936 and March 1937, *The Dike Breaks* carries on Vũ Trọng Phụng's sympathetic but qualified engagement with communism first expressed in *The Storm.*[78] Set in the precise time and place in which it was written (Tonkin during the second half of 1936), the novel dramatizes the radicalization of Phú, an unemployed ex-student with strong nationalist convictions and vague leftist leanings. Phú's political commitments are shaped by a family tradition of anticolonial activism. His father died on Poulo Condore while imprisoned for a political crime and his older brother, Teacher Minh, languishes in the same island penitentiary for participating in the Vietnam Nationalist Party's failed uprising of 1930. At the start of the novel, Phú is following news reports of the recent French election while helping his mother and sister manage a small farm in the Red River delta. Just as it inspired the political storyline that starts to loom midway through *The Storm,* the victory of the Popular Front launches *The Dike Breaks*'s central narrative concerning the ideological transformation of Phú.

> The daily news about the Popular Front in France filled Phú with hope. He believed that the new government might eliminate "misunderstandings" between the two peoples. He hoped that the conquered might come to view the conquerors as benefactors if only they were not treated as enemies or threatened with extermination or enslavement. The complete victory of workers and peasants—unprecedented in the history of France—made Phú see his ideology of nationalism as narrow and flawed or worse. An independent Vietnam with an independent king or president but unable to defend its borders, enlighten its peasants, or protect its workers from hunger was perhaps no better than a Vietnam colonized by a humanitarian France that prized justice.[79]

Confronted by a village official who raises doubts about the Popular Front's commitment to reform, Phú defends the colonial policy of the new government:

> In the past, the government was not yet in the hands of the popular forces. In the past, the capitalists controlled everything. For them, colonies were only kept to be exploited and this is what made us miserable. But things will be different now that the Socialist Party has taken power. Socialism embodies universal values, advocates peace, and opposes racial discrimination. The platform of the Socialist Party includes a plan for the liberation of the colonies and the provision of justice and freedom to backward peoples. This will permit the motherland and all of her colonies to form a huge bloc, a magnificent unity that will restore the nobility of France in the eyes of the world.[80]

The first half of the novel takes place in the countryside, where Phú observes the oppression of the peasantry by corrupt local officials. His political awareness grows after he joins a gang of coolies conscripted to repair a dike threatened by rising floodwaters. He experiences the terrible working conditions for corvée laborers, including abuse from overseers and inadequate food, water, and medical care. In the overcrowded hovels where the coolies sleep, Phú witnesses the widespread alcoholism, gambling, and thievery that mark the culture of the rural poor. When the coolies clash with local officials over unpaid wages, Phú emerges as the leader of a small protest. He is arrested, accused of communist subversion, and thrown into jail. In a scene remarkable for its graphic depiction of police brutality, a team of Vietnamese jailers torture Phú. They strip him naked, bind his hands and feet, and drip hot candle wax into his anus. Phú escapes from jail with the help of Miss Dung, the district chief's romantic "modern" daughter. As he makes his way back to his mother's house, the dike breaks and floodwaters submerge the surrounding countryside, throwing local communities into chaos.

In the second half of the novel, the narrative tacks back and forth between the flooded countryside and Hà Nội, where Dung has relocated due to the demotion of her father (a consequence of his failure to protect the broken dike). Chapters set in Hà Nội introduce readers to Phú's brother, Teacher Minh, who has been released from jail thanks to the Popular Front's amnesty for political prisoners. In conversation with a friend, Teacher Minh laments the destructive impact on local society of colonial capitalism and implies that he has transferred his allegiance from nationalism to communism while in prison. He returns to live with his family in the countryside and persuades Phú to move to the capital to find work. In Hà Nội, Phú reunites briefly with Dung and meets with activist-journalists at the communist newspaper *Labor*. Meanwhile, back in his native village, Teacher Minh leads a second peasant protest, this one demanding tax relief following the onset of a ruinous drought. He is arrested and sentenced, once again, to hard labor on Poulo Condore. With Minh in prison, Phú returns home to care for his mother and, in a final scene, contemplates two courses of action. One is to return to his beloved Dung and embrace the modern urban lifestyle and reformist social vision that she embodies. The other is to join the radical journalists at *Labor*. In an internal monologue, Phú rejects the temptation of bourgeois reformism represented by Dung. But he does not commit fully to the more radical alternative and, as the novel comes to a close, the political choice confronting him remains unresolved.

The Dike Breaks testifies to the maturation of the leftist sympathies that Vũ Trọng Phụng first expressed in *The Storm*. In place of the exuberant revolutionary romanticism embodied in the communist superagent Hải Vân, *The Dike Breaks* substitutes a developmental narrative of class struggle and communist awakening. This plodding storyline resembles the transition from "spontaneity" to "consciousness" that scholars of Soviet literature have identified as the "master-plot" of socialist realism. According to Katerina Clark, "consciousness" within this tradition "is taken to mean actions or political activities that are controlled, disciplined and guided by politically aware bodies. 'Spontaneity,' on the other hand, means actions that are not guided by complete political awareness and are sporadic, uncoordinated, even anarchic or can be attributed to the workings of vast impersonal forces rather than to deliberative actions."[81] In *The Dike Breaks,* the movement from "spontaneity" to "consciousness" is dramatized most clearly in differences between the protest of coolies led by Phú and the subsequent antitax demonstration led by his brother. The former is unplanned and it descends into chaos as soon as armed police confront the protesters.[82] As the confrontation intensifies, the coolies act at cross-purposes and disband in an uncoordinated fashion.[83] Looking on in disgust, "Phú hated the coolies more than the police. Nothing could be achieved unless leaders and followers worked resolutely and in unison. Instead, the ardor of the coolies was like a straw fire, exterminated as soon as it ignited. A worthy project had been squandered by the childishness of the effort. Such a defeat could only spawn more defeats in the future."[84]

In contrast, the antitax protest led by Teacher Minh unfolds methodically following a series of secret meetings in a village communal house: "Teacher Minh, Mẫn, and several local village officials formed a supervisory committee. To recruit participants into a procession of the poor, the committee took turns issuing orders and telling people which slogans to shout. Guided by skilled, experienced leaders, the people obeyed and maintained their determination."[85] The depiction of the procession emphasizes its orderliness and unity of purpose. Confronted by the provincial governor, the mob speaks in unison, demanding tax relief and cheering the Popular Front: "The governor was dumbfounded. The slogans of the crowd and its civilized way of speaking recalled newspaper descriptions of protesters from Hà Nội and Sài Gòn. He never imagined that this kind of revolution could occur in the countryside."[86] Intimidated by the disciplined tactics of the crowd, the governor agrees to a brief postponement of the annual tax collection.

The Dike Break exhibits additional affinities for socialist realism through its admiring portrait of local left-wing activists working in Hà Nội for *Labor*—"a newspaper that supports the proletariat." Seen through the eyes of Phú, the newspaper office is a hive of purposeful activity: "Seventeen men were seated around a wide table messily strewn with newspapers. On the walls were photos of the socialist leader Jaurès, the Minister of Colonies who had recently freed Indochina's political prisoners and several pro-Vietnamese French writers."[87] The radical Vietnamese journalists working at *Labor* are a picture of critical engagement: "Embittered and enraged by the sudden arrest of Minh, they argued over the proper course of action as if they were throwing themselves into a brawl. To generate support for Minh, they spread news of his arrest to brothers and comrades who shared the same ideology. They also sent a telegram to the Governor General denouncing the official who authorized the arrest."[88] In an interior monologue toward the end of his visit, Phú praises the courage and idealism of the communist journalists: "These were resolute men who viewed prison as a school for training defenders of the exploited and opponents of those who profit from the labors of others."[89]

Given the novel's positive portrayal of communist intellectuals, its narrative sequencing of the two peasant protests, and its formal organization around Phú's journey toward political consciousness, it is tempting to view *The Dike Breaks* as a pioneering Vietnamese experiment in socialist realism. Adding to the plausibility of this reading is the fact that socialist-realist aesthetics had been worked out in the Soviet Union, translated into French, and disseminated within Vietnamese literary circles during the years just prior to the appearance of the novel.[90] On the other hand, there is no concrete evidence that formal prescriptive guidelines shaped Vũ Trọng Phụng's composition of the narrative. Hence, although similarities between *The Dike Breaks* and socialist realist fiction suggest that Vũ Trọng Phụng's flirtation with the Left persisted through the first half of 1937, they do not indicate that his work was inspired directly by communist cultural policy.

Moreover, the leftist ideals expressed in *The Dike Breaks* coexist with countervailing sentiments expressed in the narrative that might be seen as more durable elements of Vũ Trọng Phụng's worldview. For example, the novel is preoccupied with the failing health of the Vietnamese nation. During a conversation with Teacher Minh, his boyhood friend Quang laments that the Vietnamese are an "immoral, uneducated, and underdeveloped nation *[dân tộc]* lacking ideals and resigned to slavery for over one thousand years":

> The essence of our nation produces slavish intellectuals. The spirit of slavery is our precious national heritage passed down from one generation to the next. As slaves of China, we followed Chinese civilization. As slaves of the French, we view Europe as the pinnacle of civilization. If blacks from the Sahara desert colonize us, our intellectuals will demand Africanization as the new key to civilization.[91]

Teacher Minh voices agreement:

> We must consider carefully whether we ought to Europeanize or not. Many think that living like Westerners is the apex of progress and civilization. They do not know that Duhamel, Gandhi, and Oscar Wilde have already exposed and denounced the West. They do not know that the West is a rotten society based on injustice in which money and materialism pervert traditional customs. We should wait until the West evolves further before we follow it.[92]

Nationalist convictions in the novel are also apparent (ironically) in Phú's admiration for communism. While he mentions the doctrine's vision of social justice for workers and the poor, he dwells upon its capacity to unify a fragmented national community. This comes across in his admiring depiction of the social diversity of the journalist-activists working for *Labor:* "They come from such a wide array of social classes," he thinks to himself, "laborers, students, intellectuals, and the sons of mandarins and rich families. Phú was surprised that people from such different backgrounds could work together for the same ideology."[93] Phú also admires the collaborative and inclusive nature of their efforts to protest the incarceration of his brother: "Everyone eagerly contributed ideas to help craft the protest letter. One young man insisted on using prudent language that would not provoke legal retribution from the 'hammer of bourgeois law.' Another argued for stronger language.

Several greeted Phú but those busy writing continued to write. Those busy reading continued to read. And those busy speaking continued to speak. They invited Phú to join them."[94]

Phú's nationalist embrace of solidarity in diversity—including the diversity of social class—runs against the grain of his communist inclinations because the novel, like *The Storm*, emphasizes the incompatibility between the two ideologies. This conviction is restated in *The Dike Breaks* when Phú asks a communist editor at *Labor* what he thinks of nationalism. "It deserves some respect," the editor replies, "but at the moment it is a negative force. Violence will only provoke terrible repression, which threatens to set back our society by twenty years. There are some who understand socialism but who have chosen to embrace a narrow nationalism owing to the difficulty of the struggle. This is a mistake!"[95]

What impresses Phú most, however, is the apparent sincerity of the communist activists: "Meeting them inspired an indelible sensation in the heart of Phú. . . . These men were sincere *[thành thực]* in their beliefs to the point of ideological zealotry. Moreover, they were thorough internationalists and not—as reactionary colons often claim—vague, impulsive, and ignorant. They were neither phony communists nor nationalists disguised as internationalists."[96] The earnest dedication of these left-wing activists surprises Phú because the persecution of his brother by the colonial administration had diminished his earlier faith in the Popular Front's commitment to reform. In an interior monologue, Phú complains that the "arrest of Minh had occurred during a period in which both the Governor General and the resident of the province were Socialists and when everyone in France and the land of Nam was preoccupied with the masses, the proletariat, liberation, and freedom."[97] Phú expresses skepticism about the Popular Front to the assistant editor of *Labor*, who defends the Blum government by blaming reactionary colons for undermining its mission:

> Of course, what you describe is, indeed, dangerous and unacceptable, but we should not blame the Popular Front. The colonial bourgeoisie is at fault. We are weak and must continue to struggle in order to achieve our aims. An enduring problem is the lack of confidence between the two races. They fear that we are not sincere just as we doubt the sincerity of every initiative that they launch. Both sides are undermining the other. Hence, we must try to make them trust us. How can this be done? First, we must be sincere. We must also strive to give them the benefit of the doubt in some areas. If we engage in politics without sincerity and with a constantly changing ideological orientation, we will never achieve anything.[98]

Here, Vũ Trọng Phụng returns to a familiar concern with the ultimate significance of the sincerity of political commitment. With the waning of his flirtation with communism following the publication of *The Dike Breaks,* this sentiment acquires deeper importance in his political writing. It is also significant that Phú's rejection of bourgeois reformism in the final scene of the novel is not accompanied by a renewed commitment to either nationalism or communism. Phú's indecision here is striking, given the oppression and exploitation that he has witnessed during the course of the narrative and the efforts undertaken (by his brother and the *Labor* journalists) to convince him of the virtues of communism. After all he has been through, Phú—perhaps like Vũ Trọng Phụng—remains poised on the political fence.

"NOTES ON 1936"

Published in *The Future* in February 1937, "Notes on 1936" marks the apex of Vũ Trọng Phụng's brief period of conspicuous leftist sympathy.[99] The essay reviewed the remarkable political changes of the previous year—"a special year in our history"—including the electoral victory of the Popular Front, the appointment of Marius Moutet to head the Ministry of Colonies, and, most importantly, the "awakening of the Indochinese masses."[100] It praised this "awakening" as a "positive omen for socialism" *(cái triệu chứng tốt cho chủ nghĩa xã hội),* singling out the upsurge of labor activism, the campaign to form an Indochinese Congress, the amnesty movement for political prisoners, the hunger strikes of jailed members of the La Lutte group, and the proliferation of public rallies and protest demonstrations. In conclusion, the essay commended the Popular Front for helping the masses realize their humanity through political activism. "In the past, we did not know the desire to become human *[làm người],*" Vũ Trọng Phụng wrote. "But now that we have begun to feel this desire we must prepare ourselves for the difficult struggle ahead. The lower classes, the poor landless peasants, and the scum of society all want to become human: to have enough to eat, to have a job, to be able to speak their minds, to be led by the light of science so that they might be able to laugh next year without fearing to look stupid."

Although favorably disposed toward the Popular Front, "Notes on 1936" suggests that opposition to reactionary anticommunism (a kind of anti-anticommunism) may have animated Vũ Trọng Phụng's political thinking as much as a positive enthusiasm for the Left. It is instructive that the essay barely touches upon the doctrinal virtues of communism or socialism while emphasizing how the nonviolent political activism triggered by the Popular Front gave the lie to the reactionary propaganda that had circulated in Indochina since the early 1920s:

> Since Monsieur Blum took power, people have begun to talk publicly about populism *[bình dân]* and politics. In France there are seventy-two communist delegates and eight million communist workers. This should raise doubts in the minds of peasants, hidden away behind green bamboo hedges, about the description of communism in the book *The Mask of the Communists* by Trọng Khiêm (also the author of *The Tearful Story of Kim Anh*). Maybe communists are not a gang of thieves who share husbands and wives, rob and kill people for their fortunes, and eat children and rape women. In spite of what has been crammed into their heads for the past dozen years, the poorest peasants are coming to understand that France remains a civilized country even though it is now proleftist and friendly with Soviet Russia.

Vũ Trọng Phụng further rebukes reactionary ideologies by suggesting that hatred for imperialism, fascism, capitalism, and ultranationalism was the major reason that colonized peoples had turned toward socialism and communism:

> Italy's occupation of Ethiopia has helped even the dimmest brains here to realize the nature of imperialism and fascism. It also helps people to make crucial distinctions between the various groups in the colonial government; the socialist-leaning group is much more generous and easy for colonized people to bear than the capitalist group or the ultranationalist group. The chaotic situation in Spain in which Franco has borrowed the fascist armies from Germany and Italy and black soldiers from Morocco to kill his fellow countrymen has also shaped the thoughts of Vietnamese people regarding the two ideologies that seem to be driving everyone crazy at the moment. As a result of these world events, Vietnamese people have started to care about politics. They are waking up, stretching their shoulders, and overcoming the exhaustion that comes with being asleep for thousands of years.

While the passage leaves little doubt about Vũ Trọng Phụng's political sympathies at the time, the observation that the population was being "driven crazy" *(làm đảo điên)* by both the Left and the Right suggests a measure of detachment from the political passions of the day rather than a firm commitment to ideological partisanship. This diffidence foreshadowed a change in his political views. During the eighteen months following the appearance of "Notes on 1936," Vũ Trọng Phụng's writing revealed a swift erosion of his faith in the Left. It criticized the Popular Front, denounced the Soviet Union, and chided the arrogance, ignorance, and insincerity of local left-wing activists. The transformation of Vũ Trọng Phụng's views during this period must be understood in light of evolving political developments at home and abroad as well as the shifting contours of a local discourse about leftist politics during the era.

"COMMUNIST FREEDOM" AND THE LIMITS OF POPULAR FRONT REFORM

Vũ Trọng Phụng's disenchantment with the Left reflected growing disappointment, felt throughout the French Empire, in the failure of the Popular Front to deliver on its promises for colonial reform. The seeds of this popular disillusionment had been planted as early as July 1936, when the new Minister of Colonies reaffirmed official support for France's civilizing mission and rejected independence for the overseas territories.[101] Faith in the government's commitment to reform eroded gradually throughout the fall of 1936 as local French interests and colonial security forces moved decisively to thwart directives issued from Paris designed to expand freedom of the press, movement, and association.[102] Other reforms foundered owing to the obstructionism of colonial bureaucrats. Foot-dragging and a lack of funding prevented the Parliamentary Commission of Inquiry into Colonial Conditions from carrying out its work, and it was dissolved without ever setting foot in Indochina.[103] By the end of 1938, parliamentary opposition had killed the Viénot Treaty providing limited self-rule for Syria and the Blum-Violette law extending electoral rights to the Algerian elite.[104] The persistence of police repression and inadequate funding for colonial development confirmed the essential continuity of the government's policy toward the Empire.[105]

In Indochina, dissatisfaction with the Popular Front followed a parallel trajectory. Dashing the hopes of workers and union activists, Governor General Brévié cracked down upon organized labor and issued a draconian antistrike directive at the end of 1936. In April 1937, Vietnamese students bemoaned a similarly intolerant local edict against political activity in schools.[106] Newspapermen turned against the new government as the Sûreté raided editorial offices, shuttered political journals, and repressed a budding Association of Indochinese Journalists devoted to ending censorship. The cancelation of the visit by the Commission of Inquiry demoralized Vietnamese activists, given the extensive organizational efforts that it had inspired.

Equally unpopular was the government's persecution of the Indochina Congress movement, including the arrest on trumped-up charges of Tạ Thu Thâu, Nguyễn An Ninh, and Nguyễn Văn Tạo on three separate occasions (September 1936, May 1937, and October 1937). The impact of these repressive measures on local attitudes toward Leon Blum's government may be discerned in the lead editorial of the newspaper *Public Opion (Dư Luận)* penned by Vũ Trọng Phụng's colleague Phùng Bảo Thạch on August 8, 1938:

> After two years under the authority of the French Popular Front, isn't it high time we drew up a balance sheet of its accomplishments? Why not? The government freed some political prisoners and implemented a portion of the new labor law. It also drew up plans to send a commission of inquiry to Indochina. But otherwise, it is hard to see what the Popular Front government has done for us. Freedom of speech? No. Freedom of assembly? No. Freedom of movement? No. In short, no fundamental changes to the regime. In response to the paltry gains that have been achieved, we chant with all our hearts: Support the Popular Front government! Long live the Popular Front government! But despite these expressions of fidelity to the government, Minister of Colonies Moutet mistreats us and accuses us of rebellion. This is all we get for backing the government.[107]

Vũ Trọng Phụng anticipated these complaints about the stinginess of government reforms in an editorial published by the *Indochina Journal* on October 30, 1937.[108] Entitled "Communist Freedom," it opened by praising a recent decree by Attorney General Dupré that prohibited the use of criminal subversion laws to prosecute individuals for membership in communist organizations. "We were initially amazed by this sudden change in policy," he wrote.

> It made us believe in the generosity of Minister Moutet, in the power of the Left in France, and in the work of the [PCF] assemblyman Honel. But the communists here don't dare to believe it. They suspect that it may be a rumor spread by the newspaper *La Volonté Indochinoise.* Can it be that, suddenly, without drums or trumpets, the government has endorsed a freedom that the colonial capitalist clique views as dangerous? While many remain skeptical, we believe that this announcement is real. After all, not only is the communist party legal today, but it is a pillar of the government. Annamese communists are neither violent nor antigovernment like they were after the Yên Báy uprising. Moreover, if Indochina goes to war against Japan tomorrow, the

communists will certainly encourage Annamese to take up arms and fight. Hence, although it sounds absurd, granting freedom to communists may actually help to protect Indochina.

But after commending the substance of this policy, the essay chided its limited scope and the ad hoc manner of its delivery:

> Monsieur Dupré's edict draws attention to another aspiration of the people of Nam: the desire for a broader framework of freedoms characteristic of a democratic republic. If we want guaranteed freedoms, the French assembly must put into place a new legal regime. A decree issued today may be revoked easily by a different one tomorrow. The first decree promotes the illusion—widespread among noncommunists especially—that we will soon have complete freedom. But when the International Communist Party abandons the populist struggle in France or lacks the force to oppress Trotskyists of the Fourth International or loses popular support to nationalists like Nguyễn Thái Học, then perhaps a new decree will overturn M. Dupré's edict, sending the local comrades of M. Honel back to prison at Côn Lôn and Lao Bảo. Hence, what we really need is a complete menu of freedoms sanctioned by the French National Assembly. The Annamese need freedom to travel to France, freedom to go abroad, freedom of assembly, and freedom to do business; they need more than simply the freedom to be communists. When the government liberalizes, it must do so properly, meaning that it must legalize all the main parties: the party of the monarchy, the party of direct rule, the party of nationalism, the party of democracy. Our land is not under the "dictatorship of the proletariat," so why should the government only grant freedom to the communist party? (In the South, there are two formal parties: the Constitutionalist Party and the Democratic Party, but they do not represent the majority.) Hence, we hope that Dupré's announcement is simply a first step toward the introduction of a new regime of freedom that Minister Moutet has promised to the people of Indochina *[Đông Pháp]*.

While the essay may be read as an expression of support for the ICP, its portrayal of the communist movement is mixed. It depicted communist activists as nonviolent anti-Fascists victimized by colonial persecution. But it also raised questions about their vendetta against Trotsky and the sincerity of their political beliefs, which vacillated unpredictably with changes in the party line. By including the "freedom to do business" in his list of essential rights and calling for equal protection for Monarchist and

Nationalist parties, Vũ Trọng Phụng further departed from the agenda of the communist Left. Indeed, although its title implied a focus on the question of communism, the essay's larger objective was to advance a liberal republican project for the protection of civil liberties. To this end, it portrayed the government's policy shift as another autocratic decree that contributed little to the development of a truly republican regime. The point, in other words, was that the reformist rhetoric of the Popular Front masked an enduring commitment to a repressive French colonial project.

POLITICAL INSINCERITY IN *DUMB LUCK*

One difficulty in characterizing Vũ Trọng Phụng's politics during the rapidly evolving climate of late 1936 and early 1937 is that his most ardently leftist writings like *The Storm* and "Notes on 1936" appeared simultaneously with his scathing antipolitical satire *Dumb Luck*. While it did not single out the communists for special ridicule, the novel's across-the-board mockery of all political movements encompassed parties of the Left. *Dumb Luck*'s frontal attack on the insincere populism and frivolous reformism of the Vietnamese urban elite may also be read as an indirect criticism of the Comintern's Popular Front strategy that required parties on the Left to form alliances with bourgeois reformists such as Mr. and Mrs. Civilization, Miss Snow, and Dr. Straight-Talk. Moreover, *Dumb Luck*'s derisive portrayal of its central character, the casual laborer Red-Haired Xuân, may be read as a subversive commentary on an idealized social and political group within communist discourse. While clearly the victim of class oppression, Xuân is motivated by little more than sex and survival. In a similar vein, the novel's portrayal of professional activists echoes suspicions raised in *The Storm* about the authenticity of political discourse. Toward the end of the novel, a rival of Xuân hires two clownish political operatives to disrupt a procession, leading the King of Siam to observe Xuân compete in a politically significant tennis match. Xuân eavesdrops on the plotters and learns of their subterfuge.

> "I will print up leaflets saying 'Down with the King of Siam!' When the King makes his entrance, I will sneak up behind Xuân and you will stand next to him."
>
> "What then?"
>
> "You will slip several leaflets into the pockets of his shirt and pants."
>
> "What about you?"
>
> "Me? My role is even more heroic than yours. I will scream 'Long live the Popular Front Government! Long live Democratic France!' Naturally, policemen and undercover security agents will arrest us immediately . . ."

"Oh no!"

"But then only those found to have leaflets in their pockets will be taken into custody. The two of us will bear witness to the fact that it was Xuân who yelled the slogan. We will be released immediately."

"I see! But why will they arrest someone for yelling 'Long live the current government! Long live Democratic France!'?"

"That's easy! Although France, which rules over us, is a democracy, we are a monarchy with a king. Siam is also a monarchy! To welcome kings with slogans supporting democracy implies a desire to overthrow the monarchy! The Protectorate Government is very sensitive to this sort of thing. If we scream: 'Long live Democratic France!' I guarantee that somebody will be arrested."[109]

Moments later, Xuân spies two police agents charged with providing security for the parade. Listening in on their conversation as well, he overhears an analogous plan to selectively crack down on different types of protesters—communists, nationalists, monarchists, fascists, and liberal democrats—so as to influence popular perceptions of the composition and strength of the political opposition. The juxtaposition of this exchange with the plotting of the clownish provocateurs underlines the breadth of Vũ Trọng Phụng's scorn for the sincerity of both revolutionary and counterrevolutionary speech.

Dumb Luck displays similar doubts about the sincerity of recent reformist discourse in a satire of two "civic-minded" orations presented to mark the opening of a new tennis court. As described by the narrator, the first speech, delivered by the idiotic social reformer Mr. Civilization, "possessed all the necessary attributes of a formal oratorical address by a great man of letters or an important politician: embellishment, fabrication, exaggeration, fantasy, and duplicity—all dressed up in the dishonest language of literature. The crowd applauded enthusiastically."[110] The second speech, delivered by Xuân himself, comprised a hodgepodge of political slogans, ceremonial homilies, and advertising jingles arbitrarily strung together and delivered in a loud and confident voice. Despite its evident absurdity, Xuân's speech is warmly received after the audience overhears an unrelated expression of approval from an inattentive member of the crowd who had been reading his newspaper during the course of the presentation:

Xuân concluded his speech. Hip. Hip. Hip . . . Hoorah!

Just then Joseph Thiết read in his newspaper that royalist journalists were calling for the head of the socialist Léon Blum. Joseph Thiết, originally a member of the Fire-Cross party, slapped his thigh and yelled out approvingly: "Bravo! Bravo!"

> Following his lead, the crowd broke into thunderous applause. . . . Several skeptics in the crowd applauded as well but only because Red-Haired Xuân had delivered his own extemporaneous speech instead of relying on a pre-recorded gramophone announcement.[111]

As with his depiction of the manipulation of political slogans during the parade for the King of Siam, Vũ Trọng Phụng's account of the tennis court orations raises doubts about the reliability of the public language of politics. In this second case, however, the artificiality of political language stems as much from the ignorance of the Vietnamese public as from the bad faith of political elites. This implies that Vũ Trọng Phụng viewed the insincerity of political expression and commitment as an intractable problem rooted in local society that could not be ameliorated merely through the reform of elite behavior. The persistence of this preoccupation in his subsequent journalistic writing suggests that cynicism toward all manner of partisan discourse may have trumped Vũ Trọng Phụng's preference for the views any particular political camp.

VŨ TRỌNG PHỤNG AND THE MOSCOW SHOW TRIALS

The doubts about the Left conveyed obliquely in Vũ Trọng Phụng's early political writings found full-throated expression in a lengthy essay on Soviet politics that he published in *Indochina News* during the autumn of 1937.[112] Entitled "The Schism between the Third and Fourth Internationals: A Reexamination of the Communist Revolution in Russia from Its Origins until Today," it was serialized in three installments between September 25 and October 9. In a brief introduction, the editors explained that the purpose of the essay was to educate readers about the history of the conflict between Stalin and Trotsky so that they could form learned opinions about analogous infighting within the Vietnamese Left:

> The division within the communist party in the world today has spread to Indochina. The newspaper *Friends of the People [Bạn Dân]* is exchanging insults with the band of Tạ Thu Thâu, while the band of Tạ Thu Thâu cannot forgive the gang at *Avant Garde*. Each faction claims to be the true followers of Lenin. In the last analysis, the workers of Annam in the middle of this mess are left to observe a noisy, topsy-turvy scene—a tangled situation that is truly hard to unravel. Standing outside the biases of each party, we feel that all ideologies

(isms) in the world today have their good and bad points, and the good and the bad can vary according to circumstance. In addition, practical implementation can turn the good into the bad and vice versa. But the most important thing to do first is to try to figure this all out. Once we have a clear understanding, we can strive to form a correct opinion about the ideologies that most people simply cheer or denounce in a vague, apish, or slavish way. . . . We hope that the following article by Vũ Trọng Phụng which summarizes information from several French newspapers will enlighten many people in this regard.

Mentioned at the outset of the text, "The band of Tạ Thu Thâu" referred to a small group of southern political activists (including Tạ Thu Thâu, Phan Văn Hùm, Huỳnh Văn Phương, Trần Văn Thạch, Phan Văn Chánh, and Hồ Hữu Tường) that gravitated toward Trotskyism while studying in France during the late 1920s.[113] Returning to Sài Gòn in the early 1930s, these youthful radicals promoted Trotsky's ideas through newspapers and Marxist study groups. They also worked with a small southern labor movement to further Trotsky's strategy for working-class revolution. The emergence of the group irked local Stalinists who had recently formed the ICP under Comintern auspices and Hồ Chí Minh's leadership. But the destruction of the ICP in the wake of the Depression rebellions preempted sectarian bickering between the two Marxist factions.[114] The ICP reemerged toward the middle of the decade, but its fragility discouraged its leadership from attacking the "leftist deviationism" of the local Trotskyists. Not only was open conflict avoided but, starting in 1933, Nguyễn An Ninh brokered a remarkable alliance between Stalinists and Trotskyists in Sài Gòn. Together, they formed the La Lutte group, which published an eponymous muckraking newspaper and promoted a unified list of candidates in Sài Gòn's municipal elections. La Lutte was rooted in the South but its activities were widely followed throughout Indochina. On May 25, 1935, Phan Khôi devoted a column to La Lutte in the Huế newspaper *Enduring Peace* that explained how four members of the group—Trần Văn Thạch, Nguyễn Văn Tạo, Tạ Thu Thâu, and Dương Bạch Mai—had won electoral victories despite their "communist views."[115] Stimulated by the Popular Front victory, La Lutte diversified its activities, founding grassroots action committees and spearheading the movement for an Indochina Congress.

But the rise of Popular Front, on the one hand, and Stalin's escalating persecution of "Trotskyism" at home and abroad, on the other, precipitated the dissolution of La Lutte. Caught off guard by the formation of hundreds of action committees sponsored by the group, the colonial administration cracked down on its leadership, arresting Tạ Thu Thâu, Nguyễn An Ninh, and the Stalinist Nguyễn Văn Tạo on trumped-up charges of political subversion in September 1936.[116] In their absence, the newspaper fell under the control of Hồ Hữu Tường, the most doctrinaire partisan of Trotsky among the original founders of the group.[117] As a result, La Lutte began giving voice to Trotsky's criticism of Moscow's Popular Front strategy as an unprincipled betrayal of the working class.[118] The growing anti-Stalinism of the newspaper dovetailed with the bitter aftermath of the first Moscow show trial in August 1936. La Lutte plunged into the recriminations between Vietnamese Trotskyists and Stalinists—a malicious political cross fire reinforced by an analogous global discourse covered closely in the local press. Rent by this public schism, the collaborative initiative behind La Lutte suffered a fatal blow in 1937 when both the Comintern and the PCF ordered the ICP to withdraw from the alliance. Retrospective efforts to apportion blame for the break may be seen in the forum "Why Did La Lutte Break Apart?" published in Sài Gòn's *Daily News (Nhựt Báo)* on September 4, 1937.[119] It featured a Trotskyite account entitled "Because of the Stalinists" and a Stalinist account entitled "Because of the Trotskyists."

In addition to partisan barbs, the Indochinese press published a range of sober, informed commentary on the Soviet political scene, much of it negative. In 1937 alone, excerpts and summaries of eyewitness accounts of the Soviet Union (many in Vietnamese translation) appeared by Paul Vaillant-Couturier, Roland Dorgeles, Jean Raynaud, Louis-Ferdinand Céline, Walter Citrine, Jean Giono, and Victor Serge.[120] A profile of Boris Souvarine reprinted his meticulous account of the punishments and executions carried out during the purge. "Does Stalin Maintain Power by Murder?" Souvarine asked, "What is the truth?"[121] The most influential eyewitness accounts were two works by André Gide: *Retour de l'U.R.S.S.* (1936) and the sequel *Retouches à mon "Retour de l'U.R.S.S"* (1937).[122] Both featured harsh criticism of the absence of freedom in the Soviet Union and signaled the great writer's famous flight from the communist Left.[123] Hugely popular among the Vietnamese intelligentsia, Gide and his infamous political about-face were the subject of scores of articles and editorials in the local press. In 1936, two of Vũ Trọng Phụng's's close colleagues—Lê Tràng Kiều and Lưu Trọng Lư—issued a literary-political manifesto (together with the critic Hoài Thanh) based on Gide's opaque postcommunist humanist politics. Entitled *Literature and Action,* it defended Gide's rejection of communist cultural and political orthodoxy, while endorsing his support of complete intellectual freedom.[124] It also provided an approving summary of Gide's complex ideological project, which it depicted as a mélange of individualism, socialism, classicism, symbolism, and historicism.

It was within this context that Vũ Trọng Phụng's essay appeared. It provided a brief history of the Russian Revolution, including Lenin's early political activities, the upheavals of 1905 and 1917, the first years of the Soviet Union, and the metastatic growth of schisms and purges within the Party, culminating in the first two show trials of 1936–37. It praised Lenin's early revolutionary efforts, but it also commented warily on his unnerving single-mindedness, which it contrasted to "weaker revolutionaries such as Trotsky, Krassine [Kautsky], and Marsov [Martoff]." Lenin's relentless will to power echoed even after his death since he made arrangements "to be worshiped by later generations as a red Christ." The essay then traced the history of Stalin's drive to "rule Russia as an absolute dictator" and the brutal consequences of his rise to power: "Even though they have not yet lost faith in the mystical ideals of communism, one hundred and sixty million Russians are now facing starvation." Turning to Soviet politics under Stalin, the essay detailed the exile of Trotsky, recurring waves of police repression, the persecution of political rivals, and the trials and executions of the Old Bolsheviks: "During this period, Stalin has acted without the slightest shred of humanity. But what did he want? What did he hope for? Was his heartlessness simply an arrogant plot to live up to the name: the Man of Iron and Steel?" The essay also condemned Stalin's groundless denunciation of political enemies as Trotskyists and Fascists. The fantastic nature of these charges suggested that the confessions proffered at the Moscow show trials may have been coerced. While these suspicions brought discredit upon Stalin, the essay stressed the general duplicity of communist political culture by acknowledging the plausibility of the charge that "Trotsky may have colluded with Nazi Germany, given the legacy of sneaky and treacherous communist tactics dating from the earliest days of the revolutionary struggle."

Near the conclusion of the essay, the "Machiavellianism" of communist politics emerges as its central theme. Vũ Trọng Phụng located the origins of this political impulse in the conditions of illegality and persecution within which the communist movement developed. "Under the monarchical regime," he explained, "the Bolshevik faction . . . was fiercely repressed; Lenin's father and brother were both executed for communist subversion. This explains why the Bolsheviks became masters of stealth and disguise." Vũ Trọng Phụng attributed the penchant to "do whatever is necessary to achieve victory" to the influence of Lenin. "This mode of operation, originating with Lenin, infiltrated gradually into the souls of the revolutionaries. Like Lenin, Bolsheviks are two-faced. . . . They appear gentle on the outside, but they never forget the revolution or the notion that to achieve it: *Tous les moyens sont bons*. The cunning trickery promoted by Machiavelli in the past endures in this modern form of politics *(machiavélisme politique).*" A Machiavellian approach to politics persisted after the revolutionary victory: "Once communism had gained power, Lenin continued to use treachery to exterminate opponents, crush remnants of the old order, and eliminate outdated customs and corrupt royalist sentiments so that Russians might enter a new spiritual era free from the old prejudices of the past." The point here was not to single out Lenin for criticism, but to demonstrate that his political proclivities embodied communism's general penchant for sectarianism and amoral instrumentalism.

> Trotsky opposes situational tactics because he believes that it damages the world revolution and the souls of the Russian people. He wants to rouse the groups that ignite rebellious fire and, if necessary, send the Red Army to attack capitalist countries—make communism by blood and fire. . . . Stalin, on the other hand, acts as if he doesn't care about the wider world. He focuses on the fate of one country, allowing Russia to join the League of Nations—the organization that Lenin once referred to as an association of bandits devoted to raping backward nations. Stalin is accused by Trotsky of taking the Russian people down the road of imperialism. On the other hand, Stalin is willing to temporarily halt the world revolution to address the interests of the Soviet Union so as to stop the encroachments of Japan and Germany.

In a concluding passage, the essay warned of the dire global consequences of the schisms dividing the Soviet political elite:

> Stalin and Trotsky denounce each other as counterrevolutionaries. The truth is that both sides are undermining the revolution through their divisiveness, their sniping, and their very destructive shooting at each other. This benefits only Mammon, who claps his hands and roars with laughter. And the workers of the world, in addition to bearing the burdens of exploitation, tomorrow will have to shoot each other because of Stalin and because of Trotsky.

"The Schism between the Third and Fourth International" gained notoriety in the DRV during the mid-1950s when it was cited by powerful conservative critics as proof of Vũ Trọng Phụng's Trotskyite leanings.[125] Its republication as a stand-alone pamphlet by a Trotskyite press in Sài Gòn in 1938 bolstered this tendentious interpretation.[126] But even a superficial reading of the essay discloses an equal degree of contempt for Lenin, Stalin, and Trotsky as well as disdain for the divisive impact of Soviet sectarian infighting on Vietnamese politics. Moreover, the central criticism advanced in the essay was a general assault on the Machiavellian nature of communist politics and the amoral hunger for power of communist politicians. This line of attack may be seen as a more forceful version of the reservations about the Left and about partisan political commitment that Vũ Trọng Phụng raised in his earlier writing.

THURSDAY NOVEL, 1938

During the ten months between his essay on the Soviet purges and his most stridently anticommunist journalistic composition (published in August 1938), Vũ Trọng Phụng published three articles in the short-lived Hà Nội journal *Thursday Novel* that shed additional light on his political views. Two of them departed from his established concern with colonial policy and party politics to explore the plight of a particular Vietnamese social class. "The Failure of the Petty Bourgeoisie to Achieve Consciousness during a Social Revolution" depicted the economic insecurity and political malaise of the local petty bourgeoisie (defined as "owners of enterprises with fewer than ten employees").[127] It expressed sympathy for their economic predicament, but it chided their conservative politics and urged them to ally with the working class rather than "the bankers and big capitalists." Shifting focus to the bottom of the social ladder, the second article, "We See Nothing," sketched pathetic portraits of the poor, including thieves, beggars, and scavengers in the towns and destitute vagrants in the countryside.[128] "Today's most urgent struggle is the struggle of the masses," the essay concluded. "It is more pressing than the struggle for democratic freedoms or the emancipation of women or anything else. Priority must be given to the people's livelihood." This preoccupation with the plight of the poor is consistent with priorities that Vũ Trọng Phụng expressed throughout his career. But his comments here may also be read as a veiled criticism of the Left's fidelity to a Popular Front strategy that subordinated the promotion of the global class struggle to the national security interests of the Soviet Union. This critique overlapped with Trotsky's well-known warning that Stalin's focus on anti-Fascist alliance-building threatened to water down the revolutionary agenda of the Left. But rather than embrace the equally tactical alternative program promoted by the Fourth International, Vũ Trọng Phụng demanded merely that the interests of the poor remain at the center of the local political agenda.

These two articles reveal that Vũ Trọng Phụng's growing contempt for the political behavior of the Left did not diminish his outrage at social injustice or his sympathy for the subaltern classes. Moreover, the analytic language, explanatory frameworks, and sympathy for the underdog on exhibit in the essays suggest the persistence of a crude Marxian approach to social problems. For example, "The Failure of the Bourgeoisie" opened by asserting the materialist premise that ideological orientation is isomorphic with class identity before dissecting the shifting dynamics of the local class struggle. Indeed, Vũ Trọng Phụng's decision to write a pair of discrete essays on the state of the petty bourgeoisie and the working poor confirms the enduring significance of class analysis within his political thinking. In short, Vũ Trọng Phụng's political views in 1938 combine disdain for the organized Left with a persistent fidelity to a Marxist analytic sensibility and core leftist principles, including, most importantly, the imperative of maintaining sympathy for the poor.

The third article from the period—"An Unplanned Interview with an Old and Troublesome Councilman"—comprised a transcript of an impromptu dialogue between Vũ Trọng Phụng and Nguyễn Phương Đạm, an elderly representative from Bắc Ninh Province on the Tonkin Council of Notables.[129] Although the Council possessed little formal power, elections for seats on it were fiercely contested, involving partisans of the monarchy, the urban elite, the provincial gentry, big business, and eventually local Stalinist and Trotskyite factions. As a member of the Council, Nguyễn Phương Đạm earned praise from Vũ Trọng Phụng for criticizing parties on both the Right and the Left. "And what is your opinion of our own communist party?" Vũ Trọng Phụng asked. "It disappoints me," Nguyễn Phương Đạm responded. "By forming an alliance with the petty bourgeoisie and supporting conservatives like Nguyễn Đình Tiếp and Phạm Hữu Chương simply in order to isolate [the Trotskyist] Huỳnh Văn Phương, they reveal how weak they really are. Let's speak no more of them." Toward the end of the interview, Vũ Trọng Phụng pressed Nguyễn Phương Đạm to define his own political orientation. The representative answered: "Not to brag, but I resemble Deputy Bergery in France. He shows that you can be effective without joining a political party. Bergery attacks the two hundred families, but he also attacks bad things going on in Moscow. Right-wing zealotry is harmful but so is left-wing zealotry, perhaps even more so. Our society needs more people like Bergery." Vũ Trọng Phụng responded by praising this "special old man" for his "eloquence" and for upsetting the expectations of his "disastrous" colleagues on the Council of Notables.

The exchange with Nguyễn Phương Đạm supports the general picture of Vũ Trọng Phụng's post-1936 politics sketched so far. His admiration for Nguyễn Phương Đạm was linked to the latter's refusal to join a political camp—a decision that parallels Vũ Trọng Phụng's well-known allergy to party membership. Nguyễn Phương Đạm's evenhanded criticism of both the Right and the Left dovetails as well with Vũ Trọng Phụng's doubts about established political projects. These tendencies were also associated with the French deputy Gaston Bergery, whom Nguyễn Phương Đạm singled out as a political model. A militant anti-Fascist during the early 1930s, Bergery founded the Front Commun contre le Fascism; but he was also a strident anticommunist whose newspaper *La Flèche* railed against the Moscow show trials.[130] It is instructive that Bergery's newspaper published Victor Serge, whose anti-Stalinist writings were discussed in the Indochinese press during this period. Reading the same journalism and debating the global economic slump, the coming World War, and the international strategy of the Comintern, Vũ Trọng Phụng, Nguyễn Phương Đạm, Victor Serge, and Gaston Bergery participated in a shared transglobal political culture that nurtured common commitments and sensibilities.

CHANNELING STALINISM

One week after amplifying Nguyễn Phương Đạm's scorn for the ICP, Vũ Trọng Phụng published in *Thursday Novel* a biting satire of local communist discourse using the sardonic pseudonym "The Mallard." Entitled "A Stalinist's Appeal: Down with the Trotskyist Huỳnh Văn Phương!" the essay was presented as a verbatim transcript of a monologue by a "revolutionary communist."[131] "If you want to be a good communist fighter," the transcript begins, "the most important thing is to obey the Party. After seeing hundreds of brothers and sisters bravely denounce Huỳnh Văn Phương at his home, I wish—as a genuine communist party member—to add my support to the slogan: down with Huỳnh Văn Phương."

The remainder of the essay featured a hysterical denunciation of Huỳnh Văn Phương, a leading southern Trotskyist best known as a founding member of La Lutte. But he was also an important figure in the neglected history of northern Vietnamese Trotskyism. After falling out with Tạ Thu Thâu in 1935, Huỳnh Văn Phương moved to Hà Nội, where he became known as "the only Trotskyist with a clear political orientation in all of Tonkin."[132] In September 1936, he joined forces with the ICP activists Trần Huy Liệu and (the future general) Võ Nguyên Giáp to found *Le Travail*, a leftist French-language newspaper modeled on *La Lutte*.[133] Born at a time when "the term 'Trotsykist' had not yet been heard on anyone's lips," the collaboration between Huỳnh Văn Phương and the Stalinists came together around a "minimalist" agenda endorsed by the Comintern that was anti-imperialist, pro-worker, and crudely Marxist-Leninist.[134] But this improbable alliance fell apart amid mutual recriminations in April 1937. "*Le Travail* dispersed and fighting broke out among its ex-members," recounted Trương Tửu, who witnessed the breakup and reported on its aftermath. "A number of clear political tendencies emerged from this terrible period and the term 'Trotskyist' appeared on the lips of people debating the struggle against capital."[135]

Stalinist efforts to blame Huỳnh Văn Phương for the rupture of *Le Travail* may be seen in Trần Huy Liệu's one-sided account of the episode:

> Huỳnh Văn Phương was a Trotskyist but he was unable to subvert our support for the Popular Front—an attempt to merge the people's struggle of Vietnam with the people's struggle of France. At this time we had not absorbed the lessons that Nguyễn Văn Tạo, Dương Bạch Mai, and Nguyễn Văn Nguyên learned when they worked with Tạ Thu Thâu's gang. But because we were more resolute, Huỳnh Văn Phương could not usurp the direction of the newspaper as he had in the South. His influence was limited. Huỳnh Văn Phương in the North made up lies to gain supporters and persuade some to move *Le Travail* against the Popular Front government and the People's Democratic Front in Indochina, in opposition to the policy of the French Communist Party. But during two important meetings of our group, this tendency was defeated.[136]

From then on, Huỳnh Văn Phương's old comrades contrived absurd allegations against him, and he withdrew from the political arena. On July 8, 1938, a crowd mobilized by the ICP in Hà Nội to voice support for the waning Popular Front encountered Huỳnh Văn Phương on the street during the course of a public rally: "They shouted 'down with Huỳnh Văn Phương' and subjected his name to all manner of slander, but he refused to respond and remained silent."[137] Published three weeks later, Vũ Trọng Phụng's parody was inspired directly by this incident.

Vũ Trọng Phụng's satirical Stalinist monologue presented a sequence of increasingly fanatical accusations. It condemned Huỳnh Văn Phương as "an enemy of communism, the Soviet Union, and Comrades Zhu De, Stalin, and Honel." It denounced him as a spy for Franco and the "Chinese reactionaries," and it attacked his links to the southern Trotskyist movement.[138] The essay charged Huỳnh Văn Phương with "committing a big crime at the newspaper *Le Travail*" and causing the arrest of its publishers, Nguyễn Văn Tiến and Trịnh Văn Phú: "Thankfully, not all of our comrades have been entrapped by this agent of Japanese Fascism." Alluding to Huỳnh Văn Phương's opposition to the ICP's tactical alliance with the bourgeoisie, the essay poked fun at its conservative new comrades.[139] The "revolutionary communist" then switched to an indictment based on guilt by association: "The people you befriend reveal the kind of person you are. Your friend in the South is Thâu, whom our good friends Hải Triều and Đào Duy Kỳ have bravely denounced as a spy for the Fascists. Thâu *pretended* to write articles supporting the proletariat in La Lutte. He then *pretended* to be jailed until today. Even more contemptibly, Tạ Thu Thâu *pretended* to stage a hunger strike for twenty-eight days in order to win the hearts of the Vietnamese masses. This cruel fraud cannot be forgiven—we must unmask this fake revolutionary!" Building to a frenzied conclusion, the essay accused Huỳnh Văn Phương and his Trotskyist colleagues of wrecking, political assassination, and controlling the weather:

> After hearing all this, brothers and sisters may be able to guess the next disgusting deed of Phương that I am about to denounce? On July 23, the subversive culprit Huỳnh Văn Phương called up a violent storm off the coast of Tourane which destroyed over twenty boats. Wherever they go, the damn Trotskyists sow subversion. In Russia, they shot down the plane of Maxim Gorky and tried to sabotage the Dniepostroi Dam and an electrical factory in the Ukraine. They have seized oil fields in Mexico and plotted to assassinate the son of Mussolini in Spain. And here, it seems, they even conjure up storms at sea.

Vũ Trọng Phụng may have decided to make Huỳnh Văn Phương's fall from political grace the centerpiece of an anti-Stalinist diatribe because the ICP's role in this affair embodied everything that he had come to dislike about communist political behavior. It was brutish, bullying, hypocritical, and opportunistic. It justified any means to achieve and maintain power. It bent the truth and employed vulgar modes of argument such as character assassination and guilt by association. *Le Travail*'s breakup also highlighted the divisive impact of the communists on the Left, a theme explored as well in Vũ Trọng Phụng's essay on Soviet history. Even more significantly, the Huỳnh Văn Phương affair exposed the Vietnamese Stalinists as a handmaiden of foreign communist powers as alluded to at the outset of the piece by the reference to Stalin, the FCP deputy Maurice Honel, and Zhu De, the head of CCP armed forces.

The reference to Honel was especially pointed since he was widely seen, at the time, as personally responsible for the breakup of *Le Travail*. According to Trương Tửu, the catalyst for the schism occurred when Honel, on orders from the Comintern, instructed the ICP in Tonkin to terminate its collaboration with Huỳnh Văn Phương and the Trotskyists. His account, corroborated by Trần Huy Liệu, is worth quoting at some length:

> From the moment Honel of the FCP arrived in Indochina, he cruelly split the struggle movement of the proletariat fighters from North to South into two halves: Stalinist and Trotskyist. I do not make this comment to criticize or to praise the actions of Honel. I am only recording a truth of history. Let me repeat: Honel came to Indochina with one mission: to divide the group of fighters into two antagonist fronts. I don't fear that anyone will object to this. I myself helped to greet Honel. I participated, from the outset, in every discussion that took place between the communist party members. I heard clearly the slogans that Honel ordered the comrades here to use in their activities. On another occasion, I shall relate my memories of all of the meetings between Honel and our comrades here. I only want to reiterate the point—so that everyone is clear—that the division between the Third and Fourth Internationals, especially in the North, was the work of Honel. I still hear echoes in my ears of the words this French communist spoke to the brothers at *En Avant* and *The Times [Thời Báo]:* "I warn you, my friends, be on careful guard against the Fascists since they are brutal and dangerous. But I also warn you to reject the Trotskyists. This group is one hundred times more dangerous than the Fascists." . . . These were the first words spoken by Honel when he set foot in Hà Nội. This is also what he repeated in each of his meetings. And it was the last word he spoke before he left Indochina. After carrying out the Party's orders, he returned to France. After hearing the words of Honel, *En Avant* and *The Times* dared to insult Trotskyism. They also insulted those veering toward Trotskyism. It is no surprise that one target of these insults was someone that the group of *Le Travail* had previously loved and respected. I'm speaking of Huỳnh Văn Phương. Trotskyism then spread to every mouth. To confront these insults, Huỳnh Văn Phương and several like-minded friends founded *Le Progress Social*. But this newspaper closed after several issues. In this case it was thwarted from the inside, not from the authorities. Men desire monopolies when they engage in political activity. *Progress Social* failed. Huỳnh Văn Phương retired and stopped his activism. The Third International maintained its monopoly over propaganda.[140]

Trương Tửu's account cannot be dismissed as partisan propaganda since there is no evidence that he possessed Trotskyite leanings at this time.[141] Although historians have never explored Honel's role in the breakup of *Le Travail*, documentary sources hint at the accuracy of Trương Tửu's account.[142] An ICP report from October 1937 alludes to the divisive impact of Honel's visit, stating that "he addressed the problem of factionalism facing our Party."[143] A Central Committee resolution from March 1938 describes a confrontation between Honel and southern

Trotskyists during a public meeting in Sài Gòn.[144] Most importantly, Trần Huy Liệu confirms the thrust of Trương Tửu's account, noting that Honel ordered local Stalinists in Hà Nội not to work with Trotskyists at a meeting at the office of the ICP paper *En Avant,* where he denounced them as "offspring of the Fascists."[145] As a close friend of Trương Tửu and an acquaintance of Trần Huy Liệu, Vũ Trọng Phụng was certainly aware of Honel's role in the breakup of *Le Travail.* This dimension of the story may have fed a growing concern on his part that local communists were instruments of foreign powers.

CONCLUSION

This chapter has shown that in addition to fluctuating in response to the fast-moving political developments of the 1930s, Vũ Trọng Phụng's attitude toward communism was shaped by two enduring political sentiments. The first was a form of colonial nationalism that prized communal unity and resisted foreign interference in local politics. The second was a form of late colonial republicanism that rejected the despotism, duplicity, and pervasive unfreedom of communist political culture. Vũ Trọng Phụng's writing between the fall of 1938 and his death less than a year later focused on psychological issues and avoided direct discussion of politics.[146] Hence, the extremely critical portrayal of communism that he expressed in "A Stalinist's Appeal: Down with the Trotskyist Huỳnh Văn Phương!" remains his final word on the topic.

It is tempting to dismiss the assortment of complaints about the communist movement raised by Vũ Trọng Phụng as the personal preoccupations of an unaffiliated, self-educated loner. But the expression of related concerns by some of his colleagues in the northern press suggests that Vũ Trọng Phụng's views belonged to a small but important strain of local anticommunism that was institutionally weak but nevertheless collectively felt by a significant number of intellectuals during the period. They included such eminent figures as Phan Khôi, Trương Tửu, Ngô Tất Tố, Lê Tràng Kiều, Vũ Ngọc Phan, Lưu Trọng Lư, Hoài Thanh, Vũ Bằng, and Phùng Bảo Thạch. Members of this cohort were professional writers of modest means and education who never traveled abroad or formed organized groups. In this way, they differed from the southern activists of La Lutte whose anti-Stalinism derived from a Trotskyite critique that they had encountered while studying in France. Whereas members of La Lutte crafted political and philosophical treatises, Vũ Trọng Phụng and his colleagues wrote some of the most accomplished novels, poetry, and criticism of the era.[147] A perusal of northern newspapers between 1936 and 1938 turns up numerous echoes of Vũ Trọng Phụng's views on communism in the writing of this cohort. In an essay published in 1936 condemning communist despotism and duplicity, Phan Khôi suggested that "Lenin and Stalin are no different than Mussolini or Hitler."[148] Writing in 1937, the brilliant literary critic Vũ Ngọc Phan dismissed local expressions of communist commitment as "more like a 'fad' than a real belief."[149] In 1938, the journalist Phùng Bảo Thạch complained that "Annamese people are being driven crazy by the so-called fighters of the Third International" due to their shifting tactics and sectarian bickering.[150] That same year, the novelist Ngô Tất Tố compared the infighting of Lenin's heirs to the petty sectarianism of the disciples of Confucius.[151] In short, these men affirmed the substance of Vũ Trọng Phụng's criticism of communism in Indochina as a movement that was despotic, derivative, and divisive.

Perhaps the most striking rehearsal of Vũ Trọng Phụng's views was expressed by Hoài Thanh, Lê Tràng Kiều, and Lưu Trọng Lư in their jointly authored essay "Literature and Action." The essay attacked censorship and other forms of political despotism practiced by "dictatorial regimes" in Germany and the Soviet Union, and it ridiculed the faddishness of local left-wing activists who "lurch rashly toward utopian theories or vague metaphysics."[152] Its most scathing invective, however, was reserved for the insincerity of communist culture. "Poetry that is not sincere is worthless," it argued, in a dismissive analysis of a formulaic communist poem entitled "A Drop of Proletarian Sweat."[153] Calling on writers to "cherish the concept of sincerity within our conception of literature," it concluded: "In short, freedom and sincerity are the two essential pillars necessary for the construction of a rich literature."[154] Of central concern to Vũ Trọng Phụng as well, this commitment to sincerity had complex intercultural roots in the writing of Rousseau, the Sino-Vietnamese Confucian tradition, and the pervasive insincerity of politics and society in colonial Indochina. For the authors of "Literature and Action," however, the high priest of the cult of sincerity was André Gide, who urged artists to strive for truthfulness in order to unmask hypocrisy and duplicity. In a follow-up essay entitled "The Solitary Road of an Intellectual," Lưu Trọng Lư defended Gide's controversial exposé of Soviet life since it "came from a place of sincerity."[155] Vũ Trọng Phụng never disclosed the precise source of his own fixation with the virtues of sincerity, but his friendship with the authors of "Literature and Action" suggests that their shared preoccupation was not coincidental. Vũ Trọng Phụng dedicated *The Storm* to Lê Tràng Kiều. And Lưu Trọng Lư delivered the eulogy at his funeral.

The common critique of communism expressed by these men developed in an uncoordinated fashion as a kind of shared remonstration against the disagreeable behavior of local communists and the ruthlessness, hypocrisy, and sectarianism of Stalin and his rivals. This view differed from the anticommunism of the Church and the Confucian elite, which was linked to a defensive posture toward traditional authority that Vũ Trọng Phụng and his colleagues did not share. It also diverged from the anticommunism of the colonial state and business community since it was not animated by a philosophical or a self-interested desire to protect capitalism. The neglect of this strain of anticommunism in the historical record reflects the success of the communist movement in disseminating an image of its enemies as right-wing extremists. However, although Vũ Trọng Phụng and his friends never created an institutional vehicle for the expression of their views about communism, their remarkable popularity as writers and journalists during the interwar era raises the possibility that a larger audience may have existed for their message.

CHAPTER FOUR • The Crisis of Vietnamese Sexuality

As with the rise of capitalism and the emergence of communism, the growth of sexual deviance and immorality in colonial Vietnamese society figured prominently in Vũ Trọng Phụng's writing. While he rejected, as prudish and ill-informed, charges of pornography launched against his graphic, and sometimes lurid, treatment of prostitution, rape, infidelity, and the reckless sexual behavior of Vietnamese youth, he also acknowledged a deep professional interest in these topics. In response to an interview that attempted to probe his priorities as a writer, Vũ Trọng Phụng volunteered the following account of his literary mission:

> There are three kinds of work that I must do. The first, which I call social work *[công việc xã hội]*, involves describing the obscenity *[dâm đãng]* of wealth and power—the obscenity of Nghị Hách, for example. Here is a man with eleven wives who still rapes a young peasant girl, destroys entire families, and disgraces and humiliates many people. My second task is to describe the sexual urges of pubescent girls who lack sufficient education. I address this issue in *To Be a Whore*. . . . My third task is to address the grief and suffering caused by poverty and, in particular, the epidemic of prostitution that I describe in *Venereal Disease Clinic*.[1]

Given the wide array of current events, cultural trends, and political issues that he wrote about during the tumultuous 1930s, it is striking that Vũ Trọng Phụng singled out the promotion of sex education for girls and the "epidemic of prostitution" as two of his three most pressing concerns as a writer. Moreover, the links that he posited between prostitution and poverty, on the one hand, and obscenity and wealth and power, on the other, point to a consistent conflation, within his thinking, of class oppression and sexual immorality.[2]

Vũ Trọng Phụng's fixation with sexuality and sexual deviance was noted by the major critics of his day. Vũ Ngọc Phan complained about his taste for "sexual theories" *(thuyết tình dục)*, a preoccupation that he detected in a crude form of "sexual determinism" that structured many of his narratives.[3] Phan Khôi—an outspoken admirer of Vũ Trọng Phụng—claimed that his "obsession with female sexuality" stood out as his only literary vice.[4] Less sympathetic critics such as Thái Phỉ, Nhất Chi Mai, and Hoài Thanh condemned his work as "filthy," "perverted," and "decadent."[5] Likewise, allegations of obscenity played a central role in the decisive indictment that the politburo member Hoàng Văn Hoan issued against Vũ Trọng Phụng in 1960.[6]

The most interesting analysis of this controversial aspect of his work may be found in the literary memoir of his close friend Lan Khai, who claimed that Vũ Trọng Phụng's sexual obsession was a direct symptom of the two diseases that eventually killed him: tuberculosis and opium addition.[7] Lan Khai suggested that Vũ Trọng Phụng's poverty and physical frailty frustrated his burgeoning erotic imagination and prevented him from achieving sexual satisfaction during his life. In this view, Vũ Trọng Phụng's salacious prose should be read as a textual manifestation of the repression of an artificially inflated libido: "He wrote literature to release the passions that boiled in his blood."[8] Whatever the merits of Lan Khai's crude physiological explanation, its invocation of a localized version of the "repressive hypothesis" draws attention to the importance of a crypto-Freudian orientation in some of Vũ Trọng Phụng's own writing that may have contributed to his reputation for sexual obsession.

Unfortunately, the available scholarship on discourses about female sexuality and prostitution in colonial Vietnam provides a poor guide to Vũ Trọng Phụng's large body of writing on the topic. While the intensity of interwar debates over the "question of women," in general, and prostitution, in particular, has been mentioned in passing by many scholars, there have been few attempts to describe the content of this discourse, to account for its characteristic features, or to analyze its significance.[9] Moreover, the handful of studies that do exist share a dubious assumption that debates on these issues should be interpreted as metaphorical expressions of political concerns that colonial censorship prevented from being aired in public. According to Hue-Tam Ho Tai, "gender acted as a coded language for debating a whole range of issues without overstepping the limits imposed on public discourse by colonial censorship."[10] These included "abstract issues of morality, social structure, independence, collaboration, empowerment, liberty and equality."[11] In a similar vein, Huỳnh Sanh Thông claimed that, "by the second decade of this century, among those scholars who actively or passively resisted French domination, prostitution had become a tacitly understood metaphor for a willingness to submit to foreign rule."[12]

There are good reasons to question this approach to Vietnamese public discourse about prostitution and female sexuality. Most importantly, the notion that these issues functioned discursively as metaphors for more "important" political matters assumes the presence of a hierarchy of significance within the thinking of interwar Vietnamese writers and readers that may not, in fact, have been present. While high politics and anticolonial struggles have dominated the agenda of postcolonial historians of Vietnam, they may not have loomed quite as large in the thinking of educated Vietnamese during the 1930s. After all, anticolonial movements were fragmented and ineffectual for much of that decade while the colonial state managed to maintain an aura of invincibility that was only shattered by the Japanese occupation during World War II.

Vũ Trọng Phụng's extensive writing about the growth of prostitution and sexual immorality does not appear to have functioned merely as a strategic metaphor to attack colonialism. Rather, his work on the topic suggests both an appreciation of the potency of sexuality as an instrument of social critique and a genuine preoccupation with the degeneration of Vietnamese sexual norms and behavior as a pressing social problem. These contrasting approaches to sexuality are on display in two major novels by Vũ Trọng Phụng that address sexual themes almost exclusively: *Dumb Luck* and *To Be a Whore*. *Dumb Luck* employs representations of sexual deviance and dysfunction to satirize the superficiality and hypocrisy of virtually every major group in colonial society. This approach drew upon an older Sino-Vietnamese literary tradition as well as a popular republican tradition that satirized the sexual deviance of the rich and powerful to undermine the existing political order. *To Be a Whore* features a narrative structure based on Freudian theory to explain the growth of prostitution and the erosion of traditional morality in Indochina, especially among women. It conjoins this Freudian analysis with an examination of the impact of materialism and individualism on Vietnamese sexual norms. The result is an explanatory mongrel, faithful to no school, but further evidence of Vũ Trọng Phụng's relentlessly empirical approach to social problems.

DUMB LUCK AND THE UBIQUITY OF SEXUAL DEVIANCE

Set in Hà Nội around the year it was written, *Dumb Luck* follows the absurd social ascent of the uneducated Vietnamese vagabond and sidewalk lothario Red Haired-Xuân. While working as a ball boy at the municipal tennis court, Xuân is fired and arrested after spying on the female changing room and ogling the "milky white thighs" of Mrs. Civilization, a Westernized Vietnamese "modern woman." He is rescued from jail by Mrs. Deputy Customs Officer, a twice-widowed menopausal nymphomaniac, renowned in elite circles for "literally screwing a former husband to death." Back at her house where she tries in vain to seduce him in the shower, Xuân meets Mrs. Deputy Customs Officer's oversexed infant son, Little Master Blessing, who refuses to wear pants and sports a permanent erection. With help from Mrs. Deputy Customs Officer, Xuân is hired at the Europeanization Tailor Shop, a pricey boutique that sells women's lingerie. Using skills he mastered while hawking venereal disease ointment during his vagabond days, he learns to advertise the latest fashions in women's underwear, including the "Wait-a-Minute Panties," the "Happiness Slip," and the "Watch-Those-Hands Brassiere." At the tailor shop, he meets the "cuckolded Senior Clerk," the cross-dressing Mr. Civilization, and Miss Snow, a "romantic modern girl" and "semivirgin" whom he successfully woos. He also encounters Dr. Straight-Talk, a Freudian quack who discourses nonsensically on the latest theories in European psychology and sexology. Additional characters include an archetypically lascivious monk, the businessman Victor Ban (who deals in prostitutes and venereal disease treatment), and a traditional herbalist who reveals, in public, the details of Ms. Snow's chronic vaginal itch. The countless twists of the madcap plot include an episode in which Red-Haired Xuân pretends to deflower Miss Snow in the Fairyland Hotel and another in which Mrs. Deputy Customs Officer and Xuân engage in an illicit but comically loud bout of sexual intercourse.

Critical reaction to *Dumb Luck* emphasized the sociological breadth of its satire. According to the critic Hồ Xanh, the panoramic scope of the novel's critical vision was embodied in the range of occupations and social positions held successfully by the dissolute and doltish Red-Haired Xuân: ball boy, peanut vendor, adman for venereal disease medicine, medical student, public orator, poet, social reformer, tennis instructor, and national athletic champion. The extensiveness of *Dumb Luck*'s critique may also be seen in its unusually large cast of uniformly silly characters. Hồ Xanh wrote,

> Many minor figures surround the main character, and each one represents a type, or to be more accurate, a class of people *[giai cấp người]* in contemporary

> society. Mrs. Deputy Customs Officer represents the "me tây" type [local women who wed Westerners]; Miss Snow represents the "new girl" *[gái mới];* Grandpa Hồng represents those people caught between the old and the new. Stubborn and childish, he resembles the policeman, the doctor, the herbalist, the fortune-teller, the tailor, the journalist, and the monk. Vũ Trọng Phụng's mocking laugh spares nobody. After reading the novel, it is clear that the majority of people in our society are phonies.[13]

While the ubiquitous sexual deviance on display in *Dumb Luck* serves to lampoon a wide range of social groups, it also reflects real concerns about the degeneration of Vietnamese sexual morality that Vũ Trọng Phụng expressed throughout his career. Both *To Be a Whore* and *Venereal Disease Clinic* asserted that the growth of prostitution and the erosion of sexual morality had reached a crisis. In *To Be a Whore,* the problem was depicted as a "riot of lust" *(loạn dâm)* embodied in "the rapid enrichment of venereal disease specialists, the growing prosperity of dance halls, the explosive spread of prostitution, the epidemic of illegitimate pregnancy, the proliferation of crimes of passion as reported in our newspapers, the ennui and suicidal tendencies of many of our youth, and the epidemic of rape."[14] Although the novelistic form of *To Be a Whore* discouraged the citation of documentary evidence to support this sensational claim, Vũ Trọng Phụng substantiated it through references in the text to sex scandals and off-color stories that appeared in the daily press. These included news items about "the daughter of a wealthy family found naked in a brothel," a violent altercation between a jealous wife and her husband's mistress, and the case of a "dignified young girl" impregnated by her chauffeur.[15] The circulation of such salacious stories in the press deepened a public impression that sexual immorality had reached epidemic proportions. Huyền—the main character of *To Be a Whore*—recalled the "harsh uproar of public opinion" *(cái dư luận rất nghiêm)* that occurred in response to a newspaper story about "the supervisor of a high school dormitory who caught two female students in an act of mutual masturbation with a rubber implement":[16]

> Members of the upper classes, intellectuals, and concerned parents discussed it around the dinner table and rickshaw pullers would talk about it out on the street and around the public water taps. The story dominated the conversations of the fat and the thin, the short and the tall, members of every rung of society's ladder. It was as if the entire society possessed only a single tongue that they used to express a unified sentiment of indignation at this notorious case of masturbation.[17]

In a similar vein, *Venereal Disease Clinic* referred to the capital as "Hà Nội-Sodom."[18] As a work of nonfiction reportage rather than a novel, however, it was able to verify this portrayal of the city by assembling a wealth of documentary evidence, including statistical data, expert testimony, and "scientific" research. The extent of the problem was underlined further through a tongue-in-cheek analysis of the devastating consequences that would occur were the sex industry in Hà Nội to be "miraculously eliminated" in the manner of "a hammer blow to the head of a poisonous snake."[19] Nine hundred soldiers in the city would be deeply discontented, especially if they proved "unable to endure what Freud would refer to as the repression of their sexual instincts—what the French described as 'refoulement Freudien.'"[20] Sixteen "modern madams" and 185 registered prostitutes would become jobless overnight. Thirty-seven cheap hotel owners, over one hundred bellhops, and 613 opium den proprietors would likewise be thrown out of work. Five thousand illicit prostitutes would sow discord throughout the city. The municipal treasury would lose the equivalent of fifty taels of gold each year in addition to the losses of tax revenue it would incur from the closing down of bars, cafes, and dance halls. And an army of unemployed bellhops, pimps, and rickshaw pullers would lead a crime wave throughout the city.

Although Vũ Trọng Phụng's concern with the saturation of Vietnamese society by immorality, perversity, and venal sex peaked in *To Be a Whore* and *Venereal Disease Clinic*, a preoccupation with the topic runs like an unbroken thread throughout his entire body of work. "Vũ Trọng Phụng has a weird obsession," wrote the critic Nguyễn Vỹ in 1937. "There are always obscene thoughts running through his head. He finds constant enjoyment in writing about sex. His works feature nakedness that disturbs the soul. He does not go halfway and his explicitness makes his readers uncomfortable. . . . Women don't like him; most dare not mention his name."[21] In *The Storm,* Tú Anh warns Long about the ubiquity within Hà Nội of sexual temptations and "pornography": "Wherever you go, in your office or out in the street, all you see is lustfulness posing as literature and art. We are surrounded by pornographic literature, pornographic films, pornographic theaters, pornographic pictures, dance halls, brothels, rickshaw pullers who offer you the virginity of every kind of woman for only five *đồng*. Music is also pornographic. Fashion becomes more and more pornographic. In short, we are surrounded by sights and sounds that encourage immorality. Don't you see that we are sinking in it—that we are flooded up to our necks in a swamp of lust."[22] The totalizing description of Hà Nội in *Venereal Disease Clinic* as "a spider's web of madams, pimps, cyclo drivers, and opium dens" makes the same point.[23]

Given Vũ Trọng Phụng's preoccupation in numerous works with the degeneration of Vietnamese morality and sexual behavior, the humorous treatment of the topic in *Dumb Luck* represented a new approach to an old concern. At the same time, the novel deployed representations of sexual deviancy to skewer a range of social groups that had long been targets of Vũ Trọng Phụng's writing. Consistent with the anticapitalist project that he had been expressing since the start of the decade, that *Dumb Luck* reserves its most scathing invective for members of the urban bourgeoisie and their opportunistic embrace of a shallow and hypocritical Popular Front progressivism is no surprise. "While other writers are promoting the 'new civilization,'" wrote Lê Thanh in a review of the novel written in 1937, "Vũ Trọng Phụng stands alone to attack it. He is especially critical of the 'civilization of materialism' and the 'civilization of superficiality.'"[24] The mocking portrayal of the vagabond Red-Haired Xuân is also consistent with Vũ Trọng Phụng's long-standing refusal to idealize the poor as demanded by his critics on the Left. In other words, the strategic deployment of humorous representations of deviant sexuality in *Dumb Luck* confirmed Vũ Trọng Phụng's familiar republican opposition to both the cultural vulgarity of nouveau riche and the sacred ideals of its communist opponents.

TO BE A WHORE AND THE CAUSES OF PROSTITUTION

To Be a Whore was serialized between August 1936 and March 1937 in the Huế newspaper *Perfume River*. Its considerable notoriety originated with an exchange of public letters between the editor Phan Khôi and the priest J. M. Thích, who took issue with the novel's scandalous title and threatened to lead a Catholic boycott of *Perfume River*. The novel attracted additional buzz by appearing at the height of Vũ Trọng Phụng's greatest literary success (the four novels of 1936–37) and consequent fame. The release of the first part of *To Be a Whore* coincided with the publication of the final chapters of *The Storm*, while later chapters of the novel came out simultaneously with the start of *Dumb Luck*.

Set, once again, in contemporary Hà Nội, *To Be a Whore* takes the form of an edited autoethnography of the life of a wealthy girl who becomes a prostitute. In the first of two scenes that frame the narrative, the first-person narrator and his depressed friend Quý spend a night on the town—"stopping at the cinema and a few dance halls"—and end up in a licensed brothel: "On the walls were countless pictures of beautiful, naked Western women, like photos in the pornographic magazines *Paris Plaisirs*, *Eros*, and *Sex Appeal*." The arrival of a prostitute named

Huyền gives them a shock as they recognize her as a rich and popular classmate from high school: "the beautiful and obedient daughter of a judge and the granddaughter of a doctor." After a tearful conversation and several bowls of opium, Huyền agrees to tell the narrator and Quý how she came to her shameful state by reading aloud from her diary. The remainder of the novel relates Huyền's life story in her own voice. In a concluding chapter, the narrator returns and discusses with his friend the storm of controversy that the release of the novel is likely to provoke.

The primary objective of Huyền's narrative is to explain why she became a prostitute. This interest in the causes of prostitution was expressed in two questions posed by Quý at the outset of the book: "Why does the creator make this miracle and let her be sullied so? Why does society create such a debauched creature and yet feel no remorse?"[25] Later, the narrator refines the question further, taking into account Huyền's upper-class background: "How does a girl from a good family end up wicked *[hư]*? What is wickedness? What has made her wicked? Who is responsible?"[26] In a review of *To Be a Whore* published in 1939, the critic Minh Tước lauded the seriousness of its focus on the dynamics of causality. "There is a rigorous order to the 'lesson' presented in the novel," he observed. "The writer wants us to understand a system of 'cause and effect' *[nhân-quả]* but this is not the same kind of cause and effect that we find in Buddhism. Rather, it is a mode of cause and effect derived from science and morality. One cause generates a specific effect that, in turn, causes a different effect."[27]

Given this palpable interest in causality, it is not surprising that the language and methods of social-scientific investigation loom large in the novel. "This is an age of science," the narrator writes in the final chapter, "and it is our duty to investigate and research." He also emphasizes that the narrative is based on verifiable material from Huyền's private diary and on interview data that the narrator and Quý gathered over the course of several evenings: "We tried to understand this difficult issue through the indirect means of questioning Huyền. From that night on, the three of us met many times. My friend told his family that he was staying in Hà Nội to be treated for an illness. But, in fact, we 'researched' *[khảo cứu]* the wickedness of Huyền."[28]

This emphasis on "research" and the dynamics of causation is consistent with Vũ Trọng Phụng's republican sensibility, but it may also have served as a protective shield against "moralistic" critics opposed to the graphic subject matter of the novel.[29] "Aren't you afraid that the false moralists are going to attack you?" asks Quý in the novel's final chapter. "Such people deserve only silence and scorn," the narrator replies. "Fortunately, this is an era of science *[khoa học]*. People now accept the necessity of observation, investigation, and research."[30] In the preface to the novel, Vũ Trọng Phụng fortified this defensive gambit by pointing out that many eminent Western thinkers, including Freud, Goethe, and Schiller, had written about the power and social significance of sexual desire. "In civilized countries, it is not taboo to talk about lust," he pointed out.

> On the contrary, people there view lust as a valid topic for research and analysis. This useful research reveals the proper way to lust. The research, study, and experience of so many white-haired scholars regarding this topic have led to the perfection of lust as an aesthetic object. The production of books and the delivery of public presentations on the topic have saved countless young people from debauchery.[31]

In conclusion, he cited the argument of the "social gynecologist" Wilhelm G. Liepmann from the University of Berlin on the benefits to young people, in particular, of the development of the field of modern sexology.

Vũ Trọng Phụng's preoccupation with venal sex was by no means unusual among writers of the interwar era, but there is something extraordinary about the complexity and intensity of his approach to the problem. Like *Venereal Disease Clinic*, *To Be a Whore* refuses to trade in conventional wisdom about the causes of prostitution and its rapid growth in Indochina. Instead, it conjoins an investigation into the corrosive impact of colonial modernity on traditional morality with a rudimentary Freudian analysis of the psychological dynamics that compelled elite women to enter the sex trade. The deployment of Freudianism, in particular, underlines the pioneering, scientific ambition of Vũ Trọng Phụng's approach to the problem.

FREUD AND *TO BE A WHORE*

Given its belated penetration into France during the 1920s, it is not surprising that Freudian theory barely figured in Vietnamese intellectual life during the early years of the interwar era.[32] For example, Freud is never mentioned in *Southern Wind*, the encyclopedic journal that between 1917 and 1934 introduced Vietnamese readers to hundreds of influential European scientists, philosophers, and writers.[33] In 1933, one of the first summaries of Freudianism to appear in Vietnamese lamented its insignificance in Indochina: "In our country, we never hear writers mention the name of Freud."[34] However, by providing a lucid summary of Freudian theory (and even contrasting it with historical materialism), the essay signaled a budding interest in the topic that was to grow significantly during the late 1930s.[35] In 1936, Nguyễn Văn Hanh delivered a public lecture at the Association Mutuel de l'Enseignement de Cochinchine on the relationship between Freudian theory and the verse of the eighteenth-century poetess Hồ Xuân Hương that provoked a lively debate among southern intellectuals in the journal *Mai*.[36] The following year, Nguyễn Văn Hanh published *Hồ Xuân Hương: Work, Life, and Literary Genius,* the first sustained Vietnamese-language effort to employ Freudian theory as an instrument of literary criticism.[37] While this book provides evidence of a growing awareness of Freud within Vietnamese intellectual circles, Nguyễn Văn Hanh's introduction drew attention to the public's ignorance of the topic: "Many people don't know who Freud is or what Freudian theory is, or what its strengths and weakness are. They hear rumors that Freud studies mental illness that comes from sexual repression *[sự nén tình dục]* and they conclude that those who follow his theories must be morally corrupt."[38]

A cursory reference in *Dumb Luck* confirms that Vũ Trọng Phụng was familiar with Freud in early 1936, but it also underlines the interwar Vietnamese intelligentsia's superficial grasp of his ideas. In chapter 13 of the novel, Freud is invoked only to be caricatured and absurdly misinterpreted by the pretentious Dr. Straight-Talk as part of his diagnosis of the sexual deviance of Little Master Blessing. "You have identified the physiological crux of the matter," Dr. Straight-Talk announces pompously to Red-Haired Xuân during the course of their joint medical consultation:

> There is no avoiding the truth. Once again, Freud provides the solution. The boy is exhibiting signs of early puberty brought on by too much rich food, too many nice clothes and excessive pampering of the body. These factors combine to enhance his lechery. The problem is exacerbated by the particular environment in which he lives. Wouldn't you agree, Sir?[39]

Later in *Dumb Luck,* Dr. Straight-Talk cites and comically mangles ideas about menopause put forward by Pierre Vachet, the famous French sexologist hailed during the interwar era as the "Le Freud français."[40] Such farcical citations betray little presentiment of the earnest and remarkably sustained engagement with Freudianism presented in *To Be a Whore.*

As in *Dumb Luck,* Freud is mentioned directly only once during the course of *To Be a Whore* (in the introduction), but the impact of Freudian ideas on the novel may be found within several aspects of its narrative structure. First, Huyền presents the history of her sexual life—the longest and most important section of the book—by reading aloud to the narrator from her own private notebooks. Although Huyền compares it to Catholic confession *(cuộc thú tội),* this intimate and apparently spontaneous first-person narration also brings to mind the "uncensored talking" that psychoanalysis famously employs as its primary investigative device.[41]

Second, the core narrative is divided into four chapters that mark distinct phases in Huyền's psychosexual evolution. The first chapter—"Puberty"—covers her sexual maturation between the ages of seven and sixteen. The second—"Entering Life"—chronicles the transitional years after she leaves school and before she gets married, a period in which she engages in a quasi-incestuous affair and loses her virginity. "Getting a Husband" describes the tumultuous early years of her marriage during which her husband battles syphilis and she succumbs to the temptation of infidelity. The final chapter—"Debauchery"—chronicles the breakup of her marriage and her descent into professional prostitution. These phases do not correspond to Freudian counterparts (there is no attention to Freud's famous stages of infantile sexuality, for example), but the division of her sexual life history into significant sequential periods echoes an important orientation of psychoanalytic thought. Moreover, the primacy that the novel attributes to Huyền's sexual experiences during adolescence dovetails with Freud's view, expressed in the third essay of his *Three Essays on Sexuality,* that sexual identity is consolidated during puberty. At the outset of the chapter, Huyền points out that many of the episodes that prefigured her descent into prostitution occurred during this stage of her life.[42] "Puberty made me what I am today," she says, "it was an unhealthy environment in which I was surrounded by bad friends and learned the wrong things."[43]

What made puberty (broadly defined as the years from the ages of eight to fifteen) especially "unhealthy," according to Huyền, is that it was during this period that she was first subjected to sexual repression. Vũ Trọng Phụng's treatment of this theme draws upon a basic understanding of Freud's "repressive hypothesis," which locates the etiology of psychological problems in the suppression, metamorphosis, and return of innate or deeply rooted libidinal desires.[44] To dramatize this idea, the novel establishes the existence within Huyền of powerful natural drives. It explains her enthusiasm for dolls at the age of eight as a product of a "god-given maternal nature" *(mẫu tính do sự nhiệm màu của tạo vật)*.[45] And it emphasizes the instinctive character of her libido and of her adolescent curiosity about sex. "Since lust is a function of biology, morality cannot restrain it," Vũ Trọng Phụng states in the introduction to the novel. "The flesh needs sex just as it needs to eat and drink *[tình dục đã cần cho xác thịt cũng như sự ăn uống].*"[46]

Forces conspire, however, to frustrate Huyền's libidinous drives. She describes, for example, how formal prohibitions against the discussion of sex in public were enforced through harsh punishments. In one instance, she was beaten by her father with a bamboo cane after she raised the subject of childbirth over the dinner table: "Naturally, I never forgot that whipping," she explains, "because it was the first time in my life that my father had ever hit me."[47] A more pervasive form of repression in the novel is the tendency of adults to disregard questions from children about sex or, worse still, to provide deliberate misinformation. For example, Huyền's pregnant mother tells her that her baby will be born from her armpit, while her older sister insists that it will emerge from her naval. Since no sexual organs are mentioned in these explanations, Huyền assumes that the vagina plays no part in sexual reproduction and functions only for urination. Later, Huyền's mother brushes off her questions about the meaning of her first menstruation with the vague assurance "you will understand this clearly once you are married."[48] She also receives mixed messages about male sexuality from her mother, whom she observes fiddling with the penis of her baby brother while repeating, "hate, hate this prick of men" *(ghét, ghét cái con bòi ông đây này)*.[49] Her growing sense of anxiety that sex is shameful is deepened when she overhears a common term for copulation being used by adults as a curse word. Reflecting on the counterproductive consequences of this proliferation of repressive sexual misinformation, Huyền asserts that "the more I was confined to a state of ignorance, the more curious I became."[50]

While it is difficult to confirm that Vũ Trọng Phụng's engagement with Freud provided the direct inspiration for these varied scenes of sexual repression, the general influence of Freudian theory on *To Be a Whore* was widely recognized by educated readers of the day. For example, Vũ Ngọc Phan, the most important literary critic of the interwar era, argued that Vũ Trọng Phụng's characterization of the sexual hunger of Little Master Blessing in *Dumb Luck* and Thị Mịch in *The Storm* strongly suggested that the writer was "a disciple of Freud" *(một đồ đệ của Freud)*.[51] Zeroing in on Vũ Trọng Phụng's description of the intensity of the sex drives of his characters, he asked: "Did not Freud compare human lust to hunger and thirst?" For Vũ Ngọc Phan, *To Be a Whore* confirmed this connection since, in his view, "the basic foundation *[nền tảng]* of the novel rests on the sexualism *[chủ nghĩa tình dục]* of Freud."

In 1939, the critic Minh Tước advanced a more elaborate case for the significance of Freudian influence on the novel:

> With *To Be a Whore,* Mr. Vũ Trọng Phụng has moved his pen in the direction of science. In particular, he has knocked on the door of Professor Sigmund Freud and asked to join his school. This novel demonstrates that he has already mastered the Austrian professor's theories of psychoanalysis *[tâm lý giải phẫu]*.

Can there be any question that *To Be a Whore* is a novel constructed on the basis of Freud's lectures?[52]

To support this claim, Minh Tước emphasized parallels between the confessional style of the novel and the psychoanalytical method. He also underlined the Freudian character of the novel's careful delineation of different stages in Huyền's psychosexual evolution:

> Has this reportage writer understood those lectures well enough to provide our society with a real psychoanalytical novel? By borrowing the voice of an educated prostitute, I believe that he has found a successful method for carrying out this psychoanalytical work. The prostitute describes for us her different life stages *[từng thời kỳ của đời]*, starting when she was a bourgeois little girl and ending with her descent into decadence. The first stage is her family stage. Here, we see the bourgeois prejudices and awkward education of the Vietnamese family. Because she is an intelligent girl, she grows curious *[tò mò]* about what is happening around her and what is occurring within her own body. And the strongest and most difficult-to-satisfy source of her curiosity is her own flesh. As sexual tension grows, her obsessive curiosity burns like a flame. Her family environment both represses and provokes her sexual feelings and this contradiction *[sự trái ngược]* makes her seek out unnatural methods to satisfy herself. . . . The second period is her married life, during which she experiences the misery of sexual dissatisfaction and, eventually, adultery. This leads naturally to a new period marked by her descent into prostitution.[53]

SEXOLOGY, TAOISM, AND THE TEMPTATIONS OF MASTURBATION

As Minh Tước's reference to "unnatural methods" suggests, the conflict between the forces of repression and Huyền's surging libido finds further expression in her struggle against the temptations of masturbation. She first encounters mutual masturbation at the age of nine when she and a male classmate named Ngôn fondle each other while playing together in a flower garden.[54] The sensations she experiences lead her to explore her body "in a new way" and to "discover liquid secretions there never noticed before":[55]

> That night, I experienced a significant spiritual crisis. My feeble nine-year-old soul trembled before my stimulated curiosity and disgusting thoughts. Unable

> to sleep, I tossed and turned in my bed. "Will this ever end?" I asked myself. . . . I felt ashamed and feared that my parents would find out.[56]

In the days that follow, Ngôn does not leave his house and his mother informs Huyền that he has grown feverish and tired. The following week, gossip spreads that Ngôn has been violently beaten by his father after being caught masturbating. Huyền's father forbids her from seeing Ngôn again, exclaiming: "How terrible! Who would have guessed that such an angelic looking boy would become so corrupt at such a young age."[57]

Frightened by this incident, Huyền vows to "suppress her passions," but the inflation of her libido during puberty enhances her masturbatory desire. "From the age of thirteen," she explains, "I began to struggle tenaciously on a daily basis with sexual urges *[dục tính]*. . . . The maturation of my genitalia aroused my flesh to a nearly uncontrollable degree."[58] At fifteen she starts giving in to the temptation: "Spring awakening *[tuổi xuân]* came on with such strange fury that my flesh could not be restrained and my precious womanly modesty was overwhelmed by the intensity of my sexual desire."[59] She compares her state of mind during this period to a "horse galloping crazily."[60] Huyền's surrender to masturbatory desire is facilitated by the encouragement of a "treasured friend" named Ngân, whom she describes as "the smartest, most upright girl in her class":

> "Older sister Huyền, I tell you this, but you must promise not to laugh. It is very hard not to become bad on the journey to adulthood, especially during the particular stage that we are in. But certain forms of naughtiness are trifling and will not destroy us—for example, being naughty with ourselves. We must avoid taking real lovers in order to maintain our marriage prospects. But we can act as our own lovers while we wait. Do you understand what I mean? If we keep it secret, no one will know and we will have no regrets." She held up her hand and added: "Here is our most treasured and faithful lover—one who will never harm our reputations." That afternoon, my friend introduced me to this fascinating vocation *[nghề nghiệp hay]*. She showed me how to be gentle so as not to break the hymen, and I used this method repeatedly to satisfy my throbbing flesh. I didn't realize it clearly but as the days passed, my ears rang, my eyes glazed over, my head started to hurt, my back ached, and my face grew paler.[61]

Huyền's growing awareness of the enervating consequences of chronic masturbation is reinforced by admonishments she receives from a "chaste and pure" girlfriend named Vân who learns of her "wicked" habit. Vân warns her that if she continues to play this "wretched game" she will "lose all strength, lose all control, lose all human dignity" and that "physical changes made apparent on her face will expose this vice of hers to the world."[62] To underline the point, Vân lends her a "scientific" sexual advice manual full of "illustrations of male and female genitals."[63]

Up to this point, the treatment of masturbation in *To Be a Whore* conforms, in a general way, with modernist notions about "solitary sex" that gained currency during the early twentieth century among a wide array of European thinkers including Freud.[64] This approach combined an old, pejorative view of masturbation as irredeemably harmful (to both the individual masturbator and society at large) with a new conviction that autoeroticism was bad not because it was a sin or an agent of disease but because of its damaging psychological consequences. As Thomas Laqueur has argued with regard to the twentieth-century transition in attitudes toward masturbation: "Guilt and its consequences—neurosis, tiredness, anxiety, hysteria, physical discomforts of all sorts, failure to achieve what life promised, moral collapse, abjection—replaced death and imbecility as the primary wages of solitary sex, which still carried the ethical burdens of its early modern history."[65] Consistent with this picture, Vũ Trọng Phụng's description of the negative impact of masturbation on Ngôn and Huyền emphasizes symptoms of psychological distress rather than physical or biological consequences such as insanity, impotence, or degeneration.

Vũ Trọng Phụng's relatively modern attitude toward masturbation reflects a general familiarity, on his part, with a broader scientific and pseudoscientific discourse on sexuality that circulated globally and was widely influential throughout Asia during the early twentieth century. Indeed, his psychologically oriented views on the topic probably owed as much to Freud as to popular sexual advice manuals, medical literature on neurasthenia, and the works of prominent European sexologists such as Pierre Vachet and Magnus Hirshfeld.[66] Vachet is cited in *Dumb Luck* and Vũ Trọng Phụng mentions Hirshfeld briefly in a letter written in 1936, the same year that *To Be a Whore* was published.[67] More influential still was a relatively obscure Jewish "social gynecologist" named Wilhelm Liepmann who was active in German sexological circles during the interwar era and served as the director of the Museum for the Study of Women in Berlin.[68] As with many prominent sexologists of the Weimer period, Liepmann viewed sex education as the key to stemming the growth of unwanted pregnancies, the spread of venereal disease, and the rise of various forms of sexual neuroses.[69] Vũ Trọng Phụng quoted Professor Liepmann at length in the preface to *To Be a Whore*, and he opened the novel with a short epigram from his book *Jugend und Eros*. During his interview in 1937 with Lê Thanh, Vũ Trọng Phụng acknowledged that a French translation of *Jugend und Eros* published in 1932 had inspired him to write *To Be a Whore:*[70]

> I wrote *[To Be a Whore]* after reading the translation of a German book that compiles the darkest confessions of young students. After reading this brave, scientific book, I imagined that all of our youth today are being driven by puberty toward masturbation and perversity, and I began to see the necessity of sex education for adolescents.[71]

While the treatment of masturbation in *To Be a Whore* draws attention to Vũ Trọng Phụng's idiosyncratic engagement with a mottled array of European ideas, it also points to the influence on his thinking of traditional Sino-Vietnamese beliefs. The coexistence of these discourses may be seen in the depiction of the sexual advice manual that Vân lends Huyền in order to demonstrate to her the evils of masturbation. "The book employed a combination of textual explanations and illustrations of male and female genitalia," Huyền explained, "and it led me toward science. The knowledge I gained did not dangerously pique my curiosity as before. On the contrary, my wayward, lustful thoughts were quickly replaced by a righteous and obedient frame of mind."[72] No author or title is identified, but the text in question was likely a real book in Vũ Trọng Phụng's possession since the novel reproduces verbatim two lengthy subsections from it entitled "Love with Genitals" ("Ái tình với sinh thực khí") and "The Damage Caused by Masturbation and Lustful Thoughts" ("Những sự hại về thủ dâm và ý dâm").

The notion that Huyền might be saved from the temptations of masturbation by a "scientific" sexual advice manual reflects the modern empirical orientation of Vũ Trọng Phụng's approach to the issue, as does his remark that science alone possesses the capacity to provide valuable sex education for youth without inflicting on them the collateral damage of inadvertent sexual stimulation. On the other hand, the precise ideas about masturbation advanced by this (allegedly) panacean book clearly reflect premodern Taoist notions that run directly counter to the sexual modernism that Vũ Trọng Phụng promotes elsewhere in the novel:[73]

> [Masturbators] think that what they are doing is the same as sexual intercourse. But what they don't understand is that sexual intercourse between a man and a woman reconciles and harmonizes yin and yang, facilitating the circulation of the blood. As a result, it produces no damaging hygienic consequences.

> Masturbation, on the other hand, only involves yin or yang, never both, so how can the arteries clear? Hence, masturbation is extremely dangerous.[74]

The notion expressed in Huyền's "scientific" book that masturbation is an unhealthy sexual act because it fails to establish a harmonious equilibrium between opposing yin and yang essences may be traced to premodern Taoist sexology texts.[75] Moreover the book describes dramatic physical and biological symptoms caused by chronic masturbation that reflect traditional Sino-Vietnamese beliefs utterly at odds with the careful emphasis on psychological consequences typically found in modernist approaches:

> Men will lose all their sperm. Their penises will shrivel up and become crooked and their testicles will grow uneven in size and shape. They will suffer from impotence, diseased sperm, and premature ejaculation. Eventually their health will break down completely and they will give in to imbecility, insanity, and infertility. Women will suffer as well. Their vaginal fluid will dry up and blood will appear in their urine. Their vaginas will be damaged and their faces will grow weak and pale like a flower that fades before it blooms.[76]

Finally, it advises "boys and girls who wish to resist such perverse thoughts to read stories of heroes and heroines in order to nurture their nobler virtues"—a move which suggests that the conceptual underpinning of Huyền's putatively scientific manual may owe a greater debt to a historically more recent strain of neotraditionalist nationalism than to a premodern Taoist tradition. As David Marr has demonstrated, Vietnamese sexual advice manuals from the era often appealed to patriotism to legitimize their efforts.[77]

The description of the development of Huyền's adolescent libido in the first chapter of *To Be a Whore* sheds light on the remarkable complexity of Vũ Trọng Phụng's views on sexuality as well as on the diversity of influences that shaped his understanding of the topic. Ideas drawn from Freud, modern sexology, and traditional and neotraditional Sino-Vietnamese discourses about sex comingled in his thinking, making it difficult to attach a meaningful label to his approach to this issue. Moreover, within the context of the novel's objective to shed light on the growth of commercial sex in colonial Vietnam, the distorted evolution of Huyền's adolescent sexuality represents only one part of Vũ Trọng Phụng's explanation. Equally important in this regard is the impact of powerful forces of modernity such as materialism and individualism. The pernicious effects of these forces on Huyền dominate the remainder the novel.

PROSTITUTION AND MATERIALISM

Given the novelty and intensity of Vũ Trọng Phụng's effort to link the growth of commercial sex to Freudian theory, it is not surprising that critics have focused on this thematic aspect of the novel to the near exclusion of all others. However, the remaining sections of *To Be a Whore* advance a significantly different argument, one that links the expansion of prostitution in Indochina to broader cultural and socioeconomic changes associated with the onset of modernity. The most significant is the spread throughout Vietnamese society of *chủ nghĩa vật chất*—literally "materialism" in the sense of an inflated yearning for modern consumer goods and a new Westernized lifestyle:[78]

> The materialism movement *[phong trào vật chất]* blew through our society like a violent typhoon. . . . It exhibited almost supernatural powers of deception, and many of our customs *[lề thói]* and our decent orderly values *[nền nếp]* were blown away in the storm. The discipline of a society that had once revered the spirit *[tinh thần]* was overthrown by the forces of materialism.[79]

As dramatized in *To Be a Whore*, the items most coveted by those under the spell of this powerful sensation included fashionable clothes, European food, and modern medicine as well as high-tech gadgets such as automobiles, wireless radios, cameras, and phonographs. Materialism also fostered demand for new Western forms of leisure such as dancing, dating, outdoor festivals, horse racing, the cinema, cocktail parties, and recreational sports, especially tennis, bicycling, and paddleboating.[80] As she moves into adulthood, Huyền's growing fascination with these symbols of material prosperity coincides with her involvement in two calamitous romances—an incestuous affair with a first cousin and an adulterous affair with a friend of her husband. The former leads to the loss of her virginity and to her cousin's suicide, while the latter destroys her marriage, forcing her into a life of prostitution. Since these tragic affairs function as gateways for Huyền's entrance into the sex trade, their pointed juxtaposition with her intensified fixation with consumer goods suggests an effort on the part of Vũ Trọng Phụng to link the rise of materialism with the growth of prostitution.

But what is the precise mechanism that connects these two developments? Since Huyền is financially well off throughout most of the narrative, the novel provides little support for the conventional Marxist thesis that prostitution and capitalism are linked because the sex trade is simply a specific expression of wage labor under capitalist relations of production.[81] Rather, it suggests that colonial capitalism fosters the generalized growth of an acquisitive mentality that fuses a desire for commodities with a wanton craving for sex.[82] This conflation works in a variety of different ways, but in the case of certain commodities such as revealing clothes, pornography, and forms of leisure such as dancing and cocktail parties, the transformation of materialist longing into sexual hunger is facilitated by the inherently erotic nature of the desired item itself.

An example of this may be seen in Huyền's account of the first dancing party that she attends in her early twenties with a group of wealthy friends. The party takes place in a rented room "decorated with photographs of nude Western women and glossy movie stills."[83] The men sport Western suits and wear their hair in elongated ringlets following the "philosopher's style." Their bodies reek of perfume. The women dress in gaudy colors, their faces caked with power and adorned with false eyelashes and bright red lipstick that configures their mouths into the shape of a heart. Some wear translucent, paper-thin pants that highlight the contrast between their "too-tight panties, their peach-colored buttocks, and their creamy white thighs." Huyền describes their behavior as affected and sexually suggestive: "They poured each other cocktails, passed around expensive Western sweets, and smoked little English cigarettes." The women claimed that their friendships with the men were purely platonic, but Huyền could sense romance in the air: "Their jokes, their sidelong glances, their playful asides, their feigned jealousy—all of these 'friendly' gestures served as a thinly veiled pretense for flirtation and seduction."

While Huyền views the modern accoutrements at the party as stimulants of lustful desire, she experiences dancing as a direct surrogate for sex:

> Paul Sanh turned on the music, and Ngân and I sat and happily watched the three couples dancing. This was the first time that I had seen dancing up close. I quickly came to realize that both the dancers and the spectators like me were becoming sexually aroused. Still, my friends insisted that it was an art form and that there was nothing dirty about it.[84]

Moments later, Huyền is invited to dance for the first time:

> Before I could refuse, the young man grabbed my hand, put his arm around my waist, and started pressing his leg between my thighs. My cheeks reddened with shame and my body felt as if an electric current had surged through it. My mind went blank as if my soul had departed my body. I allowed my partner to carry me along and tried to move my knees and feet so that they would not rub

> up against his. Suddenly my flesh was overcome with a sensation I could not fully suppress. It was not quite pleasure, but it was filled with passion. It increased gradually without dissipating, surging forward in small rhythmic waves. I felt excited but not fully satisfied.[85]

Huyền continues to describe the erotic sensations she experiences dancing until "a moment of climax" abruptly occurs. "I shuddered and went completely motionless. The young man released me and plopped down in a chair, panting heavily."[86] Recalling her earlier struggle with the temptations of masturbation, Huyền states, "those dirty passions that I had originally experienced in private had now found an outlet in dancing."[87]

Automobiles, films, and romantic novels have a similar impact on Huyền in the way that she feels both drawn to them as modern consumer goods and morally compromised by the erotic sensations that they stimulate. For example, the shiny new automobile in which she regularly meets her lover Tân for romantic trysts functions for Huyền as both a modern status symbol and a powerful aphrodisiac. When Huyền's husband learns of the role it plays in his wife's affair, he curses the automobile as a "whorehouse," but Huyền describes it as an erotic paradise:[88]

> The car was a truly magical instrument. It saved time and offered complete privacy. So many times we experienced the ecstasy of love, in a total and complete way, inside that car on the outskirts of the city . . . and no one on the outside had even the faintest idea what we were doing. Tân would stop the car along the side of the road, turn on the green and red parking lights, and then . . . "Do you love me? Kiss me please!" . . . We often finished before the engine had had time to cool. Tân would then start up the motor—thì-xình-xình-xình—and we would speed at one hundred kilometers per hour back to the city. . . . I will never forget those happy days. I didn't feel bad about cheating on my husband since it all seemed so romantic, like in a film or in a novel.[89]

The final reference underlines Huyền's view that foreign films and modern "romantic" novels contributed to her corruption by presenting conventionally immoral behavior regarding love, sex, and marriage as "modern," "civilized," and even "revolutionary." "Novels present a different society, indeed, a different world," she observes. "There, a woman who gets pregnant out of wedlock is depicted as someone who sacrifices nobly for love. Promiscuous whores who grow ill and die tragic deaths are depicted as romantic new women full of poetry and ardent passion. . . .

And wives who abandon their old-fashioned husbands and in-laws are depicted as leaders of a revolution to secure individual happiness for women."[90]

While these episodes dramatize how modern consumer goods and illicit sexuality tend to bleed into each other when the specific objects of materialist desire happen to possess a seemingly inherent sexual charge (as with modern fashions, dancing, movies, novels, and cars), other episodes in the novel compare the dynamics of this conflation to a kind of slippery slope, in which stimulated desires provoked by commodities slide inadvertently toward objects of sexual longing.[91] "It cannot be denied that my corruption began with white pants," Huyền asserted, "since they not only changed my attitude toward my clothes but toward my behavior *[cử chỉ]* as well."[92] These behavioral changes, in turn, triggered a move down another link in this chain of moral decay by encouraging her to enter into various forms of "social relations" *(sự xã giao)*: to engage in "natural conversations" with men, to flirt, and to have boyfriends. Because expanded "social relations" tend to take place at unsupervised sites such as movie theatres, parks, outdoor exhibits, and dancing halls, they provide further opportunities for moral corruption: "You may ask, what is so bad about a woman entertaining a man in these places? But how many illegitimate pregnancies and broken homes have resulted from a single moment of harmless flirtation!"[93]

Rather than viewing the growth of materialism as a structural outgrowth of capitalism, the second half of *To Be a Whore* portrays it as a cultural consequence of the colonial encounter: "The meeting *[sự gặp gỡ]* of East and West on this land of ours has had a huge influence on our material life *[đời vật chất]*," he states in the introduction to the novel. "While there is no doubt that new activities *[cuộc tân sinh hoạt]* such as the theater, the cinema, modern fashions, dance halls, perfume, and cosmetics make us progressively more lustful every day, we fail to recognize the need for 'educating our lust' *[giáo dục cái sự dâm]* so that young people can distinguish lust that is moral and honest from lust that will harm our race *[giống nòi]*."[94] The West also promotes materialism through local cultural and intellectual compradors that spearhead public campaigns in favor of the Europeanization of Vietnamese society. The novel does not identify members of this group by name, but it is clear (from his writing elsewhere) that Vũ Trọng Phụng is referring to writers and journalists connected to the Self-Strength Literary Group and its influential magazines *Phong Hóa (Customs)* and *These Days*. "I am against the movement for the Europeanization of external forms promoted over the past several years by the leaders of the Self-Strength Literary Group," he explained during his interview with Lê Thanh. "They argue that the progressive renovation of external forms will trigger the progressive renovation of our spirit. They say that once external forms begin to evolve, a spiritual evolution will follow automatically. They teach people to progressively reform their appearance. They introduce new fashions and teach us how to apply powder and lipstick. Their project of Europeanization has already achieved some results. The recent growth of lust, for example, is a consequence of their efforts."[95]

In *To Be a Whore,* Vũ Trọng Phụng argued that these agents of materialism hypocritically mask the destructive cultural impact of their efforts through "cunning terms" such as "progress" *(tiến bộ),* "reform" *(duy tân),* "happiness" *(vui vẻ),* "social relations" *(xã giao),* "emancipation" *(giải phóng),* "civilization" *(văn minh),* and "new activities" *(tân hoạt động).* Their promotion of "women's rights" *(nữ quyền)* and "gender equality" *(bình quyền)* also contributed to female sexual immorality and to the related growth of prostitution by stimulating the aspirations of women for a more glamorous life and increasing their social and physical mobility:

> This group of insincere journalists and writers locks away their wives, daughters, and sisters, while encouraging the wives and daughters of other people to break into society and to live a new kind of life—a life of festivals, dancing, fashions constantly in flux, and progressively more revealing outfits. Newspapers that do not revere the new *[hiếu tân]* or flatter women *[nịnh đầm]* are forced out of business. Nationalism and social responsibility are shunted aside. Those who refuse to shut their eyes and dash toward material commodities *[vật chất]* are derided as dotty, old-fashioned relics and urged to consider committing suicide. The press overflows with advice on how to find pleasurable satisfaction for the flesh. Youth are left without ideals to follow other than the ideal of the material commodity.[96]

PROSTITUTION AND INDIVIDUALISM

A second characteristic feature of modernity that plays a role in Huyền's moral deterioration is the growth of individualism.[97] While the novel rails forthrightly and at great length against the evils of materialism, it dramatizes the pernicious influence of individualism indirectly through the character of Tân, the self-absorbed playboy whose adulterous affair with Huyền precipitates the final stage of her moral decline. Huyền first encounters Tân—an old school friend of her husband—at the race track and is attracted immediately to his good looks, apparent wealth, and cosmopolitan demeanor: "I noticed a well-coifed man in a Western suit, with binoculars and a portable Contex camera. Although he was an Annamite, he carried himself with the air of a Parisian."[98] As both an earnest proponent of "social relations" for women and a disingenuous critic of traditional marital jealousy, Huyền's husband encourages her to strike up a friendship with Tân. Their relationship blossoms into love and is consummated during an outing to the countryside in Tân's erotically charged automobile. When Huyền's husband learns of the affair, Tân breaks it off and flees Hà Nội, traveling to Cambodia and Sài Gòn before setting sail for France. Huyền pursues Tân to the South, but she runs out of money in Sài Gòn and is eventually enticed by a hotel manager to sleep with his wealthy patrons in order to pay for room and board. Upon returning to Hà Nội, she heads immediately for the city's old quarter and begins to work, in earnest, as a professional prostitute.

Recalling the individualist heroes of nineteenth-century French romantic literature that Vũ Trọng Phụng consumed throughout his life, Tân is handsome, young, independently wealthy, and plagued by acute self-consciousness and neurotic introspection.[99] Divorced, childless, and unburdened apparently by the conventional demands of kinship, he "lives alone in order to better enjoy a life of leisure."[100] As with the prototypical romantic hero, he is well traveled—having earned a degree in France—and highly mobile, as evidenced by his impulsive, frenetic sojourning during the final stages of the narrative. Just as the absence of family members from his daily life signals his independence from kinship ties, his easy penchant for travel (to study or to escape a failed affair) and for driving his own car at top speed (during an era when chauffeurs were the norm) symbolizes his freedom from both social conventions and geographical constraints. "He is the happiest person I know," exclaims Huyền's husband. "He is respected, educated, and wealthy, and yet he is not working for the French *[Tây]* nor burdened with a wife and children."[101]

Tân reveals a more philosophical streak of romantic individualism through his unorthodox views on marriage. "Love and marriage are completely different things," he tells Huyền. "How many passionate lovers grow bored and stop loving each other after becoming husband and wife. Marriage is a form of regulation, while love is an ideal. You can't confine an ideal through regulation. Since marriage will inevitably destroy love, it is better to remain unmarried and forever miserable, meaning forever in love!"[102] Later, Tân expresses his antimarriage sentiments to Huyền more emphatically: "I hate marriage. Marriage will kill our love for each other. Our love will only last as long as it remains secret. . . . Marriage only brings down love to a petty, everyday level. . . . This is why in civilized countries, the ideal is for men to have a loyal wife and many lovers and it is the same for women. . . . Cuckoldry is a sign of civilization."[103] Tân's casual willingness to pursue a love affair with the wife of a friend points to the radical character of his individualist proclivities since it underscores his belief that neither marriage nor male friendship ought to restrain the pursuit of personal desires. Huyền recognizes this more extreme quality of Tân's individualism when he refuses to visit her husband following the exposure of the affair: "He would not dare to show his face again at the house of a friend, especially a friend who believed so deeply in friendship during an era in which society celebrated the individual."[104]

Tân's romantic individualism may also be seen in his vanity, penchant for self-dramatization, and moody pessimism. Such qualities come across in his interminable musings to Huyền about the difficulties of achieving true love. "My opinions about love differ utterly from the views of the majority," he insists.

> My youthful happiness was shattered long ago by the pain of failed love, and family difficulties have prevented me from living an ordinary life like the rest of the world. I have still not recovered from the scars inflicted ten years past. These have sapped my willpower and my desire to study; I am incapable of accomplishing anything important and live only for useless pleasures. I have money, health, status, education, and yet I remain unhappy. I have everything but true love. I searched for love in the West, but I could not find it or anything of real value there. I am incapable of loving those I want to love and those who I don't love seem to fall in love with me. For people to love each other, they must first understand each other, and this is not as easy for me as for others since I understand the word "understand" in a different way than the rest of the world.[105]

In response to this self-absorbed rant, Huyền's heart starts to "flutter just like the revving up of an engine."[106] *To Be a Whore* devotes less attention to the contribution of individualism to the growth of prostitution than to inadequate sex education for girls or to the growth of materialism. But the corrupting influence on Huyền of Tân's egoistic musings on love and alienation confirms that the rise of romantic individualism plays an important supporting role within Vũ Trọng Phụng's understanding of the forces promoting the moral decay of Vietnamese society.

CONCLUSION

The remarkable complexity of *To Be a Whore*'s account of Huyền's descent into the sex trade cannot be aligned with the conventional notion that representations of prostitution during the colonial era functioned primarily as metaphors for colonial relations. If Vũ Trọng Phụng's treatment of the topic was, indeed, intended to symbolize the dynamics of colonial collaboration, it is unlikely that he would have devoted so much attention to the psychosexual subtext of the phenomenon. Moreover, while the effort to link excessive materialism with the rise of prostitution might conceivably be read as a critique of the venal economic motives of colonialism's native collaborators, *To Be a Whore* does not assert that Huyền was driven to enter the sex trade by the allure of material gain. Rather, it shows how the spread of materialism enhanced her youthful desire for sex and romance, making her more susceptible to multiple forms of moral corruption that stemmed, in fact, from a wide variety of sources. The conventional argument is also belied by Vũ Trọng Phụng's tireless efforts to determine the origins of prostitution by mobilizing insights from Freudian psychology, modern sexology, social gynecology, sociology, and investigative journalism as well as from local East Asian intellectual traditions such as Taoism and Confucianism. The wide-ranging intensity of this intellectual quest supports the idea that Vũ Trọng Phụng and members of his large audience were genuinely preoccupied with prostitution and sexual immorality as pressing social problems that deserved sustained attention from researchers, intellectuals, policy makers, and the public at large.

CHAPTER FIVE · Banning Vũ Trọng Phụng

In 1960, the Vietnamese Workers' Party (VWP) politburo member Hoàng Văn Hoan condemned Vũ Trọng Phụng in a twenty-page essay entitled "Thoughts on the Problem of Vũ Trọng Phụng's Work within Vietnamese Literature." The essay attacked Vũ Trọng Phụng's politics, smeared his character, and disparaged, in considerable detail, his most important novels. "Vũ Trọng Phụng's writing represents the most dangerous kind of literature," Hoàng Văn Hoan alleged, "because it deceptively conveys a positive impression even though it is filled with poison." Denouncing the recent promotion of Vũ Trọng Phụng's legacy by "the Nhân Văn–Giai Phẩm clique," he concluded: "Instead of praising his work or holding it up as a source of pleasure or edification, we must expose and condemn the reactionary filth hidden within it."[1] Circulated internally but never published, the essay triggered a ban on Vũ Trọng Phụng's work within communist-ruled Vietnam for almost thirty years. The genesis of this posthumous repression requires explanation. Not only had Vũ Trọng Phụng been dead for more than twenty years at the time that the ban was imposed, but his writing had been well regarded within official circles throughout the previous decade. Indeed, only three years before the release of Hoàng Văn Hoan's essay, Vũ Trọng Phụng's work had been reissued by state publishing houses, excerpted in the Party press, and commemorated during a public forum at the National Opera House cosponsored by the official Association of Arts and Letters.

As remarkable as the sudden collapse of Vũ Trọng Phụng's reputation was Hoàng Văn Hoan's leading role in the campaign against him. Hoàng Văn Hoan was a founding member of the Indochinese Communist Party and the DRV's first ambassador to China, and his membership in the politburo marked him as one of the eleven most powerful men in the country.[2] His direct intervention in this episode suggests that the ban against Vũ Trọng Phụng enjoyed support at the highest levels of the regime.

This chapter explores Vũ Trọng Phụng's dramatic fall from favor, a by-product of the official repression of Nhân Văn-Giai Phẩm (NVGP), a "reform communist" intellectual movement that flourished briefly in Hà Nội during the mid-1950s.[3] Led by disenchanted artists and intellectuals inspired by de-Stalinization in the Eastern Bloc and the Hundred Flowers policy in China, the movement appealed for enhanced democracy, freedom, and "socialist legality" within the existing single-party communist system. The main media for this message were two spirited journals—*Nhân Văn (Humanity)* and *Giai Phẩm (Masterworks)*—published in Hà Nội during the final months of 1956. Contributors to the journals included northern Vietnam's most eminent philosopher (Trần Đức Thảo), historian (Đào Duy Anh), literary critic (Trương Tửu), musician (Văn Cao), and journalist (Phan Khôi)—all of whom had built their reputations during the late colonial era—as well as many of northern Vietnam's most promising younger writers, poets, and artists (such as Trần Dần, Lê Đạt, Hoàng Cầm, Sỹ Ngọc, and Phùng Quán). The Party press condemned *Nhân Văn* and *Giai Phẩm* during the three months that they circulated openly, and officials shut down the journals in December 1956. After a brief pause in the persecution of the movement in 1957, officials moved decisively against it in 1958. In January of that year, leaders of NVGP were subjected to a vicious punitive campaign that included public denunciations by colleagues, coerced self-criticism, termination of employment, and ideological rectification through hard labor. Those designated as "ringleaders" received prison terms in 1960, and all members of NVGP suffered extrajudicial discrimination, surveillance, and harassment that continued into the mid-1980s.

In addition to their well-known efforts in favor of creative freedom and political liberalization, the leaders of NVGP celebrated and promoted Vũ Trọng Phụng, the only domestic writer so honored by the group. Members of the movement organized the republication of his novels, excerpted his writing in *Nhân Văn* and sponsored a high-profile public commemoration of his life and legacy. They also published a provocative memorial volume in his honor that drew attention to connections between the writer's aesthetic and political agenda and their own.[4] At the same time, a young literary scholar with connections to NVGP named Văn Tâm published the first book-length study of Vũ Trọng Phụng's work—*Vũ Trọng Phụng: Realist*

Writer (Vũ Trọng Phụng: Nhà văn hiện thực)—that extolled the virtues of his politics and the genius of his art.[5] Featuring an introduction by Trương Tửu—who was both a leading member of NVGP and a mentor to Văn Tâm—the monograph deepened official suspicions about Vũ Trọng Phụng's political project.

The reasoning behind the veneration of Vũ Trọng Phụng by NVGP has never been adequately explained. According to some conservative critics, NVGP paid tribute to Vũ Trọng Phụng in order to trumpet the artistic superiority of prerevolutionary literature over state-sponsored socialist realism. Others have suggested that NVGP was drawn to Vũ Trọng Phụng's famous condemnation of sectarian communist power struggles during the 1930s in Indochina and the Soviet Union. Some members of NVGP insisted that they admired Vũ Trọng Phụng because of the "progressive" and "realist" character of his writing, while others justified their enthusiasm for him in terms of a nationalist impulse to commemorate a Vietnamese literary master.

In light of the argument presented in this book, NVGP's promotion of Vũ Trọng Phụng during the 1950s may reflect a general congruence between the group's explicitly anti-Stalinist political project and the writer's late colonial republicanism. Both projects challenged political despotism and championed the virtues of an independent civil society. Both saw a free and activist press as a key instrument of political struggle. Both supported the authority of science and technical knowledge over the power of political orthodoxy and entrenched intellectual dogma. In spite of sharing doubts about the Machiavellian character of communist political culture, both projects remained suspicious of unfettered capitalism. In short, colonial republicanism and reform communism shared a commitment to an Enlightenment project that was fundamentally antithetical to both French colonialism of the 1930s and Vietnamese Stalinism of the 1950s.

While NVGP's reasons for promoting Vũ Trọng Phụng remain open to debate, there is no question that the Party attacked his legacy as part of a larger campaign to silence NVGP. Not only did the repression of the movement between late 1956 and 1960 coincide precisely with the appearance of harshly negative reappraisals of the writer in the communist press, but every piece of published criticism targeting Vũ Trọng Phụng during this period (and most that were published thereafter) made a point to disparage the inflated praise showered on him by the "Nhân Văn Giai Phẩm clique" *(bọn NVGP)*. The punishment of Văn Tâm for publishing an essay in support of NVGP the year after the publication of *Vũ Trọng Phụng: Realist Writer* facilitated further an official strategy to tarnish Vũ Trọng Phụng through guilt by association. The linkage between the repression of NVGP and the persecution of Vũ Trọng Phụng crystallized in Hoàng Văn Hoan's double-barreled attack against the writer and the "counterrevolutionary clique" that promoted him. The climactic intervention of Hoàng Văn Hoan underlines the extent to which the debate over Vũ Trọng Phụng had come to be viewed in symbolic terms as a proxy war between the communist regime and its domestic opponents.

VŨ TRỌNG PHỤNG IN THE POST–WORLD WAR II ERA

Vũ Trọng Phụng attracted critical attention immediately following his death in 1939, but his work was ignored for almost a decade by communist cultural officials whose energies were absorbed by the Việt Minh war effort against France (1946–54). This period of neglect came to an end in September 1949 when Vũ Trọng Phụng was discussed briefly at the Việt Minh's Conference on Literary Debate held in the liberated zone at Việt Bắc.[6] Presided over by the hard-line revolutionary poet and cultural official Tố Hữu, the conference staged a series of discussions designed to amplify the superiority of socialist realism over the prerevolutionary fine arts. Participants in the conference included the leading lights of the Việt Minh cultural elite, a group dominated by literary figures from the late colonial era. Since their aesthetic proclivities had been corrupted by colonial schooling and French high culture, a major objective of the four-day conference was to "reeducate" this influential group about the cultural policies and preferences of the Việt Minh's communist leadership.

Initial references to Vũ Trọng Phụng at the conference praised his critical portrayal of prerevolutionary society. "When progressive literature needs to attack a social order or a way of life," explained Nguyễn Đình Thi, "its main task is to expose the true face of that society or that way of life. A work that accurately records those realities possesses real revolutionary value, as with the writing of Balzac or Vũ Trọng Phụng."[7] The comparison to Balzac anticipated subsequent efforts to label Vũ Trọng Phụng as a "critical realist," a communist literary category reserved for prerevolutionary writers who were critical of capitalism but indifferent (or openly hostile) toward "radical" alternatives. For the Hungarian Marxist Georg Lukács, the essence of critical realism is "that it can perceive the problems of human existence in a given time and place but not their solution" because "it lacks the overarching perspective which socialist realism has."[8] As opposed to unambiguously "reactionary" aesthetic categories such as "romanticism," "naturalism," or "bourgeois realism," "critical realism" allowed communist cultural officials in China and Eastern Europe to "critically assimilate" into the revolutionary literary canon politically suspect works that were highly esteemed by the public (such as Lu Xun in China or Dostoyevsky in

Eastern Europe).[9] It also helped to shore up the prestige of socialist-realist works by placing them within a literary genealogy that included genuinely popular prerevolutionary writing. By comparing him to Balzac and underlining his critical-realist affinities, Nguyễn Đình Thi was proposing a mechanism that allowed Vietnamese communist critics to endorse Vũ Trọng Phụng despite his lack of a "revolutionary perspective."

Dissatisfied with this cautious strategy of "critical assimilation," Nguyên Hồng—the great colonial-era novelist turned midlevel Việt Minh cultural official—offered a more robust defense of Vũ Trọng Phụng at the conference by insisting that a constructive "revolutionary perspective" could, in fact, be found in his work:

> Art must create something positive. But during a "destructive period," a positive creation may not necessarily reflect reality. The society of Red-Haired Xuân and Mrs. Deputy Customs Officer is a depraved and corrupt society; it fills people with disgust. In creating *Dumb Luck*, Vũ Trọng Phụng expresses a perspective *[thái độ]* marked by a refusal to accept such a society. Without this perspective, Vũ Trọng Phụng could describe the piss and shit of that society and it would not disgust us. To describe accurately is not enough. One must have a revolutionary perspective.[10]

Nguyên Hồng's strategy here was to redefine Vũ Trọng Phụng's destructive ("critical realist") attack on colonial capitalism as a "revolutionary" perspective on par with a constructive ("socialist realist") promotion of socialism. It is possible that Nguyên Hồng's own journey from "critical realism" during the late colonial era to "socialist realism" following the August Revolution motivated this eleventh-hour gambit to blur the boundaries between the two.

Bringing the exchange to a close, Tố Hữu sided with Nguyễn Đình Thi's more conservative approach by drawing attention to the difficulty of aligning Vũ Trọng Phụng's famously gloomy vision with the forward-looking character of socialist realism: "We must recognize a certain form of realism that doesn't lead anywhere but only seeks to destroy. Such realism may be referred to as 'Vũ Trọng Phụng realism.'"[11] Mitigating somewhat the ominous suggestion that Vũ Trọng Phụng's writing did not ultimately "lead anywhere," Tố Hữu also offered qualified praise (and even gratitude) that was to be invoked repeatedly by the writer's defenders throughout the remainder of the century: "Vũ Trọng Phụng's mode of realism is not socialist realism. Vũ Trọng Phụng was not a revolutionary, but the revolution thanks Vũ Trọng Phụng for exposing the corrupt and depraved reality of society at that time. Had Vũ Trọng Phụng pursued a revolutionary life, he would have met with success."[12] Owing to Tố Hữu's unrivaled power within the Vietnamese communist cultural establishment, his negative remarks boded ill for future assessments of Vũ Trọng Phụng. But his positive comments plus the endorsements of Nguyễn Đình Thi and Nguyên Hồng left Vũ Trọng Phụng's reputation intact, more or less, until the 1950s when the aggressive promotion of his work by the leaders of NVGP triggered a backlash that destroyed his reputation and prohibited the open circulation of his work for over thirty years.

VŨ TRỌNG PHỤNG AND NHÂN VĂN-GIAI PHẨM

Published on October 15, 1956, the third issue of *Nhân Văn* featured a range of articles promoting the "revisionist" project that had animated NVGP since its inception earlier in the year. Among these were the transcript of an interview with Dr. Đặng Văn Ngữ that called for less dictatorship within the VWP and more "freedom and democracy" and an article by Thanh Bình that objected to the regime's tight control over artists and intellectuals.[13] The issue also included an "Open Letter to Readers" that attempted to defuse the controversy ignited by the first two issues of the journal, which it characterized as a "struggle between brothers of the same family." "Many have approved of our recent efforts," the letter stated, "but others have opposed our journal and belittled and attacked its contributors. We have paid no attention to this opposition, viewing it as a hasty and erroneous attitude of friends toward friends."[14] Perhaps the most well-known contribution to the issue was a front-page essay by the philosopher Trần Đức Thảo—"Development of Democratic Freedoms"—which applauded Khrushchev's rebuke of Stalin at the Twentieth Congress of the CPSU and denounced the persistence within the VWP of Stalinist vices such as bureaucratism, commandism, partisanship, and the personality cult.[15]

In addition to these articles that expressed the "reform communist" agenda of NVGP, this issue of *Nhân Văn* included a series of items designed to promote the reputation of Vũ Trọng Phụng. The most dramatic was a large portrait of the writer that appeared in the top left-hand corner of the front page, adjacent to both the masthead of the journal and Trần Đức Thảo's anti-Stalinist essay. A caption beneath the portrait read: "On the Death Anniversary of Vũ Trọng Phụng (October, 13, 1939)."[16] Turning to page 2, readers found the following notice entitled: "Indifference to Vũ Trọng Phụng Is a Big Mistake":

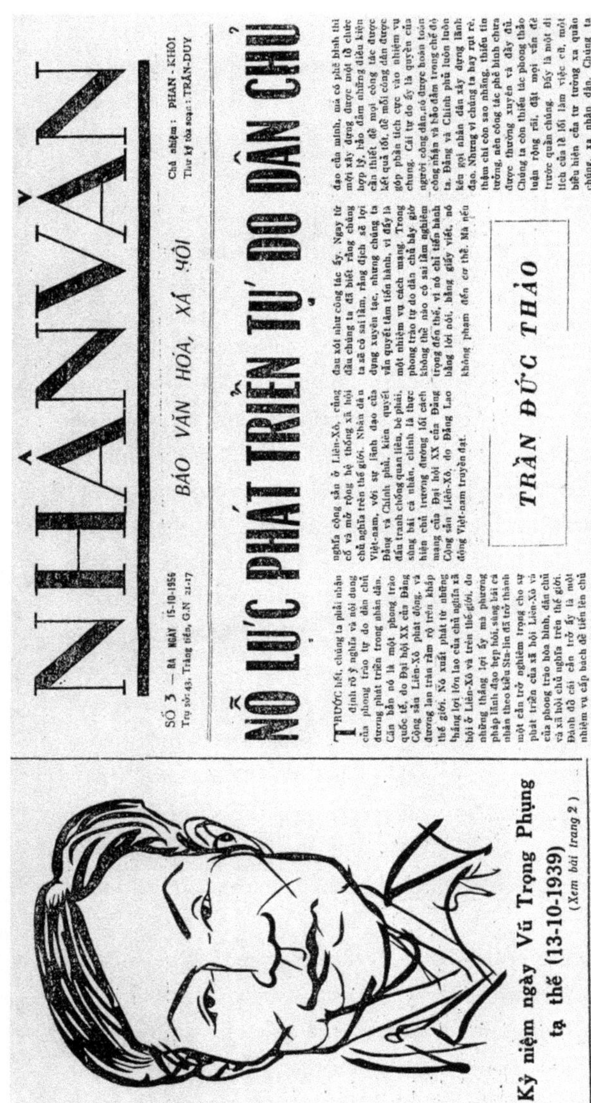

NHÂN VĂN

SỐ 3 — RA NGÀY 15-10-1956
Trụ sở: 43, Tràng tiền, G.N 21-17

BÁO VĂN HÓA, XÃ HỘI

Chủ nhiệm: PHAN-KHÔI
Thư ký tòa soạn: TRẦN-DUY

Kỷ niệm ngày Vũ Trọng Phụng tạ thế (13-10-1939)

(Xem bài trang 2)

NỖ LỰC PHÁT TRIỂN TỰ DO DÂN CHỦ

TRẦN ĐỨC THẢO

TRƯỚC hết, chúng ta phải nhận định rõ ý nghĩa và nội dung của phong trào tự do dân chủ đương phát triển trong nhân dân. Căn bản nó là một phong trào quốc tế, do Đại hội XX của Đảng Cộng sản Liên-Xô phát động, và đương lan tràn rầm rộ trên khắp thế giới. Nó xuất phát từ những thắng lợi lớn lao của chủ nghĩa xã hội ở Liên-Xô và trên thế giới, do những thắng lợi ấy mà phương pháp lãnh đạo hẹp hòi, sùng bái cá nhân theo kiểu Sta-lin đã trở thành một cản trở nghiêm trọng cho sự phát triển của xã hội Liên-Xô và của phong trào hòa bình, dân chủ và xã hội chủ nghĩa trên thế giới. Đánh đổ cái cản trở ấy là một nhiệm vụ cấp bách để tiến lên chủ nghĩa cộng sản ở Liên-Xô, củng cố và mở rộng hệ thống xã hội chủ nghĩa trên thế giới. Nhân dân Việt-nam, với sự lãnh đạo của Đảng và Chính phủ, kiên quyết đấu tranh chống quan liêu, bè phái, sùng bái cá nhân, chính là thực hiện chủ trương đường lối cách mạng của Đại hội XX của Đảng Cộng sản Liên-Xô, do Đảng Lao động Việt-nam truyền đạt.

Xét đến tình hình trong nước thì phong trào tự do dân chủ cũng có ý nghĩa trọng đại. Sau khi chúng ta đã đánh bại đế quốc và hoàn thành Cải cách Ruộng đất ở miền Bắc, chính những bệnh quan liêu, bè phái, sùng bái cá nhân là những di tích của chế độ cũ trong tổ chức mới. Đấu tranh chống những bệnh ấy là nhiệm vụ của nhân dân và đường lối của Đảng, một trọng tâm công tác để đẩy mạnh công cuộc kiến thiết kinh tế và văn hóa, nhanh chóng tiến lên chủ nghĩa xã hội. Tất nhiên trong phong trào có thể có những sai lầm cá nhân, những lời lẽ lệch lạc: với sự lãnh đạo của Đảng, những khuyết điểm ấy nhất định sẽ được sửa chữa. Nhưng đấy chỉ là chi tiết. Xét về căn bản và toàn bộ, phong trào hiện tại chống quan liêu, bè phái, sùng bái cá nhân là ...

... đau xót như công tác ấy. Ngay từ đầu chúng ta đã biết rằng chúng ta sẽ có sai lầm, rằng địch sẽ lợi dụng xuyên tạc, nhưng chúng ta vẫn quyết tâm tiến hành, vì đấy là một nhiệm vụ cách mạng. Trong phong trào tự do dân chủ bây giờ không thể nào có sai lầm nghiêm trọng đến thế, vì nó chỉ tiến hành bằng lời nói, bằng giấy viết, nó không phạm đến cơ thể. Mà nếu địch có thể tìm cách lợi dụng một vài chi tiết, thì về căn bản nó sẽ bị một gánh đòn rất nặng, có thể là quyết định, vì căn bản tuyên truyền của địch là kêu rằng chúng ta không có dân chủ, mà chính đây chúng ta lại chứng minh bằng sự việc rằng chúng ta có dân chủ rõ ràng. Không phải vì một vài vấn đề vụn vặt mà chúng ta lại bỏ cái căn bản, không vì thấy cây mà chúng ta không trông thấy rừng.

Có anh em lo rằng với tự do dân chủ được phát triển, giai cấp tư sản sẽ « ngóc đầu lên ». Chính như thế là đánh lạc vấn đề. Từ ngày hòa bình trở lại, chúng ta mở rộng phạm vi kinh doanh tư sản, chúng ta hô hào họ đầu tư; như thế họ cũng đã được thỏa mãn một phần khá, mà họ cũng không có đủ sức để làm gì khác. Những người ...

... đạo của mình, mà có phê bình thì mới xây dựng được một tổ chức hợp lý, bảo đảm những điều kiện cần thiết để mọi công tác được kết quả tốt, để mỗi công dân được góp phần tích cực vào nhiệm vụ chung. Cái tự do ấy là quyền của người công dân, nó được hoàn toàn công nhận và bảo đảm trong chế độ ta. Đảng và Chính phủ luôn luôn kêu gọi nhân dân xây dựng lãnh đạo. Nhưng vì chúng ta hay rụt rè, thậm chí còn sao nhãng, thiếu tin tưởng, nên công tác phê bình chưa được thường xuyên và đầy đủ. Chúng ta còn thiếu tác phong thảo luận rộng rãi, đặt mọi vấn đề trước quần chúng. Đấy là một di tích của lề lối làm việc cũ, một biểu hiện của tư tưởng xa quần chúng, xa nhân dân. Chúng ta phải nỗ lực mở rộng dân chủ, phát triển phê bình trong nhân dân. Đảng đã chỉ đường vạch lối, nhưng không thể làm thay: Tự do không phải là cái gì có thể ban ơn.

Trong nhiệm vụ thực hiện phương châm của Đại hội XX của Đảng Cộng sản Liên-Xô, đáp hưởng ứng lời kêu gọi của Đảng Lao động Việt-nam, hưởng ứng phong trào phát triển tự do dân chủ trong những nước dân chủ nhân dân anh em, người trí thức Việt-nam có phần trách nhiệm quan trọng. Người trí thức hoạt động văn hóa, cần tự do như khí trời để thở. Có tự do thì mới đầy mạnh được sáng tác văn nghệ, nghiên cứu khoa học, cải tiến kỹ thuật. Phát triển tự do là nhu cầu thiết thân đồng thời là nhiệm vụ ...

B.S. ĐẶNG-VĂN-NGỮ TRẢ LỜI

về mở rộng tự do và dân chủ

1 — Theo ý ông, lúc này giới trí thức nói chung và giới văn nghệ nói riêng cần phải làm gì để góp phần thực hiện mở rộng tự do và dân chủ?

2 — Theo ý ông và căn cứ vào nhu cầu phát triển của ngành y tế, có những vấn đề gì cần đem thảo luận rộng rãi?

Trả lời câu thứ nhất:

Một dân tộc càng bị áp bức thì càng thiết tha ham muốn tự do dân chủ. Dân tộc Việt-nam, hàng mấy trăm năm nay sống dưới áp bức ...

... nhân dân mà ra. Trình độ nhân dân cao đến đâu thì trình độ Đảng và Chính phủ cao đến đấy.

Mỗi người trong nhân dân có thể có sai lầm thì mỗi người trong ...

... của ta đã thiếu tự do tư tưởng, thiếu dũng cảm nên không dám phê bình xây dựng. Một số đông trong hàng ngũ trí thức chúng ta không phê bình vì sợ bị hiểu nhầm, sợ bị nghi là lập trường không vững. Một số khác có phê bình một vài lần nhưng chưa thấy sửa chữa thì sinh ra tiêu cực, không tiếp tục phê bình nữa. Cả hai thái độ đều sai vì nó đều là những hiện tượng thiếu tin tưởng vào tính chất dân chủ của chế độ ta, thiếu ý thức chủ nhân ông đất nước.

FIGURE 6.
Front Page of *Nhân Văn* (Humanity), October 15, 1956.

> Vũ Trọng Phụng published his first work at twenty-one and died at twenty-seven. His seventeen works from these six years are *a shining page in Vietnamese literary history.* Vũ Trọng Phụng's fierce pen stamped a black mark on the forehead of a corrupt, absurd society, leaving behind eternally typical figures such as Nghị Hách, Xuân Tóc đỏ, Văn Minh, and Típ-phờ-nờ. These characters step off the page and into real life. The era of *Dumb Luck* has come to an end. The revolution attacked with weapons the same things that Vũ Trọng Phụng attacked with his pen and toppled that regime of "dumb luck." But vestiges of Vũ Trọng Phụng's characters persist in our current regime. We wish for a Vũ Trọng Phụng of the revolution to struggle against the rot that endures in the North and that continues to reign under Ngô Đình Diệm in the South. For a long time, our attitude toward Vũ Trọng Phụng has not been unified. Some praise him strongly, while others denounce him. But above all, an attitude of neglect reigns supreme. This is not good. Indifference toward Vũ Trọng Phụng reflects a misunderstanding of our literary history and a neglect of *a master of the Vietnamese novel.* We must extol and understand Vũ Trọng Phụng not only to honor the dead but to discover, for the living, the deep *humanist [nhân văn]* lessons in his work. It is not enough to commemorate Vũ Trọng Phụng with newspaper articles or a memorial event. We hope that critics, theorists, and *literary historians of Vietnam* will research and assess Vũ Trọng Phụng in a manner that does justice to his monumental work.[17]

The article takes issue with Vũ Trọng Phụng's exclusion from the pantheon of writers that had gained approval within VWP literary circles during the anti-French resistance. By emphasizing Vũ Trọng Phụng's strong critique of feudal society, it rehearses the defense of his work as a form of politically acceptable critical realism. It also makes clear that its objection to the neglect of Vũ Trọng Phụng was grounded, partially at least, in nationalist concerns (embodied in references to Vũ Trọng Phụng as "a master of the Vietnamese novel" and to his work as "a shining page in Vietnamese literary history"). Less clear, however, is the precise content of the "humanist lessons" that the article identifies in his work.

Adding to this puzzle is a third commemorative item published in the issue: the full text of the lengthy letter that Vũ Trọng Phụng had published in the newspaper *The Future* on March 5, 1937, entitled "Pornographic or Not?"[18] In the letter, Vũ Trọng Phụng defended his work against charges of obscenity that had been raised by Nhất Linh's Self-Strength Literary Group. The selection of this particular piece for republication is odd since, as a letter rather than an excerpt from his creative work, it did not highlight the literary qualities that had been underlined in the accompanying article. Moreover, the letter's robust defense of the risqué content of Vũ Trọng Phụng's writing (including profanity and explicit sexuality) called attention to one aspect of his work that made puritanical communist critics most uneasy. The same goes for Vũ Trọng Phụng's defense, in the latter part of the letter, of his own "pessimist outlook" since this clashed with the morale-building imperatives of Vietnamese socialist realism. On the other hand, the letter featured elements likely to appeal to communist critics such as a strong affirmation of the merits of literary realism, a harsh attack on the anodyne romantic style of the Self-Strength Literary Group, and clear traces of class resentment in Vũ Trọng Phụng's rejoinder to accusations by his critics that his work was coarse and uncouth.

Arguments advanced throughout the third issue of *Nhân Văn* regarding the benefits of greater intellectual freedom and a more open society within the DRV raise the possibility that the decision to republish "Pornographic or Not?" was motivated less by a desire to highlight its content than to celebrate the spirit of open intellectual exchange that it embodied. Indeed, a subtitle provided by the editors referred to the letter as a "pen-war essay" *(bài bút chiến)*. It may be no coincidence that this vivid artifact of the lively intellectual battlefield of the late colonial era appeared alongside an essay by Trần Đức Thảo that asserted: "The development of forms of freedom—including freedom of the press, of speech, of assembly, and so on—is the main prerequisite for liberating the people's creative forces and for throwing into relief the rich and democratic substance we have acquired."[19] In other words, the republication of the letter might be read as an endorsement by NVGP of the lively late-colonial-era public sphere that had once nurtured the rise of feisty and iconoclastic national literary treasures such as Vũ Trọng Phụng.

VŨ TRỌNG PHỤNG IS WITH US

Two weeks after the republication of Vũ Trọng Phụng's letter in *Nhân Văn*, leading figures associated with NVGP helped to organize a high-profile commemorative event at the Hà Nội Opera House designed to honor the writer and to keep his work in the public eye. The event was publicized in the following notice printed in all the major newspapers in the city.[20]

> To commemorate a writer who brought glory to Vietnamese literature, the literary board and publishing house of the Vietnamese Association of Art and Literature *[Hội Văn Nghệ Việt Nam]* together with the Minh Đức Publishing House will organize a memorial for Vũ Trọng Phụng at the Hà Nội Opera House starting at 8:00 P.M. on October 27, 1956. At this event, the two writers

> Trương Tửu and Nguyên Hồng will speak about the life and work of Vũ Trọng Phụng. On this occasion, the Minh Đức Publishing House will launch the collection *Vũ Trọng Phụng Is with Us [Vũ Trọng Phụng với chúng ta]*. All money raised from the sale of this volume will be used by the publishing house to repair the tomb of Vũ Trọng Phụng.[21]

The commemoration occurred in the midst of the NVGP affair, six weeks after the first six issues of *Nhân Văn* and *Giai Phẩm* had come out and six weeks before both journals were forcibly shut down in early December 1956. It is remarkable, therefore, that the event was organized cooperatively by the leading cultural organ of the DRV, on the one hand, and the leading institution supporting NVGP, on the other. The Party was represented by the Vietnam Arts and Literature Association, an official body founded along Soviet lines in 1948 to mobilize and police creative intellectuals.[22] The Minh Đức Publishing House was a private publishing enterprise that printed and marketed *Nhân Văn* and *Giai Phẩm* as well as other short-lived independent periodicals such as the incendiary student magazine *New Land (Đất Mới)*.[23] In addition to cosponsoring the event, both organizations republished works by Vũ Trọng Phụng during this period. The Vietnam Arts and Literature Association released *The Storm* in 1956 and Minh Đức reissued *The Dike Breaks* and *Dumb Luck* in 1957.[24] The collaboration between the two entities is more striking given the role that the Vietnam Arts and Literature Association would come to play in the repressive campaign against NVGP later in the decade. Less than two years after they joined forces to organize the Hà Nội Opera House event, the Association condemned NVGP as "revisionist" and "counterrevolutionary" and moved to purge from its ranks the leadership of the movement. It sanctioned the banning of *Nhân Văn* and *Giai Phẩm*, the shuttering of Minh Đức, and the arrest and imprisonment of its founder, Trần Thiếu Bảo.[25]

The main speakers at the commemoration—Nguyên Hồng and Trương Tửu—were also strange bedfellows, but in a more complex sense. While the institutional cosponsorship of the event embodied an alliance between quintessentially establishment and antiestablishment forces, the joint keynote speeches of Nguyên Hồng and Trương Tửu represented a partnership between a pliable political moderate and an unorthodox anti-Stalinist radical. Nguyên Hồng had produced his greatest literary work—the novel *Bỉ vỏ (Girl thief)*—as a politically uncommitted teenager during the late 1930s, but he joined the Party in 1948 and rose to a reasonably high position within the Việt Minh cultural bureaucracy.[26] Between 1947 and 1956, he served on the executive committee of the Vietnam Arts and Literature Association and as an editor of its official organ, *Literary Arts Magazine (Tạp chí Văn Nghệ)*. In 1957,

Nguyên Hồng ascended to a higher position, serving as the editor-in-chief of *Literature (Văn)*, the weekly journal of the newly formed Vietnam Writers' Association (Hội Nhà văn Việt Nam). Inspired by the reformist tenor of the time, he provided modest support for NVGP's agenda before recanting and retiring prematurely from his official posts in early 1958.[27] After being disciplined, Nguyên Hồng managed to accommodate himself to life under the regime, serving within the provincial cultural bureaucracy in his native Hải Phòng for the remainder of his life.[28]

As with Nguyên Hồng, Trương Tửu established his reputation in the late colonial era (as a prolific Marxist literary critic) and joined the Việt Minh during World War II.[29] Unlike Nguyên Hồng, however, Trương Tửu actively resisted Party discipline, an oppositional stance that made him a natural leader of NVGP as well as one of the most beleaguered scapegoats of the subsequent official campaign against the movement.[30] Unwilling to compromise in the manner of Nguyên Hồng, Trương Tửu remained unemployed, marginalized, and under a cloud of suspicion until his death in 1999. Although relations between the two were not openly antagonistic, Nguyên Hồng signed an open letter to *The People (Nhân Dân)* less than two months after the Hà Nội Opera House event that denounced Trương Tửu along with the rest of the leadership of NVGP.[31]

Although NVGP and VWP cultural officials are typically seen as bitter enemies, their cooperation on the commemoration reveals that relations between the two were complex and evolved considerably between 1956 and the decisive repression of the movement in 1958. Members of both groups were dominated by veterans of the Việt Minh and many had worked on newspapers together and run in similar social circles during the late colonial era. Moreover, as a "revisionist" movement devoted to the perfection of communism (rather than its elimination), members of NVGP shared with cultural officials an earnest fidelity to the VWP and to Marxism-Leninism. Since both groups looked to the Soviet and Chinese communist parties for ideological leadership, they each acknowledged the virtues of de-Stalinization and the Hundred Flowers policy. The crux of their disagreement lay in the extent to which they believed that these liberalizing initiatives ought to be applied in the DRV. Officials of the VWP paid lip service to these initiatives, while members of NVGP demanded their full implementation in the DRV in the form of greater democracy within the Party, enhanced freedom for artists and intellectuals, and heightened respect for "socialist legality." As the precise parameters of these opposing positions (supportive rhetoric versus decisive action) waxed and waned throughout 1956 and 1957, the attitude of cultural officials toward NVGP during this era vacillated between tolerance and persecution.

While transcripts of the speeches delivered at the Hà Nội Opera House have not survived, an indication of the messages conveyed there may be gleaned from a slim volume of commemorative essays produced for the event by Minh Đức and suggestively entitled *Vũ Trọng Phụng Is with Us*.[32] It included original contributions by five of the most eminent members of NVGP. The first three by Nguyễn Mạnh Tường, Đào Duy Anh, and Hoàng Cầm were each entitled "Remembering Vũ Trọng Phụng."[33] A fourth, authored by Phan Khôi, was called "Don't Extol Vũ Trọng Phụng. Merely Evaluate Him Correctly."[34] A fifth item was Trương Tửu's introduction to a new edition of *The Dike Breaks* that was published by Minh Đức the following year.[35] The volume also included a brief excerpt from a soon-to-be-published book about Vũ Trọng Phụng by the young literary scholar Văn Tâm, a student of Trương Tửu.[36] It also republished one chapter from *The Dike Breaks* and another from *Dumb Luck*. The cover featured a portrait of Vũ Trọng Phụng by Sỹ Ngọc, a prominent artist closely associated with NVGP.

The essays discussed various aspects of Vũ Trọng Phụng's life and work, but they also addressed a handful of common themes. First, each essay made a point to shower Vũ Trọng Phụng with fulsome praise. Đào Duy Anh asserted that Vũ Trọng Phụng was a "brave and talented writer that the nation *[dân tộc]* would remember forever."[37] Nguyễn Mạnh Tường likened him to Tolstoy and compared his gift for satire to Cervantes and Moliere. "Looking back at our literary history during the interwar period," he wrote, "I don't see a single work as remarkable *[đặc sắc]* or as exemplary *[tiêu biểu]* as the books that he left behind."[38] Phan Khôi underlined Vũ Trọng Phụng's greatness as a novelist by touting the superiority of his writing, in terms of quantity and quality *(lượng của tiểu thuyết Vũ Trọng Phụng đã trỗi rồi mà chất cũng trỗi)*, over all of his contemporaries.[39] He was significantly more prolific than the pioneers of northern Vietnamese prose fiction such as Nguyễn Bá Học, Phạm Duy Tốn, and Hoàng Ngọc Phách, and his work avoided the pitfalls of petty-bourgeois sentimentality and supernaturalism found in the work of Nhất Linh, Khái Hưng, and Thế Lữ. While admitting that Ngô Tất Tố and Nguyễn Công Hoan had each produced one good novel during the era, Phan Khôi pointed out that they had failed to keep pace with Vũ Trọng Phụng's remarkable level of output. Only Lê Văn Trương rivaled Vũ Trọng Phụng, but only in terms of productivity, not, Phan Khôi asserted, in terms of literary quality.

While paying tribute to Vũ Trọng Phụng, contributors to the volume voiced anxiety that expressions of admiration for the author were likely to be misunderstood in politically reactionary terms. Nguyễn Mạnh Tường worried aloud that critics might misconstrue support for Vũ Trọng Phụng as nostalgia for a prerevolutionary past. "There are those that wish to lead us to a fresh, beautiful tomorrow," he wrote, "but who dampen our spirit of struggle by accusing us of pining for the old days." In anticipation of an attack that misinterpreted his praise of Vũ Trọng Phụng as nostalgia for the colonial era, Nguyễn Mạnh Tường staged a preemptive defense, condemning the colonial regime for its neglect and mistreatment of Vũ Trọng Phụng. Colonial-era neglect was responsible, he argued, for the dilapidated current condition of the writer's grave site. "How can we possibly feel nostalgia for a regime that drove its intellectuals into this kind of a dead end?" he wrote, referring to Vũ Trọng Phụng's untended tomb. "How stupid must we be to desire the return of a regime that treated its artists and intellectuals like the living dead, compelling them, in essence, to die twice? To cry for Vũ Trọng Phụng today is to adopt a political attitude. To commemorate Vũ Trọng Phụng is a political act. The great family of intellectuals is determined that the wheels of history will never take us backward into the past."[40]

Equally anxious about the possible backlash that his tribute to Vũ Trọng Phụng might provoke, Phan Khôi opened his essay with a lengthy digression on the dangers—given the paranoid political climate within the DRV—of extolling in public politically suspect figures. Illustrating the point with a recklessly inflammatory example, he pointed to the recent critical firestorm over Hoàng Cầm's sympathetic portrayal of Trần Dần in the first issue of *Nhân Văn*. "How very strange," he wrote. "Why was Hoàng Cầm criticized for inappropriate 'extolling' when he simply defended an ordinary, innocent man like Trần Dần, who has been abused and oppressed by powerful forces within our Democratic Republic?" Turning to the case of Vũ Trọng Phụng, Phan Khôi continued: "I wish to write a little about the deceased writer Vũ Trọng Phụng, but I am afraid that people will criticize me for extolling him. Hence, I must take certain precautions. Please note, dear readers, that in a society such as ours, one must be very careful when writing about a person such as Vũ Trọng Phụng."[41]

It is difficult to overstate the provocative character of Phan Khôi's analogy between his own tribute to Vũ Trọng Phụng and Hoàng Cầm's infamous profile of the soldier-poet Trần Dần. Appearing in *Nhân Văn* one month before the appearance of Phan Khôi's essay, Hoàng Cầm's article—"Toward the Revision of a Literary Case: Trần Dần the Person"—detailed the persecution of Trần Dần by communist military officials after he spearheaded an insurgent campaign for greater intellectual freedom within the army during 1955.[42] The article dwelled on the suffering of Trần Dần's pregnant wife during his term of confinement, and it implied that harsh treatment during "reeducation" had driven him to attempt suicide. Owing to its portrayal of Trần Dần as an earnest, idealistic, and loyal reformer crushed by the grinding bureaucratic machinery of the Party state, the article emerged as among the most famous essays published by NVGP, and it cemented Trần Dần's status as a personification of the movement. Phan Khôi's analogy therefore highlighted a potentially hazardous link between Vũ Trọng Phụng and the most controversial contemporary symbol of domestic opposition to the VWP.

As with the contributions to the volume by Nguyễn Mạnh Tường and Phan Khôi, Đào Duy Anh's essay betrayed awareness that excessive praise of Vũ Trọng Phụng ran the risk of triggering a conservative backlash. To contain the risk, Đào Duy Anh cited the authority of a Soviet literary scholar to support his affirmative assessment of Vũ Trọng Phụng:

> One day, I was speaking about Vietnamese literature with a Soviet professor who was here researching the Vietnamese language. Stricken with a kind of national inferiority complex, I complained to her that our modern literature did not have any great works like the ones found in the early literature of other countries. "What about Vũ Trọng Phụng?" she responded in a robust, combative tone. Her comment startled and embarrassed me. Something had happened to me during my years in the Resistance that had allowed me to forget this young writer who was most worthy of love, sympathy, and admiration and who shone brightly during the most painful historical period in our country's history.[43]

Returning to the Soviet professor at the conclusion of the essay, Đào Duy Anh offered her his "profound gratitude for helping to jog my memory."[44] While this framing device served to highlight one key theme of the essay—the persistence among DRV intellectuals of a national inferiority complex—it also functioned to shield Đào Duy Anh's tribute to Vũ Trọng Phụng with the protective cloak of Soviet authority.

Finally, all the essays argued a similar case: that Vũ Trọng Phụng's body of work qualified as politically virtuous literature according to the new evaluative standards put in place by the DRV cultural bureaucracy. The highest literary achievement based on these standards was socialist realism—a genre marked, in its most elemental form, by the coexistence of a negative attitude toward colonialism, feudalism, and capitalism and an endorsement of communist revolution as the only solution to economic exploitation, social inequity, and political oppression. Less exalted than socialist realism but still tolerated and considered worthy of republication was critical realism, which shared socialist realism's negative (or destructive) attitude toward the old society, but not its positive (or constructive) attitude toward the communist solution. Since Vũ Trọng Phụng's checkered perspective on communism made it difficult to align his writing with the standards of socialist realism, contributors to the volume adopted an intermediate position, arguing that his work represented an advanced form of critical realism that possessed within it an incipient socialist-realist embryo struggling to be born. The challenge of making this particular argument persuasive was to identify even rudimentary evidence for the presence of a positive and constructive attitude toward revolutionary communism within Vũ Trọng Phụng's dark and pessimistic body of work.

Phan Khôi presented the clearest version of this argument but with the least supporting evidence. At the conclusion of his essay, he asserted abruptly, "Perhaps we can say that Vũ Trọng Phụng was a critical-realist novelist with socialist tendencies on the eve of the August Revolution."[45] Nothing in the body of the essay, however, illustrates the presence in Vũ Trọng Phụng's work of "socialist tendencies." Indeed, Phan Khôi seems to admit as much when he writes that "all of Vũ Trọng Phụng's writing reveals the misery and ugliness of life under French colonialism although it does little more than reveal it."[46] Đào Duy Anh's essay follows Phan Khôi's in emphasizing the critical-realist elements of Vũ Trọng Phụng's work exclusively. "Vũ Trọng Phụng dealt bravely with poverty, social vices, and violence," he wrote. "He used his pen to expose all the cruelties of society at that time, to denounce those with wealth and power who live decadent lives by exploiting the blood and sweat of the people."[47]

Hoàng Cầm offered a slightly more involved (but no more convincing) case that Vũ Trọng Phụng should be read as an incipient socialist realist. After detailing his critical-realist credentials, including the way that his work stimulates hatred for colonial society, he admitted that Vũ Trọng Phụng "does not offer a concrete alternative way of life." But by discouraging his readers from following the road of "vagabonds like Red-Haired Xuân" or "colonial mimic-men like Dr. Straight-Talk" or "decadent whores like Mrs. Deputy Customs Officer," he indirectly encouraged his readers to explore other roads. "When we read Vũ Trọng Phụng today," he writes, "we need to think about the implicit point that he doesn't state directly but that remains hidden in the page: the hope to build and to live in a beautiful and humane society."[48] Faced with the absence of evidence of a clear revolutionary consciousness on the part of Vũ Trọng Phụng, Nguyễn Mạnh Tường floated an equally unverifiable theory: that the writer's revolutionary commitment was hard to detect because it was lodged in his "subconscious." He wrote: "Speaking of

Tolstoy, Lenin wrote, 'A truly great artist finds a way to reflect in his work the main aspects of the revolution.' I am not sure if Vũ Trọng Phụng understood this explicitly. But I believe that he felt it subconsciously."[49]

The most elaborate case devised to align Vũ Trọng Phụng's writing with the political standards of the new regime may be found in the contribution of Trương Tửu. The case was based on readings of two episodes from Vũ Trọng Phụng's work—one plausible and suggestive and the other tendentious and misleading. The misleading argument opened by quoting, out of context, the following passage from *To Be a Whore:*

> When a country is overrun by invaders we must join the army and face one of two possible outcomes: either kill the invaders or be killed by them. Should we advise our soldiers not to kill the invaders or to fear being killed on the battlefield? If so, we might as well advise them to stay home.[50]

The "invaders" in the original passage refers to censorious literary critics predisposed to object to the sexually graphic description of the psychological origins of the modern Vietnamese sex trade presented in *To Be a Whore*. As even a cursory reading of the original passage indicates, the "two outcomes" that it describes refer to the choice between self-censorship and open defiance of hypocritical and counterproductive puritanical moral norms. For Vũ Trọng Phụng, this dramatic metaphorical language (in which censors are "invaders" that must be "killed" by truth-speaking realists) reflected the life-or-death urgency of the numerous social problems associated with the growth of prostitution. Wrenching the passage out of its context, Trương Tửu ignored its original meaning, reading it instead as an anticolonial appeal to "use literature as a weapon of struggle to eliminate the enemy"—an enemy that he defined as "French capitalism, the feudal landlord class, and the comprador bourgeoisie." In conclusion, Trương Tửu glossed the passage as clear evidence of Vũ Trọng Phụng's "revolutionary attitude toward literature."

In addition to offering this disingenuous argument, Trương Tửu opened a significantly more plausible line of defense by drawing attention to the genuine novelty and significance of Vũ Trọng Phụng's sympathetic account of a mass political protest in *The Dike Breaks*. "In all the literature produced between 1930 and 1940," he wrote, "I have found no work that depicts peasant struggles with a mass character in such a thoroughly realistic and sympathetic way as in *The Dike Breaks*."[51] Turning to the portrayal of the ex–political prisoners who work for the newspaper *Labor* in the latter part of the novel, Trương Tửu argued further that Vũ Trọng Phụng

FIGURE 7.
Cover of *Vũ Trọng Phụng với chúng ta* (Vũ Trọng Phụng is with us) (Hanoi, 1956).

celebrated directly the political effort of "revolutionary fighters struggling for the rights of the oppressed and exploited masses." Here, Trương Tửu zeros in on the defining feature of socialist realism—the explicit endorsement of communist revolution and praise of communist revolutionaries—according to orthodox Vietnamese critics of the era: "With reference to this point—the veneration of communist fighters—Vũ Trọng Phụng was more progressive than any other realist writer of his era."[52]

The consensus view expressed in each of the essays in *Vũ Trọng Phụng Is with Us* that Vũ Trọng Phụng was a budding socialist realist extended even to Sỹ Ngọc's portrait of the writer that graced the front cover of the volume. The portrait depicts the famously skinny and sickly writer as a typical "new man" from socialist-realist iconography—square-jawed and steely eyed with a full shock of hair, a thick muscular neck, and a confident expression. This rendering contrasts sharply with newspaper caricatures of Vũ Trọng Phụng from the 1930s that tended to portray him as frail and slightly effeminate. Sỹ Ngọc's distorted portrait mimicked the improbable arguments about the protocommunist nature of Vũ Trọng Phụng's political and aesthetic project put forward in *Vũ Trọng Phụng Is with Us.*

VŨ TRỌNG PHỤNG: REALIST WRITER AND THE PUNISHMENT OF VĂN TÂM

Several months after the Hà Nội Opera House event, a twenty-three-year-old literature scholar at the Hà Nội Teachers Training College named Văn Tâm published a remarkable research monograph, over two-hundred pages in length, attempting to ground within a Marxian analytical framework the flimsy arguments about Vũ Trọng Phụng's socialist-realist proclivities advanced in *Vũ Trọng Phụng Is with Us.* Entitled *Vũ Trọng Phụng: Realist Writer,* Văn Tâm's book explored the deterministic relationship between the socioeconomic conditions of the interwar era and Vũ Trọng Phụng's portrayal of social mobility, class consciousness, and revolutionary commitment. It also assembled extensive evidence to verify Vũ Trọng Phụng's alleged procommunist sympathies. Văn Tâm's redemptive reading was more ambitious than its predecessors because it did not ignore obvious features of Vũ Trọng Phụng's writing that undermined the case for the socialist-realist character of his work. Rather, it attempted to explain (and excuse) the limitations of Vũ Trọng Phụng's socialist-realist vision as a by-product of his petty-bourgeois class background. Despite the thoroughness of his scholarship, Văn Tâm's defense of Vũ Trọng Phụng's reputation was ineffective and arguably counterproductive.

During the same year that his study was published, Văn Tâm was disciplined by the Ministry of Education for expressing public support for NVGP. The punishment of Văn Tâm served to discredit his research in the eyes of the authorities and to strengthen an impression that a connection existed between Vũ Trọng Phụng and domestic opposition to the Party state.

Văn Tâm was not a member of NVGP (he never published in *Nhân Văn* or *Giai Phẩm*), but he came of age intellectually under the influence of members of the movement. Born in 1933, Văn Tâm was first drawn to Vũ Trọng Phụng's work during the late 1940s while living in Interzone 4, a liberated area under Việt Minh control that included his native Thanh Hóa Province.[53] Administered by Nguyễn Sơn—a charismatic Việt Minh general renowned for his patronage of the arts—Interzone 4 attracted a large community of intellectuals, including future leaders of NVGP such as Đào Duy Anh, Sỹ Ngọc, Nguyễn Mạnh Tường, and Trương Tửu. Văn Tâm studied with several of these figures at the Preparatory Academy *(Dự bị Đại học)* in Interzone 4 during the early 1950s. As he fell under the influence of these figures, Văn Tâm began to collect material for *Vũ Trọng Phụng: Realist Writer* by purchasing hard-to-find copies of the writer's work from bourgeois families who had evacuated from Hà Nội to Interzone 4 with their private libraries in tow. "During those years," he recalled decades later, "I limited my spending on food and clothes in order to save money for used-book buying sprees."[54]

Settling in Hà Nội following the end of the war in 1954, Văn Tâm enrolled in an elite humanities class made up of students recruited from the new Teachers Training Department of the College of Letters (Ban Sư phạm Đại học Văn Khoa). Students in the class studied literature with Trương Tửu, philosophy with Trần Đức Thảo, and history with Đào Duy Anh.[55] For a literature colloquium led by Trương Tửu, Văn Tâm utilized the sources that he had collected in Interzone 4 to produce a fifty-page paper that became the foundation of *Vũ Trọng Phụng: Realist Writer*. Trương Tửu praised the paper and encouraged his promising pupil to submit it to the Literary Arts Publishing House (NXB Văn Nghệ). One editor there—the writer Tô Hoài—urged him to revise it into a book-length study, while another—the poet Hoàng Trung Thông—demanded a more critical treatment of Vũ Trọng Phụng's naturalist orientation. Taking the former advice but not the latter, Văn Tâm extended the scope of his manuscript and, after false starts with several publishers, submitted it to the privately owned Kim Đức Publishing House early in 1957. Kim Đức accepted the manuscript, but not before Văn Tâm had agreed to pay production costs and to persuade Trương Tửu to help market it by penning an introductory essay. As Trương Tửu came under withering public attack for his leading role in

NVGP, his preface to *Vũ Trọng Phụng: Realist Writer* marked the book as an easy target for conservative critics.

Trương Tửu's brief introduction heralded Văn Tâm's monograph as a major watershed in the study of Vũ Trọng Phụng. "The literary world and the reading public have long recognized the great value of Vũ Trọng Phụng's work," he wrote. "But they have also longed for the appearance of serious research that clarifies the contribution of this realist writer to modern Vietnamese literature. With Văn Tâm's monograph, this hope has been realized."[56] Trương Tửu highlighted Văn Tâm's research effort, which entailed scouring libraries and private manuscript collections for obscure works and criticism, interviewing members of Vũ Trọng Phụng's family, and tracking down copies of his letters, notebooks, photographs, and identity papers. He also praised Văn Tâm's "spirit of struggle," "enthusiasm for realism," and deployment of "the newest literary theories from China and the Soviet Union to analyze and assess Vũ Trọng Phụng's complex body of work."[57] Echoing reassurances invoked repeatedly in *Vũ Trọng Phụng Is with Us,* these comments underlined the politically acceptable character of Văn Tâm's project. But Trương Tửu's description of Văn Tâm's painstaking research signified how *Vũ Trọng Phụng: Realist Writer* departed from the narrow political instrumentalism of the essays published in that volume. Indeed, it was the rigorous and wide-ranging quality of this research, carried out within the inhospitable scholarly environment of the postwar DRV, that endowed Văn Tâm's monograph with its enduring value.

Following Trương Tửu's introduction, the first chapter of *Vũ Trọng Phụng: Realist Writer* presented the first history of the critical reception of Vũ Trọng Phụng's work.[58] Echoing complaints about the neglect of the writer raised in *Nhân Văn,* Văn Tâm observed that controversy had relegated Vũ Trọng Phụng's work to a "forbidden zone" for over ten years. Prior to this decade of critical inattention, Vũ Trọng Phụng's most vocal detractors were "moralistic critics" from Phạm Quỳnh's *Southern Wind* and Nhất Linh's Self-Strength Literary Group whose conservative "class viewpoint" (aristocratic for the former, bourgeois for the latter) clashed with his "denunciatory realism" (synonymous with "critical realism"). Since their aesthetic standards derived from outdated notions of "beauty" and "refinement," these critics misconstrued as crude or pornographic Vũ Trọng Phụng's harsh, unflinching brand of realism. The opening chapter's emphasis on his conservative opponents cast the writer in the most "progressive" possible light. Văn Tâm buttressed this exculpatory gambit by emphasizing the practical political benefits of reading Vũ Trọng Phụng's "critical-realist" depictions of colonial society. Negatives depictions of the colonial past, he argued, brought the virtues of the revolutionary present into bold relief. They also shed light on the neocolonial character of life in the southern Republic of Vietnam. Just as he emphasized the conservative nature of Vũ Trọng Phụng's antagonists, Văn Tâm gently chided critics on the Left for failing to appreciate the progressive orientation of his work. He also detailed a lengthy list of colonial-era critics who recognized Vũ Trọng Phụng's talent and admired his progressive politics. Finally, Văn Tâm brought the story of Vũ Trọng Phụng's reception up to the present day by describing the checkered assessment of his work at the Việt Bắc Conference on Literary Debate and the praise it received in *Vũ Trọng Phụng Is with Us*.

The second chapter—"Social Circumstances"—presented the economic and political history of the interwar era as structural determinants of Vũ Trọng Phụng's creative work.[59] It opened with a detailed account of the boom and bust of the interwar colonial economy followed by a narrative of the rise of global and local incarnations of revolutionary communism. Turning from economics and politics to culture, Văn Tâm analyzed the lively intellectual ferment of the era as a dependent level of historical experience. Among the myriad transformations underway, Văn Tâm viewed the acceleration of class differentiation, especially within the petty bourgeoisie, as crucial in explaining the emergence of Vũ Trọng Phụng. In response to the jolting economic and political transformations of the era, members of the petty bourgeoisie splintered; some ascended into the bourgeoisie and the ruling class, while others joined the proletariat or descended into a lumpen-proletarian world of crime and hooliganism. Owing to political opportunities provided by the growth of the ICP, some members of the petty-bourgeois intelligentsia underwent a revolutionary transformation and developed a "vanguard consciousness." The emergence of "realism" was the achievement of writers and creative artists shaped by this historical process.[60] The realist movement peaked, according to Văn Tâm, with the appearance of Vũ Trọng Phụng, whose work and life as an impoverished member of the petty bourgeoisie reflected the key changes in Vietnamese society during the era. "Vũ Trọng Phụng evolved into a full-blown realist in his later works," explained Văn Tâm. "His genius was an indirect product of a socialist consciousness that emerged in Vietnam with the foundation of the ICP. Vũ Trọng Phụng never studied theories of communism or revolutionary struggle, but the Party—by leading the struggle of the masses—taught him concrete and worthwhile lessons."[61]

Chapter 3—"Life and Personality"—provided a relatively detailed biography of the writer and cited numerous eyewitness reports to sketch a portrait of his character.[62] The biographical narrative dwelled on Vũ Trọng Phụng's efforts to overcome poverty, family tragedy, and poor health. Accounts of his character stressed his personal modesty and frugality as well as his famous work ethic. Văn Tâm also contrasted his reputation for honesty, gentility, and a kind of naïve artlessness with the risqué content and wised-up tone of his writing. Finally, he attempted to establish a link between Vũ Trọng Phụng's limited education and his omnivorous curiosity and passion for research.

The fourth chapter—"The Secretary of His Time"—explored four themes threaded throughout Vũ Trọng Phụng's body of work.[63] Congruent with the history of the interwar economy presented in chapter 2, the first theme concerned the acceleration of "class differentiation" within Vietnamese society. Citing examples of numerous figures from Vũ Trọng Phụng's fiction that rose and fell within the prevailing social hierarchy, Văn Tâm argued that the persistent dramatization of this theme reflected intensified processes of social mobility triggered by the economic crisis of 1929–34. The capacity to reflect this important socioeconomic development distinguished Vũ Trọng Phụng's fiction from the fiction of the Self-Strength Literary Group, which tended to portray characters immobilized within a fixed class position over time. In Văn Tâm's reading, it was this aspect of his writing that made Vũ Trọng Phụng more of a "realist" than the Self-Strength writers. Vũ Trọng Phụng's second major theme, according to Văn Tâm, was "the omnipotent power of money in bourgeois society." This referred to the idea, cited by Văn Tâm from the *Communist Manifesto*, that everything within bourgeois society, including beauty, happiness, love, morality, righteousness, and family relationships, was determined by money and the laws of supply and demand. As the frenzied pursuit of money eroded morality, spiritually disoriented individuals turned to sex as an alternative source of fulfillment. The permissive nature of French culture, the ubiquity of sexual imagery in modern advertising, and the promotion of new forms of leisure by capitalists and the colonial state (especially during the Popular Front era) stimulated further the collective libido of the population. This argument allowed Văn Tâm to mitigate the significance of Vũ Trọng Phụng's much maligned sex obsession by interpreting it as an indirect critique of colonial capitalism. A third major theme was the interrelationship between imperialism, feudalism, and capitalism, an idea dramatized in his fiction and reportage through portrayals of collusion between businessmen, colonial officials, and members of the traditional elite.

While his indictments of colonial capitalism confirmed Vũ Trọng Phụng's status as a critical realist, the final theme identified by Văn Tâm—"the misery of the people and the appearance of resolute characters"—pointed to the presence in his work of a budding socialist-realist sensibility. Rejecting the notion that Vũ Trọng

Phụng was a political nihilist, Văn Tâm pointed out that his later works featured ardent political activists who "provided a ray of light illuminating the way toward a new society." Văn Tâm suggested that the growing sophistication over time of Vũ Trọng Phụng's portrayal of such figures resembled the heightened politicization of Zola's novels during the course of his career. He then traced the evolution of revolutionary political consciousness in Vũ Trọng Phụng's characters from Thuận's desperate turn to a life of crime in *No Echo* to Hải Vân's emergence as a fantastic communist superhero in *The Storm* and finally to the plausible radicalization of Phú through political struggle and contact with communist journalists in *The Dike Breaks*. Consistent with his conjecture that Vũ Trọng Phụng's fiction was veering toward socialist realism at the time of his death, Văn Tâm insisted, in a concluding subsection of the chapter, that the writer was coming to sympathize with communism. As evidence, he excerpted (decontextualized) procommunist passages from Vũ Trọng Phụng's articles "The Schism between the Third and Fourth Internationals" and "Communist Freedom." He also rehearsed rumors that Vũ Trọng Phụng was close to the ICP member Trần Huy Liệu. Most dramatically, he cited interviews with the writer's family that revealed that he had started to collect revolutionary material, prior to his death, including a portrait of Stalin![64]

Partially mitigating the persuasiveness of the case for Vũ Trọng Phụng's communist sympathies and socialist-realist orientation, the fifth chapter—"Petty-Bourgeois Limitations of a Realist Perspective"—identified countervailing instances of the writer's failure to meet "progressive" standards.[65] Văn Tâm singled out for criticism a host of "inaccuracies" within Vũ Trọng Phụng's writing regarding the portrayal of colonial officials, patriotic capitalists, peasants and workers, national culture, the Soviet Union, and the local communist movement. He also took issue with Vũ Trọng Phụng's fatalism and xenophobia as well as with enduring traces of conservatism and reformism within his political project. In each instance, Văn Tâm attributed Vũ Trọng Phụng's shortcomings to his petty-bourgeois background and his failure to participate directly in the revolutionary struggle led by the ICP. Although he underlined a raft of petty-bourgeois weaknesses in Vũ Trọng Phụng's work, Văn Tâm insisted that these deficiencies were less severe than those found in the work of feudal or capitalist writers. He noted, moreover, that similar shortcomings could be found in the work of many great prerevolutionary writers, such as Balzac, Zola, Tolstoy, Gogol, and Nguyễn Du.

In the final chapter—"Special Artistic Features"—Văn Tâm cited aesthetic standards for progressive literature from the writings of Mao and Engels to praise certain formal and stylistic qualities in Vũ Trọng Phụng's work.[66] These included the construction of "typical characters," the description of "realistic" details and dialogue, and the strategic use of satire as an "instrument of class struggle." Văn Tâm placed Vũ Trọng Phụng's political satire within a global tradition that included Boccaccio, Rabelais, Moliere, and Lu Xun as well as a parallel national lineage of subversively bawdy folklore and rustic humor.

While many suppositions in the book resembled the contrived claims put forward by NVGP about Vũ Trọng Phụng's socialist-realist tendencies and communist sympathies, Văn Tâm's argument that Vũ Trọng Phụng's petty-bourgeois class identity hindered his "progressive" vision represented a significant new line of defense. The power of this thesis derived from two sources. One was the communist intellectual culture of the DRV, which placed a high value on even the most rudimentary forms of class analysis. More important, however, was the charitable posture of the VWP toward the petty-bourgeois ancestry of its own intelligentsia. This tolerant attitude was enshrined at the Việt Bắc Conference on Literary Debate, which opened with expressions of anxiety by leading artists and intellectuals that their status within the revolutionary regime might be diminished due to their petty-bourgeois backgrounds. "How can members of the rural and urban petty bourgeoisie participate in the creation of a people's literature?" asked the critic and translator Đỗ Đức Dục. "Everyone recognizes that most teaching cadres in the field of literature come from the petty bourgeoisie. How will this affect their ability to do their jobs?"[67] During subsequent deliberations in which participants including Nguyễn Đỗ Cung, Nguyễn Xuân Khoát, Anh Thơ, and Nguyễn Tuân guiltily acknowledged their own petty-bourgeois class identities, Tố Hữu offered a solution to this predicament.

> Brother Dục has raised an important point. It is true that our brothers in the literary sphere originate from the ranks of the petty bourgeoisie. How are these men of letters to play a constructive role in the establishment of a new people's literature? In my opinion, although the petty-bourgeois class is ideologically fickle and influenced strongly by individualism, the oppression and exploitation of our nation has inspired the petty bourgeoisie to embrace human liberation, the revolution, and the resistance. As long as members of this class willingly follow the revolutionary road illuminated by workers, they can contribute to the creation of a new life.[68]

Seen within this context, Văn Tâm's central argument functioned to defuse harsh criticism of Vũ Trọng Phụng by pointing out that his flaws stemmed from a defective class identity that happened to be shared by all of his critics. While it is difficult to know for certain if Văn Tâm designed this explanation to ensnare the writer's critics within the web of accusations that they had spun themselves, it is noteworthy that learned readers of the monograph tended to emphasize its novelty and importance.[69]

The impact of Văn Tâm's elaborate defense of Vũ Trọng Phụng was blunted by the growth of an official campaign of repression against NVGP that began in late 1956, the precise moment when *Vũ Trọng Phụng: Realist Writer* was being prepared for publication. A central target of the campaign was Trương Tửu, who was denounced viciously and repeatedly in the Party press for his leading role in the movement. Needless to say, the temporal coincidence of the campaign against NVGP and the appearance of Trương Tửu's introduction to *Vũ Trọng Phụng: Realist Writer* made Văn Tâm especially vulnerable to accusations of guilt by association.

But Văn Tâm was linked to NVGP in other ways as well. In 1956, he loaned copies of *Dumb Luck* and *The Dike Breaks* to Trần Thiếu Bảo—the publisher of *Nhân Văn* and *Giai Phẩm*—who used them to republish the novels under the Minh Đức imprint.[70] Trần Thiếu Bảo also helped to promote Văn Tâm's research by including a prepublication excerpt from his monograph in *Vũ Trọng Phụng Is with Us*. Featured alongside essays by such core NVGP members as Phan Khôi, Nguyễn Mạnh Tường, Đào Duy Anh, Hoàng Cầm, and Trương Tửu, Văn Tâm's brief contribution to the volume confirmed the impression that he was associated, somehow, with the movement.

Văn Tâm's most visible connection with NVGP, however, was an essay he penned in support of the movement for *New Land*, a controversial student magazine that was shut down after the appearance of a single issue on November 10, 1956.[71] As with *Nhân Văn* and *Giai Phẩm*, the magazine was published by Trần Thiếu Bảo's Minh Đức Publishing House. According to Văn Tâm, it was the brainchild of the philosopher Trần Đức Thảo, who pitched the project to Trần Thiếu Bảo as a "student version of *Giai Phẩm*."[72] A "note from the publisher" explained that the mission of the magazine was "to strengthen freedom of expression following the Hundred Flowers guidelines and to strengthen ideological freedom within the student movement."[73] *New Land* featured essays, poetry, and fiction that criticized the Party's control over student life in a manner reminiscent of NVGP's attack on DRV cultural policy. Its lead article, "Criticizing the Leaders of the Students," was modeled directly on Phan Khôi's famous article in the first issue of *Giai Phẩm*, "Criticizing the Leaders of the Arts and Letters."[74] As with Phan Khôi's essay, it endorsed de-Stalinization in Eastern Europe, while chiding university officials for partisanship, dogmatism, and promoting "cults of personality." Văn Tâm's essay in *New Land*—"What Do They Want?"—provided a full-throated defense of NVGP in response to charges issued against it in *The People* by the professor Hoàng Xuân Nhị. In particular, Văn Tâm took issue with Hoàng Xuân Nhị's contention that the movement enjoyed little support among university students. "The voice of the student body in recent meetings," he wrote, "has been mostly in harmony with the voice of NVGP."[75]

Although he does not figure within Văn Tâm's essay, Vũ Trọng Phụng made two appearances in *New Land*, both of which hinted at a connection between the writer and the reformist project of NVGP. The first was an advertisement for Minh Đức's upcoming edition of *The Dike Breaks* that highlighted framing material added to the novel by leading members of NVGP: a new preface by Trương Tửu and cover art by Sỹ Ngọc.[76] A significant reference to Vũ Trọng Phụng also occurred in a short story by Bùi Quang Đoài entitled "History of a Love Story." Set in a university dormitory, the story related the wicked efforts of a "secretary of the communist party cell within the student union" (named Bằng) to thwart the love affair of two students from different class backgrounds (named Tân and An). During their courtship Tân lends An a copy of *Dumb Luck*, which he describes as "a typical story of a guy named Xuân who lives a life of deception in order to be recognized as a 'hero.'"[77] When Bằng's villainous effort to drive a wedge between the lovers is revealed, An recognizes the real-world relevance of Tân's critical depiction of Red-Haired Xuân. "She recalled Tân's statement about *Dumb Luck: Dumb Luck* is the typical story of a guy named Xuân who lives a life of deception in order to be recognized as a 'hero.' Outside of this mode of deception, there is another form of manipulative deceit designed to destroy the love of human beings."[78] The passage suggests that *Dumb Luck* may have appealed to reform-minded students because its dramatization of the over-the-top "opportunism" and "sycophancy" of Red-Haired Xuân dovetailed with an important agenda item of NVGP's reform communist project.

Following the shuttering of *New Land*, the Ministry of Education established a disciplinary council to investigate Văn Tâm and other contributors to the magazine. As part of the investigation, Văn Tâm was required to undergo self-criticism, a process that required him to admit his errors in a detailed written document. The document provided verification for the accusation that he had fallen under the pernicious influence of "reform communist" movements within the Eastern Bloc:

> By the end of 1956, Stalin's speech at the Twentieth Congress of the CPSU had influenced my thinking a great deal. While I remained optimistic about the

> future, the mistakes of our government in the areas of land reform, household registration, and the management of the arts began to shake my faith in the Party and the government. The influence of reactionary speeches and the events in Poland and Hungary led me to the mistaken belief that Stalinism had given birth to a "bureaucratic system" within socialism. This "bureaucratic system" undermined the public interest and provoked risings in Poland and Hungary. Among the progressive forces battling this "bureaucratic system" were Khrushchev and Gomulka in Europe and Lê Duẩn in Vietnam. Following the Twentieth Congress of the CPSU, I came to feel that the international socialist system was entering a revolutionary phase that would eliminate the remnants of partisanship, authoritarianism, and the "cult of personality." These errors of Stalin, I believed, had deprived the people of their freedom and happiness. At that time, I came under the influence of two ideological currents. On the one hand, the courage of the Soviet Union in admitting errors fortified my loyalty toward socialism and the People's Democracy in Vietnam. On the other hand, I fell under the spell of reactionary forces at home and abroad. One document that strongly influenced me was Comrade Gomulka's speech at the Eighth Congress of the Polish Worker's Party. Comrade Gomulka provided a thorough analysis of the cult of personality and of bureaucratism and partisanship in Poland. His conclusions seemed relevant to the current situation in Vietnam, and I devoured every word of his speech.[79]

Văn Tâm's self-criticism also confirmed suspicions about the poisonous impact on his thinking of NVGP and of Trương Tửu, in particular:

> I came into contact with Trương Tửu during this period, and I became intoxicated by his views on the Vietnamese Workers' Party. He pointed out that few members of the Party are workers, while most are intellectuals, farmers, and members of the petty bourgeoisie. This is the cause of the growth within the Party of dogmatism, bureaucratism, partisanship, and the cult of personality. Given my belief that socialism had been corrupted by Stalinism, I threw my support behind *Nhân Văn* and *Giai Phẩm* and participated in *New Land*. . . . My sympathies for NVGP grew as I came to view it as part of an international movement for the promotion of artistic expression. While I criticized *Nhân Văn*'s excesses in front of the ninth-grade students at the Tân Trào School, I also affirmed my belief in the constructive nature of the journal. In addition, I forwarded issues of *Nhân Văn* and *Giai Phẩm* to several friends.[80]

After concluding its investigation, the disciplinary council ruled that Văn Tâm's essay in *New Land* had "disseminated false material" and "distorted the nature of the regime" and that he had "spread indecent ideas" in the classroom.[81] As punishment, the council recommended that he be fired from his post at the Teachers Training College and prohibited from teaching at the postsecondary level. The decision against Văn Tâm was disseminated to every college and university in the DRV, ensuring that he would never again find work within the system of higher education. After several years during which he eked out a living as a private tutor and as a poorly paid clerk in the Ministry of Education, Văn Tâm was allowed to teach literature at the Nguyễn Trãi high school, a position that he held from 1961 until his retirement in 1993. He continued to conduct research on modern literature, however, publishing extensively under the pen name Tầm Dương.[82]

MIXED REVIEWS DURING 1957

After closing down *Nhân Văn* and *Giai Phẩm* in December 1956, the Party state pulled back from the brink, adopting a vacillating, inconsistent stance toward NVGP during 1957 that combined equal measures of repression and tolerance. Party officials heaped slanderous abuse on the movement in the press and in public forums throughout the year. But they allowed the leaders of NVGP to remain at large, to retain their official positions, and to carry out and circulate their creative work. A shift toward greater repression only occurred toward the end of the year, perhaps due to the abrupt termination of the Hundred Flowers policy in China. Assessments of Vũ Trọng Phụng during 1957 dovetailed with the erratic but increasingly repressive nature of official policy toward NVGP. While continuing to acknowledge his "critical-realist" virtues, accounts published during this transitional year dwelled on the presence of serious flaws in his political and aesthetic vision. As a result, treatments of the writer during 1957 tended to take the form of a literary-critical balance sheet registering a small number of strengths and a large number of weaknesses. While the strengths tended to be drawn from the positive accounts of Vũ Trọng Phụng published in late 1956, many of the weaknesses had never before been amplified in print.

The most elaborate example of this trend may be found in a long essay by the literary scholar Văn Tân (not to be confused with Văn Tâm) entitled "Vũ Trọng Phụng through *The Storm*, *The Dike Breaks*, and *Dumb Luck*."[83] Published in *Literature, History, Geography (Văn Sử Địa)*—the preeminent journal for humanities research during the era—Văn Tân's essay addressed the modest virtues and numerous deficiencies in Vũ Trọng Phụng's work. On the positive side of the ledger, Văn Tân listed the writer's critical portrayal of the colonial regime and the Vietnamese "lackeys" who collaborated with it. "Prior to Vũ Trọng Phụng," Văn Tân explained, "a handful of writers from the revolutionary underground exposed the cruelty of colonialism. But Vũ Trọng Phụng was the first nonrevolutionary writer with the courage to denounce the colonial regime while it was still in power."[84] Văn Tân also approved of the presence of revolutionary characters in Vũ Trọng Phụng's work such as Hải Vân in the *The Storm* and the ex–political prisoners working for the *Labor* newspaper in *The Dike Breaks*. Finally, he singled out for special praise the depiction of the peasant antitax protest in *The Dike Breaks* as the first instance in which a "public writer" accurately perceived the "force of the people." For Văn Tân, this passage provided evidence of a shift in Vũ Trọng Phụng's work toward socialist realism since it "expressed a hope for a regime of social justice even though the depiction of the regime is vague."[85]

Following this perfunctory survey of Vũ Trọng Phụng's strengths, Văn Tân discussed five major points of weakness. The first concerned Vũ Trọng Phụng's views of two minor characters in *The Storm:* a compassionate French colonial scholar-bureaucrat (writing a study of the nationalist hero Trần Hưng Đạo) and a reformist local Vietnamese official (who had once demonstrated for the release of Vietnamese political prisoners). Văn Tân argued that the positive portrayal of these characters violated Engels's "principle of typicality" since the vast majority of French and Vietnamese colonial officials were treacherous. "If we accept that the issue of typicality is always a political issue," he wrote, "then Vũ Trọng Phụng's characterization of these colonial officials indicates a vague understanding of politics and confusion regarding the distinction between friends and enemies."[86] Văn Tân especially objected to the humane portrayal of the French official, which he attributed to Vũ Trọng Phụng's cowardice in the face of colonial censorship.

Vũ Trọng Phụng's second major shortcoming was his unflattering representation of the masses. Singling out crowd scenes from *The Dike Breaks,* Văn Tân chided Vũ Trọng Phụng for depicting a "peasantry that does little but squabble, insult one another, and fight over scraps of food and drink."[87] A related problem concerned the writer's inaccurate portrayal of revolutionaries. In *The Storm,* according to Văn Tân, the communist activist Hải Vân resembled a "gangster from an American detective novel more than a revolutionary."[88] A portrayal of communist journalists in *The Dike Breaks* discussing the propaganda value of various political tactics appalled him as well. "Communists do not struggle to *be perceived* as courageous heroes," he insisted. "Instead, they struggle to liberate the people and hence their only concern is with achieving victory."[89] It is significant that Văn Tân's criticism of Vũ Trọng Phụng's portrayal of colonial officials, revolutionaries, and the masses undercuts approving comments he made about the writer's treatment of these groups in the first section of the essay.

Văn Tân's fourth complaint concerned Vũ Trọng Phụng's penchant for obscenity. "Why does Vũ Trọng Phụng describe so many obscene scenes?" he asked. "Is it to reflect the true social reality of the French era? Or could it be to satisfy a demand for pornography from readers and especially from young readers?"[90] Whatever the reason, Văn Tân suggested that exposure to such scenes damaged Vietnamese youth just as pornographic novels corrupted the French and American bourgeoisie. Finally, Văn Tân chided Vũ Trọng Phụng's work for its pessimism, as embodied in Tú Anh's despondent monologues in *The Storm* and the "comprehensive contempt for all of society" expressed in *Dumb Luck*. "If everyone in society is bad," Văn Tân wrote, "both the exploiter and the exploited, then who will overthrow the bad regime? If 'there is nothing worthwhile in life,' if 'life itself is without meaning,' then what's the point of struggle? What's the point of making a revolution?"[91] In the conclusion to the essay, Văn Tân returned to Vũ Trọng Phụng's pessimism as the "most dangerous" aspect of his work owing to the comfort it provided to "colonialists and the feudalists."

Văn Tân's mixed review of Vũ Trọng Phụng was echoed by the literary scholar Trương Chính in *A Short History of Vietnamese Literature*, also published in 1957.[92] As in Văn Tân's essay, Trương Chính's praise of Vũ Trọng Phụng's work focused narrowly on the portrayal of antitax protests and communist journalists in *The Dike Breaks*. These episodes were remarkable, according to Trương Chính, because they suggested that Vũ Trọng Phụng admired revolutionary fighters even though he was not a revolutionary himself. Trương Chính's criticism of Vũ Trọng Phụng, on the other hand, addressed three broad deficiencies threaded through his body of work. The first was the privileging within his novels of sexual desire over economic exploitation. As an example, Trương Chính contrasted Vũ Trọng Phụng's meticulous account of Thị Mịch's psychosexual deterioration in *The Storm* with his cursory treatment of the rise of Nghị Hách's capitalist empire. Second, Trương Chính expressed disapproval at the xenophobic parody in *Dumb Luck* of the rage for Europeanization among the urban middle classes during the 1930s. For Trương Chính, Europeanization helped to break the "chains of feudalism" in Vietnamese society by attacking gender inequality and arranged marriages. He reproached Vũ Trọng Phụng for advocating the preservation of "the old order, the old customs, and the old discipline" along with the "spirit of feudal society." While acknowledging that

Vũ Trọng Phụng could not be seen as a disciple of Confucius, Trương Chính argued that his relentless belittlement of "the new" inadvertently buttressed a conservative Confucian project. Third, Trương Chính accused Vũ Trọng Phụng of supporting reform over revolution based on his positive portrayal of the socialist-leaning local official in *The Dike Breaks*. He found a similar reformist impulse in the thesis advanced in *To Be a Whore* that the growth of prostitution in Hà Nội could be stemmed through sex education in schools rather than revolutionary political action.

Another major assessment published in 1957 that added to the controversy surrounding the writer was an odd "special issue" of the independent magazine *The Journal of Criticism (Tập san Phê bình)* entitled "Vũ Trọng Phụng: Life and Times."[93] What made the special issue so unusual was that it featured five articles about Vũ Trọng Phụng by a single author—the relatively obscure literary scholar Thiều Quang, who was also the founder and editor-in-chief of the journal.[94] The first two articles provided snippets of biographical information on Vũ Trọng Phụng based on Thiều Quang's interaction with him during the 1930s. The last three addressed "problems" in the writer's treatment of sexuality and politics. Thiều Quang's discussion of the risqué character of Vũ Trọng Phụng's work juxtaposed contrasting views on the topic by Văn Tân and Văn Tâm. He concluded that Văn Tân viewed the obscene content in Vũ Trọng Phụng's work as a cynical marketing tool, whereas Văn Tâm interpreted it as an instrument to depict "realistically" the depravity of the bourgeoisie. Thiều Quang ultimately sided with Văn Tâm's more charitable reading, arguing that Vũ Trọng Phụng's use of graphic obscenity was consciously designed to induce a shock of recognition within his bourgeois readers regarding their own depraved condition. Nevertheless, he provided ammunition for future critics by acknowledging that the level of obscenity in Vũ Trọng Phụng's work was extreme "even by French standards." Since the dissemination of such filth threatened to damage the "national spirit," he proposed the publication of bowdlerized versions of Vũ Trọng Phụng's novels. On Vũ Trọng Phụng's politics, Thiều Quang challenged Văn Tân's suggestion that flaws in the writer's ideological orientation flowed from certain insidious personal qualities. Rather, he saw them as a product of colonial censorship and historical conditions that discouraged a true understanding of communism's world-historical mission. However, Thiều Quang accepted Văn Tân's basic charges that Vũ Trọng Phụng misrepresented both the masses and communist activists and that he exhibited troubling proclivities toward pessimism and nihilism.

Given the defensive tone exhibited in the writings about Vũ Trọng Phụng by members of NVGP and Văn Tâm, it is reasonable to assume that some of the criticisms voiced by Văn Tân, Trương Chính, and Thiều Quang had been circulating informally prior to the publication of their essays in 1957. Still, the essays are noteworthy as the first published depiction of the myriad political shortcomings that orthodox cultural officials identified in his work. They were also the first printed accounts from the postcolonial era that accused Vũ Trọng Phụng of serious character flaws, including cowardice, venality, moral and sexual perversity, and a negativity bordering on nihilism. Criticisms first expressed in 1957 in both of these areas were to become part of the standard condemnation of Vũ Trọng Phụng's work that crystallized in the following years and that was to be repeated in communist literary histories up through the early 1980s. The essays of 1957 differed from many of these subsequent assessments, however, because they did not explicitly link Vũ Trọng Phụng's political deficiencies to the promotion of his work by the leaders of NVGP. This attribution of guilt by association emerged during the final years of the decade as a key charge against the writer put forward by conservative officials and as a central justification for the banning of his work.

BANNING VŨ TRỌNG PHỤNG

Following the onset of the Anti-Rightist campaign in China and the growth of antirevisionist measures throughout the Eastern Bloc, the VWP moved decisively against the leadership of NVGP starting in 1958. On January 6, it passed a "Resolution on Literary Affairs" that denounced NVGP as a "revisionist clique" and ordered all "artists and cultural cadres" to oppose the movement in mandatory "struggle classes," some of which stretched on for weeks. During the final phase of these classes, officials staged vicious denunciations of members of the movement, who, in turn, performed public self-criticism. Between March and June, the Party press published transcripts of both the denunciations and the self-criticisms before announcing formal sanctions against members of the movement. Most were fired from their jobs, expelled from professional organizations, and issued terms of reformatory labor in the countryside. A handful were arrested and sentenced to prison, and all remained subject for decades to harassment by local security services. Unable to work in their professional fields, many members of the movement suffered extreme poverty and social isolation until they were partially rehabilitated following the onset of Renovation during the mid-1980s.

Given NVGP's promotion of Vũ Trọng Phụng, it is not surprising that the crackdown against the movement in 1958 coincided with a hardening of official attitudes toward the writer. In place of the juxtaposition of strengths and weaknesses that had characterized the critical discourse in 1957, assessments of Vũ Trọng Phụng between 1958 and 1960 took the form of shrill political indictments that highlighted linkages between the writer's shortcomings and the support he received from NVGP. According to the conservative literary scholar Vũ Đức Phúc, this new approach was triggered by the confessions delivered at the anti-NVGP struggle sessions. "The attitude of the leadership changed for two reasons," he recalled. "First, members of NVGP revealed during the struggle sessions how the Trotskyist clique and the reactionary bourgeoisie had used Vũ Trọng Phụng to advance their own interests. In addition, several old-timers such as Bùi Huy Phồn explained how Trương Tửu and the Minh Đức Publishing House had been using Vũ Trọng Phụng for nefarious purposes since 1945 or 1946."[95] Vũ Đức Phúc's account is disingenuous, given that VWP officials stage-managed the confessions and oversaw their content. Nevertheless, it confirms that the timing of the shift dovetailed with the official campaign against the movement. The second reason for the shift, according to Vũ Đức Phúc, was the discovery of journalistic writing by Vũ Trọng Phụng that verified suspicions about his opposition to communism. Again, Vũ Đức Phúc's account is misleading in that it was less the discovery of new works that prompted a reassessment of Vũ Trọng Phụng than the tendentious reinterpretation of familiar texts designed to cast the writer in the most villainous possible light.

The shift in the official assessment of Vũ Trọng Phụng may be seen in two articles published just seven months apart by the critic and cultural official Hoài Thanh. The first was a review of Văn Tâm's *Vũ Trọng Phụng: Realist Writer* that appeared during the comparatively relaxed atmosphere of September 1957.[96] The second, entitled "In Order to Assimilate Prerevolutionary Literature, We Must Subject It to Criticism," was published in *The People* in April 1958 in the midst of the decisive repressive campaign against NVGP.[97] Hoài Thanh's first article exhibited an evenhanded posture toward Vũ Trọng Phụng consistent with the accounts published in 1957. While praising the writer's "populist" spirit and critical-realist hatred for colonial society, the essay criticized his obscene prose and wrongheaded attitude toward French officials and the Vietnamese peasantry. But on balance, the essay determined that "the progressivism of Vũ Trọng Phụng's writing overshadows the backward elements." Regarding Văn Tâm's monograph, the essay pointed out minor flaws but lauded his "reading, research, and thinking" as a "remarkable achievement." The most charitable feature of Hoài Thanh's essay, however, was its refusal to allow Trương Tửu's preface or Văn Tâm's political troubles to negatively impact its assessment of the monograph.

Animated by the intensity of the recent attacks against NVGP as well as the new campaign against revisionism within the communist world, Hoài Thanh's second essay adopted a harder line. The essay condemned the revisionist tactic of tarnishing the achievements of communist culture by showering praise on prerevolutionary writers and, in particular, reactionary, anticommunist writers such as Vũ Trọng Phụng. "Why didn't Vũ Trọng Phụng dare to attack the colonialists directly?" Hoài Thanh asked. "And why did he sometimes celebrate them? Why was he filled with contempt for peasants and the urban poor? Why did he misrepresent the true nature of revolutionary fighters and why does all of his work exhibit a morally corrupt tone?"[98] Hoài Thanh identified Trotskyist sympathies in Vũ Trọng Phụng's essay "The Schism between the Third and Fourth Internationals," published in1937. "This document proves that Vũ Trọng Phụng misrepresented the Party," he wrote, "in a manner that recalls the tactics of the Trotskyist clique. . . . We must strive to understand the extent to which Vũ Trọng Phụng embraced this reactionary ideology."[99] Finally, Hoài Thanh called attention to the incriminating association between Vũ Trọng Phụng and the "revisionist clique" led by Trương Tửu. "We oppose the random republication of deviant romantic works," he wrote. "We oppose the veneration of backward and reactionary literature. We oppose the wicked tactic of using old literature to attack the Party and the regime. Most of all, we oppose Trương Tửu's baseless claim that Vũ Trọng Phụng was more radiant than the Indochinese Communist Party."[100]

Later that month, Phan Cự Đệ—a junior teaching cadre in the Literature Department at Hà Nội Teachers Training College —deepened the assault against the perceived nexus between Trương Tửu and Vũ Trọng Phụng. In an essay entitled "The Pedagogical Methods and Attitudes of Trương Tửu," Phan Cự Đệ attacked Trương Tửu both for his writings on Vũ Trọng Phụng and for comments about the writer that he had made in class.[101] The ugliness of the attack was heightened because Phan Cự Đệ and Trương Tửu were departmental colleagues and because Phan Cự Đệ relied on reports about the content of Trương Tửu's lectures provided by a student informer. "In class, Trương Tửu pays no attention to patriotic literature," Phan Cự Đệ wrote. "The only figures he praises are Vũ Trọng Phụng and Tản Đà." After establishing Trương Tửu's preoccupation with Vũ Trọng Phụng, Phan Cự Đệ asked: "But does Vũ Trọng Phụng deserve this level of acclaim. What, in fact, was his political attitude?"[102]

To answer this question, Phan Cự Đệ cited evidence from the writer's fiction and journalism. He chastised *The Storm* for "viewing the masses with a sarcastic eye and depicting them with a cruel pen." He criticized *The Dike Breaks* for implying—"in the manner of Trotsky"—that the ICP leadership had embraced reformism during the Popular Front era. He misinterpreted Vũ Trọng Phụng's infamous essay—"The

Schism between the Third and Fourth Internationals"—as an effort to "distort the October Revolution, denounce Lenin, praise Trotsky, and slander Stalin." In conclusion, Phan Cự Đệ addressed directly the reasons behind Trương Tửu's support of Vũ Trọng Phụng:

> We must understand why Trương Tửu praised Vũ Trọng Phụng more this year than in the past. Prior to the emergence of NVGP, the antiparty, antiregime, and antisocialist ideology of Trương Tửu remained hidden. But last year, Trương Tửu took advantage of the opportunity provided by the appearance of the group to excessively praise Vũ Trọng Phụng in order to diminish the significance of writers who had joined the Party such as Ngô Tất Tố, Nguyễn Công Hoan, and Nguyên Hồng. Trương Tửu extolled Vũ Trọng Phụng and praised *The Dike Breaks* in order to exaggerate the role of artists and to diminish the role of the Party. Trương Tửu made his students understand that "Vũ Trọng Phụng did not need the leadership of the Party in order to be a magnificent realist writer." Here, Trương Tửu implied that artists can be wiser than the Party and stand above the Party and that they have a greater capacity than the Party to discover universal truths.[103]

Phan Cự Đệ's harsh analysis was elaborated the following month by Nguyễn Đình Thi—the VWP's second most powerful cultural official after Tố Hữu—who described Vũ Trọng Phụng and reactionary writers such as Nhất Linh and Khái Hưng as "two sides of the same coin" since they were both examples of "prewar bourgeois literature."[104] It was no coincidence, Nguyễn Đình Thi concluded, that the "NVGP clique" promoted and republished Vũ Trọng Phụng, since members of the movement shared with the writer a "politically reactionary class character." The comparison to Nhất Linh and Khái Hưng was especially damning. Not only were both men leaders of the "reactionary" Self-Strength Literary Group, but they had openly opposed the Việt Minh after the August Revolution. Nhất Linh eventually fled to the South, while Khái Hưng was murdered at the hands of Việt Minh partisans in 1947. Contrasting sharply with his earlier portrayal of the writer (at the Conference on Literary Debate in Việt Bắc) as a progressive critical realist on par with Balzac, Nguyễn Đình Thi's new assessment demonstrates the extent to which Vũ Trọng Phụng's official reputation had plummeted.

Hoàng Văn Hoan's intervention in the debate occurred roughly two years later following a conference organized at the Institute of Literature to try to establish a standard official view about Vũ Trọng Phụng. The literary scholar Việt Trung (aka

Nguyễn Đức Đàn) circulated an essay prior to the conference that introduced the central issues to be discussed there. "In regard to the teaching of literature," Việt Trung stated, "the difficulty of evaluating Vũ Trọng Phụng has been our most complex and enduring problem."[105] He then traced the evolution of interpretations of the writer from the late colonial era to the present. His account dwelled on controversies over politics and pornography, but its attention to positive and negative assessments was relatively evenhanded. Việt Trung's treatment of NVGP's promotion of Vũ Trọng Phụng, however, echoed the harsh assessments put forward by Hoài Thanh, Phan Cự Đệ, and Nguyễn Đình Thi in 1958. "The NVGP clique showered Vũ Trọng Phụng with inflated praise in order to attack revolutionary literature and the leadership of our Party in the cultural sphere," he stated. "There are also some among us who overestimate him."[106] In conclusion, Việt Trung reiterated the imperative to reach a consensus about the writer so as to facilitate teaching and research.

According to the eyewitness account of Bùi Huy Phồn, the conference in 1960 was attended by over one hundred writers, scholars, and critics.[107] Formal presentations were delivered by a group of literary scholars including Vũ Đình Liên, Như Phong, Thiều Quang, Bùi Huy Phồn, Đoàn Nồng, Nguyễn Đức Đàn, and Phan Cự Đệ. A partial transcript of the proceedings reveals that assessments of Vũ Trọng Phụng were mixed but that even the writer's defenders acknowledged his serious defects.[108] First, conference participants complained about Vũ Trọng Phụng's friendships with Huỳnh Văn Phương ("a notorious Trotskyist") and Nguyễn Triệu Luật (who was reputed to have "distorted communism") as well as his abiding affection for the conservative Phạm Quỳnh. Second, they denounced three of his journalistic essays that criticized communism directly.[109] Indeed, the transcript from the conference indicates that Hoài Thanh read aloud from "The Schism between the Third and Fourth Internationals." Third, younger participants in particular rehearsed criticisms regarding Vũ Trọng Phụng's positive portrayal of French officials and negative depiction of "the masses" as well as his disparaging comments about the "national character." And fourth, Vũ Trọng Phụng was tarred with reactionary labels; he was called a Trotskyist, a feudalist, a conservative, a nihilist, and an anarchist.

On the other hand, several conference participants qualified the attacks against the writer by portraying him as indecisive and politically innocent. For Bùi Huy Phồn, Vũ Trọng Phụng's political commitments fluctuated erratically through four different stages. An aversion to petty factionalism led him to move from a pro-VWP position to an anti-VWP position following the Party's assault on its Trotskyist rivals during the mid-1930s. The indiscriminate hostility he displayed toward Lenin, Stalin, and Trotsky in his essay "The Schism between the Third and Fourth Internationals" indicated a subsequent movement toward anarchism. Toward the end of his life, he displayed a soft spot for the feudal ideal of a harmonious society ruled by a just monarch and a bureaucracy of virtuous men. In a similar vein, Thiều Quang insisted that Vũ Trọng Phụng's political viewpoint was marked by an incoherent admixture of reformism, Trotskyism, antinationalism, and conservatism (embodied in his admiration for Phạm Quỳnh). Further complicating this picture, Thiều Quang claimed that while Vũ Trọng Phụng loved metropolitan France, he hated the French Empire. Như Phong suggested that Vũ Trọng Phụng considered all politics to be a cynical game played by rival elites rather than a substructural reflection of class struggle. He continued that Vũ Trọng Phụng was especially skeptical of revolutionary politics, which he believed was tarnished by an immoral instrumentalism.[110]

Perhaps the most remarkable defensive tactic put forward at the conference was Bùi Huy Phồn's suggestion that the connection between Vũ Trọng Phụng and Trương Tửu had been overblown. "People say that Vũ Trọng Phụng and Trương Tửu are on the same team," he explained, "but the truth is that if Vũ Trọng Phụng, Trương Tửu, and Vũ Bằng happened to sit together, they would fight to the death. Vũ Trọng Phụng despised Trương Tửu's stupidity and duplicity. And Trương Tửu despised Vũ Trọng Phụng. Trương Tửu eulogized him after his death but only to promote his own writing. After 1954, Trương Tửu pretended that they were close friends but this was a lie."[111] Bùi Huy Phồn's comments confirm that some DRV intellectuals refused to conflate the projects of Vũ Trọng Phụng and NVGP. Moreover, the range of opinions expressed at the conference (and elsewhere) suggests that fault lines regarding Vũ Trọng Phụng's reputation split the literary community according to generational differences and official rank. In short, it appears that Vũ Trọng Phụng was judged most harshly by high-ranking cultural officials and orthodox younger scholars.[112] Older scholars and low-ranking cultural officials, on the other hand, harbored an enduring affection for Vũ Trọng Phụng based on a fondness for his work and, in some cases, firsthand experience with him during the late colonial era.

Hoàng Văn Hoan's unexpected presence at the conference weakened the position of the moderates, and his subsequent contribution to the discourse made moot their modest defense of Vũ Trọng Phụng. According to Bùi Huy Phồn, Hoàng Văn Hoan decided to attend the conference after hearing rumors that Vũ Trọng Phụng had once written an article that insulted communism.[113] Although Hoàng Văn Hoan did not speak at the conference, Bùi Huy Phồn suggests that the failure to reach a consensus there persuaded him of the necessity of attacking Vũ Trọng Phụng through a "scientific discussion" that conveyed an "aura of objectivity." Several weeks later, Hoàng Văn Hoan sent a ten-page report entitled "Thoughts on the Problem of Vũ Trọng Phụng within Vietnamese Literature" to the editors of *The Journal of Literature (Tạp Chí Văn Học)*.[114]

The essay opened with an extensive discussion of the link between Vũ Trọng Phụng and NVGP that was to be the final word on the topic for over twenty-five years:

> In 1956, members of the NVGP clique launched an insane attack on the Party leadership, in general, and the literary leadership, in particular. They promoted the work of Vũ Trọng Phụng as the greatest achievement in Vietnamese literature during the interwar years. Members of the NVGP clique bypassed the monopolistic control of our cultural institutions to republish thousands of copies of Vũ Trọng Phụng's novels, distribute them among the people, and use them as teaching material in our schools. Their purpose was to prove that only prerevolutionary literature had any value. They tried to show that after the revolution, under the leadership of the VWP, authors were forced to serve politics and to write for workers, soldiers, and peasants. Hence, writers lost their freedom and our literature lost its soul. They claimed that a genius like Vũ Trọng Phụng needed neither the revolution nor the leadership of the Party in order to produce great literature. They argued that Vũ Trọng Phụng was our most brilliant realist writer, whose work will live forever in the history of our literature. They said that Vũ Trọng Phụng was a literary master and that he was more revolutionary than the Party. But their efforts have failed. Many people wrote letters to newspapers and cultural institutions demanding an immediate end to the publication of Vũ Trọng Phụng's work and to the teaching of his writing in school. We have met these demands, and after a period of intense struggle, the NVGP clique has been neutralized. They bowed their heads and acknowledged their mistakes before the people. Later, it was discovered that Vũ Trọng Phụng had worked as an editor of *Indochina Journal* and had once written an essay insulting communism and international communism. Recently, the question of Vũ Trọng Phụng's work was raised again because the Institute of Literature wants to create guidelines for the study of literature during the interwar period. . . . I am concerned by the fact that our comrades are aware that Vũ Trọng Phụng publicly insulted the VWP and the international communist movement and yet they remain deeply interested in his work and consider it to have great value. To deal with this

> concern, I have read three of Vũ Trọng Phụng's novels—*Dumb Luck, The Storm,* and *The Dike Breaks*—that were published during the revolutionary high tide of 1936 and that are considered "masterly" and "the highest literary achievements." I have also examined Văn Tâm's very meticulous research and analysis of Vũ Trọng Phụng's work. After reading this material, I wish to contribute the following opinions about the problem of Vũ Trọng Phụng's work within Vietnamese literature for the consultation of my colleagues.[115]

Hoàng Văn Hoan's introduction brought together all of the arguments that had been put forward to date regarding the sinister motives behind NVGP's support of Vũ Trọng Phụng. His only new line of attack was the "revelation" that NVGP's effort had provoked popular outrage in the form of a letter-writing campaign demanding a ban on Vũ Trọng Phụng's work. Traces of this campaign are not found in newspapers of the era, and it is likely that the charge was false. While the VWP had mobilized members of the population to write to newspapers condemning NVGP as part of its repression of the movement starting in 1956, there is no evidence that it employed similar tactics to damage the reputation of Vũ Trọng Phụng.

The remainder of the essay extracted and amplified from the existing critical discourse the most extreme and aggressive attacks against Vũ Trọng Phụng and his body of work. It supplemented this chorus of invective with a raft of new accusations. For example, to disparage Vũ Trọng Phụng's character, Hoàng Văn Hoan related a series of illustrative episodes that had never appeared previously in print. "Vũ Trọng Phụng lived the dirty, debauched life of a playboy," he began. "He did not know how to choose friends. High on drugs, he often wandered aimlessly up and down Mã Mây Street. When he worked at *Indochina Journal* he made a lot of money and was driven to the office in a chauffeured automobile. But he continued to be an addict and to frequent opium dens. He lived only for pleasure and he lacked healthy ideals."[116] It is noteworthy that Hoàng Văn Hoan's account contrasts with numerous descriptions of the writer put forward by supporters and detractors alike that emphasized his upright character and frugal lifestyle.

Hoàng Văn Hoan's treatment of Vũ Trọng Phụng's political orientation was equally over the top. He denounced the writer's alleged support of French colonialism and his sympathy for the conservative projects of Phạm Quỳnh and Nguyễn Văn Vĩnh. But he also labeled him a Trotskyite for opposing the collusion of the ICP with anti-Fascist forces during the Popular Front era. Extending this litany of abuse, Hoàng Văn Hoan found evidence of counterrevolutionary sentiments and antinationalist impulses within extracts from Vũ Trọng Phụng's novels. He also belittled the portrayal of sexuality in Vũ Trọng Phụng's work, describing it as "pornography" designed deliberately to stimulate lust among the youth and to sell books.

In conclusion, Hoàng Văn Hoan addressed the question of the proper classification of Vũ Trọng Phụng's work. He dismissed the argument—associated with NVGP—that the writer exhibited latent socialist-realist tendencies. "The NVGP clique boasted that Vũ Trọng Phụng was more revolutionary than the Party," he wrote, "and that his work was socialist realist. But no one believes this falsehood anymore."[117] He also challenged the notion that Vũ Trọng Phụng should be seen as a critical realist, denying that his work was sufficiently "realistic" or appropriately "critical." "During the period from 1936 to 1938, Vietnamese society underwent radical changes and the light of dawn brightened the sky. But the works of Vũ Trọng Phụng only reveal a society in darkness. How, therefore, can this be considered realism?"[118] Regarding the "critical" nature of the writer's work, Hoàng Văn Hoan detailed Vũ Trọng Phụng's flawed appraisal of characters such as Nghị Hách, Red-Haired Xuân, and Mrs. Deputy Customs Officer and his failure to grasp the origins of social injustice. "Critical-realist literature must exhibit a populist or humanist sensibility," he wrote. "But in *The Storm*, *The Dike Breaks*, and *Dumb Luck*, we see only oppression, exploitation, decadence, and perversity. We also see a writer who insults the people, despises the nation, flatters the imperialists, and cynically distorts the revolution. Vũ Trọng Phụng's works lack a revolutionary spirit, a popular spirit, and even a trace of humanism. Hence, not only is it wrong to view it as socialist realism, but we cannot call it critical realism either."[119] He concluded by offering four alternative classifications for Vũ Trọng Phụng's work: "degenerate literature," "profit-seeking literature," "hooligan literature," and "naturalist literature." Given that the original effort undertaken at the Conference on Literary Debate in 1949 to classify Vũ Trọng Phụng as a "critical realist" was designed to assimilate him into a Vietnamese communist literary canon, it is perhaps no coincidence that Hoàng Văn Hoan's rejection of the label in 1960 coincided with the banning of his work.

The precise mechanism triggering the ban remains mysterious to this day. Not only was no formal directive against Vũ Trọng Phụng's work ever issued, but the editors of *The Journal of Literature* refused, in the end, to publish Hoàng Văn Hoan's essay. Vũ Đức Phúc cited these facts decades later in an essay rejecting the notion that a ban had ever existed. "My close friend Như Phong who headed a publishing house for many years insists that nobody ever banned Vũ Trọng Phụng's work," he explained. "Rather, the republication of his writing simply did not accord with an era of bitter warfare. Printing paper had to be conserved for more important works."[120] Bùi Huy Phồn also underlined the absence of a central directive regarding the official status of Vũ Trọng Phụng's writing. But in contrast to Vũ Đức Phúc's depiction of the ban as a natural occurrence that emerged in response to the requirements of the era, Bùi Huy Phồn traced its origins to the influence of shadowy rumors about Hoàng Văn Hoan's essay. "Who ordered the ban?" he asked. "Was a document issued from a mass organization or from a government office that stipulated a concrete policy for dealing with Vũ Trọng Phụng's work? Nothing was stated publicly and no order was issued outside of a ten-page typed letter by Hoàng Văn Hoan that circulated internally among a small, close-knit group. Only one or two people possessed copies of the letter, but its subterranean power radiated in a fierce and cruel manner."[121] Nguyễn Hoành Khung confirmed Bùi Huy Phồn's description of the strange role—both informal and catalytic—played by Hoàng Văn Hoan's essay in the banning of Vũ Trọng Phụng: "Hoàng Văn Hoan's rigid analysis resembled a final indictment, but the Institute of Literature did not publish it and hence few people actually read it. The literary world, however, heard vague echoes of the essay, and this generated a general wariness about Vũ Trọng Phụng's work." Reflecting on the enforcement of the ban as opposed to it origins, Văn Tâm pointed to collusion among an array of cultural and educational institutions:

> In the library, Vũ Trọng Phụng was placed in a "special research zone" that could only be accessed with a formal introductory letter. His work was eliminated from the literature curriculum in both high schools and universities. Students caught reading Vũ Trọng Phụng could be cited by their organizational unit for severe ideological problems. Teachers of literature were not allowed to possess research works about the writer or to read aloud in class excerpts of his famous exchange with Nhất Chi Mai. Perpetrators informed on by friends from the Party cell were typically referred to the Academic Council for punishment.[122]

The accounts of Văn Tâm and others confirm that despite the absence of a formal decree, schools, libraries, bookstores, and publishing houses moved in lockstep and at roughly the same time to eliminate public access to Vũ Trọng Phụng's work. The closing down of private publishing houses and independent newspapers and journals within the DRV by the end of the 1950s doubtless facilitated this process. The mobilization of the population for war during the 1960s and 1970s, including the periodic evacuation of northern cities, stifled efforts at cultural liberalization and encouraged intellectual uniformity. Moreover, Vũ Trọng Phụng's ironic and gloomy body of work was ill suited to the DRV's wartime cultural policy that was fixated on the enhancement of public morale. Indeed, it is hard to imagine a less hospitable environment for the rehabilitation of this complex writer. Hence, in addition to falling victim to the official political campaign against NVGP, Vũ Trọng Phụng's reputation remained a casualty over the longer term of larger historical processes.

CONCLUSION

Although an argument could be made that the complex content of Vũ Trọng Phụng's writing ensured that it would eventually run afoul of communist censors, the documentary record confirms that the fate of his work within the DRV was sealed by NVGP's zealous promotion of it. Less clear, however, is the precise reason that NVGP singled out Vũ Trọng Phụng for public veneration. This lack of clarity stems from the difficulty of interpreting public statements about the writer made within the DRV during the 1950s, given constraints on intellectual discourse imposed by the Party state. The impact of these constraints is most apparent in the efforts undertaken to align Vũ Trọng Phụng's work with critical realism, socialist realism, or the political project of the communist party. There is little doubt that some of Vũ Trọng Phụng's advocates genuinely believed in these arguments, but it is also likely that others perceived them as the only effective tactic to safeguard the writer's work. Moreover, retrospective analyses of the promotion of Vũ Trọng Phụng by members of NVGP whose reputations were partially rehabilitated during the late 1980s continue to be shaped by the continuity of communist cultural institutions, the endurance of censorship, and the legacy of past repressions.

The preceding narrative suggests a number of possible explanatory factors that may shed light on this question. First, older members of NVGP who were contemporaries of Vũ Trọng Phụng had observed firsthand his meteoric career throughout the 1930s. Armed with this knowledge, they felt confident in their independent assessment of the writer regardless of official interpretations. The reality of Vũ Trọng Phụng's exalted standing within the competitive literary marketplace of the late colonial era fortified their high assessment of his literary merit. Moreover, some knew Vũ Trọng Phụng personally and all were familiar with the remarkable features of his life: his modest background, his precocious talent, his relentless productivity, his battle with illness and addiction, and his tragic premature death. In short, there is a strong likelihood that members of NVGP singled out Vũ Trọng Phụng's work for veneration because they genuinely loved and admired it.

A second important factor was the timing of Vũ Trọng Phụng's death prior to the August Revolution in 1945 since it left unresolved the crucial question of his attitude toward the Vietnamese revolution. Indeed, it is no coincidence that the other modern literary figures whose reputations remained a source of controversy in the DRV during the 1950s—Thạch Lam, Hàn Mạc Tử, and Tản Đà, to take three examples—also died prematurely at roughly the same time. The assimilation into the communist cultural establishment of individualistic new poets (such as Xuân Diệu, Huy Cận, Chế Lan Viên, Thế Lữ, and Lưu Trọng Lư) who joined the revolution during the 1940s underlines further the extent to which literary reputations in the DRV were determined on the basis of political affiliation. The enduring uncertainty over Vũ Trọng Phụng's attitude toward the revolution made him one of the few figures available to serve as the focus of genuine debate over literary standards within the DRV.

It is also possible that Vũ Trọng Phụng attracted the leaders of NVGP because themes embedded in his work buttressed aspects of their own agenda. Inspired by the rise of "reform communist" movements in Eastern Europe following the death of Stalin, NVGP pursued a political project dominated by two issues. The first was a concern with the failings of Stalinist government—a concern expressed through critiques of institutional bureaucracy, on the one hand, and a culture of political leadership marked by flattery, opportunism, and authoritarianism, on the other. The high profile of these concerns within the discourse of NVGP may help to explain the intensity of the movement's affection for Vũ Trọng Phụng's widely acknowledged masterwork, *Dumb Luck*, the republication of which it organized in 1957. Indeed, direct evidence from Bùi Quang Đoài's short story in *New Land* suggests that NVGP's admiration for *Dumb Luck* derived from a perception that the fantastic social ascent of the uneducated protagonist of the novel—based on little more than a talent for flattery and opportunistic mimicry—dramatized the precise dynamics behind the rise of the new communist elite. Echoes of a "reform communist" critique of the dehumanizing character of modern bureaucracy may also be found in the absurd portrayal of the mechanical functioning of the colonial police station in the famous second chapter of the novel. Given NVGP's opposition to authoritarian political culture, it is easy to imagine how *Dumb Luck*'s caustic portrayal of the manipulation of an ignorant and gullible population by a cynical and arrogant leadership (using empty slogans venerating the common people) may have struck a chord with members of the movement.

The second issue that loomed large within the agenda of NVGP was the repression of creative and intellectual freedom. Indeed, many of the best-known essays published in *Nhân Văn* and *Giai Phẩm* dealt with the persecution of writers, the silencing of critics, the manipulation of literary awards, the heavy hand of government censorship, and the official intimidation of independent and quasi-independent periodicals. As suggested above, the decision to republish in *Nhân Văn* Vũ Trọng Phụng's famous letter from 1937 opposing calls for the censorship of his work suggests that the leaders of the movement recognized in the writer something of a kindred spirit on this particular issue. Indeed, the fact that debates over Vũ Trọng Phụng embodied the remarkably open public sphere of the late colonial era may be the primary reason that NVGP was drawn toward the writer and his work.

CONCLUSION • Rehabilitating Vũ Trọng Phụng

Following the ban imposed upon it in 1960, Vũ Trọng Phụng's work remained off limits in communist-ruled Vietnam for over twenty-five years. The lifting of this ban is typically seen as an outcome of Renovation, the "conservative" reform policy launched by the Communist Party in the mid-1980s that sought to liberalize the economy while maintaining the Party's monopoly over political power. Renovation's Janus-face may be seen in its impact on local intellectual life. It permitted the growth of limited forms of journalism, scholarly inquiry, and the fine arts, while prohibiting exploration of sensitive political issues or historical topics such as the merits of multiparty democracy, the life of Hồ Chí Minh, the crimes of Stalinism, or the fratricidal history of Vietnamese communism. Reflecting this general context, Vũ Trọng Phụng's *Selected Works* appeared in 1987, the year after Renovation was unveiled, along with a new body of criticism and commentary that reflected the conflicted political imperatives of the new policy.

But, in spite of obvious connections to the reformist agenda of the mid-1980s, the resurgence of public interest in Vũ Trọng Phụng and the lifting of the ban on his work should not be seen as exclusive products of Renovation. While 1987 was, without a doubt, a turning point in his official reputation, the public reassessment of the writer started over a decade prior to Renovation and evolved gradually, in three phases, between the early 1970s and the late 2000s. At the start of the first phase around 1970, several respected literary figures challenged Hoàng Văn Hoan's derogatory depiction of Vũ Trọng Phụng by dusting off the failed defense of the writer crafted by NVGP in the 1950s. The first phase concluded with the republication of his most left-leaning work, the novel *The Dike Breaks,* in 1982, and the public commendation of *Dumb Luck* the following year. The second phase coincided with the introduction of Renovation in 1987 and was marked by the release of Vũ Trọng Phụng's *Selected Works,* a watershed event that made his writing widely available for the first time since the late 1950s. It also witnessed major academic conferences and the publication of multiple edited volumes that publicized the dramatic reversal in his official standing. While critical views of Vũ Trọng Phụng evolved during this phase, most interpretations continued to emphasize his opposition to colonial capitalism and to downplay the significance of anticommunist sentiment in his writing. Finally, a nascent third phase in the reassessment of Vũ Trọng Phụng, spearheaded since the early 1990s by the brilliant literary critic Lại Nguyên Ân, has refocused attention on some of the late colonial republican concerns—the dangers of censorship, the value of empiricism, and the dark side of communism—that preoccupied the writer during his life and that shaped the reception of his work after his death. Hence, although the significance of Renovation cannot be denied, the recent return to prominence of Vũ Trọng Phụng in Vietnam may also owe something to the contemporary relevance of the late colonial republican project with which he remains associated.

PHASE ONE

After a decade in which Vũ Trọng Phụng was viciously disparaged and the publication and circulation of his work suppressed, two memoirs by eminent literary figures quietly challenged this campaign of vilification. The first was by Nguyên Hồng, the famous novelist and cultural official who had represented the Vietnam Arts and Literature Association during the notorious commemoration of Vũ Trọng Phụng at the Hà Nội Opera House in 1956. In his otherwise politically orthodox literary memoir, *The Road of a Writer (Bước đường viết văn),* published in 1970, Nguyên Hồng described Vũ Trọng Phụng sympathetically as a talented, modest, and poor individual who made ends meet by running a small bookstore on Conical Hat Street in Hà Nội's Old Quarter.[1] While acknowledging enduring questions about the writer's views on "politics, economics, and philosophy," Nguyên Hồng praised his "strict and responsible spirit."[2] Moreover, he cited personal experience from the 1930s to assert that Vũ Trọng Phụng "strongly respected revolutionary fighters, especially communists, ex–political prisoners, and comrades who worked at the Party paper *News [Tin Tức].*"[3] As evidence, he claimed that Vũ Trọng Phụng was friendly with the famous communist journalist Trần Huy Liệu and an admirer of the Party's official poet and cultural czar, Tố Hữu.

The following year, another eminent colonial-era author turned communist cultural official—Nguyễn Công Hoan—presented a more elaborate defense of Vũ Trọng Phụng in his literary memoir, *My Life as a Writer (Đời viết văn của tôi)*.[4] Nguyễn Công Hoan maintained that Vũ Trọng Phụng ought to be judged within the historically specific context of late-colonial-era journalism, a milieu in which writers were driven by commercial concerns rather than political imperatives. He also claimed that the suspect, shifting positions expressed in Vũ Trọng Phụng's writing were determined by the vacillating views of his publishers. "To research a writer who produced both progressive and regressive works," he explained, "we must pay attention to the sequence of his production and to the newspapers in which he published. Who were his publishers? What was their agenda? And what was the dominant ideology that reigned over society during the period?"[5] In addition to this plea for historical relativism, Nguyễn Công Hoan suggested that Vũ Trọng Phụng's erroneous political views should be excused because, as with many late colonial-era writers who joined the Vietnamese revolution after World War II, "he had not yet been touched by the hand of the Party."[6] "Had he lived longer," Nguyễn Công Hoan continued, "he would have certainly followed the Party, given his hatred of the colonial regime, his contempt for the era, and his sympathy for the poor."[7]

Nguyễn Công Hoan also attempted to debunk the slanderous charge that Vũ Trọng Phụng had been an informer for the French security police:

> It is rumored that he worked for the French security police. But Vũ Trọng Phụng had many ways to make money. He did not need to do it in this way. And, if he did take French money, why was he dirt-poor until the day he died? There were not many writers during this era and we all knew one another. If someone poor and miserable started to work for the police, it would have been hard to hide it and he would have been ostracized by his friends. I never once heard that he was a police spy. Indeed, no one from that era imagined that he would do such a terrible thing.[8]

In conclusion, Nguyễn Công Hoan reiterated his appeal to soften harsh assessments of Vũ Trọng Phụng with a dose of historical relativism. "When we look at writers from the pre-1945 era, we should not praise or condemn them in too extreme a manner," he wrote. "Rather, we must take into consideration their social situation, the literary and intellectual atmosphere of their era, and the professional pressures under which they worked in order to pass judgment in a more judicious way."[9]

It is unclear what drove Nguyên Hồng and Nguyễn Công Hoan to publicly defend Vũ Trọng Phụng at this time, but it is unlikely that their efforts were sanctioned by the Party. The war-torn early 1970s was a tense period in the DRV during which Party officials viewed even modest challenges to cultural orthodoxy as a threat to the nation's "fighting spirit" or as harbingers of political dissent. Hence, the defense of Vũ Trọng Phụng struck a discordant note within a tightly policed intellectual environment marked by compliance and uniformity. That it was tolerated at all is a testament to the high prestige enjoyed by Nguyên Hồng and Nguyễn Công Hoan—a status that derived less from their official posts in the DRV cultural bureaucracy than from the literary celebrity that they had earned during the late colonial era. Indeed, their defense of Vũ Trọng Phụng might be seen as a reassertion of the authority of late-colonial-era aesthetic standards over the philistine prescriptions for art and culture that the Party zealously enforced during decades of war.

Further confirming that the movement to rehabilitate Vũ Trọng Phụng predated Renovation, the Literature Publishing House released a new edition of *The Dike Breaks* in 1982, five years prior to the introduction of the reform policy.[10] This new edition, released without fanfare, marked the first republication of any work by Vũ Trọng Phụng in almost twenty-five years. A lesser novel than *Dumb Luck* or *The Storm, The Dike Breaks* was selected to challenge the ban because its left-leaning politics cast the writer in the most revolutionary possible light. In a cautious and apologetic introduction to the new edition, an anonymous editor admitted that the novel's strengths—including "its portrayal of the rotten inhumanity of the feudal-colonial regime" and its promotion of a "spirit of resistance"—coexisted with a host of unfortunate "mistakes and distortions."[11] These included "a misunderstanding of the essence of the Socialist Party and the French Popular Front," "a vague grasp of the class viewpoint, tactics, and strategies of the communists," and a "lack of respect for the peasantry."[12] Nevertheless, the introduction concluded by praising the novel for "painting a relatively general social portrait with a sharp pen" and "introducing readers, especially young readers, to a realistic slice of life prior to the August Revolution."[13] Building upon the momentum signaled by the appearance of *The Dike Breaks*, the respected writer Nguyễn Khải praised *Dumb Luck* the following year in a speech delivered at the Third Congress of the Vietnam Writers' Association (Đại hội lần thứ ba Hội Nhà Văn Việt Nam) as "a staggering work that ennobles Vietnamese literature."[14] Later that year, Vũ Trọng Phụng and several of his works were included in an official literary dictionary published in Hà Nội.[15]

While a thorough reversal of the ban on Vũ Trọng Phụng was not to be achieved until the start of Renovation four years later, these gestures from the early 1980s paved the way for his rehabilitation.

It is probably no coincidence that the uptick in Vũ Trọng Phụng's official standing in the early 1980s followed soon after the infamous defection to China of his harshest critic, the ex–politburo member Hoàng Văn Hoan. Long associated with a pro-China faction in the communist leadership, Hoàng Văn Hoan fell under suspicion and was expelled from the politburo after a spike in Sino-Vietnamese hostilities in 1976. As a border war raged between Vietnam and China in 1979, he left for a medical procedure in Berlin, disappeared during a stopover in Pakistan, and turned up, weeks later, in Beijing.[16] Hoàng Văn Hoan remained an exile in China until his death in 1991, paying the price of his sanctuary by publicly denouncing his ex-comrades in the Vietnamese politburo for betraying their Chinese allies.[17] In an essay published in 1987, the literary critic Nguyễn Đăng Mạnh alluded directly to the role of Hoàng Văn Hoan's defection in the rehabilitation of Vũ Trọng Phụng, stating that it was only after the person responsible for "dragging his work through the mud" had "been exposed as a great national traitor *[một tên đại phản quốc]* that the first steps in his exoneration could begin."[18]

PHASE TWO

The second phase in Vũ Trọng Phụng's rehabilitation began in 1987 and witnessed both a surge in the republication of his work and a change in his critical reputation. The most significant event, by far, was the publication of his *Selected Works*, which appeared in three volumes and ran over twelve hundred pages.[19] It was edited and compiled by Nguyễn Đăng Mạnh and Trần Hữu Tá, northern academic scholars with moderately "progressive" track records. Reflecting an understandable uncertainty about the staying power of the new Renovation policy, the first volume included three relatively "safe" works: *No Echo*, *The Prisoner Is Released*, and *The Storm*. The second volume published excerpts from three pieces of reportage and reprinted *The Dike Breaks*. The third volume was more daring, featuring *Dumb Luck*, *Winning the Lottery*, a handful of short stories, and some criticism. Although it was oddly organized and ignored major texts such as *To Be a Whore* and *Venereal Disease Clinic*, the collection included Vũ Trọng Phụng's most important works and succeeded in capturing something of his talent, productivity, and range. It also served to publicize the end of the ban on his work. Vũ Trọng Phụng's return to respectability was signaled even more widely by the integration of selections from his oeuvre into public school curricula and by the adaptation of *Dumb Luck* (1989) and *The Storm* (1991) into successful feature films. Over the following two decades all of his fiction and literary nonfiction would be reprinted multiple times, and in 1999, the Vietnam Writers' Association released *Vũ Trọng Phụng: Complete Works,* a canonical collection that ran five volumes and over thirty-six hundred pages.[20]

In addition to making Vũ Trọng Phụng's writing broadly available, the release of *Selected Works* in 1987 inaugurated a new tradition of criticism by including a pathbreaking forty-seven-page introduction by Nguyễn Đăng Mạnh.[21] Unlike the defenses of Vũ Trọng Phụng crafted in the previous phase, Nguyễn Đăng Mạnh did not base his high regard for the writer on the fiction that he was a budding communist revolutionary. Rather, he argued that Vũ Trọng Phụng's significance derived from the complexity of his vision, his massive popularity, and the intensity of the controversies surrounding him. Such a contention may seem unremarkable, but it broke new ground in Hà Nội after a generation of criticism that defined literary excellence in political terms exclusively. Nguyễn Đăng Mạnh also adopted a new approach to Vũ Trọng Phụng's incriminating connection to NVGP. Blaming the leaders of the movement for contriving a fraudulent common cause with the writer, he argued that NVGP had "taken advantage" of Vũ Trọng Phụng to launch a "devious political plot."[22] In attempting to thwart it, officials overreacted and unfairly attacked Vũ Trọng Phụng. But this approach began to lose favor in the early 1960s, coming to a definitive end with the recent publication of The *Dike Breaks.*

By trumpeting recent progress and maintaining the disapproving attitude toward NVGP that had dominated public discourse since the late 1950s, Nguyễn Đăng Mạnh's defense of Vũ Trọng Phụng reflected an enduring conservatism that marked early Renovation discourse. But it also signaled a loosening of the rigid politicized standards that had long governed Vietnamese communist cultural criticism. Instead of assessing the writer solely on his fidelity to socialist-realist norms, Nguyễn Đăng Mạnh celebrated Vũ Trọng Phụng's richness, complexity, and popular appeal. The essay made a persuasive case that Vũ Trọng Phụng's work was animated by two ideological impulses: a pessimistic fatalism with strong traditionalist undertones and a fierce indignity at injustice and social inequality. The body of the essay tracked the ebb and flow of these dual impulses in the writer's work over three successive periods of his career. It concluded with a searching exploration of his socially panoramic vision, the central role of fate in his stories, and his mastery of satire and parody. In short, it provided the deepest and most wide-ranging examination of the writer since Văn Tâm's book-length study thirty years earlier. Although it expressed a spectrum of "progressive" and "conservative" views characteristic of Renovation discourse, the introduction made an irrefutable case for Vũ Trọng Phụng's historical importance and pointed to the range of interpretative approaches that might usefully be applied to his work.

Nguyễn Đăng Mạnh's essay kicked off an explosive upsurge in critical writing about Vũ Trọng Phụng. Four waves of criticism were produced in conjunction with four major academic conferences organized in 1987 (Hồ Chí Minh City), 1989 (Hà Nội), 1992 (Hồ Chí Minh City), and 2002 (Hà Nội).[23] Participants produced essays on many aspects of the writer's work and organizers circulated newly unearthed documents and memoirs about his life. Many conference essays were released in the national media before being preserved in edited volumes for future scholarly use. The latter included a five-hundred-page volume released by the Hồ Chí Minh City Publishing House entitled *The Writer Vũ Trọng Phụng Is With Us* and a massive seven-hundred-page collection prepared by the Education Publishing House entitled *Vũ Trọng Phụng: On the Writer and His Work*.[24] The republication of Vũ Trọng Phụng's novels and reportage as stand-alone texts provided another venue for short criticism in the form of introductory essays. Between 1989 and 1997, for example, the critic Hoàng Thiếu Sơn penned appreciative introductions to five separate works: *Marry for Love* (*Lấy nhau vì tình*; 1989), *Winning the Lottery* (1990), *The Man Trap* (1993), *To Be a Whore* (1994), and *Venereal Disease Clinic* (1998).[25] This same period witnessed the first wave of in-depth, locally produced academic scholarship on Vũ Trọng Phụng. In 1990, the influential organ of the Institute of Literature, *The Journal of Literature*, published a special issue on the writer to mark the fiftieth anniversary of his death.[26] Full-length Ph.D. dissertations completed in the aftermath of Renovation and subsequently published as books include "Character in Vũ Trọng Phụng's Novels," "The Art of Time in Vũ Trọng Phụng's Novels," "Humor in Vũ Trọng Phụng," and "Special Literary Characteristics of Vũ Trọng Phụng."[27]

While most of the new criticism and scholarship continued to portray Vũ Trọng Phụng as a fellow traveler whose protorevolutionary critical realism had been temporarily obscured from view during the fog of the Second Indochina War, aspects of the discourse succeeded in pushing the boundaries of the Renovation agenda. The first volume of criticism to appear, Trần Hữu Tá's *Vũ Trọng Phụng: Yesterday and Today* (1992), featured essays by long-silenced figures such as Trương Tửu and Văn Tâm.[28] It also included an essay from 1966 by the anticommunist author Dương Nghiễm Mậu, a major literary figure from the southern Republic of Vietnam (RVN) whose work had been banned in the North.[29] Subsequent volumes of criticism reprinted more essays by RVN writers such as Phạm Thế Ngữ and Vũ Bằng. Perhaps more significantly, every volume of criticism was organized chronologically and featured a range of positive and negative assessments—a format that drew attention to the fluctuation of attitudes toward the writer over time. The relativism and historicism implicit in this approach contrasted with the rigid standards of assessment that had dominated Vietnamese literary criticism prior to Renovation and signaled the opening of a more freewheeling public sphere inside the country.

PHASE THREE

Since the mid-1990s, scholarship on Vũ Trọng Phụng has been dominated by Lại Nguyên Ân, a prolific critic, anthologist, and literary historian whose broad intellectual project dovetails with core concerns of late colonial republicanism. In particular, his research has amplified the virtues of empiricism, the negative consequences of censorship, and the checkered history of communism—all concerns that preoccupied Vũ Trọng Phụng. Lại Nguyên Ân's approach suggests that the writer's enduring appeal may owe something to the capacity of the colonial republican project that he embraced to address pressing Vietnamese political concerns during the current late communist era.

In 1994 and 1997, Lại Nguyên Ân edited two essential volumes of essays and historical documents: *Vũ Trọng Phụng: Man and Work* and *Vũ Trọng Phụng: Talent and Truth* (the former coedited with Nguyễn Hoành Khung).[30] In 1999, he served as the main editor *(biên tập chính)* for the massive collection *Vũ Trọng Phụng's Complete Works*. In 2000 and 2001, he published two volumes of Vũ Trọng Phụng's journalistic writing—*Clown Makeup* and *Hobbling along the Road*—that he unearthed (with my assistance) in old newspaper collections in Hà Nội, Hồ Chí Minh City, and Berkeley, California.[31] He also authored a series of groundbreaking essays during this period that focused on the history, politics, and "textology" *(văn bản học)* of Vũ Trọng Phụng's work.[32] His unprecedented research in textology (a branch of philology) climaxed with the release in 2007 of *Textual Research on "The Storm,"* a comparative analysis of multiple editions of the famous novel from 1936 that brilliantly illuminated the distorting impact on Vietnamese literary history of multiple regimes of state censorship.[33]

Both Lại Nguyên Ân's writing and his editorial work reveal a zealous commitment to documentary research that is unusual within contemporary Vietnamese literary studies. Virtually alone among scholars and critics who have written about Vũ Trọng Phụng since the late 1980s, his essays are grounded in close readings of the period press and original editions of literary texts. His earliest essay—"An Aspect of Vũ Trọng Phụng the Journalist: Summarizer of International News"—explored the coverage of Soviet politics in the interwar Vietnamese press to suggest that the writer's notorious article from 1937 on the Moscow show trials reflected widely held anticommunist views of the era.[34] In "Several Documents about Vũ Trọng Phụng's Trial in 1932," he mobilized a rich trove of press clippings from the early 1930s to reconstruct the history of Vũ Trọng Phụng's first obscenity trial and to explore the dynamics of colonial censorship.[35] Another essay—"Vũ Trọng Phụng and Two Sài Gòn Newspapers from 1937"—followed the paper trail of a long-forgotten public spat between Vũ Trọng Phụng and the left-wing critic Xuân Sa.[36] As with his literary-historical essays, Lại Nguyên Ân's editorial projects privilege the presentation of new documentary material. For example, his edited collection from 1997, *Vũ Trọng Phụng: Talent and Truth,* recovered and reprinted verbatim a series of letters in which the writer defended himself against obscenity charges. "Below, please find a collection of long-neglected documents from Vũ Trọng Phụng's pen wars," Lại Nguyên Ân wrote in a brief editorial note. "They provide direct insight into the writer's views on literature and society."[37] Several years later, *Hobbling along the Road* and *Clown Makeup* each reproduced dozens of stories, plays, articles, reviews, and editorials that Lại Nguyên Ân retrieved from old newspaper collections. Lại Nguyên Ân's interest in the potential truth-power of documents may be seen in the unusual format of his two article collections, which feature legible photographic reproductions of his archival discoveries. This documentary fetish is politically loaded in communist Vietnam because empirical data continues to represent one of the most potent weapons of "experts" in their remarkably enduring struggle with "political commissars." The wide availability of original documents and data challenges the power of the Party state to bend the human sciences to its will.

Lại Nguyên Ân's preoccupation with empirical documentation dovetails with his concern about the pervasiveness of censorship in Vietnamese history, an issue he explores with great ingenuity and originality in *Textual Research on "The Storm."* This remarkable book juxtaposes four separate editions of *The Storm:* (1) the original version serialized in *Hà Nội News* in 1936; (2) the first edition packaged as a stand-alone book in 1937; (3) a version from 1951 published in Sài Gòn under the French-controlled State of Vietnam; and (4) an edition from 1956 released in communist Hà Nội. Through a meticulous line-by-line comparison of the four texts, Lại Nguyên Ân discloses an enormously complex history of bowdlerization, sanitization, and expurgation. The discovery of large differences between the serialized edition from 1936 and the first edition published as a book in 1937 raises intriguing questions about what might constitute an "original" text in this particular context. The book also charts variation in official sensitivity toward politics, sexuality, and profanity under different political regimes. While teasing out distinctions in the repression of free speech over time, the study is remarkable for its refusal to assert any moral difference between regimes of censorship under colonial, nationalist, and communist states. This departs from official Vietnamese historiography, which refuses to acknowledge even the most obvious continuities between the repressive machinery of the colonial regime and the postcolonial communist state.

While Lại Nguyên Ân's close focus on issues of censorship and empirical documentation is easily read as an indirect criticism of the pervasive manipulation of the Vietnamese public sphere by political authorities, his efforts to publicize the troubled relationship between Vũ Trọng Phụng and the communist movement challenge more directly the hegemonic discourse of the Party state. A pernicious consequence of the Party's draconian cultural policy is that it has compelled Vũ Trọng Phụng's defenders (from members of NVGP to Renovation-era critics) to mischaracterize him as a slightly flighty ally of the revolution. At the same time, official textbooks treat the censorship and suppression of Vũ Trọng Phụng euphemistically, further whitewashing, in effect, the history of antagonism between the writer and the revolution. In contrast, Lại Nguyên Ân has endeavored to illuminate this difficult history by arranging the rerelease of Vũ Trọng Phụng's anticommunist writing along with the most vicious communist screeds against him. For example, in the collection of criticism that he coedited in 1994, he presided over the first publication of Hoàng Văn Hoan's infamous essay from 1960.[38] More surprising still, in 1999, he was able to include Vũ Trọng Phụng's controversial article from 1937 on the history of the Moscow show trials in the final volume of *Vũ Trọng Phụng: Complete Works*.[39] The publication of this essay is notable, not only because of its hostility to the Machiavellian nature of communist politics, but because the ever-cautious Vietnamese Party state has never permitted a full public airing of the crimes of Stalinism. Hence, Vũ Trọng Phụng's recently republished eighty-year-old account may represent the only widely available treatment of the topic published in communist Vietnam. In 2001, Lại Nguyên Ân managed to include in the anthology *Clown Makeup* Vũ Trọng Phụng's blistering denunciation from 1938 of the ICP's malicious campaign against Trotskyist rivals.[40] Given that histories produced in Vietnam almost never reproduce local criticism of the Party or its policies, the release of such an essay by a state publishing house represents a small but significant wrinkle in the officially sanctioned historical record.

CONCLUSION

As the brief accounts above and in the previous chapter indicate, discussions about Vũ Trọng Phụng in Vietnam since the onset of Renovation in the mid-1980s have been more diverse, less ideological, and certainly less fraught with risk than the heated exchanges of the 1950s. But these changes coexist with more durable features of the discourse that stem from the unbroken continuity of communist power in Vietnam throughout the postcolonial era. Perhaps the most consistent and consequential feature of the Party's cultural policy, from its inception, is its keen sensitivity to direct criticism of communist power. Hence, with notable exceptions, such as in the work of Lại Nguyên Ân, the significance of Vũ Trọng Phụng's relatively extensive anticommunist writing, as detailed in chapter 3, has been minimized. By incorporating this anticommunist perspective, however, into the writer's larger views about political economy and social policy (as described in chapter 2), including his opposition to unrestrained capitalism and state censorship and his support for empirical science, legal universalism, and mass education, a picture of Vũ Trọng Phụng's political vision emerges that resembles the late republican project associated with the Third Republic's moderate political center. As explained in chapter 1, the origins of this vision may be found in Vũ Trọng Phụng's wide exposure to the writings of French republican authors and journalists and in his personal experiences in key institutions and cultural contact zones of French colonial society.

The "colonial" dimension of Vũ Trọng Phụng's republicanism is apparent in his fixation with the insincerity of French Indochina's political culture, which was marked by the copresence of lofty republican rhetoric and the grubby workings of a clumsy, underfunded, and deeply racist police state. *Dumb Luck* explores this theme with special intensity. The colonial character of Vũ Trọng Phụng's vision may also be found in his revulsion for the radical cultural changes that disrupted interwar Vietnamese society, the spasmodic pace of which was overdetermined by the abrupt rise of French political and economic power. As described in chapter 4, these included the breakdown of the family, the rise of the individual, the emancipation of women, and the modernization of love and sexuality. Confronting these "social problems" in a republican spirit, Vũ Trọng Phụng advocated prudent government intervention backed by social science. But the intensity of his distaste for cultural modernization reflected a nativism and traditionalism with deep colonial roots.

Just as the framework of colonial republicanism is better able than available alternatives to capture the mix of concerns present in Vũ Trọng Phụng's work, it may also help to explain his enduring appeal today. The republican tradition's historic opposition to the despotism of monarchy and the obscurantism of the Church has honed it into an effective weapon with which to challenge the deeply authoritarian and illiberal tendencies of the Vietnamese communist state. Its veneration of free speech and an uncensored press strikes a meaningful contemporary chord, as does its support for science, education, and the rule of law. While the enduring popularity of Vũ Trọng Phụng's work today owes much to its humor, sex, violence, compelling plotlines, memorable characters, and complex psychological analysis, it is also possible that many of his most enthusiastic readers feel an attraction to his moderate republican political vision. This is certainly the case for the handful of remarkable critics who have promoted his work most zealously in the wake of Renovation. The research career of Lại Nguyên Ân—which includes another massive project on the NVGP leader and fellow colonial republican Phan Khôi, as well as numerous smaller studies of silenced or controversial Vietnamese literary figures—has exhibited a consistent opposition to the repression of the public sphere by the communist state.[41] A similar political tendency may be observed in Trần Hữu Tá, a pioneer in the recuperation of censored literary voices from the Republic of Vietnam. Nguyễn Đăng Mạnh has moved into an even deeper level of political defiance, publishing a controversial, banned memoir online in 2008.[42] In short, the study of Vũ Trọng Phụng has attracted a group of intellectuals who share some of the writer's colonial republican values, including freedom of speech, empiricism, and indignity at communist despotism. There is hope that the continuing popularity of Vũ Trọng Phụng's work in Vietnam today may reflect a broader sympathy with these values among the reading public.

NOTES

INTRODUCTION

1. Since 1996, four major works by Vũ Trọng Phụng have been translated into English and one into French. Each of the English translations is accompanied by a scholarly introduction to the text and the author. See Vũ Trọng Phụng, "Household Servants," in *The Light of the Capital: Three Modern Vietnamese Classics*, ed. Greg Lockhart, trans. Greg Lockhart and Monique Lockhart (Kuala Lumpur: Oxford University Press, 1996); Vũ Trọng Phụng, *Le fabuleux destin de Xuan le Rouquin*, trans. Phan The Hong and Janine Gillon (Hà Nội: Thế Giới, 1998); Vũ Trọng Phụng, *Dumb Luck: A Novel by Vũ Trọng Phụng*, ed. Peter Zinoman, trans. Peter Zinoman and Nguyễn Nguyệt Cầm (Ann Arbor: University of Michigan Press, 2002); Vũ Trọng Phụng, *The Industry of Marrying Europeans*, trans. Thuy Tranviet (Ithaca: Cornell Southeast Asia Program Publications, 2006); Vũ Trọng Phụng, *Lục Xì: Prostitution and Venereal Disease in Colonial Hanoi*, ed. Shaun Kingsley Malarney, trans. Shaun Kingsley Malarney (Honolulu: University of Hawaii Press, 2011).

2. Peter Davidson, ed., *The Complete Works of George Orwell* (London: Secker Warburg, 1997); Lại Nguyên Ân, ed., *Vũ Trọng Phụng toàn tập* [Complete works of Vũ Trọng Phụng] (Hà Nội: Hội Nhà Văn, 1999).

3. Just as Orwell is equally well known for *Down and Out in Paris and London* (1933), *The Road to Wigan Pier* (1937), *Homage to Catalonia* (1938), *Animal Farm* (1945), and 1984 (1949), Vũ Trọng Phụng's reputation rests as much with the novels *Dumb Luck* (1936), *The Storm* (1936), and *To Be a Whore* (1937) as with reportage such as *The Industry of Marrying Westerners* (1934), *Household Servants* (1936), and *Venereal Disease Clinic* (1938). Note, as well, the temporal overlap of the two men's major work.

4. Christopher Hitchens, *Why Orwell Matters* (New York: Basic Books, 2002), 5–8.

5. Lan Khai, *Vũ Trọng Phụng—Mớ tài liệu cho văn học sử Việt Nam* [Vũ Trọng Phụng—documents for a Vietnamese literary history] (Hà Nội: Minh Phương, 1941), 19.

6. Lê Thanh, "Chúng tôi phỏng vấn ông Vũ Trọng Phụng về những tiểu thuyết *Giông tố*, *Làm đĩ*" [Interviewing Vũ Trọng Phụng about his novels *The Storm* and *To Be a Whore*], *Bắc Hà*, April 1, 1937.

7. For the history of this splintering, see Georges Boudarel, *Cent fleurs écloses dans la nuit du Vietnam: Communism et dissidence, 1954–1956* (Paris: Jacque Bertoin, 1991); Kim Ninh, *A World Transformed: The Politics of Culture in Revolutionary Vietnam, 1945–1965* (Ann Arbor: University of Michigan Press, 2002); Peter Zinoman, "Nhân Văn-Giai Phẩm and Vietnamese 'Reform Communism' in the 1950s: A Revisionist Interpretation," *Journal of Cold War Studies* 13, no. 1 (Winter 2011): 60–100.

8. Intelligent but incomplete accounts of this story can be found in Bùi Huy Phồn, "Nhớ và nghĩ về Vũ Trọng Phụng" [Remembering and thinking about Vũ Trọng Phụng], *Tuần báo Người Hà Nội* 79 (July 1, 1988); Văn Tâm, "Ba mươi năm ấy bây giờ là đây" [Here we are after thirty years], *Tuần báo Người Hà Nội* 86 (October 15, 1988); Nguyễn Hoành Khung, "Nhìn lại và suy nghĩ xung quanh một 'vụ án' văn học" [Looking back and thinking about a literary "case"], in *Vũ Trọng Phụng: Tài năng và sự thật*, ed. Lại Nguyên Ân (Hà Nội: Văn Học, 1997), 19–53.

9. Nguyễn Đăng Mạnh, "Chủ nghĩa tự nhiên trong sáng tác của Vũ Trọng Phụng" [Naturalism in Vũ Trọng Phụng's work], *Tạp chí Văn Học* 3 (1965); Vũ Đức Phúc, "Bàn về một số đặc trưng của khuynh hướng tự nhiên chủ nghĩa trong văn học Việt-Nam trước cách mạng" [Special features of the naturalist tendency in Vietnamese literature before the revolution], *Tạp chí Văn Học* 9 (1966): 54–62.

10. The key figures in this campaign were Trần Hữu Tá, Nguyễn Đăng Mạnh, Lại Nguyên Ân, and Nguyễn Hoành Khung.

11. Edited by Nguyễn Đăng Mạnh and Trần Hữu Tá, the first collection comprised three volumes and was issued by the Literature Publishing House in 1987: *Tuyển tập Vũ Trọng Phụng (ba tập)* [Selected works of Vũ Trọng Phụng], 3 vols. (Hà Nội: Văn Học, 1987). Second and third editions of this collection came out in 1993 and 1996. A more extensive collection of five volumes was edited by Lại Nguyên Ân and issued by the Writers Association Publishing House in 1999: *Toàn tập Vũ Trọng Phụng (năm tập)* [Complete works of Vũ Trọng Phụng], 5 vols. (Hà Nội: Hội Nhà Văn, 1999). In 2004, a new five-volume collection was edited by Tôn Thảo Miên and issued by the Literature Publishing House: *Vũ Trọng Phụng toàn tập* [Vũ Trọng Phụng, complete works] (Hà Nội: Văn Học, 2004). In addition, two collections of recently rediscovered journalistic writing have been published since 2000. See Vũ Trọng Phụng, *Vẽ nhọ bôi hề: Những tác phẩm mới tìm thấy năm 2000* [Clown makeup: Newly discovered work in 2000], ed. Peter Zinoman and Lại Nguyên Ân (Hà Nội: Hội Nhà Văn, 2000); and Vũ Trọng Phụng,

Chống nạng lên đường: Chùm sáng tác đầu tay mới tìm thấy cuối năm 2000 [Crutches on the road: Work newly found in 2000], ed. Lại Nguyên Ân (Hà Nội: Hội Nhà Văn, 2001). An updated issue of *Vẽ nhọ bôi hề* published in 2004 features additional material not included in the original edition.

12. On the seventy-fifth anniversary of his birth in December 1987, the Institute of Literature organized a major academic conference on Vũ Trọng Phụng in Hồ Chí Minh City that signaled his formal rehabilitation. A second conference was organized in Hà Nội on October 12, 1989, the fiftieth anniversary of his death. A third conference was held in Hà Nội in 1992 on the eightieth anniversary of his birth. A fourth conference, funded partially by the Ford Foundation, was organized in Hà Nội on the ninetieth anniversary of his birth on October 15–16, 2002.

13. See, for example, Nguyễn Bích Thuận, ed., *Vũ Trọng Phụng: Tác giả, tác phẩm, tư liệu* [Vũ Trọng Phụng: Writer, works, and documents] (Hồ Chí Minh City: Đồng Nai, 2007), 150. The book is part of the series "Bookshelf of Literary Works Used in School" (Tủ sách tác phẩm văn học dùng trong nhà trường), a Vietnamese version of *Cliffs Notes*. It includes excerpts from an essay by Nguyễn Hoành Khung on *The Storm*, which makes a case for Vũ Trọng Phụng's clumsy but earnest support for the revolutionary mission of the novel's communist lead character.

14. Criticism and scholarly essays on Vũ Trọng Phụng may be found in the following collections: Trần Hữu Tá, ed., *Vũ Trọng Phụng: Hôm qua và hôm nay* [Vũ Trọng Phụng: Yesterday and today] (Hồ Chí Minh City: Thành phố Hồ Chí Minh, 1992); Lại Nguyên Ân, ed., *Vũ Trọng Phụng: Tài năng và sự thật* [Vũ Trọng Phụng: Talent and truth] (Hà Nội: Hội Nhà Văn, 1992); Nguyễn Hoành Khung and Lại Nguyên Ân, eds., *Vũ Trọng Phụng, Con người và tác phẩm* [Vũ Trọng Phụng, life and work] (Hà Nội: Hội Nhà Văn, 1994); Trần Hữu Tá, ed., *Nhà văn Vũ Trọng Phụng với chúng ta* [The writer Vũ Trọng Phụng is with us] (Hồ Chí Minh City: Thành phố Hồ Chí Minh, 1999); Nguyễn Ngọc Thiện, ed., *Vũ Trọng Phụng: Về tác gia và tác phẩm* [Vũ Trọng Phụng: The writer and his work] (Hà Nội: Giáo Dục, 1999); and Ban Biên tập Viện Văn học, ed., *Bản sắc hiện đại trong các tác phẩm Vũ Trọng Phụng* [Modern identity in Vũ Trọng Phụng's work] (Hà Nội: Văn Học, 2003). Recent scholarly monographs include Bùi Văn Tiếng, *Thời gian nghệ thuật trong tiểu thuyết Vũ Trọng Phụng* [The art of time in Vũ Trọng Phụng's novels] (Hà Nội: Văn Hóa, 1997); Nguyễn Quang Trung, *Tiếng cười Vũ Trọng Phụng* [Laughter of Vũ Trọng Phụng] (Hà Nội: Văn Hóa Thông Tin, 2002); Trần Đăng Thao, *Đặc sắc văn chương Vũ Trọng Phụng* [Special literary features of Vũ Trọng Phụng] (Hà Nội: Thanh Niên, 2004); Đinh Trí Dũng, *Nhân vật tiểu thuyết Vũ Trọng Phụng* [The world of characters in Vũ Trọng Phụng] (Hà Nội: Khoa học Xã hội and Đông Tây, 2005); Lại Nguyên Ân, *Nghiên cứu văn bản tiểu thuyết Giông tố* [Manuscript research on *The Storm*] (Hà Nội: Trí Thức, 2007).

15. For background on republicanism as a postrevolutionary French political tradition, see Theodore Zeldin, *France, 1848–1945: Politics and Anger* (Oxford: Oxford

University Press, 1979); Claude Nicolet, *L'idée républicaine en France, 1789–1924: Essai d'histoire critique* (Paris: Gallimard, 1982); Suhir Hazareesingh, *Political Traditions in Modern France* (Oxford: Oxford University Press, 1994); Philip Nord, *The Republican Moment: Struggles for Democracy in Nineteenth-Century France* (Cambridge, Mass.: Harvard University Press, 1995); and Pamela Pilbeam, *Republicanism in Nineteenth Century France, 1814–1871* (New York: St. Martin's Press, 1995).

16. Hazareesingh, *Political Traditions in Modern France*, 66.

17. See Stephen E. Hanson, "The Founding of the French Third Republic," *Comparative Political Studies* 43, no. 8–9 (2010): 1023–1058.

18. Leo A. Loubère, "French Left-Wing Radicals and the Law as a Social Force, 1870–1900," *American Journal of Legal History* 8, no. 1 (1964): 54.

19. Ibid., 191.

20. Jean Terrier, "The Idea of a Republican Tradition: Reflections on the Debate concerning the Intellectual Foundations of the French Third Republic," *Journal of Political Ideologies* 11, no. 3 (2006): 298–308.

21. Laurent Dobuzinskis, "Defenders of Liberal Individualism, Republican Virtues and Solidarity: The Forgotten Intellectual Founding Fathers of the French Third Republic," *European Journal of Political Theory* 7, no. 3 (2008): 287–307.

22. Peter J. Lamour, *The French Radical Party in the 1930s* (Stanford: Stanford University Press, 1964). See especially chapter 8, which discusses "a phase in the history of the Radical party in which unadulterated anti-Communism gradually became the principal article of faith, perhaps filling the void left by the disappearance of anti-clericalism." On the replacement of anticlericalism with anticommunism, see also William R. Keylor, "Anti-Clericalism and Educational Reform in the French Third Republic: A Retrospective Evaluation," *History of Education Quarterly* 21, no. 1 (1981): 101.

23. Sarraut's speech is discussed in Martin Thomas, "Albert Sarraut, French Colonial Development and the Communist Threat, 1919–1930," *Journal of Modern History* 77, no. 4 (2005): 917–955. Gambetta's speech is discussed in Hanson, "The Founding of the French Third Republic," 1048.

24. The most comprehensive discussion of Sarraut's tenure in Indochina is Agathe Larcher-Gosha, "La légitimation française en Indochine: Mythes et réalités de la 'collaboration franco-vietnamienne' et du réformisme colonial, 1905–1945" (Ph.D. diss., Université de Paris VII, 2000).

25. Conklin suggests that the French colonial state failed to live up to the republican ideals expressed by its top officials, while Wilder argues that deeply illiberal impulses were an intrinsic feature of the republican tradition itself. Alice Conklin, *A Mission to Civilize: The Republican Idea of Empire in France and West Africa, 1895–1930* (Stanford: Stanford University Press, 1997); Gary Wilder, *The French Imperial Nation-State: Negritude and Colonial Humanism between the Two World Wars* (Chicago: University of Chicago Press, 2005). See also J. P. Daughton, *An Empire Divided: Religion, Republicanism*

and the Making of French Colonialism, 1880–1914 (Oxford: Oxford University Press, 2006).

26. Daniel Hémery, "L'Indochine, les droits humains, 1899–1954: Entre colonisateurs et colonisés, la Ligue des droits de l'homme," *Revue française d'Histoire d'Outre-mer* 88, no. 330–331 (January 2001): 223–239; Jacques Dalloz, "Les Vietnamiens dans la franc-maçonnerie colonial," *Revue française d'Histoire d'Outre-mer* 85, no. 320 (1998): 103–118; Phan Chu Trinh and Vĩnh Sính, *Phan Chau Trinh and His Political Writings* (Ithaca: Cornell Southeast Asia Program Publications, 2009). For a good general study of the Ligue during this period, see William D. Irvine, *Between Justice and Politics: The Ligue des Droits de l'Homme, 1898–1945* (Stanford: Stanford University Press, 2007).

27. Indeed, Hémery suggests that the legacy of colonial republicanism may be seen in the Nhân Văn–Giai Phẩm movement of the late 1950s, in domestic intellectual opposition to the RVN between 1954 and 1975, and in post-Renovation political activism after 1986, but he does not acknowledge the influence of this tradition in the broader intellectual life of the colonial era. Hémery, "L'Indochine, les droits humains," 19.

28. See, for example, David Marr, "Ho Chi Minh's Declaration of Independence," in *Essays into Vietnamese Pasts*, ed. K. W. Taylor and John K. Whitmore (Ithaca: Cornell Southeast Asia Program Publications, 1995), 221–232. Marr writes: "In deciding to open the Declaration with 1776 and 1789 quotations, Hồ Chí Minh was not only tipping his hat to Washington and Paris, but more importantly placing Việt Nam squarely within the world revolutionary line of succession. While it was not politic to mention the 1917 Bolshevik Revolution, educated listeners could draw their own conclusions. The 1776 and 1789 citations also allowed Ho to take the high philosophical and moral ground of 'natural rights' in stark contrast to French colonial barbarism and slavery."

29. Gilles de Gantès, "Protectorate, Association, Reformism: The Roots of the Popular Front's Republican Policy in Indochina," in *French Colonial Empire and the Popular Front: Hope and Disillusion*, ed. Tony Chafur and Amanda Sackur (New York: St. Martin's Press, 1999), 109–131.

30. Gail Paradise Kelly, "Interwar Schools and the Development of African History in French West Africa," in *French Colonial Education: Essays on Vietnam and West Africa*, ed. Gail Paradise Kelly (New York: AMS Press, 2000), 215. For a discussion of the depoliticized treatment of Bastille Day in the French Empire, see Gail Paradise Kelly, "The Presentation of Indigenous Society in the Schools of French West Africa and Indochina, 1918 to 1938," in ibid., 251.

31. Truong Buu Lam, *Colonialism Experienced: Vietnamese Writings on Colonialism, 1900–1931* (Ann Arbor: University of Michigan Press, 2000), 94–97. See also M. B. Hooker, "The French Legal World: French Indochina and Thailand," in *A Concise Legal History of Southeast Asia*, ed. M. B. Hooker (Oxford: Clarendon Press, 1978), 153–183;

and Alice Conklin, "Colonialism and Human Rights, a Contradiction in Terms? The Case of French West Africa, 1895–1914," *American Historical Review* 103, no. 2 (1998): 435–440.

32. Truong, *Colonialism Experienced,* 12–14.

33. Wilder, *The French Imperial Nation-State,* 167.

34. The most sophisticated account of Vietnamese nationalism as a local iteration of a global form is Christopher Goscha, *Vietnam or Indochina? Contesting Conceptions of Space in Vietnamese Nationalism, 1887–1954,* NIAS Report Series 28 (Copenhagen: Nordic Institute of Asian Studies, 1995).

35. On Vũ Trọng Phụng's exposure to French literature, see Peter Zinoman, "Provincial Cosmopolitanism: Vũ Trọng Phụng's Foreign Literary Engagements," in *Traveling Nation-Makers: Transnational Flows and Movements in the Making of Modern Southeast Asia,* ed. Caroline S. Hau and Kasian Tejapira (Kyoto: Kyoto University Press; Singapore: NUS Press, 2011), 126–152.

36. Hugo championed universal manhood suffrage, freedom of the press and popular sovereignty. Zola identified the Republic with equality, social justice, liberty, and science. Both men were anticlerical, anti-Monarchist, anticommunist, and critical of the social impact of unfettered capitalism. And both shared a preoccupation with education policy that was a hallmark of early Third Republic republicanism.

37. Vũ Trọng Phụng referred to himself as a "conservative" on the "question of women" in his interview with Lê Thanh in 1937. Lê Thanh, "Chúng tôi phỏng vấn ông Vũ Trọng Phụng về những tiểu thuyết *Giông tố*, *Làm đĩ*."

38. Daniel Hémery, *Révolutionnaires vietnamiens et pouvoir colonial en Indochine: Communistes, trotskystes, nationalists à Saigon de 1932 à 1937* (Paris: Maspero, 1975); Alexander Woodside, *Community and Revolution in Modern Vietnam* (Boston: Houghton Mifflin, 1976); David Marr, *Vietnamese Tradition on Trial, 1920–1945* (Berkeley: University of California Press, 1981); Hue-Tam Ho Tai, *Radicalism and the Origins of the Vietnamese Revolution* (Cambridge, Mass.: Harvard University Press, 1992).

39. Sophie Quinn-Judge, *Hồ Chí Minh: The Missing Years, 1919–1941* (Berkeley: University of California Press, 2002); Christoph Giebel, *Imagined Ancestries of Vietnamese Communism: Ton Duc Thang and the Politics of Vietnamese History and Memory* (Seattle: University of Washington Press, 2004).

40. Hue-Tam Ho Tai, *Radicalism and the Origins of the Vietnamese Revolution,* 1.

41. Lê Thanh, "Chúng tôi phỏng vấn ông Vũ Trọng Phụng về những tiểu thuyết *Giông tố*, *Làm đĩ*."

42. *Tao Đàn: Số đặc biệt về Vũ Trọng Phụng* [Literary circle: Special issue about Vũ Trọng Phụng], new series, no. 1 (December 1939). The issue is reprinted in its entirety in the second volume of the following collection: Nguyễn Ngọc Thiện and Lữ Huy Nguyên, eds., *Tao Đàn 1939: Sưu tập trọn bộ tạp chí văn học của nhà xuất bản Tân Dân* [*Tao Đàn* 1939: Complete collection of the literary magazine of Tân Dân Publishing

House] (Hà Nội: Văn Học, 1998), 1347–1434; and Lan Khai, *Vũ Trọng Phụng—Mớ tài liệu cho văn học sử Việt Nam.*

43. See Vũ Trọng Phụng, *Vẽ nhọ bôi hề: Những tác phẩm mới tìm thấy năm 2000*; and Vũ Trọng Phụng, *Chống nạng lên đường: Chùm sáng tác đầu tay mới tìm thấy cuối năm 2000.*

44. For a prominent example, see Huỳnh Kim Khánh, *Vietnamese Communism, 1925–1945* (Ithaca: Cornell University Press, 1982), 39. Khanh describes "two contending groups of Vietnamese" emerging during the late 1920s. "On the one side," he writes, "stood a sizable group of collaborators, who considered their fortunes intimately bound with continued colonial presence. On the other side stood revolutionary patriots, who were enemies of foreign imperialism and worked for Vietnamese independence and social transformation."

45. In an important article, Christopher Goscha discusses the political agenda of the interwar journalist Nguyễn Văn Vĩnh in republican terms. Christopher Goscha, "'The Modern Barbarian': Nguyen Van Vinh and the Complexity of Colonial Modernity in Vietnam," *European Journal of East Asian Studies* 3, no. 1 (2004): 135–169.

46. For the republican agenda of the Self-Strength Literary Group, see Martina T. Nguyen, "The Self-Reliant Literary Group (Tu Luc Van Doan): Colonial Modernism in Vietnam, 1932–1941" (Ph.D. diss., University of California, Berkeley, 2012). For a recent discussion of republican sensibilities in southern Vietnamese journalism, see Philippe M. F. Peycam, *The Birth of Vietnamese Political Journalism: Saigon, 1916–1930* (New York: Columbia University Press, 2012), esp. chap. 2, "French Republicanism and the Emergence of Saigon's Public Sphere," 34–70.

CHAPTER 1

1. *Tao Đàn: Số đặc biệt về Vũ Trọng Phụng.* The issue is reprinted in its entirety in the volume *Tao Đàn 1939: Sưu tập trọn bộ tạp chí văn học nhà xuất bản Tân Dân.* Page references are to the original issue.

2. Vũ Ngọc Phan, *Nhà văn hiện đại: Phê bình văn học* [Modern writers: Literary criticism] (Hà Nội: Tân Dân, 1942). Reprint, Hồ Chí Minh City: Văn Học, 1994.

3. Thanh Châu, "Đám tang Vũ Trọng Phụng" [Vũ Trọng Phụng's funeral], in *Tao Đàn: Số đặc biệt về Vũ Trọng Phụng*, 13.

4. For useful background on Vũ Đình Long, see his interview from 1943 with Lê Thanh in Lê Thanh, *Cuộc phỏng vấn các nhà văn* [Interviews with writers] (Hà Nội: Đời Mới, 1943), 129.

5. Lan Khai, Trương Tửu, Nguyễn Triệu Luật, and Nguyễn Tuân, in particular, were widely seen, along with Vũ Trọng Phụng, as core members of the Tân Dân Group. Nguyễn Văn Tòng, *Báo chí Việt Nam từ khởi thủy đến 1945* (Hồ Chí Minh City: Thành phố Hồ Chí Minh, 2000), 321–322.

6. Ibid., 322–323. Membership in Tân Dân was less formal and exclusive than it was in the Self-Strength Literary Group, the most influential literary circle of the period.

7. For biographical information on Lan Khai, see Trần Minh Tiến, ed., *Lan Khai: Tác phẩm, nghiên cứu lý luận và phê bình văn học* [Lan Khai: Work, critical studies, and literary criticism] (Hà Nội: Văn Hóa–Thông Tin, 2002). On Lan Khai's death, see Nguyễn Vỹ, *Văn thi sĩ tiền chiến—Chứng dẫn của một thời đại* [Prewar writers and poet—witnesses of a time] (Sài Gòn: Khai Trí, 1969), 87; Hoàng Ngọc Thanh, *Vietnam's Social and Political Development as Seen through the Modern Novel* (New York: Peter Lang, 1991), 161; and Bùi Xuân Bào, *Le Roman Vietnamien Contemporain: Tendences et evolution du roman vietnamien contemporain, 1925–1945* (Sài Gòn: Tủ sách Nhân văn Xã hội, 1972), 192–193.

8. For biographical information on Trương Tửu, see Trương Tửu, *Tuyển tập, nghiên cứu, phê bình* [Collected works: Research and criticism] (Hà Nội: Lao Động, 2007), 7–20.

9. Nguyễn Vỹ, "Điếu văn đọc trước huyệt Vũ Trọng Phụng" [Eulogy read at Vũ Trọng Phụng's grave], in *Tao Đàn: Số đặc biệt về Vũ Trọng Phụng*, 86.

10. Lưu Trọng Lư, "Anh Vũ Trọng Phụng: điếu văn ngày 15.10.1939 bên mộ Vũ Trọng Phụng" [Vũ Trọng Phụng, eulogy read at his gravesite, October 15, 1939], in *Tao Đàn: Số đặc biệt về Vũ Trọng Phụng*, 81.

11. Nguyễn Triệu Luật, "Vũ Trọng Phụng với tôi" [Vũ Trọng Phụng and me], in *Tao Đàn: Số đặc biệt về Vũ Trọng Phụng*, 35.

12. Thanh Châu, "Đám tang Vũ Trọng Phụng," 14.

13. Ngô Tất Tố, "Gia thế ông Vũ Trọng Phụng" [Vũ Trọng Phụng's family background], in *Tao Đàn: Số đặc biệt về Vũ Trọng Phụng*, 25.

14. Nguyễn Tuân, "Một đêm họp đưa ma Phụng" [A night gathering for the funeral of Phụng], in *Tao Đàn: Số đặc biệt về Vũ Trọng Phụng*, 48; Lan Khai, "Con người Vũ Trọng Phụng" [Vũ Trọng Phụng, the person], in *Tao Đàn: Số đặc biệt về Vũ Trọng Phụng*, 22.

15. Tam Lang, "Vài kỷ niệm về Vũ Trọng Phụng" [A few memories of Vũ Trọng Phụng], in *Tao Đàn: Số đặc biệt về Vũ Trọng Phụng*, 60.

16. Nguyễn Vỹ, "Điếu văn đọc trước huyệt Vũ Trọng Phụng," 87.

17. Lưu Trọng Lư, "Anh Vũ Trọng Phụng: điếu văn ngày 15.10.1939 bên mộ Vũ Trọng Phụng," 83.

18. Trương Tửu, "Địa vị của Vũ Trọng Phụng trong văn học Việt Nam cận đại" [The position of Vũ Trọng Phụng in contemporary Vietnamese literature], in *Tao Đàn: Số đặc biệt về Vũ Trọng Phụng*, 3, 5.

19. Ibid., 9.

20. Ibid., 11.

21. Birth information comes from a notarized document provided by Vũ Trọng Phụng's son-in-law entitled "Acte de notorieté tenant lieu d'acte de naissance," dated May 12, 1920. It records that he was born on Rue de la Chaux, today renamed Hàng

Vôi/Tông Đản streets. Văn Tâm suggests that he was actually born in 1912, but that the date was doctored to get him into school. Văn Tâm, *Vũ Trọng Phụng: Nhà văn hiện thực* (Hà Nội: Kim Đức, 1957), 61.

22. For an account of the conquest, see Pierre Brocheaux and Daniel Hémery, *Indochina: An Ambiguous Colonization, 1858–1954*, trans. Ly-Lan Dill-Klein, Eric Jennings, Nora A. Taylor, and Noémi Tousignant (Berkeley: University of California Press, 2009), 15–70.

23. Pierre Gourou, *Les paysans du delta tonkinois: Étude de géogaphie humaine* (Paris: Éditions d'art et d'Histoire, 1936).

24. A recent study of the Doumer administration is Amaury Lorcin, *Paul Doumer, gouverneur général de l'Indochine, 1897–1902: Le tremplin colonial* (Paris: Éditions l'Harmattan, 2004).

25. For population density in Tonkin, see Gourou, *Les paysans du delta tonkinois*, 146.

26. According to Nguyễn Văn Đạm, Vũ Trọng Phụng's mother's given name was originally Khánh but it was changed to Khách owing to an error on her identity papers. Nguyễn Văn Đạm, "Đôi điều kể thêm về Vũ Trọng Phụng," last modified October 13, 2004, http://www.truongxuantrieu.ooauthor.com/hoso-b/vutrongphung-v.htm.

27. In the "Acte de notorieté tenant lieu d'acte de naissance," she is referred to as a "couturier."

28. The following information comes from Văn Tâm, *Vũ Trọng Phụng: Nhà văn hiện thực* [Vũ Trọng Phụng: Realist writer], 61. Văn Tâm's book is perhaps the best source for biographical information on Vũ Trọng Phụng.

29. Lan Khai, *Vũ Trọng Phụng—Mớ tài liệu cho văn học sử Việt Nam* (Hà Nội: Minh Phương, 1941), 3–4.

30. For the early development of colonial Hanoi, see André Masson, *Hanoi pendant le période héroique, 1873–1888* (Paris: Librarie Orientaliste Paul Gueuthner, 1929).

31. For the later development of colonial Hanoi, see William Logan, *Hanoi: Biography of a City* (Seattle: University of Washington Press, 2000), 67–113; and Gwendolyn Wright, *The Politics of Design in French Colonial Urbanism* (Chicago: University of Chicago Press, 1991), 161–235.

32. Philippe Papin, *Histoire de Hanoi* (Paris: Fayard, 2001), 225, 251.

33. Ibid., 253, 257.

34. Vũ Bằng, "Cái tài, cái tật của Vũ Trọng Phụng" [The talents and failings of Vũ Trọng Phụng], *Văn Học* 114 (1970): 36. See also Nguyễn Đăng Mạnh, "Vũ Trọng Phụng: Tiểu sử, 1912–1939" [Vũ Trọng Phụng biography], in *Tuyển tập Vũ Trọng Phụng: tập 1* [Selected works of Vũ Trọng Phụng, vol. 1], ed. Nguyễn Đăng Mạnh and Trần Hữu Tá (Hà Nội: Văn Học, 1996), 9.

35. To Kien, "'Tube House' and 'Neo Tube House' in Hanoi: A Comparative Study on Identity and Typology," *Journal of Asian Architecture and Engineering* 7, no. 2 (2008): 257.

36. Ibid. According to To Kien's research, tube houses typically measure 2.5 to 3 meters across and 50 to 100 meters deep.

37. Đỗ Đức Hiếu, "Những lớp sóng ngôn từ trong 'Số đỏ' của Vũ Trọng Phụng" [Waves of language in Vũ Trọng Phụng's *Dumb Luck*], in Trần Hữu Tá, *Nhà văn Vũ Trọng Phụng với chúng ta*, 417.

38. Vũ Trọng Phụng, *Household Servants*, in Lockhart, *The Light of the Capital*, 144.

39. Vũ Trọng Phụng, *Giông tố* (1936; Hà Nội: Văn Học, 1996), 195.

40. Ibid.

41. Charles Robequain, *The Economic Development of French Indochina*, trans. Isabel A. Ward (London: Oxford University Press, 1944), 119. Originally published as *L'évolution économique de l'Indochine française* (Paris: Hartmann, 1939).

42. Ibid., 243–304.

43. Vũ Trọng Phụng, *Vẽ nhọ bôi hề: Những tác phẩm mới tìm thấy năm 2000*, 109–133.

44. "Qua các phố," in *Hải Phòng Tuần Báo*, January 20, 1935, January 27, 1935, February 10, 1935, February 17, 1935, February 24, 1935, March 3, 1935, March 10, 1935, March 17, 1935, March 24, 1935, March 31, 1935, April 7, 1935.

45. See Adeline Tran, "'Paris de l'Annam': On the Flâneur in Colonial Vietnam" (seminar paper, University of California, Berkeley, December 17, 2007).

46. Van Nguyen-Marshall, *In Search of Moral Authority: The Discourse on Poverty, Poor Relief, and Charity in French Colonial Vietnam* (New York: Peter Lang, 2008).

47. Electoral politics in the South have been treated by Hue-Tam Ho Tai, "The Politics of Compromise: The Constitutionalist Party and the Electoral reforms of 1922 in French Cochinchina," *Modern Asian Studies* 18, no. 3 (1984): 371–391. Electoral politics in Annam and Tonkin toward the end of the interwar era have not yet been studied closely but their intensity is apparent in press reporting from the period.

48. Alexander Woodside, "The Development of Social Organizations in Vietnamese Cities in the Late Colonial Period," *Pacific Affairs* 44, no. 1 (Spring 1971): 39–64.

49. There were seven Masonic lodges in Indochina in total. Brocheux and Hémery, *Indochina: An Ambiguous Colonization*, 114, 196.

50. Goscha, "'The Modern Barbarian,'" 144. See also Hémery, "L'Indochine, les droits humains entre colonisateurs et colonisés," 223–239.

51. Vũ Trọng Phụng, "Cộng sản tự do" [Communist freedom], *Đông Dương Tạp Chí*, October 30, 1937, 1.

52. Vũ Trọng Phụng, "Phỏng vấn tình cờ: Một ông nghị già . . . lôi thôi" [An unexpected interview with a troublesome representative], *Tiểu Thuyết Thứ Năm* 12 (July 28, 1938).

53. Larcher-Gosha, "La légitimation française en Indochine."

54. Patrice Morlat, *Indochine années vingt: Le rendez-vous manqué: La politique indigene des grands commis au service de la mise en valeur* (Paris: Les Indes savantes, 2006), 23–51.

55. Theodore Zeldin, *A History of French Passions, 1848–1945*, vol. 2, *Intellect, Taste and Anxiety* (Oxford: Clarendon Press, 1977), 139–205.

56. Pacale Bezançon, *Une colonization éducatrice? L'expérience indochinoise, 1860–1945* (Paris: L'Harmattan, 2002); Trinh Van Thao, *L'école française en Indochina* (Paris: Karthala, 1995).

57. Gail Paradise Kelly, "Colonial Schools in Vietnam: Policy and Practice," in *French Colonial Education*, 7.

58. Ibid., 9.

59. Scott McConnell, *Leftward Journey: The Education of Vietnamese Students in France, 1919–1939* (New Brunswick, N.J.: Transaction, 1989), 14.

60. Nguyễn Văn Đạm suggests that Vũ Trọng Phụng may have entered the Hàng Vôi School in 1921. This is supported by accounts of his education in Vũ Bằng's memoirs. Nguyễn Văn Đạm, "Đôi điều kể thêm về Vũ Trọng Phụng" [Additional items about Vũ Trọng Phụng], *truongxuantrieu*, last modified October 15, 2004, http://www.truongxuantrieu.ooauthor.com/hoso-b/vutrongphung-v.htm.

61. Nguyễn Triệu Luật, "Vũ Trọng Phụng với tôi," 37; Nguyễn Văn Đạm, "Đôi điều kể thêm về Vũ Trọng Phụng."

62. Vũ Bằng, "Cái tài, cái tật của Vũ Trọng Phụng," 31.

63. Liam Kelly, "Vietnam as a 'Domain of Manifest Civility' (Văn Hiến Chi Bang)," *Journal of Southeast Asian Studies* 34, no. 1 (February 2003): 63–76.

64. Alexander Woodside, *Vietnam and the Chinese Model: A Comparative Study of Vietnamese and Chinese Government in the First Half of the Nineteenth Century* (Cambridge, Mass.: Harvard University Press, 1971).

65. For evidence regarding the status of Vietnamese as a Mon-Khmer language, see Mark Alves, "Linguistic Research on the Origins of the Vietnamese Language: An Overview," *Journal of Vietnamese Studies* 1, nos. 1–2 (Fall 2006): 104–131.

66. For recent research on the origins of *quốc ngữ*, see Roland Jacques, *Portuguese Pioneers of Vietnamese Linguistics prior to 1650* (Bangkok: Orchid Press, 2002).

67. The best treatment of French language policy in Cochinchina remains Milton Osborne, *The French Presence in Cochinchina and Cambodia: Rule and Response, 1859–1905* (Ithaca: Cornell University Press, 1969).

68. Kelly, "Colonial Schools in Vietnam," 10.

69. In addition to Chinese characters, Vietnamese composed literary texts using a demotic system of modified characters known as *chữ nôm*.

70. Texts written in *chữ nôm* or in Sino-Vietnamese (i.e., composed of Chinese loan words exclusively) were "transcribed" into *quốc ngữ*, but many Chinese texts required "translation."

71. Vũ Trọng Phụng, "*Tắt Đèn của* Ngô Tất Tố" [Ngô Tất Tố's *Turn out the Lights*], *Thời Vụ Báo*, January 31, 1939, 4.

72. Vũ Bằng, "Cái tài, cái tật của Vũ Trọng Phụng," 38.

73. Zinoman, "Provincial Cosmopolitanism," 126–153.

74. Lan Khai, *Vũ Trọng Phụng—Mớ tài liệu cho văn học sử Việt Nam,* 21.

75. Ibid.

76. Trương Tửu, "Địa vị Vũ Trọng Phụng trong văn học Việt Nam cận đại," 4.

77. Nhất Chi Mai, "Dâm hay không dâm: ý kiến một người đọc" [Pornographic or not? Opinion of a reader], *Ngày Nay* 51 (March 14, 1937).

78. Vũ Trọng Phụng, "Để đáp lời Báo Ngày Nay: Dâm hay không dâm" [Answering *These Days:* Pornographic or not?], *Báo Tương Lai,* March 25, 1937.

79. Nguyễn Triệu Luật, "Vũ Trọng Phụng với tôi," 38.

80. Logan, *Hanoi: Biography of a City,* 76.

81. Rue Paul Bert is Tràng Tiền Street today. Papin, *Histoire de Hanoi,* 238.

82. Lê Tràng Kiều, "Viết về Vũ Trọng Phụng" [Notes on Vũ Trọng Phụng], *Tạp Chí Văn Học* (Sài Gòn) 94 (January 1, 1969): 53.

83. Hoàng Văn Đào, *Việt-Nam Quốc-dân Đảng: Lịch sử tranh đấu cận đại, 1927–1954* [The Vietnamese Nationalist Party: A history of modern struggle] (Sài Gòn: Nguyễn Hòa Hiệp, 1965), 146–150.

84. Louis Roubaud, *Vietnam: La tragédie indochinoise* (Paris: Valois, 1931), 115–20.

85. "Life of a Clerk" was never completed and few copies have survived. In 1938, however, the respected writer Nguyễn Đình Lạp excerpted a lengthy passage from "Life of a Clerk" in the first installment of his nonfiction narrative "The Village Bully" ["Cường Hào"], serialized in the Hanoi weekly *The Nation* [*Quốc Gia*]. Nguyễn Đình Lạp, "Cường Hào: phóng sự dài về dân quê" [The village bully: A long reportage about the peasantry], *Quốc Gia,* September 16, 1938.

86. Ibid.

87. Nguyễn Văn Đạm, "Đôi điều kể thêm về Vũ Trọng Phụng," 1.

88. Lan Khai, *Vũ Trọng Phụng—Mớ tài liệu cho văn học sử Việt Nam,* 5.

89. Shawn McHale, *Print and Power: Confucianism, Communism and Buddhism in the Making of Modern Vietnam* (Honolulu: University of Hawaii, 2004), 19, 188.

90. Vũ Bằng, "Cái tài, cái tật của Vũ Trọng Phụng," 31.

91. Trương Tửu, "Địa vị Vũ Trọng Phụng trong văn học Việt Nam cận đại," 4.

92. Tam Lang, "Vài kỷ niệm về Vũ Trọng Phụng," 54–57.

93. Thiều Quang, *Tập san phê bình: Số đặc biệt về Vũ Trọng Phụng—Đời sống và con người,* October 1957, 2–8.

94. An extended analysis of the story is provided in chapter 2.

95. Ibid., 3.

96. *Ngọ Báo* was *Hà Thành Ngọ Báo* until August 1931. It was known thereafter as *Ngọ Báo.*

97. In 1931: "Thủ đoạn," January 25, 26, 27, 28; "Cô Mai thưởng xuân," March 3; "Một cái chết," March 16, 17; "Bà lão lòa," April 7, 8; "Phép ông láng giềng," April 26; "Bẫy tình," July 11, 12; "Chống nạng lên đường," August 10, 11, 12; "Cái tin vặt," Sep-

tember 21, 22; "Bên góc giường," September 27; "Nhân quả," December 21, 22. In 1932: "Tội người cô," February 1, 2; "Câu chuyện của nhà văn sĩ vô danh," March 1, 2; "Con người điêu trá," March 14, 15.

98. "Điên," August 21, 22, 1931; "Hiu quạnh," March 10, 1932; "Tư cách nhà phê bình," November 8, 1931.

99. "Cái đặc tính của kịch lãng mạn," January 28, 1932.

100. "Một ông thầy cãi của nhà làm thơ," November 22, 1931; "Một cái án văn chương," January 23, 1932.

101. Zinoman, "Provincial Cosmopolitanism," 132–145.

102. For Hoàng Tích Chu, Đỗ Văn and *Midday News,* see Zinoman, "Vũ Trọng Phụng's *Dumb Luck* and the Nature of Vietnamese Modernism," in Vũ Trọng Phụng, *Dumb Luck,* 16–17.

103. Vũ Trọng Phụng, "Phê bình báo chí: *Ngọ Báo*" [Newspaper criticism, daily news], *Tiến Hóa* 3 (December 7, 1935).

104. Vũ Bằng, *Bốn mươi năm nói láo* [Forty years of lying] (Sài Gòn: Phạm Quang Khải, 1969), 22.

105. Thế Phong, ed., *Cuộc đời viết văn làm báo—Tam Lang—Tôi kéo xe* [The journalistic and literary life of Tam Lang—I pulled a rickshaw] (Hồ Chí Minh City: Văn Hóa-Thông Tin, 1996).

106. For useful studies of the colonial press, albeit focused in the South, see Walter Langlois, *André Malraux: The Indochina Adventure* (New York: Prager, 1966); Peycam, *The Birth of Vietnamese Political Journalism.*

107. Ho Tai, *Radicalism and the Origins of the Vietnamese Revolution,* 114–146.

108. Ibid., 126.

109. Daniel Hémery, *Révolutionnaires vietnamiens et pouvoir colonial en Indochine: Communistes, trotskystes, nationalists à Saigon de 1932 à 1937* (Paris: Maspero, 1975).

110. Marr, *Vietnamese Tradition on Trial,* 220–228.

111. Sarah Womack, "Colonialism and the Collaborationist Agenda: Pham Quynh, Print Culture and the Politics of Persuasion in Colonial Vietnam" (Ph.D. diss., University of Michigan, 2003); Stephen O'Harrow, "French Colonial Policy towards Vernacular Language Development and the Case of Phạm Quỳnh in Viet-Nam," in *Aspects of Vernacular Languages in Asian and Pacific Societies,* ed. Nguyen Dang Liem (Honolulu: University of Hawaii Press, 1973).

112. McHale, *Print and Power,* 56, 198.

113. Nguyễn Thành, *Báo chí cách mạng Việt Nam, 1925–1945* [Vietnamese revolutionary newspapers] (Hà Nội: Khoa Học Xã Hội, 1984), 31.

114. Ibid., 76.

115. Marr, *Vietnamese Tradition on Trial,* 47.

116. Vũ Trọng Phụng, "Phê bình báo chí: Báo Đông Pháp," *Tiến Hóa,* November 16, 1935.

117. Phan Thị Mỹ Khanh, *Nhớ cha tôi: Phan Khôi* [Remembering my father Phan Khôi] (Đà Nẵng: Đà Nẵng, 2001), 91; Nguyễn Vỹ, *Văn thi sĩ tiền chiến,* 192–193; Nguyễn Công Hoan, *Đời viết văn của tôi* [My life as a writer] (Hà Nộ: Văn Học, 1971), 360.

118. Zeldin, *A History of French Passions,* 2:510.

119. Nguyễn Vỹ, *Văn thi sĩ tiền chiến,* 458. In 1936, the newspaper *Nghề Mới* [New profession] lumped Vũ Trọng Phụng together with Lê Tràng Kiều, Lưu Trọng Lư, Thái Can, and Huy Thông. "Có phải cùng một vết xe? Lê Tràng Kiều và Ng. Tường Tam," *Nghề Mới,* April 10, 1936.

120. Vũ Trọng Phụng, "Phê bình báo chí: Báo Đông Pháp"; Vũ Trọng Phụng, "Phê bình báo chí: Ngọ Báo."

121. This is the opinion of Vạn Tóc Mai in *The Storm.* See Vũ Trọng Phụng, *Giông tố,* 89.

122. Zeldin, *A History of French Passions,* 2:494.

123. Philip Nord, *The Republican Moment: Struggles for Democracy in Nineteenth-Century France* (Cambridge, Mass.: Harvard University Press, 1995), 207.

124. Vũ Trọng Phụng, "Một hành vi bất lương trong nghề phóng sự và điều tra của Vũ Trọng Phụng" [A dishonest deed in the work of reportage and investigation of Vũ Trọng Phụng], *Chuyện Đời* (Hải Phòng) 5 (May 7, 1938).

125. The rival was the journalist Thao Thao, whose reportage about the clinic was serialized in *Việt News (Việt Báo)* under the titles *Gái Lục sì* (Girls of the VD clinic) and *Gái Trụy lạc* (Depraved girls) between February 16 and March 3, 1937 (the title was changed midway through the serialization). For a discussion of Thao Thao's reportage, see Shaun Malarney, introduction to Vũ Trọng Phụng, *Lục Xì: Prostitution and Venereal Disease in Colonial Hanoi,* 11, 25, 29, 30–32.

126. Vũ Trọng Phụng, "Một cái án văn chương," *Ngọ Báo,* January 23, 1932.

127. Vũ Trọng Phụng, "Chung quanh thiên phóng sự Lục sì," *Tương Lai,* March 11, 1937.

128. Ibid.

129. Vũ Trọng Phụng, "Để đáp lời Báo Ngày Nay: Dâm hay là không dâm."

130. "Một cái gương sáng cho những ông văn sĩ hay viết càn, vì tập văn 'Tiếng Chuông,' Nguyễn Văn Thìn bị án tù và tiền phạt," *Trung Lập* 6691 (March 29, 1932). Vũ Trọng Phụng's sentence was suspended and he never paid the fine.

131. Recent research confirms that the episode was unrelated to the case involving "The Ploy" described by Thiều Quang. Lại Nguyên Ân, "Vài tài liệu về việc Vũ Trọng Phụng bị gọi ra tòa năm 1932" [Documents regarding Vũ Trọng Phụng's appearance in court in 1932], in *Mênh mông chật chội: Tiểu luận phê bình văn học* (Hà Nội: Trí Thức, 2009), 287–303.

132. See "Báo giới Bắc kỳ đối với việc anh Lê Bá Chấn bị bắt" [The northern press and the arrest of Lê Bá Chấn], *Việt Báo,* April 13, 1937.

133. "Sự việc ông Lê Bá Chấn bị bắt" [On the arrest of Lê Bá Chấn], *Việt Báo,* April 5–6, 1937.

134. "Báo giới Bắc kỳ đối với án Lê Bá Chấn bị bắt" [The northern press and the arrest of Lê Bá Chấn], *Việt Báo,* April 15, 1937.

135. Nguyễn Giang, "Chương-trình tờ tạp-chí này" [The program of this journal], *Đông Dương Tạp Chí,* December 25, 1937, 1.

136. Vũ Ngọc Phan, *Nhà văn hiện đại: Phê bình văn học, Tập 1,* 504.

137. Ibid., 505.

138. Ibid.

139. Peter Monteath, "The Spanish Civil War and the Aesthetics of Reportage," in *Literature and War,* ed. David Bevan (Amsterdam: Editions Rodopi B. V., 1989), 70.

140. Ibid., 71.

141. Charles A. Laughlin, *Chinese Reportage: The Aesthetics of Historical Experience* (Durham: Duke University Press, 2002).

142. Walter Redfern, *Writing on the Move: Albert Londres and Investigative Journalism* (Bern: Peter Lang, 2004), 35.

143. Roubaud is cited in *Kỹ Nghệ Lấy Tây* [*The Industry of Marrying Westerners*], *Toàn tập Vũ Trọng Phụng* tập 1, 228. He appears in the play *Hội nghị đùa nhả* [A conference of bad jokes], *Đông Dương Tạp Chí* 34 (January 1, 1938).

144. Nguyễn Văn Đạm, "Đôi điều kể thêm về Vũ Trọng Phụng."

145. Vũ Trọng Phụng, "Những việc đáng ghi chép của năm Bính-Tý" [Notable matters of 1936], *Tương Lai,* February 18, 1937, 3.

146. Vũ Trọng Phụng, *Household Servants,* 123.

147. Vũ Trọng Phụng, "Để đáp lời Báo Ngày Nay: Dâm hay là không dâm."

148. Nguyễn Văn Đạm, "Đôi điều kể thêm về Vũ Trọng Phụng."

149. Đồ Nam, "Năm cái bí mật của Vũ Trọng Phụng" [Five secrets about Vũ Trọng Phụng], *Văn Học* 114 (1970).

150. Vi Huyền Đắc, "Vài kỷ niệm về Vũ Trọng Phụng" [Memories of Vũ Trọng Phụng], *Văn* 67 (October 15, 1970). In this memoir, Vi Huyền Đắc relates that Vũ Trọng Phụng told him that it took four months to research *The Man Trap.*

151. Vũ Trọng Phụng, *Cạm bẫy người: Phóng sự tiểu thuyết về nghề cờ gian bạc lận* [The man trap: A reportage novel about gambling] (Hà Nội: An nam xuất bản cục, Trung Bắc tân văn, 1934).

152. Thái Phỉ, "*Cạm bẫy người* của Vũ Trọng Phụng" [*The Man Trap* of Vũ Trọng Phụng], *Ngọ Báo* 1939 (February 22, 1934).

153. This review was excerpted in "Dư luận các báo về *Cạm bẫy người*" [Newspaper discussion of *The Man Trap*], *Nhật Tân,* January 23, 1935.

154. Ibid.

155. Vi Huyền Đắc, "Vài kỷ niệm về Vũ Trọng Phụng."

156. Vũ Trọng Phụng, "Kỹ nghệ lấy Tây," *Nhật Tân.* Installments appeared in December 5, 12, 19, and 26, 1934; and January 2, 9, 16, and 23, 1935.

157. Vũ Trọng Phụng, "Cơm thầy cơm cô," *Hà Nội Báo.* The eight installments appeared between March 25 and May 20, 1936.

158. Vũ Trọng Phụng, *Kỹ nghệ lấy Tây* (Hà Nội: Phương Đông, 1936); Vũ Trọng Phụng, *Cơm thầy cơm cô, Lục xì* (Hà Nội: Minh Phương, 1937).

159. Both have been republished in Vũ Trọng Phụng, *Vẽ nhọ bôi hề: Những tác phẩm mới tìm thấy năm 2000.*

160. Mai Xuân Nhân, "Xem qua *Kỹ nghệ lấy Tây,* phóng sự của Vũ Trọng Phụng" [Perusing Vũ Trọng Phụng's *The Industry of Marrying Westerners*], *Tràng An,* October 9, 1936.

161. Vũ Ngọc Phan, *Nhà văn hiện đại,* 521.

162. Lệ Chi, "Đọc sách *Lục-xì*: Phóng sự của Vũ Trọng Phụng" [Reading *Venereal Disease Clinic* by Vũ Trọng Phụng], *Phụ Nữ* 10 (April 23, 1938).

163. Phùng Tất Đắc's essay appears as the introduction to the published book of *Kỹ Nghệ Lấy Tây* in 1936.

164. Lãng Tử, "Nhân đọc 'Kỹ Nghệ Lấy Tây' của Vũ Trọng Phụng" [Reading Vũ Trọng Phụng's *The Industry of Marrying Westerners*], *Phóng Sự* 7 (December 22, 1938).

165. Vũ Trọng Phụng, *Không một tiếng vang: Dân sinh bi kịch, 3 hồi* [*No Echo:* a tragedy in three acts] (Hà Nội: Đông Tây, 1934).

166. *Dứt Tình* was serialized initially in *New Day* in 1934. It was republished in 1941 by *Phổ Thông bán nguyệt san* 49.

167. Many of these pieces are available in the two volumes: Lại Nguyên Ân, ed., *Chống nạng lên đường: Chùm sáng tác đầu tay mới tìm thấy cuối năm 2000* [Leaning on a stick by the road: Works newly found in 2000] (Hà Nội: Hội Nhà Văn, 2001); and Vũ Trọng Phụng, *Vẽ nhọ bôi hề: Những tác phẩm mới tìm thấy năm 2000.*

168. Pages numbers are based on the following editions: *Giông tố* (Hà Nội: Mai Lĩnh, 1951); *Số đỏ* (Hà Nội: Minh Đức, 1957); *Vỡ đê* (Hà Nội: Minh Đức, 1957); *Làm đĩ* (Hà Nội: Văn Học, 1996).

169. *The Storm* was serialized in *Hanoi News (Hà Nội Báo)* between January and September 1936. The serialization of *The Dike Breaks* in *Tuesday Novel (Tiểu Thuyết Thứ Ba)* began on September 27, 1936. *Dumb Luck* was serialized in *Hanoi News* between October and December 1936. *To Be a Whore* was serialized in *Perfume River (Sông Hương)* between August 1936 and March 1937.

170. Victor Hugo, *Giết Mẹ tức là chuyện nàng Lucrèce Borgia, kịch lãng mạn của Victor Hugo,* trans. Vũ Trọng Phụng (Hà Nội: Lê Cường, 1936).

171. Hồ Xanh, "Văn học bình luận *Số đỏ* của Vũ Trọng Phụng" [Literary comment on Vũ Trọng Phụng's *Dumb Luck*], *Công Thương Báo* 6 (May 1–15, 1938).

172. Nguyễn Lương Ngọc, "Đọc sách *Giông tố*" [Reading *The Storm*], *Tinh Hoa* 10 (May 15, 1937).

173. Vũ Ngọc Phan, *Nhà văn hiện đại,* 529. The discussion of *The Storm* in this book appeared originally as a review in the *Indochina Journal.*

174. Minh Tước, "Đọc sách *Làm đĩ*" [Reading *To Be a Whore*], *Mới*, May 15, 1939.

175. "Sách mới: Một cuốn xã hội tiểu thuyết mới ra đời" [New book: A new social novel], *Tiểu Thuyết Thứ Ba*, May 18, 1937, 8.

176. Mộng Sơn, *Văn học và triết luận* [Literature and theory] (Hà Nội: Đại Học Thư Xã, 1944), 17.

177. *The Storm* was republished by Văn Thanh in 1937. *Dumb Luck* was republished by Lê Cường in 1938. *To Be a Whore* was republished by Mai Lĩnh in 1939. After the first part of *The Dike Breaks* was serialized in *The Future* starting in September 1936, it was reserialized by *Tuesday Novel* throughout 1937.

178. The caricature appeared in *Loa* 50 (January 24, 1935). The cover photo appeared in *Tiểu Thuyết Thứ Năm* 11 (December 15, 1938).

179. "Ái tình là gì?," *Anh Niên*, July 2, 1937.

180. "Mừng bạn Vũ Trọng Phụng lấy vợ" [Congratulations to Vũ Trọng Phụng for getting married], *Bắc Hà*, March 19, 1938.

181. Thạch Lam, "Phê bình *Cơm thầy cơm cô* và *Lục sì*, phóng sự của Vũ Trọng Phụng" [Criticizing *Household Servants* and *Venereal Disease Clinic*, reportage by Vũ Trọng Phụng], *Ngày Nay* 99 (February 27, 1938).

182. Vũ Ngọc Phan, *Nhà văn hiện đại, tập 1*, 544.

183. Uyển Diễm, "*Làm đĩ* dưới mắt nhà văn tiểu tư sản Vũ Trọng Phụng" [*To Be a Whore* in the eyes of the petite-bourgeois writer Vũ Trọng Phụng], *Sáng*, April 14, 1939.

184. Xuân Sa, "Văn chương và giai cấp, lần thứ nhất trong văn học Việt Nam, Cuốn 'Giông tố' của Vũ Trọng Phụng bày tỏ cuộc xung đột của hai giai cấp" [For the first time in Vietnamese literature, Vũ Trọng Phụng's *The Storm* presents the conflict between two classes], *Nữ Lưu* 37 (May 28, 1937).

185. Vũ Trọng Phụng, "Chung quanh một bài phê bình" [Around a criticism], *Sài Gòn Tiểu Thuyết*, Nouvelle série, 1 (August 21, 1937).

186. Lãng Nhân, "Dâm ô," *Ích Hữu* 36 (October 27, 1936).

187. Lệ Chi, "*Giông tố*, xã hội tiểu thuyết của Vũ Trọng Phụng" [*The Storm*, Vũ Trọng Phụng's social novel], *Anh Niên*, June 18, 1937. Lệ Chi was a pseudonym for Nguyễn Vỹ.

188. Vũ Ngọc Phan, *Nhà văn hiện đại, tập 1*, 526.

189. Phan Khôi, "Một vấn đề, hai ý kiến" [One problem, two opinions], *Sông Hương* 11 (October 10, 1936). The J. M. Thích letter has not been recovered, but Phan Khôi quotes from J. M. Thích's letter in this essay.

190. Phan Khôi, "Thơ trả lời cho một ông cố đạo" [Response to a priest], *Sông Hương* 4 (August 22, 1936).

191. Thái Phỉ, "Văn chương dâm uế" [Pornographic literature], *Tin Văn* 25 (September 1–15, 1936).

192. Vũ Trọng Phụng, "Thư ngỏ cho ông Thái Phỉ, chủ báo Tin Văn về bài 'Văn chương dâm uế'" [One open letter to Thái Phỉ, publisher of *Tin Văn*, regarding the article "Pornographic Literature"], *Hà Nội Báo* 38 (September 23, 1936).

193. Vũ Trọng Phụng, "Chung quanh thiên phóng sự Lục sì" [Around the reportage *Venereal Disease Clinic*], *Tương Lai,* March 11, 1937.

194. Nhất Chi Mai, "Dâm hay không dâm: Ý kiến một người đọc."

195. Vũ Trọng Phụng, "Để đáp lời Ngày Nay: Dâm hay là không dâm."

CHAPTER 2

1. See, for example, Gareth Porter, "Proletariat and Peasantry in Early Vietnamese Communism," *Asian Thought and Society* 1, no. 3 (December 1976): 333–346; Pierre Brocheux, "Vietnamese Communism and the Peasants: Analogy and Originality in Vietnamese Experience," in *Vietnamese Communism in Comparative Perspective,* ed. William Turley (Boulder: Westview Press, 1980); Huynh Kim Khanh, *Vietnamese Communism, 1925–1945* (Ithaca: Cornell University Press, 1982); Bernard Fall, ed., *Ho Chi Minh on Revolution: Selected Writings, 1920–1966* (New York: Praeger, 1967); Cedric Sampson, "Nationalism and Communism in Vietnam, 1925–1931" (Ph.D. diss., University of California, Los Angeles, 1975).

2. For the economic history of Indochina, see Martin Murray, *The Development of Capitalism in Colonial Indochina, 1870–1940* (Berkeley: University of California Press, 1980); Robequain, *The Economic Development of French Indochina;* Brocheux and Hémery, *Indochina: An Ambiguous Colonization;* Phạm Cao Dương, *Vietnamese Peasants under French Domination, 1861–1945* (Berkeley: Center for South and Southeast Asia Studies, University of California, 1985); Le Manh Hung, *The Impact of World War II on the Economy of Vietnam, 1939–45* (Singapore: Eastern Universities Press, 2004).

3. Pierre Brocheux, *The Mekong Delta: Ecology, Economy, and Revolution, 1860–1960* (Madison: University of Wisconsin-Madison Center for Southeast Asian Studies, 1995).

4. Kimloan Hill, "Strangers in a Foreign Land: Vietnamese Soldiers and Workers in France during World War I," in *Vietnam Borderless Histories,* ed. Nhung Tuyet Tran and Anthony Reid (Madison: University of Wisconsin Press, 2006), 256–289.

5. Kimloan Vu-Hill, *Coolies into Rebels: Impact of World War I on French Indochina* (Paris: Les Indes Savantes, 2011), 17–30.

6. Andrew Hardy, "The Economics of French Rule in Indochina: A Biography of Paul Bernard, 1892–1960," *Modern Asian Studies* 32, no. 4 (1998): 807–848; Martin Thomas, "French Empire Elites and the Politics of Economic Obligation in the Interwar Years," *Historical Journal* 52, no. 4 (2009): 989–1016.

7. Rubber comprised roughly 20 percent of Indochina's export earnings by the mid-1930s.

8. The best treatment of the history of the rubber industry in Indochina is Murray, *Development of Capitalism in Colonial Indochina,* 255–314.

9. Ibid., 262. After peaking at 82 cents per pound in 1913, the price of rubber plummeted to 16 cents per pound in 1921.

10. Ian Brown, *Economic Change in South-East Asia, c. 1830–1980* (Kuala Lumpur: Oxford University Press, 1997), 48–50.

11. Martin Murray, "'White Gold' or 'White Blood'?: The Rubber Plantations of Colonial Indochina, 1910–1940," *Journal of Peasant Studies* 19, no. 3–4 (1992): 47.

12. Murray, *Development of Capitalism in Colonial Indochina*, 219.

13. Irene Norlund, "Rice and the Colonial Lobby: The Economic Crisis in French Indo-China in the 1920s and 1930s," in *Weathering the Storm: The Economies of Southeast Asia in the 1930s Depression*, ed. Peter Boomgaard and Ian Brown (Leiden: KITLV Press, 2000), 198–228.

14. The price of rice in Saigon decreased by half between 1929 and 1931, from 11.7 piastres per 100 kg to 6.6 piastres per 100 kg. See Hy Van Luong, "Agrarian Unrest from an Anthropological Perspective: The Case of Vietnam," *Comparative Politics* 17, no. 2 (January 1985): 160.

15. Robequain, *Economic Development of French Indochina*, 163.

16. Ibid., 164. By way of comparison, only 15.4 million francs were lost to bankruptcies and cutbacks during 1929.

17. Ibid., 153.

18. Ibid., 81–85. The number of wage earners in the colony decreased from 221,000 to 150,000 between 1929 and 1936. Public works alone had provided daily employment for roughly 50,000 coolies during the late 1920s.

19. Gerard Sasges, "The Landscape of Enterprise in Colonial Vietnam" (unpublished paper, 2011).

20. On the conglomerates, see Kham Vorapeth, *Commerce et colonization en Indochine, 1860–1945: Les maisons de commerce français un siècle d'aventure humaine* (Paris: Les Indes Savantes, 2004).

21. On the Bank of Indochina, see Yasuo Gonjo, *Banque coloniale ou banque d'affaires: La Banque de l'Indochine sous la IIIe République* (Paris: Comité pour l'histoire économique et financière de la France, 1993); Marc Meuleau, *Des pionniers en extrême-orient: Histoire de la Banque de l'Indochine, 1875–1975* (Paris: Fayard, 1990).

22. Sasges, "Landscape of Enterprise in Colonial Vietnam," 25.

23. Ibid., 24.

24. Pierre Brocheux, "The State and the 1930s Depression in French Indochina," in Boomgaard and Brown, *Weathering the Storm*, 265.

25. *No Echo* was first published in Hà Nội by the Đông Tây Publishing House in 1934. The final page of the play script, however, indicates that it was "completed in the autumn of 1931." Citations to the text in this chapter are from the second edition of Nguyễn Đăng Mạnh and Trần Hữu Tá, *Vũ Trọng Phụng: Tuyển tập I*, 63–119.

26. Ibid., 94. He continued: "Where is God? Where is Buddha? We are devout, good, kind, meek, and loyal, but still we are cursed by misfortune. How can I still

believe in God or Buddha? What does it matter if I live or die? What does it matter if I'm a good husband or a devoted son? What's the purpose of God and Buddha? Perhaps they are nothing but frauds who sit by while people devour one another. Dishonest, brutal, and greedy men have beautiful wives, clever children, and a life of luxury. Honest and gentle men suffer exploitation and mistreatment; they have neither clothes to wear nor food to eat. Where are God and Buddha in this picture? I don't see them. If they do exist, they must be weak, without virtue, and undeserving of our worship."

27. Ibid., 91.

28. He works for the "Entreprise Thénardier" on Victor Hugo Street. Vũ Trọng Phụng, *Không Một Tiếng Vang,* 105.

29. Vũ Trọng Phụng, "Chung quanh thiên phóng sự Lục sì: Bức thư ngỏ cho một độc giả," *Tương Lai,* March 11, 1937.

30. In 1931–32, Vũ Trọng Phụng published original translations of two Maupassant stories as well as of his prescriptive essay "Le roman," which discussed the relative virtues of realism and naturalism. His version of "Le roman" may be found in two installments: "Tư cách nhà phê bình" [The critic's personality], *Ngọ Báo,* November 3–4, 1931; and "Lối viết chuyện của phái tả chân" [The realist camp's way of writing a story], *Ngọ Báo,* November 8, 1931.

31. "Planter enfin le véritable drame humain au milieu des mensonges ridicules."

32. "Le naturalisme au théâtre." Emile Zola, *Œuvres complètes* (Paris: Cercle de Livre Précieux, 1966), 279. Thanks to Anna Gural-Migdal and Alain Pages for help tracking down this reference.

33. Cited in Christopher Innes, ed., *A Sourcebook on Naturalist Theater* (London: Routledge, 2000), 47–48. "It seems possible," Zola argued, "that the movement of inquiry and analysis which is precisely the movement of the nineteenth century can have revolutionized all the sciences and arts and left dramatic art to one side. The natural sciences date from the end of the last century; chemistry and physics are less than a hundred years old; history and criticism have been renovated, virtually recreated since the revolution; an entire world has arisen; it has sent us back to the study of documents, to experience, made us realize that to start afresh we must first take things back to the beginning, become familiar with man and nature, verify what is."

34. Zola's thoughts on this may be found in his essay "The Experimental Novel," available in translation in the collection Emile Zola, *The Experimental Novel, and Other Essays* (New York: Cassell, 1893), 1–57.

35. Zola's conflicts with his critics are described in Frederick Brown, *Zola: A Life* (New York: Farrar, Straus and Giroux, 1995).

36. The production was announced in "Vũ Trọng Phụng và anh em hướng đạo" [Vũ Trọng Phụng and the boy scouts], *Tương Lai,* March 25, 1937.

37. See Philippe Senart, "Henry Becque: Les Corbeaux," *Nouvelle Revue des Deux Mondes* (October 1982): 187–192.

38. See Henry Becque, *The Vultures, The Women of Paris, Marry-Go-Round: Three Plays*, trans. Freeman Tilden (New York: Kennerley, 1913).

39. Khái Hưng, "Diễn kịch: *Không Một Tiếng Vang*" [The play: *No Echo*], *Ngày Nay*, April 11, 1937.

40. Zola, "The Influence of the Republic on Literature," in *The Experimental Novel*, 373–413.

41. Ibid., 386.

42. Brown, *Zola: A Life*, 366.

43. Zola, "The Influence of the Republic on Literature," 387.

44. William Gallois, "Emile Zola's Forgotten History: *Les Rougon-Macquart*," *French History* 19, no. 1 (2005): 87–88.

45. References to the text *(Kỹ nghệ lấy Tây)* are from Thuy Tranviet's translation, *The Industry of Marrying Europeans*, translated with an introduction by Thuy Tranviet. Modifications to the translation have been made based on the Vietnamese text in Vũ Trọng Phụng, *Toàn tập Vũ Trọng Phụng: Phóng sự* (Hà Nội: Hội Nhà Văn, 1999), 213–297.

46. Ibid. See chapter 5, "To Want or Not to Want: Suzanne's Dilemma," 41–45.

47. Harriet M. Phinney, "Objects of Affection: Vietnamese Discourses on Love and Emancipation," *Positions* 16, no. 2 (Fall 2008): 329–358.

48. Vũ Trọng Phụng, *The Industry of Marrying Europeans*, 25.

49. Ibid. "Of course we get involved with them for money," stated Madame Kiểm Lâm, "never for love" (p. 35). A different "dame" told Vũ Trọng Phụng: "If you are going to put it in your paper then you might as well write the truth. We marry them for money. No one cares about our kind anyway so what does it matter?" When Vũ Trọng Phụng protests that some of the relationships must have been based on love, she replies: "Why wouldn't it be for money? How could we possibly marry them for love? It is certainly not love to them. They think of us merely as long term toy dolls" (p. 47). Madam Thị B echoed the sentiment later in the narrative: "So, you see how scheming we are? Please do not ever make the mistake of thinking that we marry them for love" (p. 50).

50. Ibid., 27.

51. Ibid., 34.

52. Ibid., 42.

53. Ibid., 46.

54. Lãng Tử, "Nhân đọc '*Kỹ nghệ lấy Tây*' của Vũ Trọng Phụng."

55. Mai Xuân Nhân, "Xem qua *Kỹ nghệ lấy Tây*, phóng sự của Vũ Trọng Phụng."

56. Thomas, "Albert Sarraut, French Colonial Development, and the Communist Threat," 919.

57. Mai Xuân Nhân, "Xem qua *Kỹ nghệ lấy Tây*, phóng sự của Vũ Trọng Phụng."

58. Lãng Tử, "Nhân đọc '*Kỹ nghệ lấy Tây*' của Vũ Trọng Phụng."

59. Vũ Trọng Phụng, *The Industry of Marrying Westerners*, 62.

60. Ibid., 34.

61. Ibid., 29.

62. Ibid., 49.

63. Ibid., 53.

64. Ibid., 48.

65. References to the text *(Cơm thầy cơm cô)* are from the translation of Lockart and Lockhart, *The Light of the Capital*, 122–156.

66. Ibid., 123.

67. Ibid., 145–150.

68. Ibid., 127–128.

69. Ibid., 152.

70. Ibid., 130–135.

71. Ibid., 151.

72. Ibid., 135.

73. Ibid., 136.

74. Ibid., 138.

75. The most comprehensive treatment of this issue is Emmanuelle Saada, *Les enfants de la colonie: Les métis de l'Empire français entre sujétion et citoyenneté* (Paris: Éditions la Découverte, 2007). See also Christina Firpo, "Crisis of Whiteness and Empire: The Removal of Abandoned Eurasian Children from the Vietnamese Milieu, 1890–1956," *Journal of Social History* 43, no. 3 (Spring 2010): 587–613.

76. Emmanuelle Saada, "Race and Sociological Reason: Inquiries on the *Métis* in the French Empire, 1908–37," *International Sociology* 17, no. 3 (September 2002): 365.

77. Emmanuelle Saada, "The Empire of Law: Dignity, Prestige and Domination in the 'Colonial Situation,'" *French Politics, Culture & Society* 20, no. 2 (Summer 2002): 99.

78. Vũ Trọng Phụng, *The Industry of Marrying Westerners*, 43.

79. The citations from the preceding paragraph are from ibid., 41–45.

80. Ibid., 46.

81. Ibid., 48.

82. Vũ Trọng Phụng, *Household Servants*, 130.

83. See chapter 1. "Thủ đoạn" was not republished for almost seventy years nor was it mentioned directly by critics or scholars with the exception of a brief reference by Thiều Quang in 1958. It seems to have been largely forgotten. In 2001, however, it was rediscovered by the scholar Lại Nguyên Ân, who recognized its significance and republished it. See Lại Nguyên Ân, *Chống nạng lên đường*, 23–38. Page citations hereafter refer to the recently republished version.

84. The businessman is never identified explicitly as a Frenchman but this may be inferred from the description of his "piercing blue eyes and handle-bar mustache."

85. "Thủ đoạn," 27. The publication of the episode suggests that colonial censorship of the *quốc ngữ* press at the time was significantly less stringent or more haphazard than is commonly assumed.

86. Thiều Quang, *Tập san Phê bình: Số đặc biệt về Vũ Trọng Phụng, đời sống và con người* [Critical journal: Special issue about Vũ Trọng Phụng, the man and his life] (Hà Nội: Minh Quang, 1957), 3–4.

87. See Frank Proschan, "'Syphilis, Opiomania and Pederasty': Colonial Constructions of Vietnamese (and French) Social Diseases," *Journal of the History of Sexuality* 11, no. 4 (October 2002): 610–636; and Robert Aldrich, *Colonialism and Homosexuality* (London: Routledge, 2003), 16.

88. Quoted in Proschan, "Syphilis, Opiomania and Pederasty," 631.

89. Vũ Trọng Phụng, "Thủ đoạn," 33.

90. Ibid. The term refers to young girls from the countryside lost in the big city.

91. See, for example, Ann Laura Stoler, *Carnal Knowledge and Imperial Power: Race and the Intimate in Colonial Rule* (Berkeley: University of California Press, 2002).

92. It is an "indirect" catalyst only because she commits suicide before learning that her husband has actually stood in for her as a sexual object for his French employer. Nevertheless, her suicide is triggered by the conflict with her husband over how his employer's sexual demands will be met.

93. Vũ Trọng Phụng, *Giông tố*, in *Vũ Trọng Phụng: Toàn tập* (Hà Nội: Hội Nhà Văn, 1999), 163.

94. Ibid., 346–347.

95. Ibid., 330–331.

96. Lynn Hunt, "Pornography and the French Revolution," in *The Invention of Pornography: Obscenity and the Origins of Modernity, 1500–1800*, ed. Lynn Hunt (New York: Zone Books, 1993), 301–340.

97. Lê Thanh, "Chúng tôi phỏng vấn ông Vũ Trọng Phụng về những tiểu thuyết *Giông tố, Làm đĩ*" [Interviewing Vũ Trọng Phụng about his novels *The Storm* and *To Be a Whore*], *Bắc Hà* 1 (April 1, 1937).

98. Nguyễn Triệu Luật, "Vũ Trọng Phụng với tôi" [Vũ Trọng Phụng and me], in *Tao Đàn: Số đặc biệt về Vũ Trọng Phụng*, 35.

99. Vũ Trọng Phụng, *Dumb Luck*, 59.

100. For more on this theme, see Zinoman, "Vũ Trọng Phụng's *Dumb Luck* and the Nature of Vietnamese Modernism," 14–15.

101. Vũ Trọng Phụng, *Vỡ đê*, in *Toàn tập Vũ Trọng Phụng*, 619.

102. Lê Thanh, "Chúng tôi phỏng vấn ông Vũ Trọng Phụng về những tiểu thuyết *Giông tố, Làm đĩ*."

103. References to the text are from the translation by Shaun Malarney. See Vũ Trọng Phụng, *Lục xì: Prostitution and Venereal Disease in Colonial Hanoi*.

104. Ibid., 45.

105. Ibid., 56, 109.

106. Ibid., 56.

107. For the history of prostitution in colonial Indochina, see Isabelle Tracol-Huynh, "Between Stigmatisation and Regulation in Colonial Northern Vietnam," *Culture, Health and Society* 12, no. 5 (August 2010): 73–87; Marie-Corine Rodriguez, "'L'administration de la prostitution': Réglementation et contrôle social au Vietnam pendant la période coloniale," in *Vietnamese Society in Transition: The Daily Politics of Reform and Change,* ed. John Kleinen (Amsterdam: Het Spinhuis, 2001); and Annick Guénel, "Prostitution, maladies vénériennes et medicine coloniale au Vietnam de la conquête française à la guerre d'indépendence," in Kleinen, *Vietnamese Society in Transition.*

108. For a history of the French model, see Jill Harsin, *Policing Prostitution in Nineteenth-Century Paris* (Princeton: Princeton University Press, 1985); and Alain Corbin, *Women for Hire: Prostitution and Sexuality in France after 1850,* trans. Alan Sheridan (Cambridge, Mass.: Harvard University Press, 1990).

109. For Vietnamese Marxist and traditionalist approaches to "the question of women" during this period, see Marr, *Vietnamese Tradition on Trial,* 190–252.

110. For a collection of documents and studies that address the policy options in Indochina, see Société médico-chirurgicale de l'Indochine, *Bulletin de la Société Médico-Chirurgicale de l'Indochine* (Hà Nội: Imprimerie d'Extrême-Orient, 1930). It includes the following important studies from earlier issues of the journal: B. Joyeux, "Le péril vénérien et la prostitution à Hanoi" (1930); H. Coppin, "La Prostitution, la police des moeurs et le Dispensaire Municipal à Hanoi" (1925); and Le Roy Des Barres, "Les maladies vénériennes au Tonkin" (1927).

111. Vũ Trọng Phụng described these three positions in *Venereal Disease Clinic.* See Vũ Trọng Phụng, *Venereal Disease Clinic,* 46–47, 145–150.

112. For the history of the abolitionist movement in France, see Julia Christine Scriven Miller, "The 'Romance of Regulation': The Movement against State-Regulated Prostitution in France, 1871–1946" (Ph.D. diss., New York University, 2000).

113. Corbin, *Women for Hire,* 225.

114. Société médico-chirurgicale de l'Indochine, *Bulletin de la Société Médico-Chirurgicale de l'Indochine,* 522.

115. Ibid., 531.

116. Ibid., 550.

117. Ibid., 555.

118. Ibid., 501.

119. Vũ Trọng Phụng, *Venereal Disease Clinic,* 149.

120. Ibid.

121. Ibid., 147.

122. Ibid., 145.

123. Miller, "The 'Romance of Regulation,'" 500. On Sellier and his program, see also Siân Reynolds, *France between the War: Gender and Politics* (London: Routledge, 1996),

132–137, 142–145, 150–155; and Paul Rabinow, *French Modern: Norms and Forms of the Social Environment* (Chicago: University of Chicago Press, 1989), 262–266, 337–343.

124. Vũ Trọng Phụng, *Venereal Disease Clinic,* 146.

125. Ibid., 147.

126. Ibid., 150.

CHAPTER 3

1. For an early example, see Trương Tửu, "Địa vị của Vũ Trọng Phụng trong văn học Việt Nam cận đại."

2. In 1941, Lan Khai wrote: "If near death, he [Vũ Trọng Phụng] appeared to be veering toward an ideology *[chủ nghĩa]*, it is only because critics project onto him ideas that he does not possess." Lan Khai, *Vũ Trọng Phụng: Mớ tài liệu cho văn học sử Việt Nam,* 22–23. See also Vũ Ngọc Phan's appraisal in 1942: "He did not love new or progressive ideologies, but he never flattered the rich and powerful. He was a writer with no orientation toward politics and he belonged to no party." Vũ Ngọc Phan, *Nhà văn hiện đại: phê bình văn học.*

3. See chapter 5 in Vũ Ngọc Phan, *Nhà văn hiện đại: Phê bình văn học.*

4. Marr, *Vietnamese Tradition on Trial,* 27, 82–86.

5. Peter J. Larmour, *The French Radical Party in the 1930s* (Stanford: Stanford University Press, 1964), 245.

6. See Jeffrey C. Isaac, "Critics of Totalitarianism," in *The Cambridge History of Twentieth-Century Political Thought,* ed. Terence Ball and Richard Bellamy (Cambridge: Cambridge University Press, 2005), 181–202; and Daniel Gordon, "In Search of Limits: Raymond Aron on 'Secular Religion' and Communism," *Journal of Classical Sociology* 11, no. 2 (2001): 139–154.

7. On the emergence of sincerity as a new element of Western moral life, see Lionel Trilling, *Sincerity and Authenticity* (Cambridge, Mass.: Harvard University Press, 1971).

8. Vũ Trọng Phụng, *Cạm bẫy người,* in *Vũ Trọng Phụng: Toàn tập, Tập 1: Phóng sự* (Hà Nội, Hội Nhà Văn 1999), 121.

9. Vũ Trọng Phụng, *Kỹ nghệ lấy Tây,* in *Vũ Trọng Phụng: Toàn tập, Tập 1: Phóng sự,* 227. The original installment appeared in *Nhật Tân* on December 12, 1934. The reference to fighting communism has been excised from most editions of the book published in Hanoi after 1956.

10. Tom Kemp, *Stalinism in France,* vol. 1, *The First Twenty Years of the French Communist Party* (London: New Park, 1984), 40–100.

11. Michael B. Miller, *Shanghai on the Metro: Spies, Intrigue and the French between the Wars* (Berkeley: University of California Press, 1994), 262.

12. Thomas, "Albert Sarraut, French Colonial Development and the Communist Threat," 919.

13. Patrice Morlat, *La Repression Coloniale au Vietnam, 1908–1940* (Paris: L'Harmattan, 1990), 81.

14. Nguyễn An Ninh, "France in Indochina," in *Colonialism Experienced: Vietnamese Writing on Colonialism, 1900–1931*, ed. Truong Buu Lam (Ann Arbor: University of Michigan Press, 2000), 198.

15. Larcher-Goscha, "La légitimation française en Indochine."

16. Christopher Goscha, *Thailand and the Southeast Networks of the Vietnamese Revolution, 1885–1954* (Richmond: Curzon, 1999), 41.

17. According to Martin Thomas, Sarraut expressed a "virulent loathing of communism," denouncing "the perniciousness of Soviet propaganda and the global reach of the Comintern." Thomas, "Albert Sarraut, French Colonial Development and the Communist Threat," 942, 947.

18. See Womack, "Colonialism and the Collaborationist Agenda"; and Gerard Sasges, "'Indigenous Representation Is Hostile to All Monopolies': Phạm Quỳnh and the End of the Alcohol Monopoly in Colonial Vietnam," *Journal of Vietnamese Studies* 5, no. 1 (Winter 2010): 1–36.

19. "Các đảng chính trị ở nước Nga ngày nay" [Political parties in Russia today], *Nam Phong* 7 (January 1918): 53; "Nga hòa với Đức-Áo" [Russia makes peace with Prussia], *Nam Phong* 9 (March 1918): 186.

20. Soviet news appeared frequently in a monthly world politics section called *Current Events (Thời Đàm)*.

21. See, "Thăm Hương Cảng và Quảng Đông" [A visit to Hong Kong and Guandong], *Nam Phong* 107 (July 1926): 48–63; "Une réfutation du socialism par M. Wells," *Nam Phong: Supplément en français* 113 (February 1927): 1–3.

22. Morlat, *Indochine années vingt*, 72–74.

23. William Frederick, "Alexandre Varenne and Politics in Indochina, 1925–26," in *Aspects of Vietnamese History*, ed. Walter Vella (Honolulu: University of Hawaii Press, 1973), 133. Nguyễn An Ninh publicized the exchange in *La Cloche Fêlée* on January 7, 1924.

24. Milton Osborne, "The Faithful Few: The Politics of Collaboration in Cochinchina in the 1920s," in Vella, *Aspects of Vietnamese History*, 182.

25. The accusation appeared in a July 24, 1925, editorial in *Impartial* entitled "The Bolshevik Moment—the Organization of Class Struggle." Langlois, *André Malraux*, 141.

26. Ibid., 138.

27. Cited in Marr, *Vietnamese Tradition on Trial*, 85.

28. The emergence of this discourse followed three developments that coalesced during the mid-1920s: the appointment of the socialist Governor General Alexander Varrene (1925–27), the radicalization of students in response to the trial of Phan Bội Châu and the funeral of Phan Chu Trinh (1925–26), and the infiltration into Indochina of members of the Revolutionary Youth League, founded by Hồ Chí Minh in Canton in 1925.

29. "Colonial possessions are essentially the product of capitalism," the editorial explained. "Without capitalism, there cannot be colonies. Socialism—at least in its pure doctrine—must condemn any colonial conquest and support the liberation of all subject populations." Peycam, "Intellectuals and Political Commitment in Vietnam: The Emergence of a Public Sphere in Colonial Sài Gòn" (School of Oriental and African Studies, University of London, 1999), 238.

30. Ibid., 239–242. It ran from March 29 to April 26. After the leftist intellectual Phan Văn Trường joined its editorial board in May 1926, *La Cloche Fêlée* was renamed *L'Annam* and it continued to run stories about communism and to employ a loose Marxian framework until its dissolution in February 1928.

31. The pro-Soviet leanings of the Youth League curriculum may be discerned in a handbill confiscated by the Sûreté in the spring of 1926 that read: "Here we stand on the soil of our ancestors. We should march from north to south. If the government asks the local officials where they can expel us, we reply—to Moscow. . . . The people should take up arms and drive the invaders from our land." Frederick, "Alexandre Varenne and Politics in Indochina," 136.

32. Pierre Brocheux, "L'implantation du mouvement communiste en Indochine française: Le cas du Nghe-Tinh, 1930–31," *Revue d'Histoire Moderne et Contemporaine* 24 (January-March 1977): 49–74.

33. "In 1931 and 1932, the government published a newspaper *Thanh Nghệ Tĩnh Tân Văn* to compete with Communist propaganda." Huỳnh Kim Khánh, *Vietnamese Communism*, 159.

34. Marr, *Vietnamese Tradition on Trial*, 87.

35. Ibid., 386.

36. Megan Cook, *The Constitutionalist Party in Cochinchina: The Years of Decline, 1930–1942* (Victoria, Australia: Centre of Southeast Asian Studies, Monash University, 1977), 32.

37. Ibid., 24: "Instead of trying to hear the cries of anguish of a distressed people," Bùi Quang Chiêu wrote, "it has been thought cleverer and safer to institute, in the name of order and peace, the regime of the gag. . . . To justify this rash repressive policy, the cry of Bolshevism is raised. The muffled discontent is attributed to Muscovite Communism, but exactly what that consists of, neither those who talk of it nor those who are accused of it know."

38. See McHale, *Print and Power*, 67–101.

39. For the history of the French Popular Front, see Julian Jackson, *The Popular Front in France: Defending Democracy, 1934–1938* (Cambridge: Cambridge University Press, 1988).

40. Tony Chafur and Amanda Sackur, eds., *French Colonial Empire and the Popular Front: Hope and Disillusion* (New York: St. Martin's Press, 1999).

41. Jackson, *The Popular Front in France,* 154. The appointment of Moutet provoked recollections of his support for the imprisoned nationalist leader Phan Châu Trinh in 1908 and his opposition to the repression of the Yên Báy Uprising at the start of the 1930s. For example, see Dương Trung Thực, "Ông Moutet với Bộ Thuộc địa" [Moutet and the Ministry of Colonies], *Nghề Mới,* June 10–20, 1936.

42. Hoài Thanh, "Nội các Bình dân bên Pháp với dân ta" [The Popular Front ministry in France and us], *Tràng An* 125 (May 22, 1936). At the same time, Hoài Thanh aired a cautionary note, pointing out that the Soviet Union pursued an imperialist policy toward indigenous people and recalling the failed hopes inspired by the administration of the Socialist Governor General Varenne during the mid-1920s.

43. Cook, *The Constitutionalist Party in Cochinchina,* 87.

44. Hémery, *Révolutionnaires vietnamiens et pouvoir colonial en Indochine,* 333–376.

45. Cochinchina's relatively liberal public sphere derived from its status as a direct colony that mandated the imposition there of French law. This included the Third Republic's progressive press law of 1881, which outlawed most forms of government censorship. The colonial administration prevented the full implementation of metropolitan law by issuing repressive local decrees and ordering the security police to harass muckraking newspapers and outspoken political activists. It also refused to apply the law of 1881 to Vietnamese-language publications. But the maintenance of an overarching French legal framework in Cochinchina ensured that violations of civil liberties could be challenged in court. The persistence of imperial Vietnamese law in the protectorates of Annam and Tonkin explains the comparative timidity there of public political discourse and aboveground left-wing activism. Hence, neutral or positive representations of communism within newspapers in Annam and Tonkin lagged behind their Cochinchinese counterparts until the middle of the decade.

46. "Tại Nga Sô-Viết" [In the Soviet Union], *Nhật Tân,* January 10, 1934, translated by Hồng Vân. The original author is not listed.

47. C. B., "Trí thức với bình dân" [Intellectuals and populism], *Cùng Bạn,* June 21, 1934.

48. Hoàng Tân Dân, "Văn hóa bình dân," *Văn Học tuần san* 4 (December 1, 1934).

49. J. E. Flower, *Literature and the Left in France: Society, Politics, and the Novel since the Late Nineteenth Century* (London: Methuen, 1983), 80–83.

50. Thiếu Sơn, "Văn học bình dân," *Tiểu Thuyết Thứ Bảy* 43 (March 23, 1935).

51. The relaxation of censorship by Governor General Robin in January 1935 may have been undertaken in anticipation of a shift toward the Left with French politics. Cooke, *The Constitutionalist Party in Cochinchina,* 77.

52. Peter Zinoman, *The Colonial Bastille: A History of Imprisonment in Vietnam, 1862–1940* (Berkeley: University of California Press, 2001), 240–266.

53. Examples of such hazy political radicals include Dũng in Nhất Linh, *Đoạn tuyệt* [Breaking the ties] (Hà Nội: Đời Nay, 1935); Hạc in Khái Hưng, *Gia đình* [Family] (Hà Nội: Đời Nay, 1937); Mạnh in Nguyễn Văn Phúc, *Con đường mới* [New road] (Hà Nội: Hương Sơn đường, 1939); and Duy in Hoàng Đạo, *Con đường sáng* [Bright road] (Hà Nội: Đời Nay, 1940). The most distinctly drawn communist character after Hải Vân is the ex–political prisoner Teacher Minh in Vũ Trọng Phụng's *The Dike Breaks,* originally serialized in *The Future* starting on September 27, 1936. Unlike Hải Vân, however, there is no indication that Minh is anything but a rank-and-file party member.

54. It is well known that scores of ICP members trained at the Stalin School during the 1920s and 1930s. See Quinn-Judge, *Hồ Chí Minh: The Missing Years,* 53–56; and William Duiker, *Hồ Chí Minh: A Life* (New York: Hyperion, 2000), 92–94. Duiker makes use of data from the Comintern archives published in Anotoly A. Sokolov, *Komintern I V'ietnam* (Moscow: Iv Ran, 1998).

55. Most references to the novel are from an edition published by the Literary Studies Publishing House in 1996. Vũ Trọng Phụng, *Giông tố* (Hà Nội: Văn Học, 1996), 369–371.

56. This remarkable detail appears in the first edition of the novel published in Hanoi as a stand-alone book by the Văn Thanh Publishing House in 1937. It is curious that Nguyễn Ái Quốc's name does not appear in the original serialized version of the novel published in *Hà Nội Báo* (but it is not surprising that it is consistently cut out thereafter). This suggests that Vũ Trọng Phụng inserted Nguyễn Ái Quốc into the second edition of the novel, although why he did so remains obscure. For speculation about what may have motivated this move, see Lại Nguyên Ân, *Nghiên cứu văn bản tiểu thuyết Giông tố,* 49.

57. This passage has been cut from more recent editions of the novel, but it may be found in the original serialization. See *Hà Nội Báo,* September 16, 1936.

58. The following reflections on the relationship between the election of the Popular Front and the narrative structure of *The Storm* are anticipated by Thiều Quang, "Vũ Trọng Phụng: Đời sống và con người" [Vũ Trọng Phụng: The man and his life], first published in the Hà Nội occasional journal *Tập san Phê bình—số đặc biệt* (October 1957): 23–24.

59. Beginning with the eleventh chapter of the original serialized version in *Hà Nội Báo,* her name—Thị Mịch—actually displaces *The Storm* on the newspaper's masthead as the title of the novel. This move may have been undertaken to fool censors who were uncomfortable with the first ten chapters. See the note on the publishing history of the novel in Vũ Trọng Phụng, *Vũ Trọng Phụng—Toàn tập: Tiểu thuyết Dứt tình, Giông tố, Vỡ đê* [Vũ Trọng Phụng—the complete works: The novels *Break Up, The Storm, The Dike Breaks*] (Hà Nội: Hội Nhà Văn, 1999), 147.

60. This passage appears in the versions of the novel from 1936 and 1937 but not in later editions. See Lại Nguyên Ân, *Nghiên cứu văn bản tiểu thuyết Giông tố,* 580.

61. Hirohide Kurihara, "The First Congress of the Indochinese Communist Party (1935) and Its Aftermath: A Turning Point in the Comintern-ICP Relations," *Journal of Asian and African Studies* 60 (2000).

62. Vũ Trọng Phụng, *Giông tố*, 370.

63. Ibid.

64. Ibid., 373.

65. This is the thesis of Huỳnh Kim Khánh, *Vietnamese Communism, 1925–1945*, generally considered the standard work in the field.

66. Patricia Pelley, *Postcolonial Vietnam: New Histories of the National Past* (Durham: Duke University Press, 2002).

67. Vũ Trọng Phụng, *Giông tố*, 337.

68. Ibid., 338.

69. Xuân Sa, "Văn chương và giai cấp: Lần thứ nhứt trong văn học Việt Nam cuốn Giông tố của Vũ Trọng Phụng bày tỏ cuộc xung đột của hai giai cấp."

70. Vũ Trọng Phụng, "Chung quanh một bài phê bình."

71. Vũ Trọng Phụng, *Giông tố*, 46.

72. Ibid., 47.

73. Ibid., 53.

74. Ibid., 97–98.

75. Ibid., 99.

76. Ibid., 252.

77. Ibid., 223.

78. The version of *Vỡ đê* cited here is from *Toàn tập Vũ Trọng Phụng*, ed. Lại Nguyên Ân (Hà Nội: Hội Nhà Văn, 1999), 463–695.

79. Vũ Trọng Phụng, *Vỡ đê*, 469.

80. Ibid., 475.

81. Katerina Clark, *The Soviet Novel: History as Ritual* (Bloomington: Indiana University Press, 1981), 15.

82. Vũ Trọng Phụng, *Vỡ đê*, 511–512: "None of the dike workers dared to address the officers. Instead, for almost half an hour, they whispered sheepishly, urged each other on, and fought among themselves. Observing this wretched situation, Phú raced to the front of the group to speak on their behalf."

83. Ibid., 513–514: "The three hundred coolies talked loudly among themselves. One hundred melted away gradually, followed by another hundred. Those who remained were forcibly disbanded by the curses and blows of the police."

84. Ibid., 514.

85. Ibid., 669: "Women and children took to the front lines, while young men and old men brought up the rear. Here stood a man with a tile-roofed house and a jackfruit tree whose life had been upended by the flood. There was the village head whose efforts to rebuild after the destruction of the dike were thwarted by the drought. Here was a destitute woman, widowed by the floodwaters, carrying her two children in a basket. There was an old man who had lost two sons—one fighting in the war for France, the other beaten to death by security agents of the alcohol monopoly. Each of the six

hundred protesters shelved personal grievances in order to voice a single complaint. Forming an army of the homeless and unemployed, this ragtag mob marched forward."

86. Ibid., 671.

87. Ibid., 675.

88. Ibid.

89. Ibid., 678.

90. For the French discourse on socialist realism during the early 1930s, see Flower, *Literature and the Left in France*, 98–130. Descriptions of socialist realism in Vietnamese were disseminated around the same time by the Marxist critic Hải Triều. See Hải Triều, *Văn sĩ và xã hội* [Writers and society] (Huế: Hương Giang thư quán, 1937), which includes chapters on Gorky, Rolland, and Barbusse.

91. Vũ Trọng Phụng, *Vỡ đê*, 618.

92. Ibid., 619.

93. Ibid., 677: "There were poorly dressed ex–political prisoners whose faces had been hardened by the horrible conditions in the *bagnes* of Poulo Condore and Guyana. Beside them were handsome and fashionable sons of mandarins who looked as if they had known nothing in their lives but fine food and pleasure. Could it be true that all of these men were revolutionaries? He found it strange that men dressed in expensive jackets, velvet hats, and shiny gold watches should scream about the class struggle, strikes, the oppression of the proletariat, the rights of workers, and the villainy of the bourgeoisie, mandarin officials, and the rural ruling class. . . . Following introductions, Phú learned that Mr. X was a graduate student in philosophy, fluent in French, and the eldest son of official N; that Mr. M. had been persecuted by the Parisian police while a student in France; that Mr. H. V. had been expelled from the literature department in Toulouse after joining anti-imperialist protests; and that Mr. T. Q. had been sentenced to five years in prison after attending the Whampoa Military Academy. In short, these were resolute men who considered prison as a training school for fighters determined to defend the poor and downtrodden against their oppressors."

94. Ibid., 676.

95. Ibid., 679.

96. Ibid., 678.

97. Ibid.

98. Ibid., 679.

99. Vũ Trọng Phụng, "Những việc đáng ghi chép của năm Bính-Tý," 3.

100. In addition, "Notes on 1936" surveyed a series of high-profile crimes, scandals, and corruption cases as well as factional politics at the Huế court and the visit to Indochina of Charlie Chaplin.

101. "Some think that the Left is anti-colonial; maybe some of its members, as a result of misdirected idealism, have seen colonial expansion as being nothing but brutality, violence and rape. But the greatest numbers have well understood the immense tasks

to be accomplished in taking seriously the civilizing mission which a nation can pursue without forgetting either its traditions or its principles." William Cohen, "The Colonial Policy of the Popular Front," *French Historical Studies* 7, no. 3 (1972): 376.

102. Ibid., 377.

103. Martin Thomas, *The French Empire between the Wars: Imperialism, Politics and Society* (Manchester: Manchester University Press, 2005), 288.

104. France Tostain, "The Popular Front and the Blum-Violette Plan, 1936–37," in Chafur and Sackur, *French Colonial Empire and the Popular Front*, 218–229.

105. "In Algeria the nationalist party Etoile nord-africaine was outlawed; in Morocco the Comité d'action marocaine was also suppressed and its members imprisoned and deported. A socialist from Morocco told the SFIO congress in 1937, 'the Moroccans have no reason to be glad that a Popular Front government led by socialists has been in power for a year.' . . . Explaining his repressive policies in Indochina, Moutet spoke of his determination to preserve the empire against those undermining it. He told parliament that: 'The Popular Front did not appoint me to the position I occupy to allow French sovereignty in the colonies to be attacked.' To a member of the party's colonial commission he insisted that he would not be 'the gravedigger of the colonies, he would not lose them for France.'" Cohen, "The Colonial Policy of the Popular Front," 385–386.

106. Cook, *The Constitutionalist Party in Cochinchina*, 89.

107. Phùng Bảo Thạch, "Chúng ta đã thấy rõ chánh-phủ bình dân chưa?" [Have we seen the real populist government yet?], *Dư Luận*, August 8, 1938.

108. Vũ Trọng Phụng, "Cộng sản tự do," 1.

109. Citations to Dumb Luck are from my translation: Vũ Trọng Phụng, *Dumb Luck*, 167.

110. Ibid., 113.

111. Ibid., 115.

112. Vũ Trọng Phụng, "Nhân sự chia rẽ của đệ tam và đệ tứ quốc tế: Ta thử ngó lại cuộc cách mệnh cộng sản ở Nga từ lúc khởi thủy cho đến ngày nay," *Đông Dương Tạp Chí*, September 25, 1937, October 2, 1937, October 9, 1937.

113. Their ages in 1930: Tạ Thu Thâu, 24; Phan Văn Hùm, 28; Huỳnh Văn Phương, 24; Trần Văn Thạch, 27; Phan Văn Chánh, 24; and Hồ Hữu Tường, 20. The best account of La Lutte, both the group and its eponymous journal, remains Daniel Hémery, *Révolutionnaires vietnamiens et pouvoir colonial en Indochine*.

114. There was some conflict, however. Hémery identifies four "fundamental texts of Vietnamese Trotskyism," three by Tạ Thu Thâu and one by Huỳnh Văn Phương, that provoked Stalinist attacks in 1933. Ibid., 44–57.

115. Phan Khôi, "Sau cuộc bầu cử nghị viên thành phố Sài Gòn, Đảng viên cộng sản sao cũng được dự cử và đắc cử" [Why can communists stand in elections and win elections?], *Tràng An*, May 21, 1935, 1.

116. The charges were thrown out.

117. Hồ Hữu Tường founded the first illegal and legal Trotskyist journals in Indochina including *Le Militant*. The father of Harvard historian Hue Tam Ho Tai, he was a prolific writer and a remarkable survivor. He was imprisoned in both the RVN and the SRV and died in reeducation camp in 1980.

118. In addition to Hémery's, this account of La Lutte relies on Ngô Văn, *Việt Nam 1920–1945, Cách mạng và phản cách mạng thời đô hộ thuộc địa* [Vietnam 1920–1945, revolution and counterrevolution under colonial domination] (California: Chuông Rè, 2000).

119. "Vì sao nhóm La Lutte chia rẽ?," *Nhựt Báo*, September 4, 1937.

120. An account by Roland Dorgeles appeared in "Một bức thư không niêm về thực trạng nga-sô-viết" [An open letter on the real situation in the USSR], *Vì Chúa*, March 12, 1937: "I am not in any party nor am I trying to make you join any side," Dorgeles wrote, asserting his objectivity. "I have no political position. Indeed, I have never had one. Or to be more accurate, I am simply an opponent. I oppose greed, I oppose repression, I oppose injustice; I oppose lies." Expressing grave misgivings about what he had observed during a recent trip to the Soviet Union, he wrote: "People say that the workers are masters of the USSR. This is untrue. It is a lie. They must obey their masters just like here. They must toil just like here. Indeed, they are much more wretched there than here." Other accounts may be found in "Những điều trông thấy ở Nga Xô-Viết" [Things seen in the USSR], *Vì Chúa*, July 11 and 18, 1937; "Đảng đệ tứ quốc tế hoạt động ở Pháp và Tây Ban Nha" [Party of the fourth international agitates in France and Spain], *Vì Chúa*, August 6, 1937; "Đi tìm sự thật ở Liên Xô" [Searching for truth in the USSR], *Tràng An*, February 10, 1938.

121. "Biết đâu địa ngục ở miền dương gian: Tin ai?" [A hell on earth: Who to believe?], *Tràng An*, February 11, 1938.

122. For a small sampling of Vietnamese journalism about Gide during this period, see Lộc Phương Thủy, *André Gide: Đời văn và tác phẩm* [André Gide: Life and works] (Hà Nội: Khoa Học Xã Hội, 2002), 408–483.

123. It is not clear if full translations of either book were ever published. For an excerpt from "Afterthoughts," see "Sự thực về Nga" [The truth about the USSR], *Chính Trị*, November 8, 1939.

124. Hoài Thanh, Lê Tràng Kiều, and Lưu Trọng Lư, *Văn chương và hành động* (Hà Nội: Phương Đông, 1936). The short book was republished by the Writers Association Publishing House in 1999.

125. Lại Nguyên Ân, "Một khía cạnh ở nhà báo Vũ Trọng Phụng: người lược thuật thông tin quốc tế" [One aspect of Vũ Trọng Phụng the journalist, reporting international news], in *Vũ Trọng Phụng tài năng và sự thật* (Hà Nội: Văn Học, 1997), 189–200.

126. Vũ Trọng Phụng, *Nhân sự chia rẽ của Đệ tam và Đệ tứ* (Sài Gòn: Thanh Mậu, 1938). It is not known if Vũ Trọng Phụng endorsed the republication of the essay.

127. Vũ Trọng Phụng, "Giữa cuộc cách mệnh xã hội phái tiểu tư sản chưa đủ giác ngộ," *Tiểu Thuyết Thứ Năm* 4 (June 2, 1938).

128. Vũ Trọng Phụng, "Chúng ta không trông thấy gì," *Tiểu Thuyết Thứ Năm* 2 (May 19, 1938).

129. Vũ Trọng Phụng, "Phỏng vấn tình cờ: Một ông nghị già . . . lôi thôi," *Tiểu Thuyết Thứ Năm* 12 (July 28, 1938).

130. Diane N. LaBrosse, "'La Dérive Bergery/The Bergery Drift': Gaston Bergery and the Politics of Late Third Republic France and the Early Vichy State," *Historical Reflections* 34, no. 2 (Summer 2008): 66–87.

131. Vịt Đực, "Văn hoạt kê, lời hiệu triệu của một tay Sịt-Ta-Li-Nít: Đả đảo tên Tờ-Rốt-Kýt Huỳnh Văn Phương!," *Tiểu Thuyết Thứ Năm* 13 (August 2, 1938).

132. Trương Tửu, "Những xu hướng chính trị hiện thời ở xứ ta nhóm Tia Sáng" [A political tendency in our country: The Ray of Light group], *Quốc Gia,* September 23, 1938. The article includes an interview with the leader of the Trotskyite Tia Sáng group, Thái Văn Tam. The characterization of Huỳnh Văn Phương is from Thái Văn Tam.

133. Trần Huy Liệu, *Hồi ký* (Hà Nội: Khoa Học Xã Hội, 1991), 188.

134. Trương Tửu, "Những xu hướng chính trị hiện thời ở xứ ta nhóm Tia Sáng."

135. Ibid.

136. Trần Huy Liệu, *Hồi ký,* 189.

137. Trương Tửu, "Những xu hướng chính trị hiện thời ở xứ ta: chung quanh sự chia rẽ Đệ Tam và Đệ Tứ, phỏng vấn Huỳnh Văn Phương, nguyên bút báo *le Travail*" [Current political tendencies in our country, around the split between the Third and Fourth International, an interview with Huỳnh Văn Phương, writer for *Le Travail*], *Quốc Gia,* September 30, 1938.

138. "The world knows the disloyalty of the Fourth International. Hence, revolutionary elements here are wrong to cooperate with them just because France has formed a Popular government. It was an oversight on our part that allowed the gang of Tạ Thu Thâu, Hồ Hữu Tường, and Phan Văn Hùm to provoke so many risings against the established order. This has called down imperialist repression upon the heads of the working masses." Vịt Đực, "Văn hoạt kê, lời hiệu triệu của một tay Sịt-Ta-Li-Nít: Đả đảo tên Tờ-Rốt-Kýt Huỳnh Văn Phương!"

139. "He dared to oppose our Democratic Front led by many real revolutionaries such as the revolutionary Phạm Hữu Chương (a famous doctor), the revolutionary Nguyễn Đình Thiệp (representative of beggars), the revolutionary Lemur (who has achieved victory in the revolution of women's fashion), or the revolutionary Nguyễn Tường Tam (a revolutionary celebrated for his virtue among many other things). Moscow ordered comrade Cahin to form this alliance with the middle classes. Even though we have received no direct word from Moscow, we still must follow this policy." Ibid.

140. Trương Tửu, "Những xu hướng chính trị hiện thời ở xứ ta: Nhóm Tia Sáng."

141. He explicitly denies any partisan commitment in the introduction to the article.

142. Honel is mentioned only in passing in political histories of the period by David Marr, Daniel Hémery, Ngô Văn, and Sophie Quinn-Judge.

143. "Báo cáo về tình hình Đảng Cộng sản Đông Dương" [Report on the situation of the ICP, 10/1937], in Đảng cộng sản Việt Nam, *Văn kiện Đảng Toàn tập: 1936–39* [Complete party documents] (Hà Nội: Chính Trị Quốc Gia, 2000), 6:334.

144. "Nghị quyết của toàn thể hội nghị Ban Trung ương Đảng Cộng sản Đông Dương, 20, 30 tháng, 3 năm, 1938," in *Văn kiện Đảng Toàn tập*, 6:345.

145. Trần Huy Liệu, *Hồi ký*, 203.

146. His major literary work during this period included the relatively apolitical novel *Winning the Lottery* and a handful of short stories in *Tao Đàn*.

147. Following diverse postcolonial trajectories, some of these northerners went to the South, many joined the Việt Minh, and a handful were excommunicated for their role in the revisionist Nhân Văn–Giai Phẩm Affair of 1956.

148. Phan Khôi, "Thuyết 'tịnh canh' của Hứa Hành với chủ nghĩa cộng sản" [The "agriculturalist" theory of Hsu Hsing and communism], *Sông Hương* 13 (October 25, 1936) and 14 (October 31, 1936).

149. Vũ Ngọc Phan, "Thư Hà Nội gửi vào—'Cộng sản theo nghĩa khác,'" [Letter from Hanoi about "a different meaning of communism"], *Sông Hương* 24 (January 16, 1937).

150. Phùng Bảo Thạch, "Dân chúng Annam đang bị loạn óc" [The Annamese people are being driven crazy], *Dư Luận*, August 1, 1938.

151. Ngô Tất Tố, "Lê-nin và Khổng Tử" [Lenin and Confucius], *Tuần Lễ* 15 (June 25, 1938).

152. Hoài Thanh, Lê Tràng Kiều, and Lưu Trọng Lư, *Văn chương và hành động*, 12, 34.

153. Ibid., 39–44.

154. Ibid., 38.

155. Lưu Trọng Lư, "Con đường riêng của trí thức," *Tao Đàn*, May 16, 1939, 505–515.

CHAPTER 4

1. Lê Thanh, "Chúng ta phỏng vấn ông Vũ Trọng Phụng về những tiểu thuyết *Giông tố*, *Làm đĩ*."

2. He lists the rape of the peasant girl Thị Mịch by the lascivious capitalist Nghị Hách in his novel *The Storm*, published in 1936, as an example of his exploration of this particular issue. The novel contains much more, in addition, on the sexual decadence of Nghị Hách.

3. Vũ Ngọc Phan, *Nhà văn hiện đại*, 531–532.

4. Phan Khôi, "Không đề cao Vũ Trọng Phụng, chỉ đánh giá đúng," in *Vũ Trọng Phụng với chúng ta*, ed. Trần Hữu Tá (Hà Nội: Minh Đức, 1956), 10.

5. See Thái Phỉ, "Văn chương dâm uế"; Nhất Chi Mai, "Ý kiến một người đọc: Dâm hay không dâm," *Ngày Nay*, March 21, 1937; Hoài Thanh, "Đối với văn nghệ trước cách mạng: Tiếp thu phải có phê phán," *Nhân Dân*, April 6, 1958.

6. Hoàng Văn Hoan, "Một vài ý kiến về vấn đề tác phẩm Vũ Trọng Phụng trong văn học Việt Nam," in *Vũ Trọng Phụng: Con người và tác phẩm,* ed. Nguyễn Hoành Khung and Lại Nguyên Ân (Hà Nội: Hội Nhà Văn, 1994), 219–245.

7. Lan Khai, *Vũ Trọng Phụng: Mớ tài liệu cho văn sử Việt Nam.*

8. Ibid., 22.

9. David Marr is the obvious exception here since he devotes a dense, interesting chapter to the topic in *Vietnamese Tradition on Trial, 1920–1945.* See chapter 4, "The Question of Women."

10. Ho Tai, *Radicalism and the Origins of the Vietnamese Revolution,* 90. While Ho Tai acknowledges the possibility that "debates on women" might be interpreted as a "body of reflection on their condition," her primary concern is the way in which this discourse represented "a commentary on a whole range of cultural, social, and political questions. Woman was youth; woman was also the only possible symbol of a colonized nation." In the hands of Vietnamese Marxists, she argues, "women would assume another symbolic role in public discourse as the representative of the disenfranchised masses." For Ho Tai, the "multiplicity of functions" carried out by the discourse on women explains its prominence and durability. But it also gave rise to the danger that "the condition of women would be lost from view in the welter of symbolism."

11. Ibid.

12. Huỳnh Sanh Thông, "Main Trends in Vietnamese Literature between the Two World Wars," *Vietnam Forum* 3 (Winter/Spring 1984): 106.

13. Hồ Xanh, "*Số đỏ của* Vũ Trọng Phụng" [Vũ Trọng Phụng's *Dumb Luck*], *Công Thương Báo* 6 (May 1–15, 1938).

14. Vũ Trọng Phụng, *Làm đĩ,* 35.

15. Ibid, 110–111.

16. Ibid, 110.

17. Ibid, 111.

18. Vũ Trọng Phụng, *Lục Xì,* 99.

19. Ibid, 35.

20. Ibid.

21. Lệ Chi, "*Giông tố:* Xã hội tiểu thuyết của Vũ Trọng Phụng."

22. Vũ Trọng Phụng, *Giông tố,* 206.

23. Vũ Trọng Phụng, *Lục xì,* 61.

24. Lê Thanh, "*Số đỏ:* Hoạt kê tiểu thuyết của Vũ Trọng Phụng" [*Dumb Luck:* A humorous novel by Vũ Trọng Phụng], *Phụ Nữ* 5 (March 16, 1938).

25. Vũ Trọng Phụng, *Làm đĩ,* 61.

26. Ibid., 72–73.

27. Minh Tước, "Đọc sách *Làm đĩ*" [Reading *To Be a Whore*], *Mới* 2 (May 15, 1939).

28. Vũ Trọng Phụng, *Làm đĩ,* 73.

29. French writers employed a similar strategy during this era. See Mary Lynn Stewart, "'Science Is Always Chaste': Sex Education and Sexual Initiation in France," *Journal of Contemporary History* 32, no. 3 (July 1997): 383.

30. Vũ Trọng Phụng, *Làm đĩ*, 290.

31. Ibid., 34.

32. Works by Freud were first translated into French only in 1922, and the first French psychoanalytic society was not founded until 1926. Similar societies had existed in Vienna, Zurich, Budapest, Berlin, London, and the United States since 1914. Explanations for the "stiff opposition" to Freudian theory in interwar France tend to emphasize French hostility to its putative German and Jewish origin. Florence Tamagne, *A History of Homosexuality in Europe: Berlin, London, Paris, 1919–1939* (New York: Algora, 2004), 1:221. See also Antony Copley, *Sexual Moralities in France, 1780–1980: New Ideas on the Family, Divorce, and Homosexuality* (London: Routledge, 1989), 147–154.

33. See, Nguyễn Khắc Xuyên, *Mục lục phân tích Tạp chí Nam Phong, 1917–1934* [Analytic bibliography of Nam Phong, 1917–1934] (Huế: Thuận Hóa/Trung tâm VHNN Đông Tây, 2003).

34. X. X. "Triết học và đời người: Một vấn đề triết học" [Philosphy and life: A philosophical problem], *Phụ Nữ Tân Văn* 210 (August 3, 1933): 18.

35. In 1936, another brief but informative discussion of Freud was published in the journal *Ngày Nay:* "Những cái bí mật màu nhiệm trong tâm lý Sigmund Freud và khoa tâm lý giải phẫu," *Ngày Nay* 35 (November 22, 1936): 467.

36. Judith Henchy "Performing Modernity in the Writings of Nguyễn An Ninh and Phan Văn Hùm" (Ph.D. Diss., University of Washington, 2005), 169.

37. Nguyễn Văn Hanh, *Hồ Xuân Hương: Tác phẩm, thân thế và văn tài* (Sài Gòn [?]: Aspar, 1937).

38. Ibid., 9–10.

39. Vũ Trọng Phụng, *Dumb Luck*, 79.

40. Background on Vachet can be found in Angus McLaren, *Twentieth-Century Sexuality: A History* (Oxford: Blackwell, 1999), 250.

41. See Peter Gay, *Freud: A Life for Our Time* (London: Papermac, 1988), 71. The reference to "confession" appears on page 75 of the novel.

42. Vũ Trọng Phụng, *Làm đĩ*, 74.

43. Ibid., 76.

44. Freud vacillated in his writing between viewing the drives as biological, on the one hand, and as psychically and culturally determined, on the other. See Arlene Stein, "Three Models of Sexuality: Drives, Identities and Practices," *Sociological Theory* 7, no. 1 (Spring 1989): 1–13.

45. Vũ Trọng Phụng, *Làm đĩ*, 77.

46. Ibid., 33.

47. Ibid., 82.

48. Ibid., 95.

49. Ibid., 90.

50. Ibid., 80.

51. Vũ Ngọc Phan, *Nhà văn hiện đại, Tập I* (1941; Hồ Chí Minh City: Văn Học, 1994), 526.

52. Minh Tước, "Đọc sách *Làm đĩ*."

53. Ibid.

54. The passage describing the incident is uncharacteristically discrete, and hence it is not clear if what transpires is entirely mutual. Vũ Trọng Phụng, *Làm đĩ*, 87.

55. Ibid., 88.

56. Ibid., 89.

57. Ibid., 93.

58. Ibid., 95.

59. Ibid., 96–97.

60. Ibid., 98.

61. Ibid., 101.

62. Ibid., 102.

63. Ibid., 103.

64. For Freud's view on masturbation, see George J. Makari, "Between Seduction and Libido: Sigmund Freud's Masturbation Hypotheses and the Realignment of his Etiologic Thinking, 1897–1905," *Bulletin of the History of Medicine* 72, no. 4 (1998): 638–662.

65. Thomas W. Laqueur, *Solitary Sex: A Cultural History of Masturbation* (New York: Zone Books, 2003), 372.

66. For the rapid spread of these discourses in Japan during the late nineteenth century and early twentieth, see Sabine Frühstück, "Male Anxieties: Nerve Force, Nation, and the Power of Sexual Knowledge," *Journal of the Royal Asiatic Society* 15, no. 1 (2005): 71–88. For China, see Frank Dikötter, *Sex, Culture and Modernity in China: Medical Science and the Construction of Sexual Identities in the Early Republican Period* (Honolulu: University of Hawaii Press, 1995).

67. Vũ Trọng Phụng mentions Hirshfeld in "Thư ngỏ cho ông Thái Phỉ, chủ bút báo Tin Văn về bài 'Văn chương dâm uế.'" For the reference to Vachet, see Vũ Trọng Phụng, *Dumb Luck*, 178.

68. Patricia R. Stokes, "Pathology, Danger, and Power: Women's and Physicians' Views of Pregnancy and Childbirth in Weimer Germany," *Social History of Medicine* 13, no. 3 (2000): 374.

69. Lutz D. H. Sauerteig, "Sex Education in Germany from the Eighteenth to the Twentieth Century," in *Cultures in Europe: Themes in Sexuality*, ed. Franz X. Eder, Lesley Hall, and Gert Hekma (Manchester: Manchester University Press, 1999), 9–33.

70. W. Liepmann, *Jeunesse et Sexualité: Initiation sexuelle des jeunes gens, d'aprés leurs propres confessions* (Paris: Montaigne, Fernand Aubier, 1932).

71. Lê Thanh, "Chúng ta phỏng vấn ông Vũ Trọng Phụng về những tiểu thuyết *Giông tố*, *Làm đĩ*."

72. Vũ Trọng Phụng, *Làm đĩ*, 103.

73. It is possible that the book in question was Chinese in origin since, as David Marr points out, many of the earliest Vietnamese-language sexual advice manuals were simply translations of Chinese texts. He cites the example of Nguyễn Văn Khải, *Nam nữ hôn nhân vệ sinh* [Marriage hygiene for men and women] (Hải Phòng, 1924). Marr, *Vietnamese Tradition on Trial*, 213.

74. Vũ Trọng Phụng, *Làm đĩ*, 105.

75. See Douglas Wile, *Art of the Bedchamber: The Chinese Sexual Yoga Classics Including Women's Solo Meditation Texts* (Albany: SUNY Press, 1992), 24–43.

76. Vũ Trọng Phụng, *Làm đĩ*, 105.

77. Marr, *Vietnamese Tradition on Trial*, 213.

78. *Chủ nghĩa vật chất* is not to be confused with the broader philosophical concept of "materialism"—the antithesis of "idealism"—that eventually came to be translated within Vietnamese Marxist discourse as *chủ nghĩa duy vật*.

79. Vũ Trọng Phụng, *Làm đĩ*, 112.

80. Huyền describes herself as living a "100 percent material life" *(cuộc đời một trăm phần trăm vật chất)* and itemizes her monthly expenses on such things as "radios, phonographs, movies, Western food, Western medicine, dancing, gambling on the horses, going to festivals, and going paddleboating." Ibid., 193.

81. For a useful treatment and critique of Marxist explanations for prostitution, see Lars O. Ericsson, "Charges against Prostitution: An Attempt at a Philosophical Assessment," *Ethics* 90, no. 3 (April 1980): 344–348.

82. In this sense, Vũ Trọng Phụng's position on this question resembles radical pre-Marxist views on the topic expressed by early-nineteenth-century Utopian Socialists such as Fourier and Saint-Simon. See Thanh-Dam Truong, *Sex, Money and Morality: Prostitution and Tourism in South-East Asia* (London: Zed Book, 1990), 32.

83. Vũ Trọng Phụng, *Làm đĩ*, 138–139.

84. Ibid., 144.

85. Ibid., 145–146.

86. Ibid., 147.

87. Ibid., 148.

88. Ibid., 240.

89. Ibid., 234.

90. Ibid., 137.

91. For a useful analysis of this phenomenon in a very different historical context, see Debra Curtis, "Commodities and Sexual Subjectivities: A Look at Capitalism and Its Desires," *Cultural Anthropology* 19, no. 1 (2004): 95–121.

92. Ibid., 120.

93. Ibid.

94. Ibid., 135.

95. Lê Thanh, "Chúng ta phỏng vấn ông Vũ Trọng Phụng về những tiểu thuyết *Giông tố, Làm đĩ*."

96. Vũ Trọng Phụng, *Làm đĩ*, 112–113.

97. For the emergence of a discourse about individualism in modern Vietnam, see David Marr, "Concepts of 'Individual' and 'Self' in Twentieth-Century Vietnam," *Modern Asian Studies* 34, no. 4 (2000): 769–796.

98. Vũ Trọng Phụng, *Làm đĩ*, 204.

99. For an analysis of the romantic hero in French fiction, see Allan H. Pasco, *Sick Heroes: French Society and Literature in the Romantic Age, 1750–1850* (Exeter: University of Exeter Press, 1997), 7. Pasco writes: "Though defeated, rejected and impotent, literary Romantic heroes are usually portrayed as above the common herd, either because of their great intelligence, acute sensitivity, and heightened powers of insight or wisdom, and they are not at all averse to being set off as an astonishing if not admirable spectacle. Almost always physically attractive, they come from the aristocracy or the upper reaches of the middle class. Despite the fact that they are often orphans and virtually without exception in their late teens or twenties, seldom do they have to work for a living. Nor, indeed, do they wish to find a useful occupation. They see themselves as misunderstood outsiders, fated to be imprisoned within their situation and are unequivocally impressed with their own singularity."

100. Vũ Trọng Phụng, *Làm đĩ*, 209.

101. Ibid.

102. Ibid., 217.

103. Ibid., 254.

104. Ibid., 261.

105. Ibid., 219.

106. Ibid.

CHAPTER 5

1. Hoàng Văn Hoan's essay was first published in 1994 in an anthology of criticism about Vũ Trọng Phụng edited by Nguyễn Hoành Khung and Lại Nguyên Ân. See Hoàng Văn Hoan, "Một vài ý kiến về vấn đề tác phẩm Vũ Trọng Phụng trong văn học Việt Nam."

2. For insight into Hoàng Văn Hoan's career, see Wen-huan Huang, *A Drop in the Ocean: Hoang Van Hoan's Revolutionary Reminiscences* (Beijing: Foreign Language Publishing House, 1988).

3. The key scholarship on Nhân Văn-Giai Phẩm may be found in Zinoman, "Nhân Văn-Giai Phẩm and Vietnamese 'Reform Communism' in the 1950s: A Revisionist

Interpretation"; Hirohide Kurihara, "Changes in the Literary Policy of the Vietnamese Workers' Party, 1956–1958," in *Indochina in the 1940s and 1950s,* ed. Takashi Shiraishi and Motoo Furata (Ithaca: Cornell University Southeast Asia Program Publications, 1992). Kurihara's original Japanese-language essay was published in *Ajia, Afurika gengo bunka kenkyū* [Journal of Asian and African studies]. Boudarel, *Cent fleurs écloses dans la nuit du Vietnam;* Georges Boudarel, "The Nhân-Văn Giai-Phẩm Affair: Intellectual Dissidence in the 1950s," *Vietnam Forum: A Review of Vietnamese Culture* 13 (1990): 154–174; Ninh, *A World Transformed,* chap. 4, "Intellectual Dissent: The Nhan Van Giai Pham Period"; Nguyễn Ngọc Tuấn, "Socialist Realism in Vietnamese Literature: An Analysis of the Relationship between Literature and Politics" (Ph.D. diss., Victoria University, 2004), chap. 6, "The Nhan Van Giai Pham Affair, a 'Peace Crisis.'"

4. Đào Duy Anh, Hoàng Cầm, Phan Khôi, Sỹ Ngọc, Nguyễn Mạnh Tường, Văn Tâm, and Trương Tửu, *Vũ Trọng Phụng với chúng ta* [Vũ Trọng Phụng is with us] (Hà Nội: Minh Đức, 1956).

5. Văn Tâm, *Vũ Trọng Phụng: Nhà văn hiện thực.*

6. A transcript of the conference proceeding was published in *Văn Nghệ* 17–18 (November/December 1949). This issue is available in Hữu Nhuận, ed., *Sưu tập Văn nghệ, 1948–1954: Tập 2, 1949* [Collection of *Văn Nghệ*] (Hà Nội: Hội Nhà Văn, 1999), 591–734.

7. Ibid., 607.

8. From Georg Lukács, *The Meaning of Contemporary Realism,* trans. John Mander and Necke Mander (London: Merlin Press, 1963). Cited in Gordon Graham, "Lukács and Realism after Marx," *British Journal of Aesthetics* 38, no. 2 (April 1998): 199.

9. On the "critical assimilation" of prerevolutionary literature into the Maoist literary canon, see Douwe Wessel Fokkema, *Literary Doctrine in China and Soviet Influence, 1956–1960* (London: Mouton, 1965), 104.

10. Hũu Nhuận, *Sưu tập Văn nghệ, 1948–1954: Tập 2, 1949,* 609.

11. Ibid., 610.

12. Ibid.

13. "B. S. Đặng Văn Ngữ trả lời về mở rộng tự do và dân chủ" [Dr. Đặng Văn Ngữ responds about the opening of freedom and democracy], 1; Thanh Bình, "Vài ý nghĩ về thái độ tự phê bình của ông Hoài Thanh" [Thoughts on Hoài Thanh's self-critical attitude], *Nhân Văn* 3 (October 15, 1956).

14. Nhân Văn, "Mấy lời chân tình gửi bạn đọc," 5.

15. Trần Đức Thảo, "Nỗ lực phát triển tự do dân chủ," 1.

16. The caption read "Kỷ niệm ngày Vũ Trọng Phụng tạ thế (13–10–1939)."

17. "Thờ ơ với Vũ-T-Phụng là khuyết điểm lớn," 2.

18. "Dâm hay là không dâm?," 2.

19. Trần Đức Thảo, "Nỗ lực phát triển tự do dân chủ," 1.

20. The notice appeared in *Văn Nghệ* (Literature & Arts) on October 25, in *Trăm Hoa* (Hundred Flowers) on October 28 and in *Nhân Dân* on October 29, 1956.

21. "Lễ kỷ niệm nhà văn Vũ Trọng Phụng," *Trăm Hoa*, October 28, 1956, 2.

22. The Association grew out of the Hội Văn hóa Cứu quốc (The cultural association for national salvation) formed by the Việt Minh in 1943. See Ninh, *A World Transformed*, 27.

23. Kim Ninh points out that private publishing houses were permitted to operate in the DRV through the late 1950s. They were closed as a consequence of the repression of Nhân Văn-Giai Phẩm.

24. Vũ Trọng Phụng, *Giông tố;* Vũ Trọng Phụng, *Số đỏ;* Vũ Trọng Phụng *Vỡ đê* (Hà Nội: Minh Đức, 1957).

25. See Nguyễn Ngọc Tuấn, "Socialist Realism in Vietnamese Literature," 251. "On June 4, 1958, the Vietnamese Union of Literature and Art issued a resolution accusing Nhan Van Giai Pham of being revisionist and counterrevolutionary."

26. See Hữu Nhuận, *Nguyên Hồng: Về tác gia và tác phẩm* [Nguyên Hồng: Writer and works] (Hà Nội: Giáo Dục, 2001).

27. Nguyên Hồng's controversial tenure as the editor of *Văn* is treated in Ninh, *A World Transformed*, 154–160.

28. For Nguyên Hồng's post-*Văn* bureaucratic career in Haiphong, see *Tuyển tập Nguyên Hồng* (Hà Nội: Văn Học, 1997), 1:6–7.

29. For information on Trương Tửu's life and work, see Nguyễn Hữu Sơn and Trịnh Bá Đĩnh, *Trương Tửu: Tuyển tập nghiên cứu, phê bình* [Selected works of Trương Tửu, research and criticism] (Hà Nội: Lao Động, 2007).

30. See, for example, Văn Tân and Nguyễn Hồng Phong, *Chống quan điểm phi vô sản về văn nghệ và chính trị (nhân những ý kiến của ông Trương Tửu về văn nghệ và chính trị đã đăng trên báo Nhân Văn và Giai Phẩm mùa Thu và mùa Đông)* (Hà Nội: Sự Thật, 1957). This hundred-page book is devoted to undermining the ideas of Trương Tửu.

31. The letter was published on December 16, 1956. See Ninh, *A World Transformed*, 278.

32. Đào Duy Anh et al., *Vũ Trọng Phụng với chúng ta.*

33. See Nguyễn Mạnh Tường, "Nhớ Vũ Trọng Phụng," 3–5; Đào Duy Anh, "Nhớ Vũ Trọng Phụng," 6; Hoàng Cầm, "Nhớ Vũ Trọng Phụng," 7–8.

34. Phan Khôi, "Không đề cao Vũ Trọng Phụng, chỉ đánh giá đúng," 9–11.

35. Trương Tửu, "Giới thiệu *Vỡ đê,* tiểu thuyết của Vũ Trọng Phụng" [Introducing *The Dike Breaks,* a novel by Vũ Trọng Phụng], 15–18.

36. Văn Tâm, "Vũ Trọng Phụng: Người thư ký của thời đại," 12–14.

37. Đào Duy Anh, "Nhớ Vũ Trọng Phụng," 6.

38. Nguyễn Mạnh Tường, "Nhớ Vũ Trọng Phụng," 5.

39. Phan Khôi, "Không đề cao Vũ Trọng Phụng, chỉ đánh giá đúng," 10.

40. Nguyễn Mạnh Tường, "Nhớ Vũ Trọng Phụng," 3.

41. Phan Khôi, "Không đề cao Vũ Trọng Phụng, chỉ đánh giá đúng," 9.

42. See Hoàng Cầm, "Tiến tới xét lại một vụ án văn học: Con người Trần Dần" [Toward a revision of a literary case: Trần Dần the person], *Nhân Văn* 1 (September 20, 1956).

43. Đào Duy Anh, "Nhớ Vũ Trọng Phụng," 6.

44. Ibid.

45. Phan Khôi, "Không đề cao Vũ Trọng Phụng, chỉ đánh giá đúng," 11. The passage reads: "Có thể nói Vũ Trọng Phụng là một nhà tiểu thuyết hiện thực phê phán có khuynh hướng xã hội chủ nghĩa của đêm trước Cách mạng tháng Tám."

46. Ibid., 10.

47. Đào Duy Anh, "Nhớ Vũ Trọng Phụng," 6.

48. Hoàng Cầm, "Nhớ Vũ Trọng Phụng," 8.

49. Nguyễn Mạnh Tường, "Nhớ Vũ Trọng Phụng," 5.

50. Trương Tửu, "Giới thiệu *Vỡ đê* tiểu thuyết của Vũ Trọng Phụng," 15.

51. Ibid., 18.

52. Ibid.

53. The origins and evolution of Văn Tâm's work on Vũ Trọng Phụng are described in an informative memoir that he published in 1993 and the following account draws heavily on this. Văn Tâm, "Một thuở ban đầu" [Once upon a time], *Nha Trang: Tạp chí Sáng Tác Nghiên Cứu Phê Bình Văn Nghệ* [Nha Trang: Journal of literary creative work, criticism and research] 20 (1993): 64–70.

54. Ibid., 64.

55. Trần Hữu Tá, "Văn Tâm, Người nặng tình với văn học dân tộc" [Văn Tâm, devotee of the national literature], *Nghiên Cứu Văn Học* 12 (2005): 73. Other students included Cao Xuân Hạo, Hà Thúc Chỉ, Bùi Quang Đoài, Phan Kế Hoành, and Trần Hữu Tá.

56. Văn Tâm, *Vũ Trọng Phụng: Nhà văn hiện thực*, 4.

57. Ibid.

58. "Chương 1: Vấn đề Vũ Trọng Phụng—Ý thức chiến đấu của Vũ Trọng Phụng" [Chapter 1: The problem of Vũ Trọng Phụng and his will to struggle], in ibid., 9–36.

59. "Chương 2: Hoàn cảnh xã hội," in ibid., 37–60.

60. According to Văn Tâm, an early realist current included the work of Phạm Duy Tốn, Vũ Đình Long, Nguyễn Đình Nghi, Vũ Đình Chí, Nguyễn Trọng Khiêm, and Nam Xương, while a more mature wave was dominated by Nguyễn Công Hoan, Đồ Phồn, Tam Lang, Ngô Tất Tố, and Nam Cao.

61. Ibid., 59.

62. "Chương 3: Thân thế và cá tính," in ibid., 61–76.

63. "Chương 4: Người thư ký của thời đại," in ibid., 77–141.

64. Ibid., 139: These documents were allegedly destroyed in a French bombing raid in 1947.

65. "Chương 5: Lập trường tiểu tư sản giới hạn nhãn quan hiện thực," in ibid.,142–195.

66. "Chương 6: Vài nét về đặc tính nghệ thuật," in ibid., 196–229.

67. Hữu Nhuận, *Sưu tập Văn nghệ: 1948–1954, Tập 2 1949*, 597.

68. Ibid. Raising the requirements slightly for political "naturalization," Tố Hữu underlined the importance for petty-bourgeois intellectuals of "revolutionizing *[cách mạng hóa]* their ideology" and "massifying *[quần chúng hóa]* their behavior."

69. For Trương Tửu, one of Văn Tâm's "most original discoveries" was his thesis that "Vũ Trọng Phụng's petty-bourgeois class outlook diminished the realist orientation of his work." Likewise, Hoài Thanh singled out for praise Văn Tâm's insight that Vũ Trọng Phụng's class background led him to produce novels that "revealed extreme class differentiation within Vietnamese society during the era, especially with regard to the petty bourgeoisie." Hoài Thanh, "Đọc sách *Vũ Trọng Phụng Nhà văn hiện thực*" [Reading *Vũ Trọng Phụng: Realist Writer*], *Văn Nghệ*, September 4, 1957, 103.

70. Interview with Văn Tâm, December 19, 1999. Văn Tâm also furnished Trần Thiếu Bảo with photographs of Vũ Trọng Phụng and his family that were reproduced and included in the new editions of the novels.

71. Minh Đức, ed., *Đất Mới Tập 1: Chuyện sinh viên* [New Land: Student stories] (Hà Nội: Hiến Nam, 1956).

72. Văn Tâm, "Bản tự kiểm thảo" [Self-criticism] (1957). Unpublished handwritten manuscript provided by Văn Tâm's wife, Mrs. Cao Xuân Cam.

73. "Lời của nhà xuất bản," *Đất Mới*, 2.

74. Q. Ngọc and T. Hồng, "Phê bình lãnh đạo sinh viên," *Đất Mới*, 3–19.

75. Văn Tâm, "Những người ấy muốn gì?," *Đất Mới*, 47.

76. It is also significant that one of only two other advertisements to appear in the issue was a full-page notice for the winter issue of *Giai Phẩm*. The notice appeared on the back cover of the issue and included a complete table of contents.

77. Bùi Quang Đoài, "Lịch sử một câu chuyện tình," *Đất Mới*, 28.

78. Ibid., 35.

79. Văn Tâm, "Bản tự kiểm thảo" (1957).

80. Ibid.

81. Decree no, 232/QN, Bộ Giáo Dục. March 9, 1957. Signed by Nguyễn Văn Huyên. Ministry of Education document provided by Cao Xuân Cam.

82. Much of his work was anthologized in a thousand-page-long collection published in 2006. Văn Tâm, *Tuyển tập Văn Tâm* [Selected works of Văn Tâm] (Hồ Chí Minh City: Văn Hóa Sài Gòn, 2006).

83. Văn Tân, "Vũ Trọng Phụng qua *Giông tố*, *Vỡ đê* và *Số đỏ*," in *Tập san Nghiên Cứu Văn-Sử-Địa* 29 (June 1957): 4–22.

84. Ibid., 8.

85. Ibid., 9.

86. Ibid., 12.

87. Ibid., 14.

88. Ibid., 15.

89. Ibid., 17.

90. Ibid.

91. Ibid., 18.

92. Nhóm Lê Quý Đôn, *Lược thảo lịch sử văn học Việt Nam* (Hà Nội: Xây Dựng, 1957). The Lê Quý Đôn Group was a team of scholars that included Vũ Đình Liên, Đỗ Đức Hiểu, Lê Trí Viễn, Huỳnh Lý, Lê Thước, and Trương Chính. The table of contents indicates that the entry on Vũ Trọng Phụng was written by Trương Chính.

93. *Tập san Phê bình—Số đặc biệt về Vũ Trọng Phụng: Đời sống và con người.* No copyright date appears in the issue but the introduction is dated October 1957.

94. Also known as Lê Quang Lộc, Thiều Quang (1913–80) was the brother of the better-known literary critic Thiếu Sơn. He wrote for the journal *Tao Đàn* in 1939 and for *Hà Nội hàng ngày* and *Thủ đô Hà Nội* in the late 1950s and 1960s. For more on Thiều Quang and *Tập san Phê bình,* see Lại Nguyên Ân, "Tập san Phê bình: Một ấn phẩm tư nhân ở miền bắc hồi 1957–58" [Journal of criticism: a private publication in the North during 1957–58], *Tạp chí Nghiên Cứu Văn Học* 8 (2009), accessed June 30, 2010, http://www.vienvanhoc.org.vn/reader/?id=646&menu=118.

95. Vũ Đức Phúc, "Vũ Trọng Phụng và những sự kiện lịch sử có thật" [Vũ Trọng Phụng and true historical events], *Tạp chí Văn Học* 4 (2000): 14–15.

96. Hoài Thanh, "Đọc sách *Vũ Trọng Phụng Nhà văn hiện thực*" [Reading *Vũ Trọng Phụng: Realist Writer*]," *Văn Nghệ* 4 (September 1, 1957): 103–106.

97. Hoài Thanh, "Đối với văn nghệ trước cách mạng tiếp thu phải có phê phán," *Nhân Dân* 1486 (April 6, 1958). Reprinted in Lại Nguyên Ân and Nguyễn Hoành Khung, *Vũ Trọng Phụng—Con người và tác phẩm (Hồi ức—chân dung—tiểu luận)*, 211–216.

98. Ibid., 216.

99. Ibid., 215.

100. Ibid., 213.

101. Phan Cự Đệ, "Thái độ và phương pháp giảng dạy của Trương Tửu," *Độc Lập* 354 (April 10, 1958): 3.

102. Ibid.

103. Ibid.

104. Nguyễn Đình Thi, "Nhà văn với quần chúng lao động" [Writers and the working masses], *Nhân Dân* 1511 (May 1, 1958).

105. The essay was published in *Nghiên Cứu Văn Học.* Việt Trung, "Trao đổi ý kiến vấn đề Vũ Trọng Phụng" [Exchanging views on the problem of Vũ Trọng Phụng], *Nghiên Cứu Văn Học* 5 (1960): 103–106.

106. Ibid., 106.

107. Bùi Huy Phồn, "Nhớ và nghĩ về Vũ Trọng Phụng" [Recalling and thinking about Vũ Trọng Phụng], *Người Hà Nội* 79 (July 1, 1988). Reprinted in Trần Hữu Tá, *Vũ Trọng Phụng: Hôm qua và hôm nay,* 114–123.

108. The transcript, entitled "Thảo luận về Vũ Trọng Phụng: Viện Văn Học, 10/6/1960," was published in *Chống nạng lên đường,* 2nd printing with supplemental

material, ed. Lại Nguyên Ân (Hà Nội: Hội Nhà Văn, 2004), 315–325. Phan Cự Đệ's comments have been excised inexplicably from the transcript, possibly because of the harshness of his assessment.

109. "The Schism between the Third and Fourth Internationals," "Down with the Trotskyist Huỳnh Văn Phương," and "Communist Freedom."

110. Như Phong argued that Vũ Trọng Phụng believed that revolutionaries were marked by a penchant for assassination, plotting, and blackmail.

111. "Thảo luận về Vũ Trọng Phụng," 322.

112. According to Bùi Huy Phồn, members of this group dismissed his work as "procolonial, conservative, or Trotskyist" without ever bothering to read it. Bùi Huy Phồn, "Nhớ và nghĩ về Vũ Trọng Phụng," 120.

113. Ibid., 119.

114. Bùi Huy Phồn reports that Hoàng Văn Hoan joined a second smaller meeting to discuss Vũ Trọng Phụng at the home of Tố Hữu that was attended by Nguyễn Công Hoan, Hoài Thanh, Lưu Trọng Lư, and Nguyên Hồng. This meeting also failed to reach a consensus. Ibid., 121.

115. Hoàng Văn Hoan, "Một vài ý kiến về vấn đề tác phẩm Vũ Trọng Phụng trong văn học Việt Nam," 220–221.

116. Ibid., 227.

117. Ibid., 34.

118. Ibid., 235.

119. Ibid., 239–240.

120. Vũ Đức Phúc, "Vũ Trọng Phụng và những sự kiện lịch sử có thật," 15.

121. Bùi Huy Phồn, "Nhớ và nghĩ về Vũ Trọng Phụng," 122.

122. Văn Tâm, "Ba mươi năm ấy bây giờ là đây" [Thirty years ago and here we are], in Lại Nguyên Ân, *Vũ Trọng Phụng: Tài năng và sự thật*, 11.

CONCLUSION

1. Nguyên Hồng, *Bước đường viết văn* (Hà Nội: Văn Học, 1970), 163.
2. Ibid., 164.
3. Ibid.
4. Nguyễn Công Hoan, *Đời viết văn của tôi* (Hà Nội: Văn Học, 1971).
5. Ibid., 391.
6. Ibid.
7. Ibid., 393.
8. Ibid., 392.
9. Ibid., 393.
10. Vũ Trọng Phụng, *Vỡ đê* (Hà Nội: Văn Học, 1982).
11. Ibid., 3–4.

12. Ibid.

13. Ibid.

14. Cited in Trần Hữu Tá, "Nhà văn Vũ Trọng Phụng với chúng ta" [The writer Vũ Trọng Phụng is with us], in Trần Hữu Tá, *Nhà văn Vũ Trọng Phụng với chúng ta,* 20.

15. Ibid., 19.

16. "Hoàng Văn Hoan, Vietnam Aide Who Defected to China, Dies at 86," *New York Times,* May 23, 1991.

17. Hoàng Văn Hoan, *Giọt nước trong biển cả: Hồi ký cách mạng* [Drop in the ocean, revolutionary memoir] (Beijing: Tin Việt Nam, 1986).

18. Nguyễn Đăng Mạnh, "Vũ Trọng Phụng và niềm căm uất không nguôi" [Vũ Trọng Phụng and the unending fury], *Thể Thao & Văn Hóa* 42 (October 17, 1987): 24–31. Reprinted in Trần Hữu Tá, *Nhà văn Vũ Trọng Phụng với chúng ta,* 349.

19. Nguyễn Đăng Mạnh and Trần Hữu Tá, eds., *Tuyển tập Vũ Trọng Phụng (Ba tập)* (Hà Nội: Văn Học, 1987).

20. Lại Nguyên Ân, ed., *Toàn tập Vũ Trọng Phụng (Năm tập)* (Hà Nội: Hội Nhà Văn, 1999). In 2004, a different edition of Vũ Trọng Phụng's "complete works" was published by Văn Học Publishing House. See Tôn Thảo Miên, *Vũ Trọng Phụng Toàn tập.*

21. Nguyễn Đăng Mạnh, "Lời Giới thiệu" [Introduction], in ibid., 13–60.

22. Ibid., 15.

23. The conferences were timed to commemorate the seventy-fifth anniversary of his birth (1987), the fiftieth anniversary of his death (1989), the eightieth anniversary of his birth (1992), and the ninetieth anniversary of his birth (2002).

24. Trần Hữu Tá, *Nhà văn Vũ Trọng Phụng với chúng ta;* and Nguyễn Ngọc Thiện, *Vũ Trọng Phụng về tác giả và tác phẩm.*

25. Hoàng Thiếu Sơn, "Từ tình yêu đến hạnh phúc vợ chồng" [From love to marital happiness], in *Lấy nhau vì tình,* by Vũ Trọng Phụng (Hà Nội: Văn Học, 1989), 6–25; Hoàng Thiếu Sơn, "Lời giới thiệu," introduction to *Trúng số độc đắc,* by Vũ Trọng Phụng (Hà Nội: Văn Học, 1990), 5–14; Hoàng Thiếu Sơn, "Cạm bẫy người: Mở đầu sự nghiệp của 'ông vua phóng sự'" [*The Man Trap:* The first work of the king of reportage], in *Cạm bẫy người,* by Vũ Trọng Phụng (Hà Nội: Văn Học, 1993), 5–21; Hoàng Thiếu Sơn, "Làm đĩ, cuốn sách có trách nhiệm và đầy nhân đạo" [*To Be a Whore,* a responsible book full of humanity], in *Làm đĩ,* by Vũ Trọng Phụng (Hà Nội: Văn Học, 1994), 3–37; Hoàng Thiếu Sơn, "Sáu mươi năm rồi, *Lục xì* cũng nên đọc lại" [Sixty years later, *Venereal Disease Clinic* is worth reading again], in *Lục xì,* by Vũ Trọng Phụng (Hà Nội: Văn Học, 1998), 5–7.

26. *Tạp Chí Văn Học* (Hà Nội) *số đặc biệt kỷ niệm 50 năm ngày mất của Vũ Trọng Phụng* [Special issue on the occasion of the fiftieth-year anniversary of Vũ Trọng Phụng's death], February, 1990.

27. Đinh Trí Dũng, *Nhân vật tiểu thuyết Vũ Trọng Phụng;* Bùi Văn Tiếng, *Thời gian nghệ thuật trong tiểu thuyết Vũ Trọng Phụng;* Nguyễn Quang Trung, *Tiếng cười Vũ Trọng*

Phụng (Hà Nội: Văn Hóa-Thông Tin, 2002); Trần Đăng Thao, *Đặc sắc văn chương Vũ Trọng Phụng.*

28. Trần Hữu Tá, *Vũ Trọng Phụng: Hôm qua và hôm nay.*

29. Dương Nghiễm Mậu, "Viết về Vũ Trọng Phụng," in Trần Hữu Tá, *Vũ Trọng Phụng: hôm qua và hôm nay,* 160–174.

30. Lại Nguyên Ân and Nguyễn Hoành Khung, eds., *Vũ Trọng Phụng: Con người và tác phẩm* (Hà Nội: Hội Nhà Văn, 1994); Lại Nguyên Ân, *Vũ Trọng Phụng: Tài năng và sự thật.*

31. Lại Nguyên Ân and Peter Zinoman, *Vẽ nhọ bôi hề: Những tác phẩm mới tìm thấy năm 2000* (Hà Nội: Hội Nhà Văn, 2000); Lại Nguyên Ân, *Chống nạng lên đường.*

32. Some of these may be found in Lại Nguyên Ân, *Mênh mông chật chội . . . : tiểu luận—phê bình văn học* (Hà Nội: Trí Thức, 2009).

33. Lại Nguyên Ân, *Nghiên cứu văn bản tiểu thuyết Giông tố.*

34. Lại Nguyên Ân, "Một khía cạnh ở nhà báo Vũ Trọng Phụng: người lược thuật thông tin quốc tế," in Lại Nguyên Ân, *Vũ Trọng Phụng: tài năng và sự thật,* 189–200.

35. Lại Nguyên Ân, "Vài tư liệu về việc Vũ Trọng Phụng bị gọi ra tòa năm 1932," in *Mênh mông chật chội—tiểu luận phê bình,* 287–302.

36. Lại Nguyên Ân, "Vũ Trọng Phụng và hai tờ báo ở Sài Gòn, 1937," in *Mênh mông chật chội—tiểu luận phê bình,* 303–314.

37. Lại Nguyên Ân, *Vũ Trọng Phụng: Tài năng và sự thật,* 203.

38. Hoàng Văn Hoan, "Một vài ý kiến về vấn đề tác phẩm Vũ Trọng Phụng trong văn học Việt Nam," 220–244.

39. Vũ Trọng Phụng, "Nhân sự chia rẽ của đệ-tam và đệ-tứ, ta thử ngó lại cuộc cách mệnh cộng sản ở Nga từ lúc khởi thủy cho đến ngày nay," in *Toàn tập Vũ Trọng Phụng (tập 5),* ed. Lại Nguyên Ân, 432–458.

40. Vịt Cái, "Văn hoạt kê: lời hiệu triệu của một tay Sịt-ta-li-nít, đả đảo tên Tờ-rốt-kýt Huỳnh Văn Phương!," in *Vẽ nhọ bôi hề,* 204–209.

41. For the Phan Khôi project, see Lại Nguyên Ân, ed., *Phan Khôi: Tác phẩm đăng báo, 1928* [Phan Khôi newspaper writing, 1928] (Đà Nẵng: Đà Nẵng, 2003); Lại Nguyên Ân, ed., *Phan Khôi: Tác phẩm đăng báo, 1929* (Đà Nẵng: Đà Nẵng, 2005); Lại Nguyên Ân, ed., *Phan Khôi: Tác phẩm đăng báo, 1930* (Hà Nội: Hội Nhà Văn, 2006); Lại Nguyên Ân, ed., *Phan Khôi: Tác phẩm đăng báo, 1931* (Hà Nội: Hội Nhà Văn, 2007); Lại Nguyên Ân, ed., *Phan Khôi: Tác phẩm đăng báo, 1932* (Hà Nội: Trí Thức, 2010); Lại Nguyên Ân, ed., *Phan Khôi viết và dịch Lỗ Tấn* [Phan Khôi writes and translates Lu Xun] (Hà Nội: Hội Nhà Văn, 2007).

42. Nguyễn Đăng Mạnh, *Hồi ký* [Memoirs] (Hà Nội, 2008), http://www.scribd.com/doc/86527507/Hoi-ky-Nguyen-Dang-Manh.

BIBLIOGRAPHY

VIETNAMESE PERIODICALS CONSULTED

Anh Niên, 1937
Bắc Hà, 1936–38
Chính Trị, 1938–39
Chuyện Đời, 1938
Công Thương, 1938
Đất Mới, 1956
Điện Tín, 1937
Độc Lập, 1958
Đông Dương Tạp Chí, 1937–38
Đông Tây, 1936
Dư Luận, 1938
Giai Phẩm, 1956
Hà Nội Báo, 1936
Hải Phòng Tuần Báo, 1934–35
Ích Hữu, 1936
Loa, 1934–35
Mới, 1939
Nam Phong, 1918

Ngày Nay, 1936–38
Nghề Mới, 1936
Nghiên Cứu Văn Học, 1960, 2005, 2008
Ngọ Báo, 1931–32, 1934
Người Hà Nội, 1988
Người Mới, 1939
Nha Trang: Tạp Chí Sáng Tác Nghiên Cứu Phê Bình Văn Nghệ, 1993
Nhân Dân, 1956, 1958
Nhân Văn, 1956, 1958
Nhật Tân, 1934–35
Nhựt Báo, 1937
Nữ Giới, 1939
Nữ Lưu, 1937
Phóng Sự, 1938
Phụ Nữ, 1938
Phụ Nữ Tân Văn, 1933
Phụ Nữ Thời Đàm, 1934
Quốc Gia, 1938
Sáng, 1939
Sông Hương, 1936–37
Tao Đàn, 1936, 1939
Tạp Chí Văn Học [DRV], 1965, 1970, 1990, 2000
Tạp Chí Văn Học [RVN], 1969
Tập San Phê Bình: Số Đặc Biệt Về Vũ Trọng Phụng, 1957
Tập San Nghiên Cứu Văn Sử Địa, 1957
Thế Giới Tân Văn, 1936
Thể Thao & Văn Hóa, 1987
Thời Vụ, 1939
Tiến Hóa, 1935
Tiểu Thuyết Thứ Bảy, 1935, 1958
Tiểu Thuyết Thứ Ba, 1937
Tiểu Thuyết Thứ Năm, 1938–39
Tin Văn, 1936
Tinh Hoa, 1937

Trăm Hoa, 1956
Tràng An, 1935–36, 1938
Trung Lập, 1932
Tuần Báo, 1935
Tuần Báo Người Hà Nội, 1988
Tuần Lễ, 1938
Tương Lai, 1937
Văn Học Tạp Chí, 1935
Văn Học Tuần San, 1934
Văn Nghệ, 1956–57
Vì Chúa, 1937
Việt Báo, 1937
Vịt Đực, 1938

VŨ TRỌNG PHỤNG'S WRITINGS

Vũ Trọng Phụng. *Cạm bẫy người: phóng sự tiểu thuyết về nghề cờ gian bạc lận*. Hà Nội: An Nam xuất bản cục, Trung Bắc Tân Văn, 1934.

———. *Chống nạng lên đường: Chùm sáng tác đầu tay mới tìm thấy cuối năm 2000*. Edited by Lại Nguyên Ân. Hà Nội: Hội Nhà Văn, 2001.

———. "Chung quanh một bài phê bình." *Sài Gòn Tiểu Thuyết, Nouvelle série*, August 21, 1937.

———. "Chung quanh thiên phóng sự Lục sì: Bức thư ngỏ cho một độc giả." *Tương Lai*, March 11, 1937.

———. "Chúng ta không trông thấy gì." *Tiểu Thuyết Thứ Năm*, May 19, 1938.

———. *Cơm thầy cơm cô, Lục xì*. Hà Nội: Minh Phương, 1937.

———. "Cộng sản tự do." *Đông Dương Tạp Chí*, October 30, 1937.

———. "Để đáp lời Báo Ngày Nay: Dâm hay không dâm." *Tương Lai*, March 25, 1937.

———. *Dumb Luck: A Novel by Vũ Trọng Phụng*. Edited by Peter Zinoman. Translated by Nguyễn Nguyệt Cầm and Peter Zinoman. Ann Arbor: University of Michigan Press, 2002.

———. *Le fabuleux destin de Xuan le Rouquin*. Translated by Phan The Hong and Janine Gillon. Hà Nội: Thế Giới, 1998.

———. *Giết mẹ tức là chuyện nàng Lucrèce Borgia, kịch lãng mạn của Victor Hugo*. Hà Nội: Lê Cường, 1936.

———. *Giông tố*. Hà Nội: Văn Học, 1996.

———. "Giữa cuộc cách mệnh xã hội phái tiểu tư sản chưa đủ giác ngộ." *Tiểu Thuyết Thứ Năm*, June 2, 1938.

———. "Household Servants." In *The Light of the Capital: Three Modern Vietnamese Classics*, by Vũ Trọng Phụng, Nguyên Hồng and Tam Lang, translated by Greg Lockhart and Monique Lockhart. Kuala Lumpur: Oxford University Press, 1996.

———. *The Industry of Marrying Europeans*. Translated by Thuy Tranviet. Ithaca: Cornell Southeast Asia Program Publications, 2006.

———. *Không một tiếng vang: dân sinh bi kịch, 3 hồi*. Hà Nội: Đông Tây, 1934.

———. *Kỹ nghệ lấy Tây*. Hà Nội: Phương Đông, 1936.

———. *Làm đĩ*. Hà Nội: Văn Học, 1994.

———. *Lấy nhau vì tình*. Hà Nội: Văn Học, 1989.

———. *Lục xì*. Hà Nội: Văn Học, 1998.

———. *Lục xì: Prostitution and Venereal Disease in Colonial Hanoi*. Edited by Shaun Kingsley Malarney. Translated by Shaun Kingsley Malarney. Honolulu: University of Hawaii Press, 2011.

———. "Một hành vi bất lương trong nghề phóng sự và điều tra của Vũ Trọng Phụng." *Chuyện Đời*, May 7, 1938.

———. *Nhân sự chia rẽ của Đệ tam và Đệ tứ*. Sài Gòn: Thanh Mậu, 1938.

———. "Nhân sự chia rẽ của đệ tam và đệ tứ quốc tế: Ta thử ngó lại cuộc cách mệnh cộng sản ở Nga từ lúc khởi thủy cho đến ngày nay." *Đông Dương Tạp Chí*, September 25, 1937.

———. "Những việc đáng ghi chép của năm Bính-Tý." *Tương Lai*, February 18, 1937.

———. "Phê bình báo chí: Báo Đông Pháp." *Tiến Hóa*, November 16, 1935.

———. "Phê bình báo chí: Ngọ Báo." *Tiến Hóa*, December 7, 1935.

———. "Phỏng vấn tình cờ: Một ông nghị già . . . lôi thôi." *Tiểu Thuyết Thứ Năm*, July 28, 1938.

———. "Qua các phố." *Hải Phòng Tuần Báo*, January 20, 1935.

———. "Thư ngỏ cho ông Thái Phỉ, chủ bút báo Tin Văn về bài 'Văn chương dâm uế." *Hà Nội Báo*, September 23, 1936.

———. *Toàn tập Vũ Trọng Phụng (năm tập)*. Edited by Lại Nguyên Ân. Hà Nội: Hội Nhà Văn, 1999.

———. *Trúng số độc đắc*. Hà Nội: Văn Học, 1990.

———. *Tuyển tập Vũ Trọng Phụng (ba tập)*. Edited by Nguyễn Đăng Mạnh. Hà Nội: Văn Học, 1987.

———. *Vẽ nhọ bôi hề: Những tác phẩm mới tìm thấy năm 2000*. Edited by Lại Nguyên Ân and Peter Zinoman. Hà Nội: Hội Nhà Văn, 2000.

———. *Vỡ đê*. Hà Nội: Minh Đức, 1957.

———. *Vỡ đê*. Hà Nội: Văn Học, 1982.

———. *Vũ Trọng Phụng—Toàn tập: "Tiểu thuyết Dứt tình," "Giông tố," "Vỡ đê."* Hà Nội: Hội Nhà Văn, 1999.

———. *Vũ Trọng Phụng: Tuyển tập I*. Edited by Nguyễn Đăng Mạnh and Trần Hữu Tá. Hà Nội: Văn Học, 1993.

———. *Vũ Trọng Phụng toàn tập*. Edited by Tôn Thảo Miên. Hà Nội: Văn Học, 2004.

VIETNAMESE-LANGUAGE SOURCES

Ban Biên Tập Viện Văn học, ed. *Bản sắc hiện đại trong các tác phẩm Vũ Trọng Phụng*. Hà Nội: Văn Học, 2003.

Bùi Văn Tiếng. *Thời gian nghệ thuật trong tiểu thuyết Vũ Trọng Phụng*. Hà Nội: Văn Hóa, 1997.

Đảng Cộng sản Việt Nam. *Văn kiện Đảng Toàn tập: 1936–39*. Vol. 6. Hà Nội: Chính Trị Quốc Gia, 2000.

Đào Duy Anh, Hoàng Cầm, Phan Khôi, Sỹ Ngọc, Nguyễn Mạnh Tường, Văn Tâm, and Trương Tửu. *Vũ Trọng Phụng với chúng ta*. Hà Nội: Minh Đức, 1956.

Đinh Trí Dũng. *Nhân vật tiểu thuyết Vũ Trọng Phụng*. Hà Nội: Khoa Học Xã Hội and Đông Tây, 2005.

Đỗ Đức Hiểu. "Những lớp sóng ngôn từ trong *Số Đỏ* của Vũ Trọng Phụng." In *Nhà văn Vũ Trọng Phụng với chúng ta*, by Trần Hữu Tá. Hồ Chí Minh City: Thành Phố Hồ Chí Minh, 1999.

Hải Triều. *Văn sĩ và xã hội*. Huế: Hương Giang Thư Quán, 1937.

Hoài Thanh. "Đối với văn nghệ trước cách mạng tiếp thu phải có phê phán." *Nhân Dân*, April 6, 1958.

Hoàng Đạo. *Con đường sáng*. Hà Nội: Đời Nay, 1940.

Hoàng Thiếu Sơn. "Cạm bẫy người: mở đầu sự nghiệp của 'ông vua phóng sự." In *Cạm bẫy người*, by Vũ Trọng Phụng, 5–21. Hà Nội: Văn Học, 1993.

Hoàng Văn Đào. *Việt-Nam Quốc-dân Đảng: Lịch sử tranh đấu cận đại, 1927–1954*. Sài Gòn: Nguyễn Hòa Hiệp, 1970.

Hoàng Văn Hoan. *Giọt nước trong biển cả: Hồi ký cách mạng*. Beijing (?): Tin Việt Nam, 1986.

Hữu Nhuận. *Nguyên Hồng: Về tác gia và tác phẩm*. Hà Nội: Giáo Dục, 2001.

———. *Sưu tập Văn nghệ, 1948–54: Tập 2, 1949*. Hà Nội: Hội Nhà Văn, 1999.

Khái Hưng. *Gia đình*. Hà Nội: Đời Nay, 1937.

Lại Nguyên Ân, ed. *Chống nạng lên đường: Chùm sáng tác đầu tay mới tìm thấy cuối năm 2000*. Hà Nội: Hội Nhà Văn, 2001.

———, ed. *Chống nạng lên đường: Chùm sáng tác đầu tay mới tìm thấy cuối năm 2000.* 2nd ed. Hà Nội: Hội Nhà Văn, 2004.

———. *Mênh mông chật chội . . . : Tiểu luận—phê bình văn học.* Hà Nội: Trí Thức, 2009.

———. *Nghiên cứu văn bản tiểu thuyết "Giông Tố."* Hà Nội: Trí Thức, 2007.

———, ed. *Phan Khôi: Tác phẩm đăng báo, 1928.* Đà Nẵng: Đà Nẵng, 2003.

———, ed. *Phan Khôi: Tác phẩm đăng báo, 1929.* Đà Nẵng: Đà Nẵng, 2005.

———, ed. *Phan Khôi: Tác phẩm đăng báo, 1930.* Hà Nội: Hội Nhà Văn, 2006.

———, ed. *Phan Khôi: Tác phẩm đăng báo, 1931.* Hà Nội: Hội Nhà Văn, 2007.

———, ed. *Phan Khôi: Tác phẩm đăng báo, 1932.* Hà Nội: Trí Thức, 2010.

———, ed. *Phan Khôi viết và dịch Lỗ Tấn.* Hà Nội: Hội Nhà Văn, 2007.

———, ed. *Tập san Phê bình: Một ấn phẩm tư nhân ở miền bắc hồi 1957–58.* 2009. http://www.vienvanhoc.org.vn/reader/?id = 646&menu = 118 (accessed June 30, 2010).

———. "Vài tài liệu về việc Vũ Trọng Phụng bị gọi ra tòa năm 1932." Hà Nội: Trí Thức, 2009.

———, ed. *Vũ Trọng Phụng tài năng và sự thật.* Hà Nội: Văn Học, 1997.

Lại Nguyên Ân and Nguyễn Hoành Khung, eds. *Vũ Trọng Phụng, Con người và tác phẩm.* Hà Nội: Hội Nhà Văn, 1994.

Lại Nguyên Ân and Peter Zinoman, eds. *Vẽ nhọ bôi hề: những tác phẩm mới tìm thấy năm 2000.* Hà Nội: Hội Nhà Văn, 2000.

Lan Khai. *Vũ Trọng Phụng—Mớ tài liệu cho văn học sử Việt Nam.* Hà Nội: Minh Phương, 1941.

Lê Thanh. *Cuộc phỏng vấn các nhà văn.* Hà Nội: Đời Mới, 1943.

Lê Tràng Kiều, Lưu Trọng Lư, Hoài Thanh. *Văn chương và hành động.* Hà Nội: Phương Đông, 1936.

Lộc Phương Thủy. *André Gide: Đời văn và tác phẩm.* Hà Nội: Khoa Học Xã Hội, 2002.

Minh Đức, ed. *Đất Mới Tập 1: Chuyện sinh viên.* Hà Nội: Hiến Nam, 1956.

Mộng Sơn. *Văn học và triết luận.* Hà Nội: Đại Học Thư Xã, 1944.

Ngô Văn. *Việt Nam, 1920–1945, Cách mạng và phản cách mạng thời đô hộ thuộc địa.* California: Chuông Rè, 2000.

Nguyễn Bích Thuận. *Vũ Trọng Phụng: Tác giả, tác phẩm, tư liệu.* Hồ Chí Minh City: Đồng Nai, 2007.

Nguyễn Công Hoan. *Đời viết văn của tôi.* Hà Nội: Văn Học, 1971.

Nguyễn Đăng Mạnh. *Hồi ký.* 2008. http://www.scribd.com/doc/86527507/Hoi-ky-Nguyen-Dang-Manh.

Nguyên Hồng. *Bước đường viết văn.* Hà Nội: Văn Học, 1970.

Nguyễn Hữu Sơn and Trịnh Bá Đĩnh, eds. *Trương Tửu: Tuyển tập nghiên cứu, phê bình.* Hà Nội: Lao Động, 2007.

Nguyễn Khắc Xuyên. *Mục lục phân tích Tạp chí Nam Phong, 1917–1934.* Huế: Thuận Hóa/Trung tâm VHNN Đông Tây, 2003.

Nguyễn Ngọc Thiện, ed. *Vũ Trọng Phụng: Về tác gia và tác phẩm.* Hà Nội: Giáo Dục, 1999.

Nguyễn Ngọc Thiện and Lữ Huy Nguyên, eds. *Tao Đàn 1939: Sưu tập trọn bộ tạp chí văn học nhà xuất bản Tân Dân.* Hà Nội: Văn Học, 1998.

Nguyễn Quang Trung. *Tiếng cười Vũ Trọng Phụng.* Hà Nội: Văn Hóa-Thông Tin, 2002.

Nguyễn Thành. *Báo chí cách mạng Việt Nam, 1925–1945.* Hà Nội: Khoa Học Xã Hội, 1984.

Nguyễn Văn Đạm. *Đôi điều kể thêm về Vũ Trọng Phụng.* October 13, 2004. http://www.truongxuantrieu.00author.com/hoso-b/vutrongphung-v.htm.

Nguyễn Văn Hanh. *Hồ Xuân Hương: Tác phẩm, thân thế và văn tài.* Sài Gòn: Aspar, 1937.

Nguyễn Văn Phúc. *Con đường mới.* Hà Nội: Hương Sơn đường, 1939.

Nguyễn Văn Tòng. *Báo chí Việt Nam từ khởi thủy đến 1945.* Hồ Chí Minh City: Thành phố Hồ Chí Minh, 2000.

Nguyễn Vỹ. *Văn thi sĩ tiền chiến—Chứng dẫn của một thời đại.* Sài Gòn: Khai Trí, 1969.

Nhất Linh. *Đoạn tuyệt.* Hà Nội: Đời Nay, 1935.

Nhóm Lê Quý Đôn. *Lược thảo lịch sử văn học Việt Nam.* Hà Nội: Xây Dựng, 1957.

Phan Thị Mỹ Khanh. *Nhớ cha tôi: Phan Khôi.* Đà Nẵng: Đà Nẵng, 2001.

"Tao Đàn: Số đặc biệt về Vũ Trọng Phụng." No. 1. New Series, December 1939.

Thế Phong, ed. *Cuộc đời viết văn làm báo—Tam Lang—Tôi kéo xe.* Hồ Chí Minh City: Văn Hóa-Thông Tin, 1996.

Thiều Quang. *Tập san Phê bình: Số đặc biệt về Vũ Trọng Phụng, đời sống và con người.* Hà Nội: Minh Quang, 1957.

Trần Đăng Thao. *Đặc sắc văn chương Vũ Trọng Phụng.* Hà Nội: Thanh Niên, 2004.

Trần Hữu Tá, ed. *Nhà văn Vũ Trọng Phụng với chúng ta.* Hồ Chí Minh City: Thành phố Hồ Chí Minh, 1999.

———. "Văn Tâm, Người nặng tình với văn học dân tộc." *Nghiên Cứu Văn Học* 12 (2005).

———, ed. *Vũ Trọng Phụng: Hôm qua và hôm nay.* Hồ Chí Minh City: Thành phố Hồ Chí Minh, 1992.

Trần Huy Liệu. *Hồi ký.* Hà Nội: Khoa Học Xã Hội, 1991.

Trần Minh Tiến, ed. *Lan Khai: Tác phẩm, nghiên cứu lý luận và phê bình văn học.* Hà Nội: Văn Hóa–Thông Tin, 2002.

Trương Tửu. *Tuyển tập, nghiên cứu, phê bình*. Hà Nội: Lao Động, 2007.

Văn Tâm. "Một thuở ban đầu." *Nha Trang: Tạp chí Sáng Tác Nghiên Cứu Phê Bình Văn Nghệ* 20 (1993): 64–70.

———. *Vũ Trọng Phụng nhà văn hiện thực (1912–1939)*. Hà Nội: Kim Đức, 1957.

Văn Tân. "Vũ Trọng Phụng qua *Giông tố, Vỡ đê* và *Số đỏ*." *Tập san Nghiên Cứu Văn-Sử-Địa* (June 1957): 4–22.

Văn Tân and Nguyễn Hồng Phong. *Chống quan điểm phi vô sản về văn nghệ và chính trị (nhân những ý kiến của ông Trương Tửu về văn nghệ và chính trị đã đăng trên báo Nhân Văn và Giai Phẩm mùa Thu và mùa Đông)*. Hà Nội: Sự Thật, 1957.

Việt Trung. "Trao đổi ý kiến vấn đề Vũ Trọng Phụng." *Nghiên Cứu Văn Học* 5 (1960): 103–106.

Vi Huyền Đắc. "Vài kỷ niệm về Vũ Trọng Phụng." *Văn*, October 15, 1970.

Vũ Bằng. *Bốn mươi năm nói láo*. Sài Gòn: Phạm Quang Khải, 1969.

———. "Cái tài, cái tật của Vũ Trọng Phụng." *Tạp Chí Văn Học Phổ Thông*, 1970.

Vũ Đức Phúc. "Bàn về một số đặc trưng của khuynh hướng tự nhiên chủ nghĩa trong văn học Việt-Nam trước cách mạng." *Tạp Chí Văn Học* (1966): 54–62.

———. "Vũ Trọng Phụng và những sự kiện lịch sử có thật." *Tạp Chí Văn Học* 4 (2000): 14–15.

Vũ Ngọc Phan. *Nhà văn hiện đại, Tập I*. Hồ Chí Minh City: Văn Học, 1994.

———. *Nhà văn hiện đại: phê bình văn học*. Hà Nội: Tân Dân, 1942.

WESTERN-LANGUAGE SOURCES

Aldrich, Robert. *Colonialism and Homosexuality*. London: Routledge, 2003.

Alves, Mark. "Linguistic Research on the Origins of the Vietnamese Language: An Overview." *Journal of Vietnamese Studies* 1, nos. 1–2 (2006): 104–131.

Becque, Henry. *The Vultures, The Women of Paris, Marry-Go-Round: Three Plays*. Translated by Freeman Tilden. New York: Kennerley, 1913.

Bezançon, Pacale. *Une colonization éducatrice? L'expérience indochinoise, 1860–1945*. Paris: L'Harmattan, 2002.

Boudarel, Georges. *Cent fleurs écloses dans la nuit du Vietnam: Communism et dissidence, 1954–1956*. Paris: Jacque Bertoin, 1991.

———. "The Nhân-Văn Giai-Phẩm Affair: Intellectual Dissidence in the 1950s." *Vietnam Forum: A Review of Vietnamese Culture* 13 (1990): 154–174.

Brocheux, Pierre. "L'implantation du mouvement communiste en Indochine française: Le cas du Nghe-Tinh, 1930–31." *Revue d'Histoire Moderne et Contemporaine* 24 (January-March 1977): 49–74.

———. *The Mekong Delta: Ecology, Economy, and Revolution, 1860–1960.* Madison: University of Wisconsin-Madison Center for Southeast Asian Studies, 1995.

———. "The State and the 1930s Depression in French Indochina." In *Weathering the Storm: The Economies of Southeast Asia in the 1930s Depression*, edited by Peter Boomgaard and Ian Brown. Pasir Panjang: Institute of Southeast Asian Studies, 2000.

———. "Vietnamese Communism and the Peasants: Analogy and Originality in Vietnamese Experience." In *Vietnamese Communism in Comparative Perspective*, edited by William Turley. Boulder: Westview Press, 1980.

Brocheux, Pierre, and Daniel Hémery. *Indochina: An Ambiguous Colonization, 1858–1954.* Translated by Eric Jennings, Nora A. Taylor, and Noémi Tousignant Ly-Lan Dill-Klein. Berkeley: University of California Press, 2009.

Brown, Frederick. *Zola: A Life.* New York: Farrar, Straus and Giroux, 1995.

Brown, Ian. *Economic Change in South-East Asia, c. 1830–1980.* Kuala Lumpur: Oxford University Press, 1997.

Bùi Xuân Bào. *Le roman vietnamien contemporain: Tendences et evolution du roman vietnamien contemporain, 1925–1945.* Sài Gòn: Tủ Sách Nhân Văn Xã Hội, 1972.

Chafur, Tony, and Amanda Sackur, eds. *French Colonial Empire and the Popular Front: Hope and Disillusion.* New York: St. Martin's Press, 1999.

Clark, Katerina. *The Soviet Novel: History as Ritual.* Bloomington: Indiana University Press, 1981.

Cohen, William. "The Colonial Policy of the Popular Front." *French Historical Studies* 7, no. 3 (1972): 368–393.

Conklin, Alice. "Colonialism and Human Rights, a Contradiction in Terms? The Case of French West Africa, 1895–1914." *American Historical Review* 103, no. 2 (1998): 419–442.

———. *A Mission to Civilize: The Republican Idea of Empire in France and West Africa, 1895–1930.* Stanford: Stanford University Press, 1997.

Cook, Megan. *The Constitutionalist Party in Cochinchina: The Years of Decline, 1930–1942.* Victoria, Australia: Centre of Southeast Asian Studies, Monash University, 1977.

Copley, Antony. *Sexual Moralities in France, 1780–1980: New Ideas on the Family, Divorce, and Homosexuality.* London: Routledge, 1989.

Corbin, Alain. *Women for Hire: Prostitution and Sexuality in France after 1850.* Translated by Alan Sheridan. Cambridge, Mass.: Harvard University Press, 1990.

Curtis, Debra. "Commodities and Sexual Subjectivities: A Look at Capitalism and Its Desires." *Cultural Anthropology* 19, no. 1 (2004): 95–121.

Dalloz, Jacques. "Les Vietnamiens dans le franc-maçonnerie coloniale." *Revue franchise d'Histoire d'Outre-mer* 85, no. 320 (1998): 103–118.

Daughton, J. P. *An Empire Divided: Religion, Republicanism and the Making of French Colonialism, 1880–1914*. Oxford: Oxford University Press, 2006.

Davidson, Peter, ed. *The Complete Works of George Orwell*. London: Secker Warburg, 1997.

Dikötter, Frank. *Sex, Culture and Modernity in China: Medical Science and the Construction of Sexual Identities in the Early Republican Period*. Honolulu: University of Hawaii Press, 1995.

Dobuzinskis, Laurent. "Defenders of Liberal Individualism, Republican Virtues and Solidarity: The Forgotten Intellectual Founding Fathers of the French Third Republic." *European Journal of Political Theory* 7, no. 3 (2008): 287–307.

Duiker, William. *Hồ Chí Minh: A Life*. New York: Hyperion, 2000.

Ericsson, Lars O. "Charges against Prostitution: An Attempt at a Philosophical Assessment." *Ethics* 90, no. 3 (April 1980): 335–366.

Fall, Bernard, ed. *Ho Chi Minh on Revolution: Selected Writings, 1920–66*. New York: Praeger, 1976.

Firpo, Christina. "Crisis of Whiteness and Empire: The Removal of Abandoned Eurasian Children from the Vietnamese Milieu, 1890–1956." *Journal of Social History* 43, no. 3 (2010): 587–613.

Flower, J. E. *Literature and the Left in France: Society, Politics, and the Novel since the Late Nineteenth Century*. London: Methuen, 1983.

Fokkema, Douwe Wessel. *Literary Doctrine in China and Soviet Influence, 1956–1960*. London: Mouton, 1965.

Frederick, William. "Alexandre Varenne and Politics in Indochina, 1925–26." In *Aspects of Vietnamese History*, edited by Walter Vella. Honolulu: University of Hawaii Press, 1973.

Frühstück, Sabine. "Male Anxieties: Nerve Force, Nation, and the Power of Sexual Knowledge." *Journal of the Royal Asiatic Society* 15, no. 1 (2005): 71–88.

Gallois, William. "Emile Zola's Forgotten History: Les Rougon-Macquart." *French History* 19, no. 1 (2005): 69–90.

Gantès, Gilles de. "Protectorate, Association, Reformism: The Roots of the Popular Front's Republican Policy in Indochina." In *French Colonial Empire and the Popular Front: Hope and Disillusion*, edited by Tony Chafur and Amanda Sackur, 109–131. New York: St. Martin's Press, 1999.

Gay, Peter. *Freud: A Life for Our Time*. London: Papermac, 1988.

Giebel, Christoph. *Imagined Ancestries of Vietnamese Communism: Ton Duc Thang and the Politics of Vietnamese History and Memory*. Seattle: University of Washington Press, 2004.

Gonjo, Yasuo. *Banque coloniale ou banque d'affaires: La Banque de l'Indochine sous la IIIe République*. Paris: Comité pour l'histoire économique et financière de la France, 1993.

Gordon, Daniel. "In Search of Limits: Raymond Aron on 'Secular Religion' and Communism." *Journal of Classical Sociology* 11, no. 2 (2001): 139–154.

Goscha, Christopher. "'The Modern Barbarian': Nguyen Van Vinh and the Complexity of Colonial Modernity in Vietnam." *European Journal of East Asian Studies* 3, no. 1 (2004): 135–169.

———. *Thailand and the Southeast Networks of the Vietnamese Revolution, 1885–1954.* Richmond: Curzon, 1999.

———. *Vietnam or Indochina? Contesting Conceptions of Space in Vietnamese Nationalism, 1887–1954.* NIAS Report Series 28. Copenhagen: Nordic Institute of Asian Studies, 1995.

Gourou, Pierre. *Les paysans du delta tonkinois: Étude de géogaphie humaine.* Paris: Éditions d'art et d'Histoire, 1936.

Graham, Gordon. "Lukács and Realism after Marx." *British Journal of Aesthetics* 38, no. 2 (April 1998): 198–207.

Guénel, Annick. "Prostitution, maladies vénériennes et medicine coloniale au Vietnam de la conquête française à la guerre d'indépendence." In *Vietnamese Society in Transition: The Daily Politics of Reform and Change,* edited by John Kleinen. Amsterdam: Het Spinhuis, 2001.

Hanson, Stephen E. "The Founding of the French Third Republic." *Comparative Political Studies* 43, nos. 8–9 (2010): 1023–1058.

Hardy, Andrew. "The Economics of French Rule in Indochina: A Biography of Paul Bernard, 1892–1960." *Modern Asian Studies* 32, no. 4 (1998): 807–848.

Harsin, Jill. *Policing Prostitution in Nineteenth-Century Paris.* Princeton: Princeton University Press, 1985.

Hazareesingh, Suhir. *Political Traditions in Modern France.* Oxford: Oxford University Press, 1994.

Hémery, Daniel. "L'Indochine, les droits humains, 1899–1954: Entre colonisateurs et colonisés, la Ligue des droits de l'homme." *Revue française d'Histoire d'Outre-mer* 88, nos. 330–331 (January 2001): 223–239.

———. *Révolutionnaires vietnamiens et pouvoir colonial en Indochine: Communistes, trotskystes, nationalists à Saigon de 1932 à 1937.* Paris: Maspero, 1975.

Henchy, Judith. "Performing Modernity in the Writings of Nguyễn An Ninh and Phan Văn Hùm." Ph.D. diss., University of Washington, 2005.

Hitchens, Christopher. *Why Orwell Matters.* New York: Basic Books, 2000.

Ho Tai Hue-Tam. "The Politics of Compromise: The Constitutionalist Party and the Electoral Reforms of 1922 in French Cochinchina." *Modern Asian Studies* 18, no. 3 (1984): 371–391.

———. *Radicalism and the Origins of the Vietnamese Revolution*. Cambridge, Mass.: Harvard University Press, 1992.

Hoang Ngoc Thanh. *Vietnam's Social and Political Development as Seen through the Modern Novel*. New York: Peter Lang, 1991.

Hooker, M. B. *A Concise Legal History of Southeast Asia*. Oxford: Clarendon Press, 1978.

Huang, Wen-huan. *A Drop in the Ocean: Hoang Van Hoan's Revolutionary Reminiscences*. Beijing: Foreign Language Publishing House, 1988.

Hunt, Lynn. "Pornography and the French Revolution." In *The Invention of Pornography: Obscenity and the Origins of Modernity, 1500–1800*, edited by Lynn Hunt. New York: Zone Books, 1993.

Huỳnh Kim Khánh. *Vietnamese Communism, 1925–1945*. Ithaca: Cornell University Press, 1982.

Innes, Christopher, ed. *A Sourcebook on Naturalist Theater*. London: Routledge, 2000.

Irvine, William D. *Between Justice and Politics: The Ligue des Droits de l'Homme, 1898–1945*. Stanford: Stanford University Press, 2007.

Isaac, Jeffrey C. "Critics of Totalitarianism." In *The Cambridge History of Twentieth-Century Political Thought*, edited by Terence Ball and Richard Bellamy, 181–202. Cambridge: Cambridge University Press, 2005.

Jackson, Julian. *The Popular Front in France: Defending Democracy, 1934–1938*. Cambridge: Cambridge University Press, 1988.

Jacques, Roland. *Portuguese Pioneers of Vietnamese Linguistics prior to 1650*. Bangkok: Orchid Press, 2002.

Kelly, Gail Paradise. *French Colonial Education: Essays on Vietnam and West Africa*. New York: AMS Press, 2000.

Kelly, Liam. "Vietnam as a 'Domain of Manifest Civility' (Văn Hiến Chi Bang)." *Journal of Southeast Asian Studies* 34, no. 1 (February 2003): 63–76.

Kemp, Tom. *Stalinism in France*. Volume 1, *The First Twenty Years of the French Communist Party*. London: New Park, 1984.

Keylor, William R. "Anti-Clericalism and Educational Reform in the French Third Republic: A Retrospective Evaluation." *History of Education Quarterly* 21, no. 1 (1981): 95–103.

Kurihara, Hirohide. "Changes in the Literary Policy of the Vietnamese Workers' Party, 1956–1958." In *Indochina in the 1940s and 1950s*, edited by Motoo Furata and Takashi Shiraishi. Ithaca: Cornell University Southeast Asia Program Publications, 1992.

———. "The First Congress of the Indochinese Communist Party (1935) and Its Aftermath: A Turning Point in the Comintern-ICP Relations." *Journal of Asian and African Studies* 60 (2000).

LaBrosse, Diane N. "'La Dérive Bergery/The Bergery Drift': Gaston Bergery and the Politics of Late Third Republic France and the Early Vichy State." *Historical Reflections* 34, no. 2 (2008): 66–87.

Langlois, Walter. *André Malraux: The Indochina Adventure.* New York: Prager, 1966.

Laqueur, Thomas W. *Solitary Sex: A Cultural History of Masturbation.* New York: Zone Books, 2003.

Larcher-Gosha, Agathe. "La légitimation française en Indochine: Mythes et réalités de la 'collaboration franco-vietnamienne' et du réformisme colonial, 1905–1945." Ph.D. diss., Université de Paris VII, 2000.

Larmour, Peter J. *The French Radical Party in the 1930s.* Stanford: Stanford University Press, 1964.

Laughlin, Charles A. *Chinese Reportage: The Aesthetics of Historical Experience.* Durham: Duke University Press, 2002.

Le Manh Hung. *The Impact of World War II on the Economy of Vietnam, 1939–45.* Singapore: Eastern Universities Press, 2004.

Liepmann, W. *Jeunesse et Sexualité: Initiation sexuelle des jeunes gens, d'aprés leurs propres confessions.* Paris: Fernand Aubier, 1932.

Logan, William. *Hanoi: Biography of a City.* Seattle: University of Washington Press, 2000.

Lorcin, Amaury. *Paul Doumer, gouverneur général de l'Indochine, 1897–1902: Le tremplin colonial.* Paris: Éditions l'Harmattan, 2004.

Loubère, Leo A. "French Left-Wing Radicals and the Law as a Social Force, 1870–1900." *American Journal of Legal History* 8, no. 1 (1964).

Lukács, George. *The Meaning of Contemporary Realism.* Translated by John Mander and Necke Mander. London: Merlin Press, 1963.

Luong Van Hy. "Agrarian Unrest from an Anthropological Perspective: The Case of Vietnam." *Comparative Politics* 17, no. 2 (January 1985): 153–174.

Makari, George J. "Between Seduction and Libido: Sigmund Freud's Masturbation Hypotheses and the Realignment of His Etiologic Thinking, 1897–1905." *Bulletin of the History of Medicine* 72, no. 4 (1998): 638–662.

Marr, David. "Concepts of 'Individual' and 'Self' in Twentieth-Century Vietnam." *Modern Asian Studies* 34, no. 4 (2000): 769–796.

———. "Ho Chi Minh's Declaration of Independence." In *Essays into Vietnamese Pasts,* edited by Keith W. Taylor and John K. Whitmore, 221–232. Ithaca: Cornell Southeast Asia Program Publications, 1995.

———. *Vietnamese Tradition on Trial, 1920–1945.* Berkeley: Universiy of California Press, 1981.

Masson, André. *Hanoi pendant le période héroique, 1873–1888.* Paris: Librarie Orientaliste Paul Gueuthner, 1929.

McConnell, Scott. *Leftward Journey: The Education of Vietnamese Students in France, 1919–1939.* New Brunswick, N.J.: Transaction, 1989.

McHale, Shawn. *Print and Power: Confucianism, Communism and Buddhism in the Making of Modern Vietnam.* Honolulu: University of Hawaii Press, 2004.

McLaren, Angus. *Twentieth-Century Sexuality: A History.* Oxford: Blackwell, 1999.

Meuleau, Marc. *Des pionniers en extrême-orient: Histoire de la Banque de l'Indochine, 1875–1975.* Paris: Fayard, 1990.

Miller, Julia Christine Scriven. "The 'Romance of Regulation': The Movement against State-Regulated Prostitution in France, 1871–1946." Ph.D. diss., New York University, 2000.

Miller, Michael B. *Shanghai on the Metro: Spies, Intrigue and the French between the Wars.* Berkeley: University of California Press, 1994.

Monteath, Peter. "The Spanish Civil War and the Aesthetics of Reportage." In *Literature and War,* by David Bevan. Amsterdam: Editions Rodopi B. V., 1989.

Morlat, Patrice. *Indochine années vingt: Le Rendez-vous manqué: La politique indigene des grands commis au service de la mise en valeur.* Paris: Les Indes savantes, 2006.

———. *La Repression Coloniale au Vietnam, 1908–1940.* Paris: L'Harmattan, 1990.

Murray, Martin. *The Development of Capitalism in Colonial Indochina, 1870–1940.* Berkeley: University of California Press, 1980.

———. "'White Gold' or 'White Blood'?: The Rubber Plantations of Colonial Indochina, 1910–1940." *Journal of Peasant Studies* 19, nos. 3–4 (1992): 41–67.

Nguyen-Marshall, Van. *In Search of Moral Authority: The Discourse on Poverty, Poor Relief, and Charity in French Colonial Vietnam.* New York: Peter Lang, 2008.

Nguyen, Martina T. "The Self-Reliant Literary Group (Tu Luc Van Doan): Colonial Modernism in Vietnam, 1932–1941." Ph.D. diss., University of California, Berkeley, 2012.

Nguyễn Ngọc Tuấn. "Socialist Realism in Vietnamese Literature: An Analysis of the Relationship between Literature and Politics." Ph.D. diss., Victoria University, 2004.

Nicolet, Claude. *L'idée républicaine en France, 1789–1924: Essai d'histoire critique.* Paris: Gallimard, 1982.

Ninh N. B. Kim. *A World Transformed: The Politics of Culture in Revolutionary Vietnam, 1945–1965.* Ann Arbor: University of Michigan Press, 2002.

Nord, Philip. *The Republican Moment: Struggles for Democracy in Nineteenth-Century France.* Cambridge, Mass.: Harvard University Press, 1995.

Norlund, Irene. "Rice and the Colonial Lobby: The Economic Crisis in French Indo-China in the 1920s and 1930s." In *Weathering the Storm: The Economies of Southeast Asia in the 1930s Depression*, edited by Peter Boomgaard and Ian Brown. Leiden: KITLV Press, 2000.

O'Harrow, Stephen. "French Colonial Policy towards Vernacular Language Development and the Case of Phạm Quỳnh in Viet-Nam." In *Aspects of Vernacular Languages in Asian and Pacific Societies*, edited by Đăng Liêm Nguyễn. Honolulu: University of Hawaii Press, 1973.

Osborne, Milton. "The Faithful Few: The Politics of Collaboration in Cochinchina in the 1920s." In *Aspects of Vietnamese History*, edited by Walter Vella. Honolulu: University of Hawaii Press, 1973.

———. *The French Presence in Cochinchina and Cambodia: Rule and Response, 1859–1905*. Ithaca: Cornell University Press, 1969.

Papin, Philippe. *Histoire de Hanoi*. Paris: Fayard, 2001.

Pasco, Allan H. *Sick Heroes: French Society and Literature in the Romantic Age, 1750–1850*. Exeter: University of Exeter Press, 1997.

Pelley, Patricia. *Postcolonial Vietnam: New Histories of the National Past*. Durham: Duke University Press, 2002.

Peycam, Philippe. *The Birth of Vietnamese Political Journalism: Saigon, 1916–1930*. New York: Columbia University Press, 2012.

———. "Intellectuals and Political Commitment in Vietnam: The Emergence of a Public Sphere in Colonial Sài Gòn." School of Oriental and African Studies, University of London, 1999.

Phạm Cao Dương. *Vietnamese Peasants under French Domination, 1861–1945*. Berkeley: Center for South and Southeast Asia Studies, University of California, 1985.

Phan Chu Trinh and Vĩnh Sính. *Phan Chau Trinh and His Political Writings*. Translated by Vĩnh Sính. Ithaca: Cornell Southeast Asia Program Publications, 2009.

Phinney, Harriet M. "Objects of Affection: Vietnamese Discourses on Love and Emancipation." *Positions* 16, no. 2 (2008): 329–358.

Pilbeam, Pamela. *Republicanism in Nineteenth Century France, 1814–1871*. New York: St. Martin's Press, 1995.

Porter, Gareth. "Proletariat and Peasantry in Early Vietnamese Communism." *Asian Thought and Society* 1, no. 3 (December 1976): 333–346.

Proschan, Frank. "'Syphilis, Opiomania and Pederasty': Colonial Constructions of Vietnamese (and French) Social Diseases." *Journal of the History of Sexuality* 11, no. 4 (2002): 610–636.

Quinn-Judge, Sophie. *Hồ Chí Minh: The Missing Years, 1919–1941*. Berkeley: University of California Press, 2002.

Rabinow, Paul. *French Modern: Norms and Forms of the Social Environment*. Chicago: University of Chicago Press, 1989.

Redfern, Walter. *Writing on the Move: Albert Londres and Investigative Journalism*. Berm: Peter Lang, 2004.

Reynolds, Siân. *France between the War: Gender and Politics*. London: Routledge, 1996.

Robequain, Charles. *The Economic Development of French Indo-China*. Translated by Isabel A. Ward. London: Oxford University Press, 1944.

Rodriguez, Marie-Corine. "'L'administration de la prostitution': Réglementation et contrôle social au Vietnam pendant la période coloniale." In *Vietnamese Society in Transition: The Daily Politics of Reform and Change*, edited by John Kleinen. Amsterdam: Het Spinhuis, 2001.

Roubaud, Louis. *Vietnam: La tragédie indochinoise*. Paris: Valois, 1931.

Saada, Emmanuelle. *Les enfants de la colonie: Les métis de l'Empire français entre sujétion et citoyenneté*. Paris: Éditions la Découverte, 2007.

———. "Race and Sociological Reason: Inquiries on the Métis in the French Empire, 1908–37." *International Sociology* 17, no. 3 (2002): 361–391.

Sampson, Cedric. "Nationalism and Communism in Vietnam, 1925–1931." Ph.D. diss., University of California, Los Angeles, 1975.

Sasges, Gerard. "'Indigenous Representation is Hostile to All Monopolies': Phạm Quỳnh and the End of the Alcohol Monopoly in Colonial Vietnam." *Journal of Vietnamese Studies* 5, no. 1 (Winter 2010): 1–36.

———. "The Landscape of Enterprise in Colonial Vietnam." Unpublished paper, 2011.

Sauerteig, Lutz D. H. "Sex Education in Germany from the Eighteenth to the Twentieth Century." In *Cultures in Europe: Themes in Sexuality*, edited by Franz X. Eder, Lesley Hall, and Gert Hekma. Manchester: Manchester University Press, 1999.

Senart, Philippe. "Henry Becque: Les Corbeaux." *Nouvelle Revue des Deux Mondes* (October 1982): 187–192.

Société médico-chirurgicale de l'Indochine. *Bulletin de la Société médico-chirurgicale de l'Indochine*. Hà Nội: Imprimerie d'Extrême-Orient, June 1930.

Sokolov, Anatolij A. *Komintern I V'ietnam*. Moscow: Iv Ran, 1998.

Stein, Arlene. "Three Models of Sexuality: Drives, Identities and Practices." *Sociological Theory* (Spring 1989): 1–13.

Stewart, Mary Lynn. "'Science Is Always Chaste': Sex Education and Sexual Initiation in France." *Journal of Contemporary History* (July 1997): 381–394.

Stokes, Patricia R. "Pathology, Danger, and Power: Women's and Physicians' Views of Pregnancy and Childbirth in Weimer Germany." *Social History of Medicine* 13, no. 3 (2000): 359–380.

Stoler, Ann Laura. *Carnal Knowledge and Imperial Power: Race and the Intimate in Colonial Rule*. Berkeley: University of California Press, 2002.

Tamagne, Florence. *A History of Homosexuality in Europe: Berlin, London, Paris*. Volume I, *1919–1939*. New York: Algora, 2004.

Terrier, Jean. "The Idea of a Republican Tradition: Reflections on the Debate concerning the Intellectual Foundations of the French Third Republic." *Journal of Political Ideologies* 11, no. 3 (2006): 289–308.

Thomas, Martin. "Albert Sarraut, French Colonial Development and the Communist Threat, 1919–1930." *Journal of Modern History* 77, no. 4 (2005): 917–955.

———. *The French Empire between the Wars: Imperialism, Politics and Society*. Manchester: Manchester University Press, 2005.

———. "French Empire Elites and the Politics of Economic Obligation in the Interwar Years." *Historical Journal* 52, no. 4 (2009): 989–1016.

To Kien. "'Tube House' and 'Neo Tube House' in Hanoi: A Comparative Study on Identity and Typology." *Journal of Asian Architecture and Engineering* 7, no. 2 (2008): 255–262.

Tostain, France. "The Popular Front and the Blum-Violette Plan, 1936–37." In *French Colonial Empire and the Popular Front: Hope and Disillusion*, edited by Tony Chafur and Amanda Sackur. New York: St. Martin's Press, 1991.

Tracol-Huynh, Isabelle. "Between Stigmatisation and Regulation in Colonial Northern Vietnam." *Culture, Health and Society* 12, no. 5 (August 2010): 73–87.

Tran, Adeline. "'Paris de l'Annam': On the Flâneur in Colonial Vietnam." Seminar paper, University of California, Berkeley, December 17, 2007.

Trilling, Lionel. *Sincerity and Authenticity*. Cambridge, Mass.: Harvard University Press, 1971.

Trinh Van Thao. *L'école française en Indochina*. Paris: Karthala, 1995.

Truong Buu Lam. *Colonialism Experienced: Vietnamese Writings on Colonialism, 1900–1931*. Ann Arbor: University of Michigan Press, 2000.

Truong Thanh-Dam. *Sex, Money and Morality: Prostitution and Tourism in South-East Asia*. London: Zed Book, 1990.

Vorapeth, Kham. *Commerce et colonization en Indochine, 1860–1945: Les maisons de commerce français un siècle d'aventure humaine*. Paris: Les Indes Savantes, 2004.

Vu-Hill, Kimloan. *Coolies into Rebels: Impact of World War I on French Indochina*. Paris: Les Indes savantes, 2011.

———. "Strangers in a Foreign Land: Vietnamese Soldiers and Workers in France during World War I." In *Vietnam Borderless Histories,* edited by Nhung Tuyet Tran and Anthony Reid. Madison: University of Wisconsin Press, 2006.

Wilder, Gary. *The French Imperial Nation-State: Negritude and Colonial Humanism between the Two World Wars.* Chicago: University of Chicago Press, 2005.

Wile, Douglas. *Art of the Bedchamber: The Chinese Sexual Yoga Classics including Women's Solo Meditation Texts.* Albany: SUNY Press, 1992.

Womack, Sarah. "Colonialism and the Collaborationist Agenda: Pham Quynh, Print Culture and the Politics of Persuasion in Colonial Vietnam." Ph.D. diss., University of Michigan, 2003.

Woodside, Alexander. *Community and Revolution in Modern Vietnam.* Boston: Houghton Mifflin, 1976.

———. "The Development of Social Organizations in Vietnamese Cities in the Late Colonial Period." *Pacific Affairs* 44, no. 1 (1971): 39–64.

———. *Vietnam and the Chinese Model: A Comparative Study of Vietnamese and Chinese Government in the First Half of the Nineteenth Century.* Cambridge, Mass.: Harvard University Press, 1971.

Wright, Gwendolyn. *The Politics of Design in French Colonial Urbanism.* Chicago: University of Chicago Press, 1991.

Zeldin, Theodore. *France, 1847–1945: Politics and Anger.* Oxford: Oxford University Press, 1979.

———. *A History of French Passions, 1848–1945.* Volume 2, *Intellect, Taste and Anxiety.* Oxford: Clarendon Press, 1977.

Zinoman, Peter. *The Colonial Bastille: A History of Imprisonment in Vietnam, 1862–1940.* Berkeley: University of California Press, 2001.

———. "Hải Vân, *The Storm* and Vietnamese Communism in the Inter-war Imagination." In *Southeast Asia over Three Generations: Essays Presented to Benedict R. O'G. Anderson,* edited by James T. Siegel and Audrey R. Kahin, 125–43. Ithaca: Cornell Southeast Asia Program Publications, 2003.

———. "Nhân Văn-Giai Phẩm and Vietnamese 'Reform Communism' in the 1950s: A Revisionist Interpretation." *Journal of Cold War Studies* 13, no. 1 (Winter 2011): 60–100.

———. "Provincial Cosmopolitanism: Vũ Trọng Phụng's Foreign Literary Engagements." In *Traveling Nation-Makers: Transnational Flows and Movements in the Making of Modern Southeast Asia,* edited by Caroline S. Hau and Kasian Tejapira, 126–152. Kyoto: Kyoto University Press; and Singapore: NUS Press, 2011.

Zola, Emile. *"The Experimental Novel," and Other Essays.* New York: Cassell, 1893.

———. *Œuvres complètes.* Paris: Cercle de Livre Précieux, 1966.

INDEX

Page numbers in italics refer to illustrations

www.ingramcontent.com/pod-product-compliance
Ingram Content Group UK Ltd.
Pitfield, Milton Keynes, MK11 3LW, UK
UKHW040914070725
460446UK00012B/100/J

9 780520 276284